TWIN SPICA

1

Kou Yaginuma

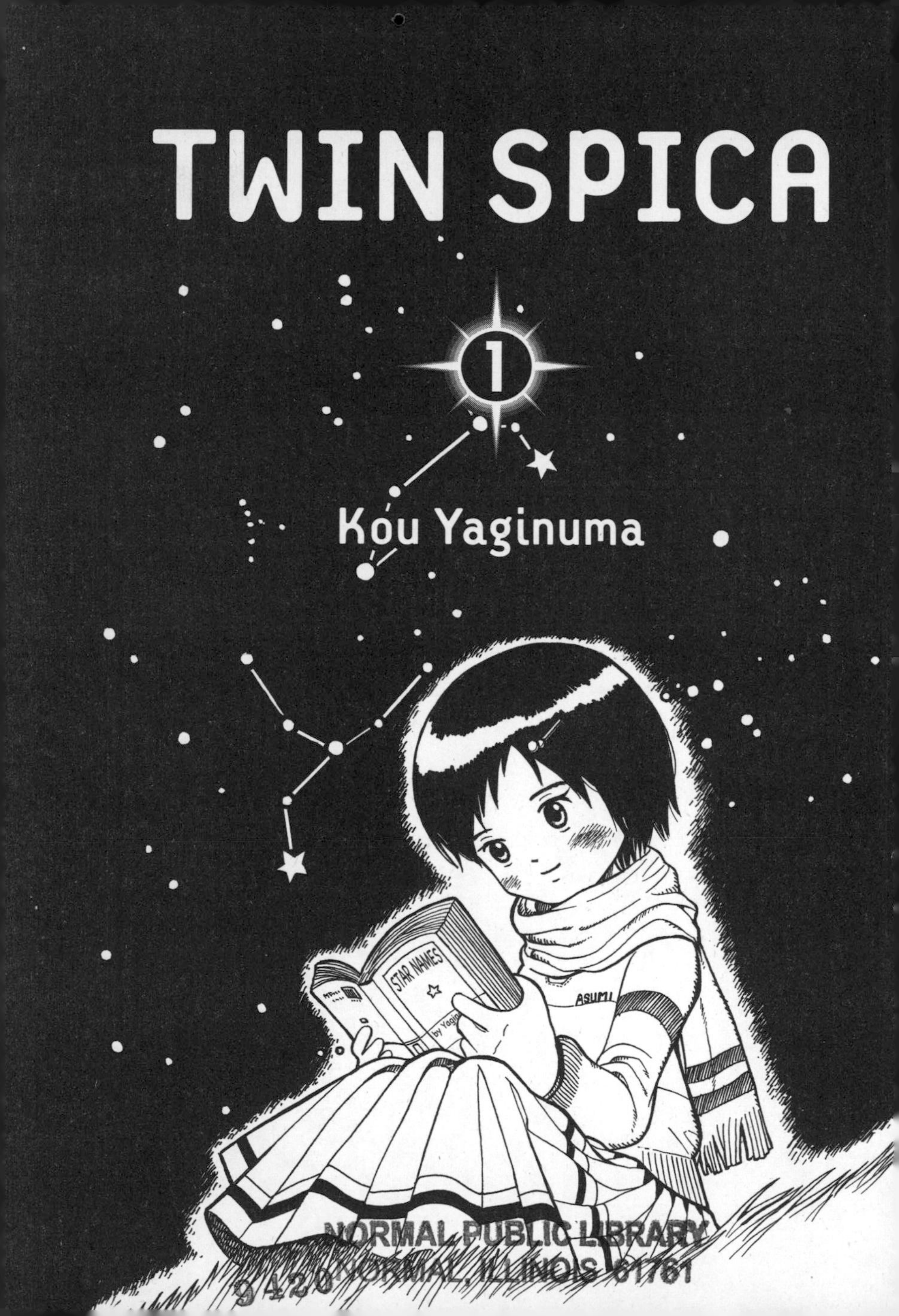
STAR NAMES
ASUMI

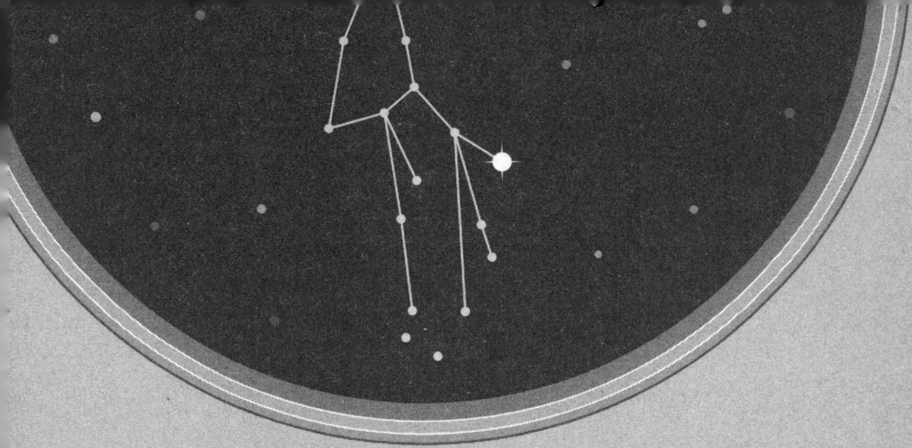

CONTENTS

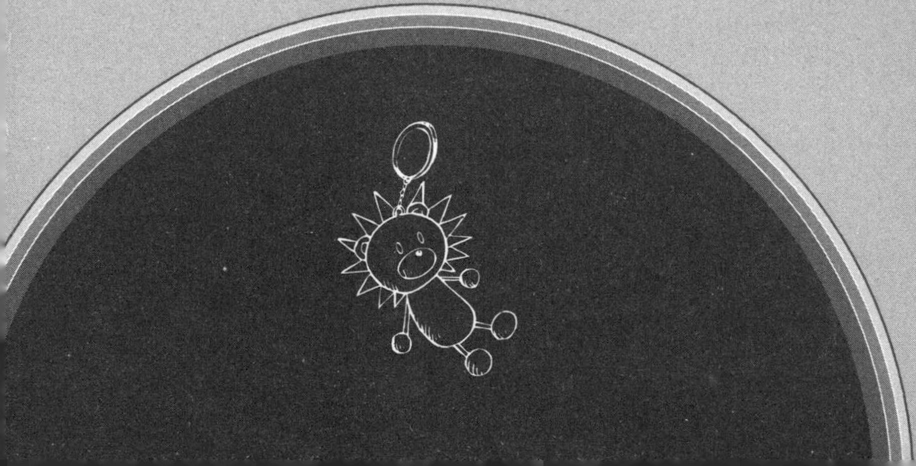

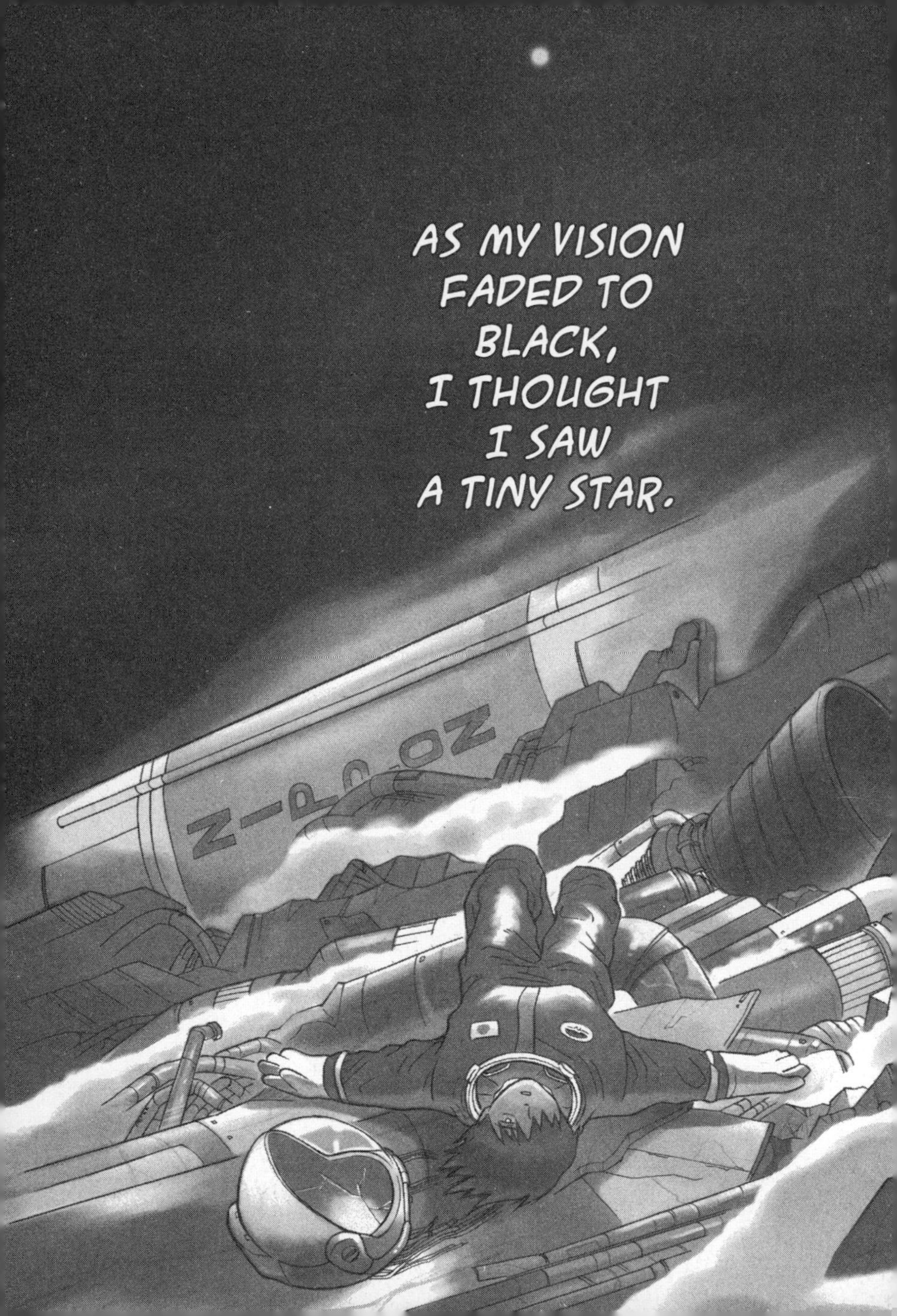
AS MY VISION FADED TO BLACK, I THOUGHT I SAW A TINY STAR.

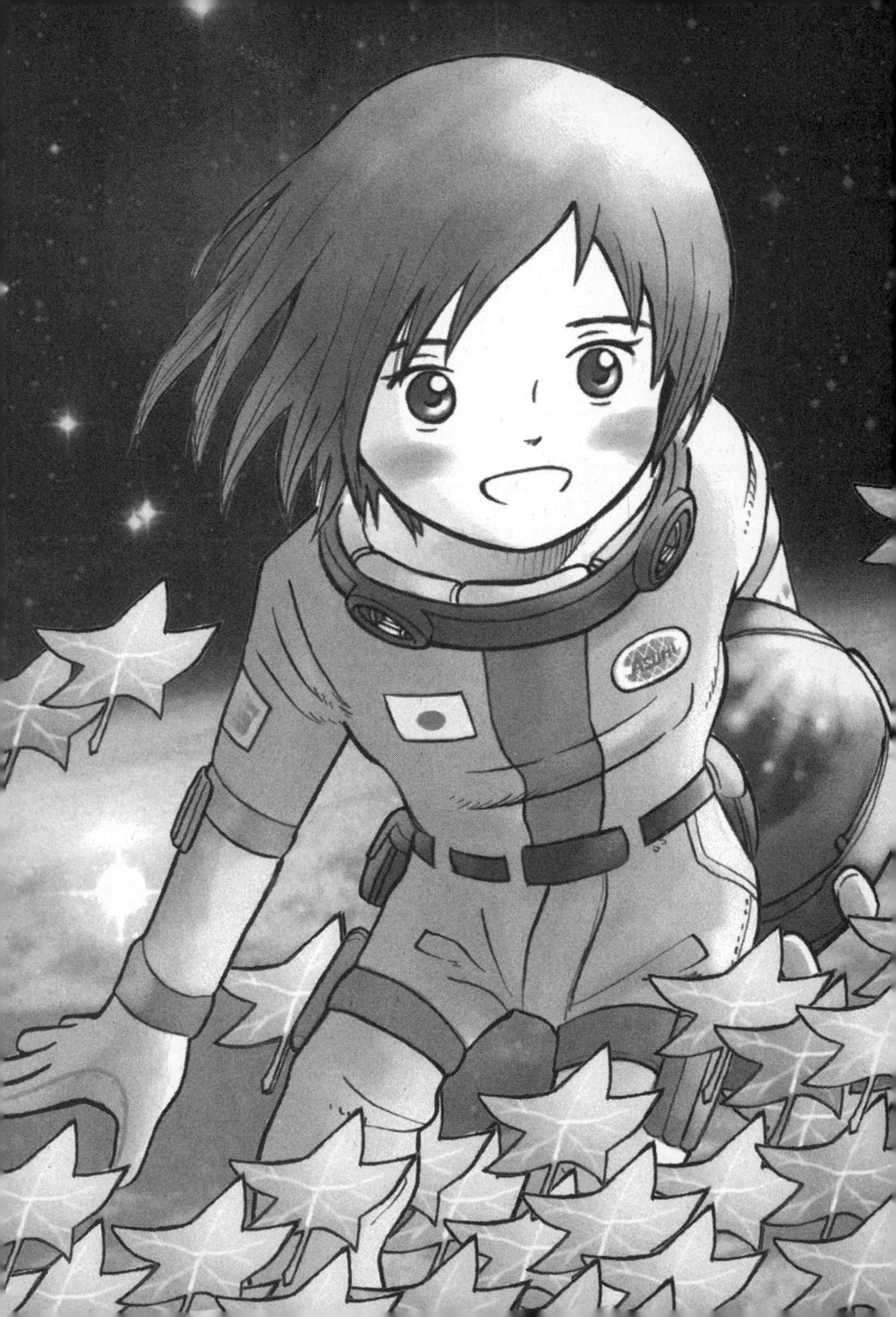

MISSION:01

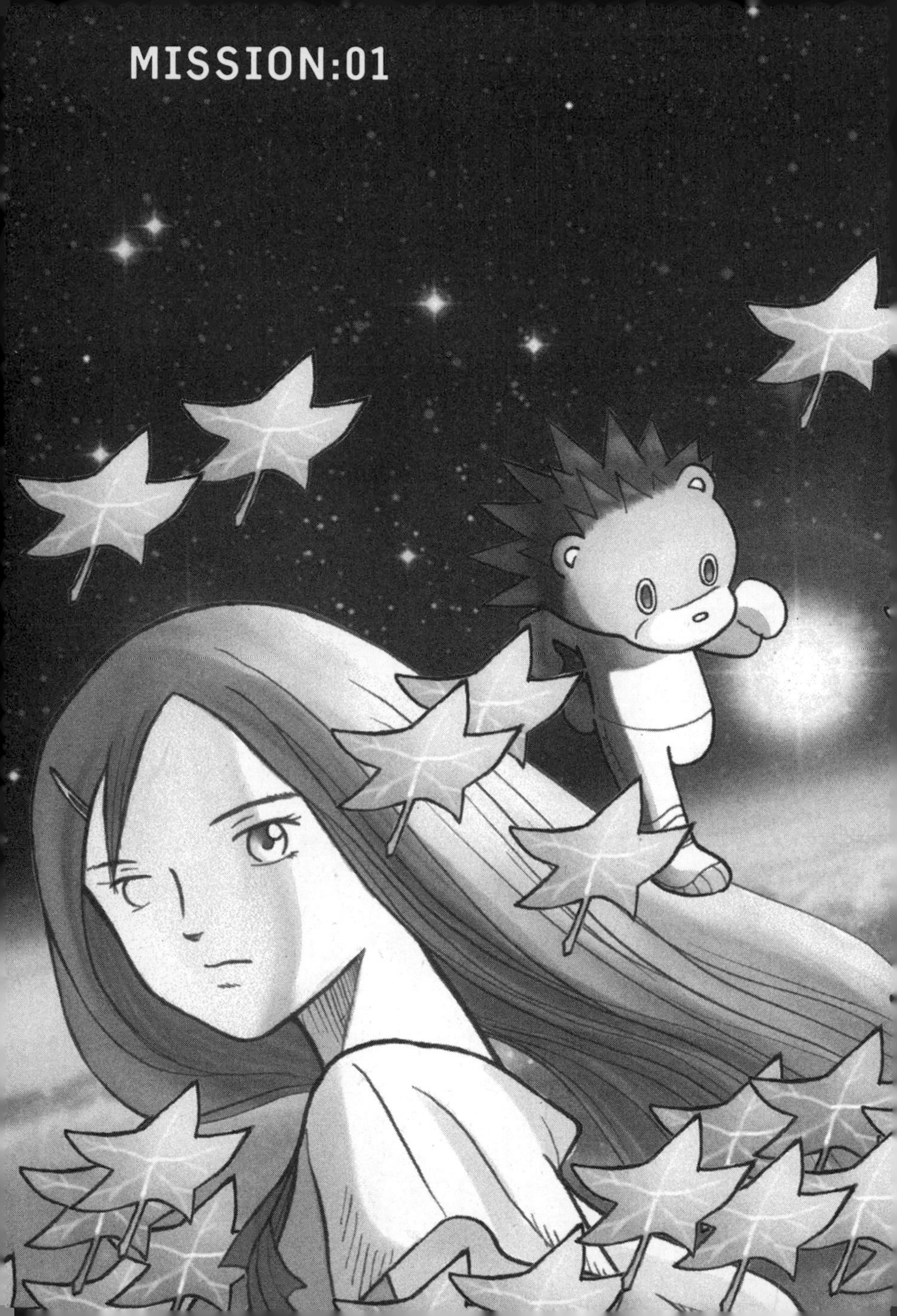

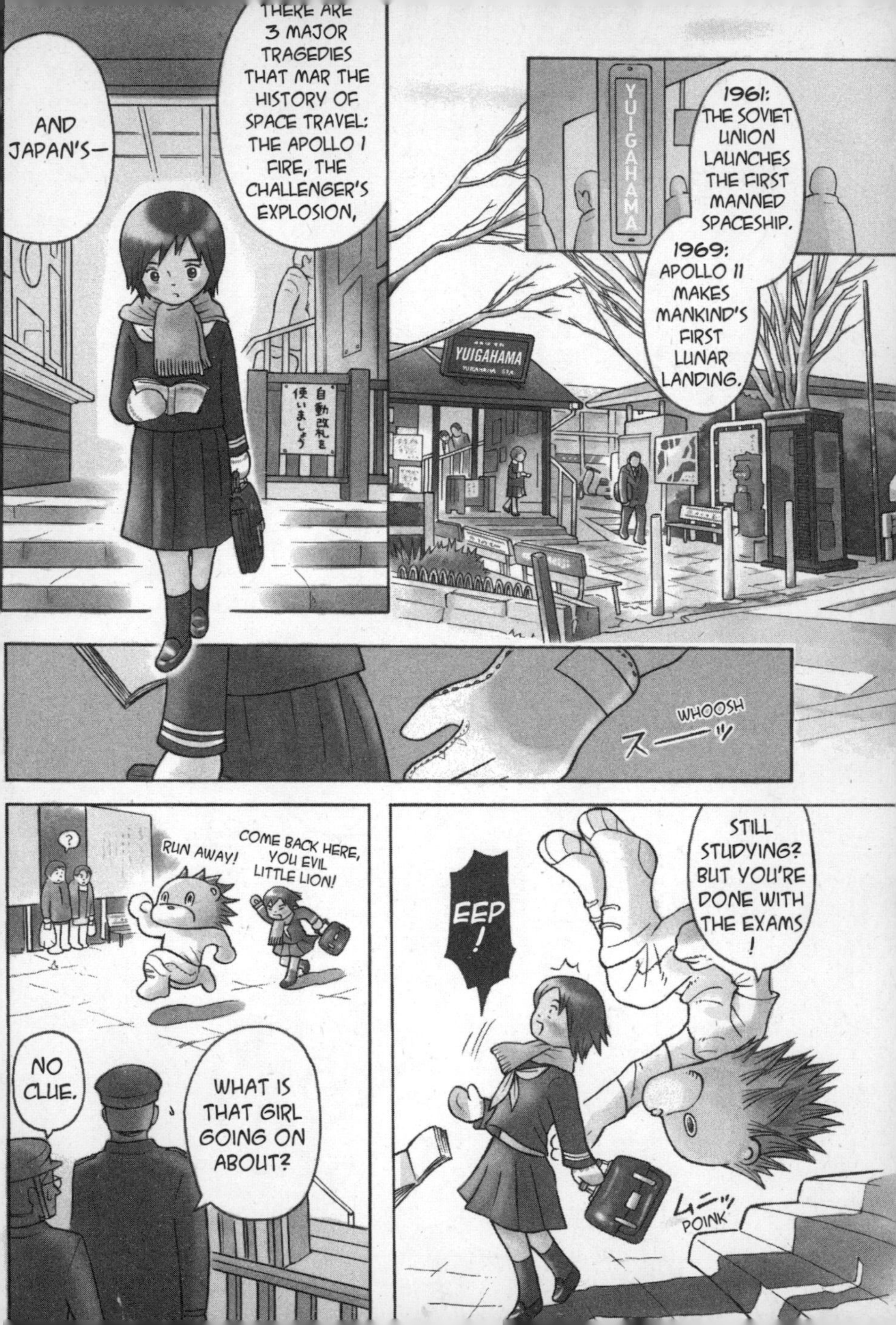
YUIGAHAMA
1961: THE SOVIET UNION LAUNCHES THE FIRST MANNED SPACESHIP.
1969: APOLLO 11 MAKES MANKIND'S FIRST LUNAR LANDING.
YUIGAHAMA
THERE ARE 3 MAJOR TRAGEDIES THAT MAR THE HISTORY OF SPACE TRAVEL: THE APOLLO 1 FIRE, THE CHALLENGER'S EXPLOSION,
AND JAPAN'S—
自動改札を使いましょう
WHOOSH
スーッ
STILL STUDYING? BUT YOU'RE DONE WITH THE EXAMS!
EEP!
ムニッ
POINK
COME BACK HERE, YOU EVIL LITTLE LION!
RUN AWAY!
?
WHAT IS THAT GIRL GOING ON ABOUT?
NO CLUE.

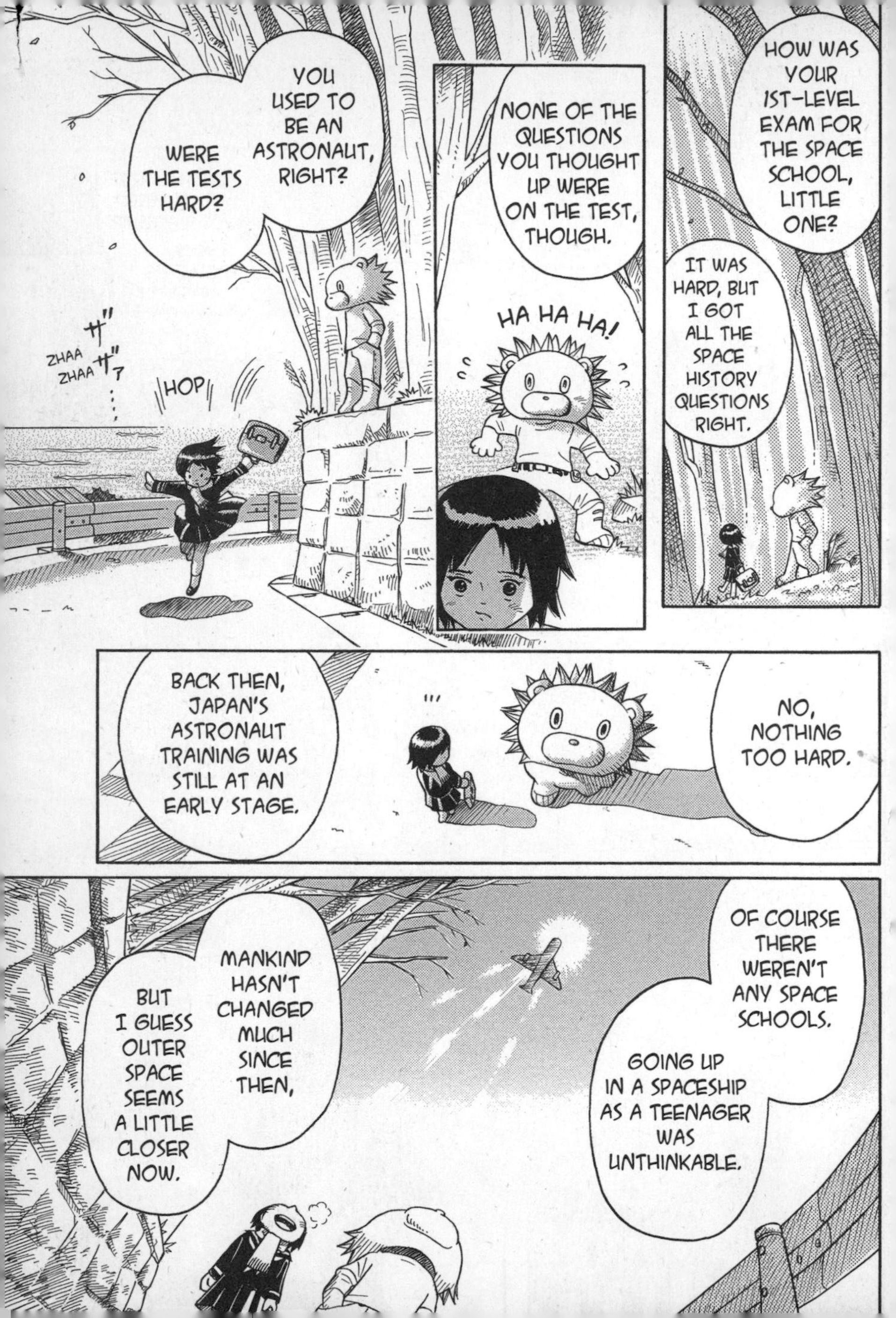
HOW WAS YOUR 1ST-LEVEL EXAM FOR THE SPACE SCHOOL, LITTLE ONE?
IT WAS HARD, BUT I GOT ALL THE SPACE HISTORY QUESTIONS RIGHT.
NONE OF THE QUESTIONS YOU THOUGHT UP WERE ON THE TEST, THOUGH.
HA HA HA!
YOU USED TO BE AN ASTRONAUT, RIGHT?
WERE THE TESTS HARD?
ZHAA ZHAA
HOP
NO, NOTHING TOO HARD.
BACK THEN, JAPAN'S ASTRONAUT TRAINING WAS STILL AT AN EARLY STAGE.
OF COURSE THERE WEREN'T ANY SPACE SCHOOLS.
GOING UP IN A SPACESHIP AS A TEENAGER WAS UNTHINKABLE.
MANKIND HASN'T CHANGED MUCH SINCE THEN,
BUT I GUESS OUTER SPACE SEEMS A LITTLE CLOSER NOW.

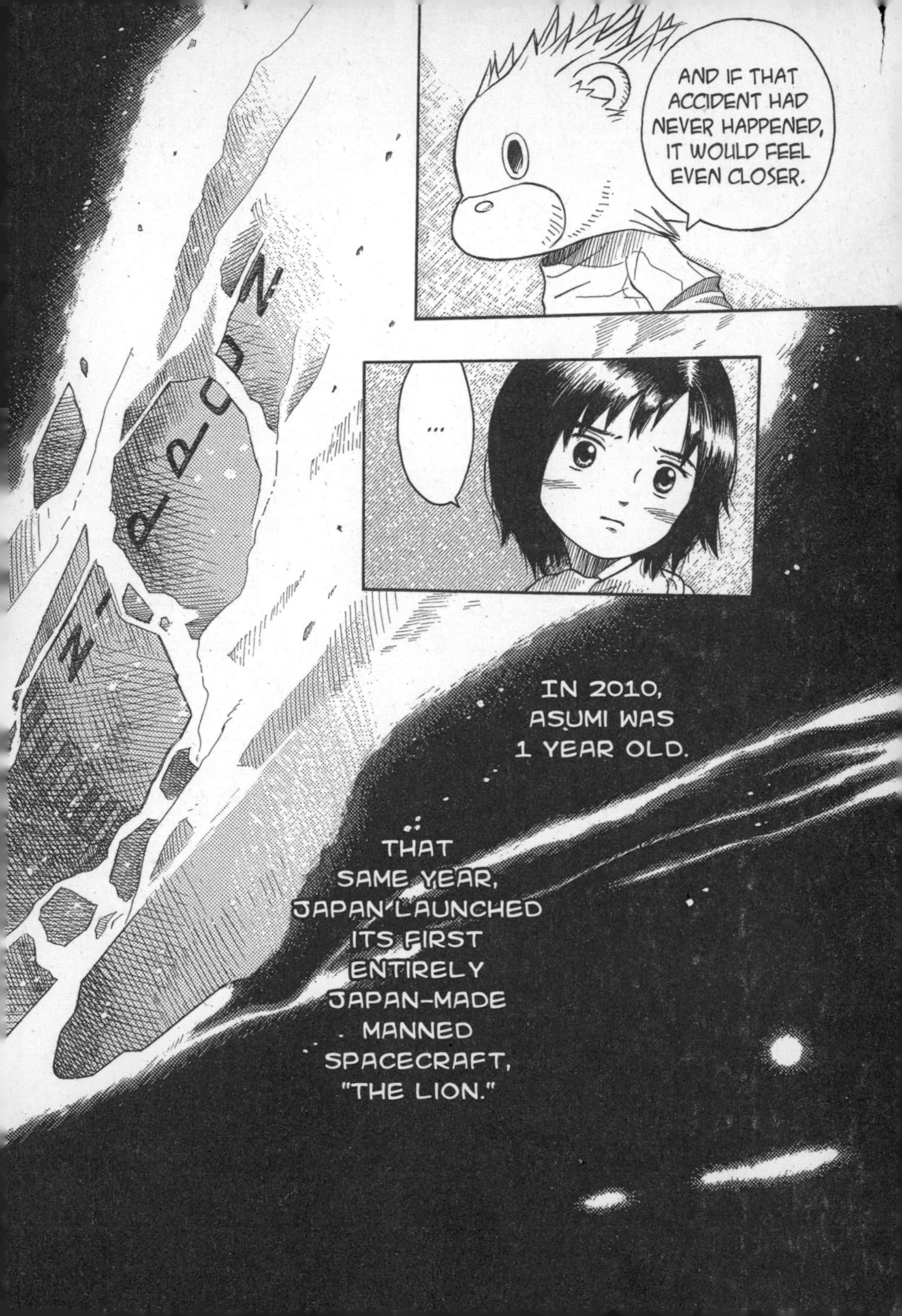
AND IF THAT ACCIDENT HAD NEVER HAPPENED, IT WOULD FEEL EVEN CLOSER.
...
IN 2010, ASUMI WAS 1 YEAR OLD.
THAT SAME YEAR, JAPAN LAUNCHED ITS FIRST ENTIRELY JAPAN-MADE MANNED SPACECRAFT, "THE LION."

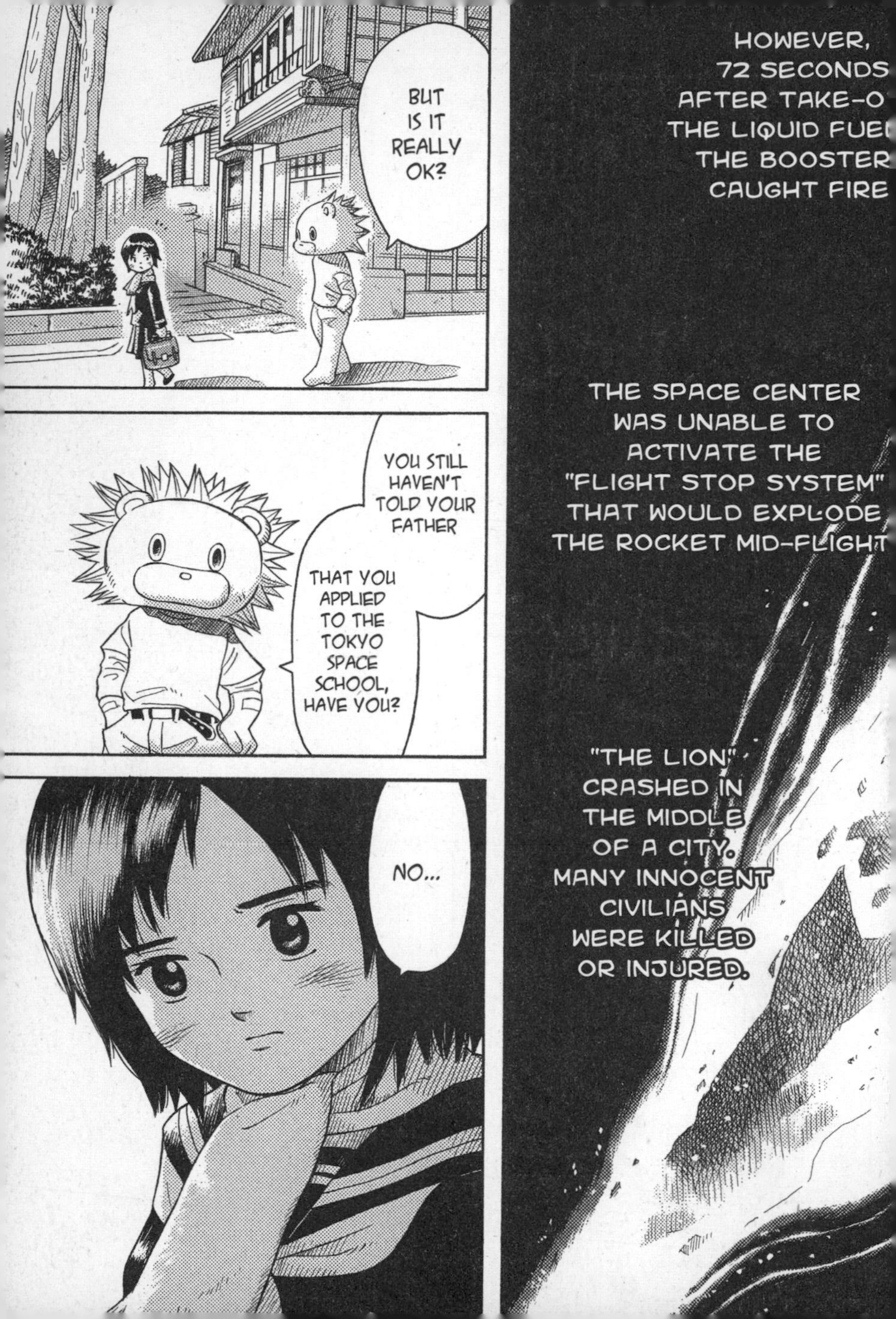
HOWEVER, 72 SECONDS AFTER TAKE-O THE LIQUID FUE THE BOOSTER CAUGHT FIRE
THE SPACE CENTER WAS UNABLE TO ACTIVATE THE "FLIGHT STOP SYSTEM" THAT WOULD EXPLODE THE ROCKET MID-FLIGHT
"THE LION" CRASHED IN THE MIDDLE OF A CITY. MANY INNOCENT CIVILIANS WERE KILLED OR INJURED.
BUT IS IT REALLY OK?
YOU STILL HAVEN'T TOLD YOUR FATHER
THAT YOU APPLIED TO THE TOKYO SPACE SCHOOL, HAVE YOU?
NO...

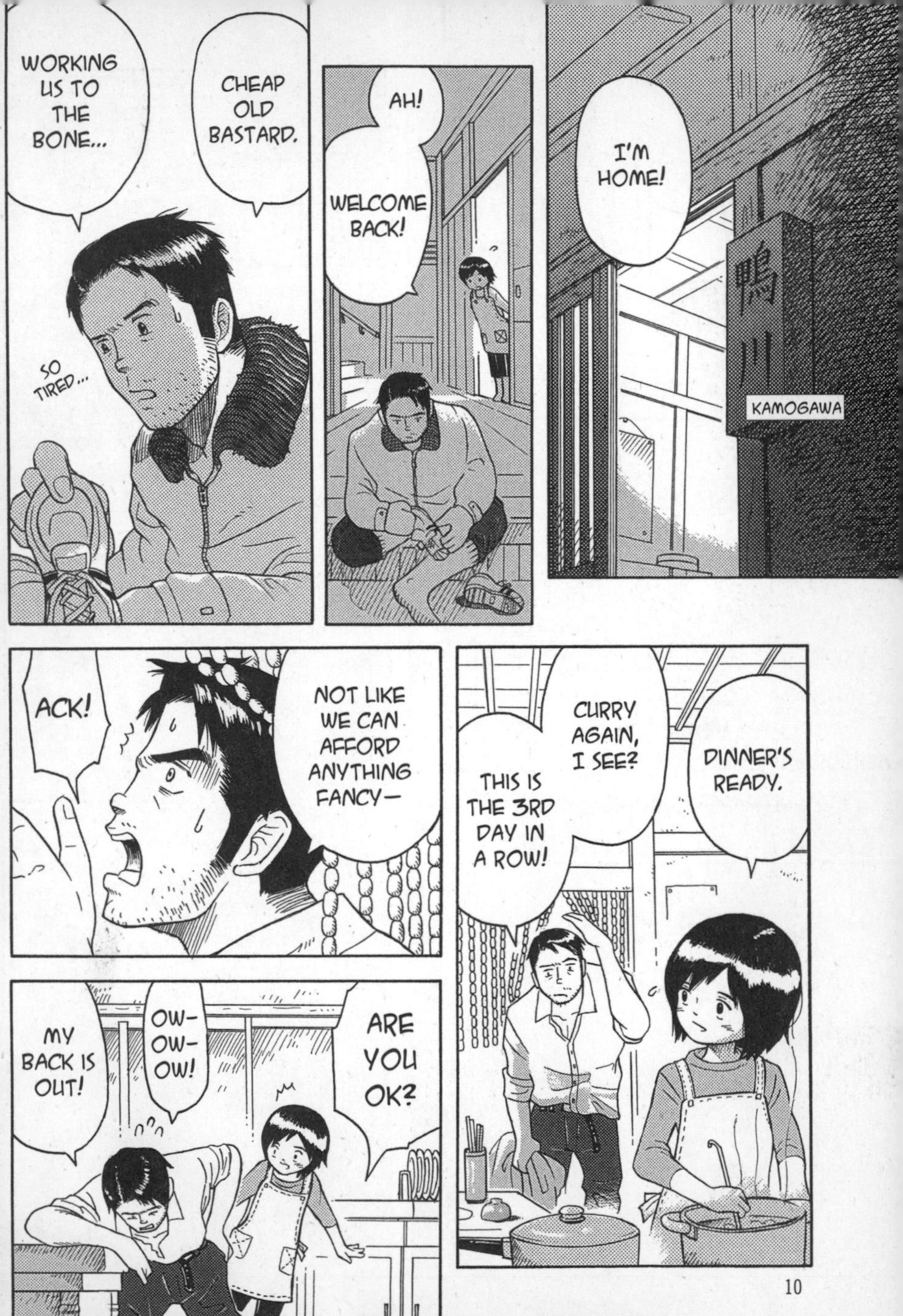
I'M HOME!
鴨川
KAMOGAWA
AH!
WELCOME BACK!
CHEAP OLD BASTARD.
WORKING US TO THE BONE...
SO TIRED...
DINNER'S READY.
CURRY AGAIN, I SEE?
THIS IS THE 3RD DAY IN A ROW!
NOT LIKE WE CAN AFFORD ANYTHING FANCY—
ACK!
ARE YOU OK?
OW-OW-OW!
MY BACK IS OUT!

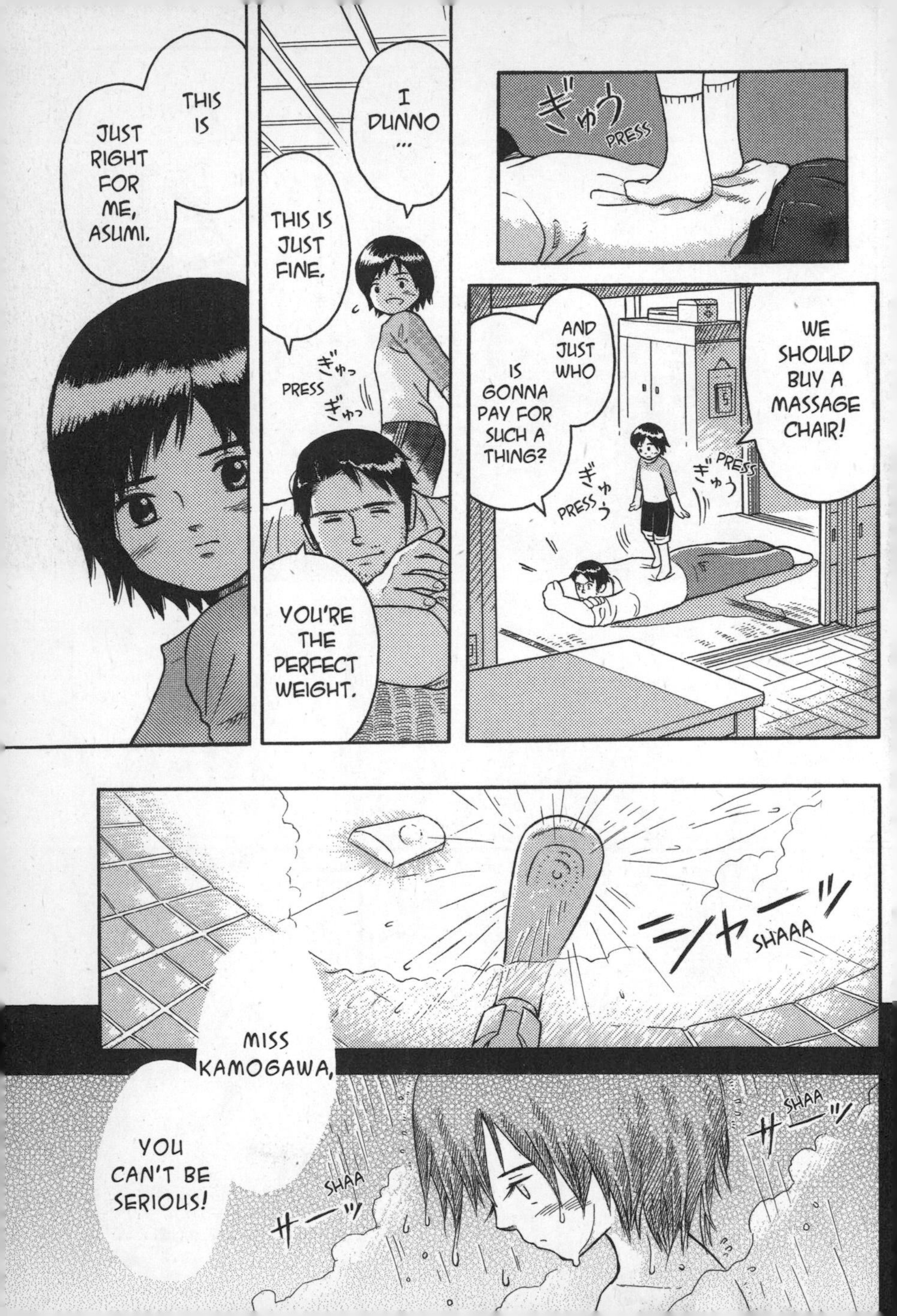
ぎゅう
PRESS
WE SHOULD BUY A MASSAGE CHAIR!
AND JUST WHO IS GONNA PAY FOR SUCH A THING?
ぎゅう PRESS
ぎゅう PRESS
I DUNNO...
THIS IS JUST FINE.
ぎゅっ
PRESS
ぎゅっ
YOU'RE THE PERFECT WEIGHT.
THIS IS JUST RIGHT FOR ME, ASUMI.
シャーッ
SHAAA
MISS KAMOGAWA,
YOU CAN'T BE SERIOUS!
サーッ
SHAA
サーッ
SHAA

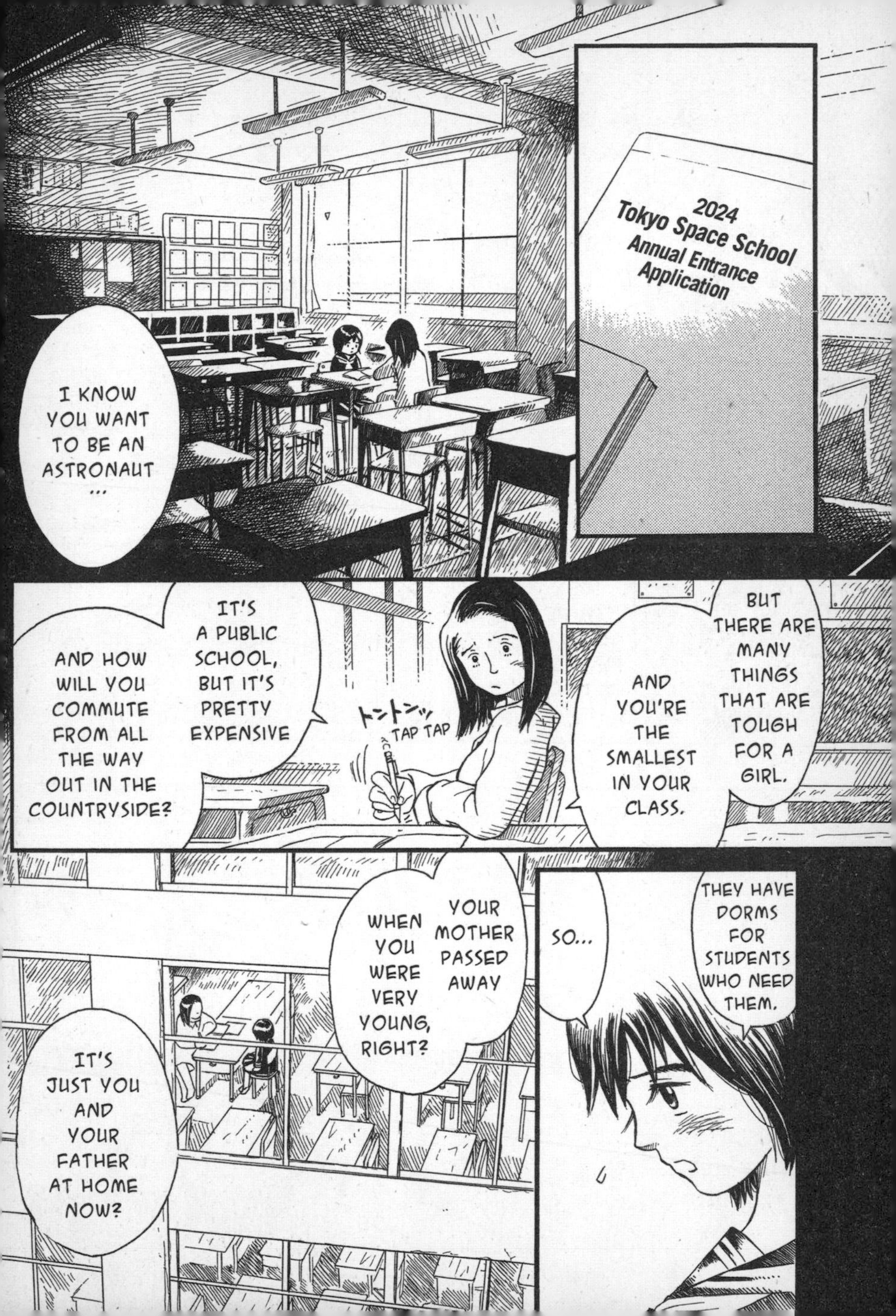
2024 Tokyo Space School Annual Entrance Application
I KNOW YOU WANT TO BE AN ASTRONAUT ...
BUT THERE ARE MANY THINGS THAT ARE TOUGH FOR A GIRL.
AND YOU'RE THE SMALLEST IN YOUR CLASS.
トントンッ TAP TAP
IT'S A PUBLIC SCHOOL, BUT IT'S PRETTY EXPENSIVE
AND HOW WILL YOU COMMUTE FROM ALL THE WAY OUT IN THE COUNTRYSIDE?
THEY HAVE DORMS FOR STUDENTS WHO NEED THEM.
SO...
YOUR MOTHER PASSED AWAY
WHEN YOU WERE VERY YOUNG, RIGHT?
IT'S JUST YOU AND YOUR FATHER AT HOME NOW?

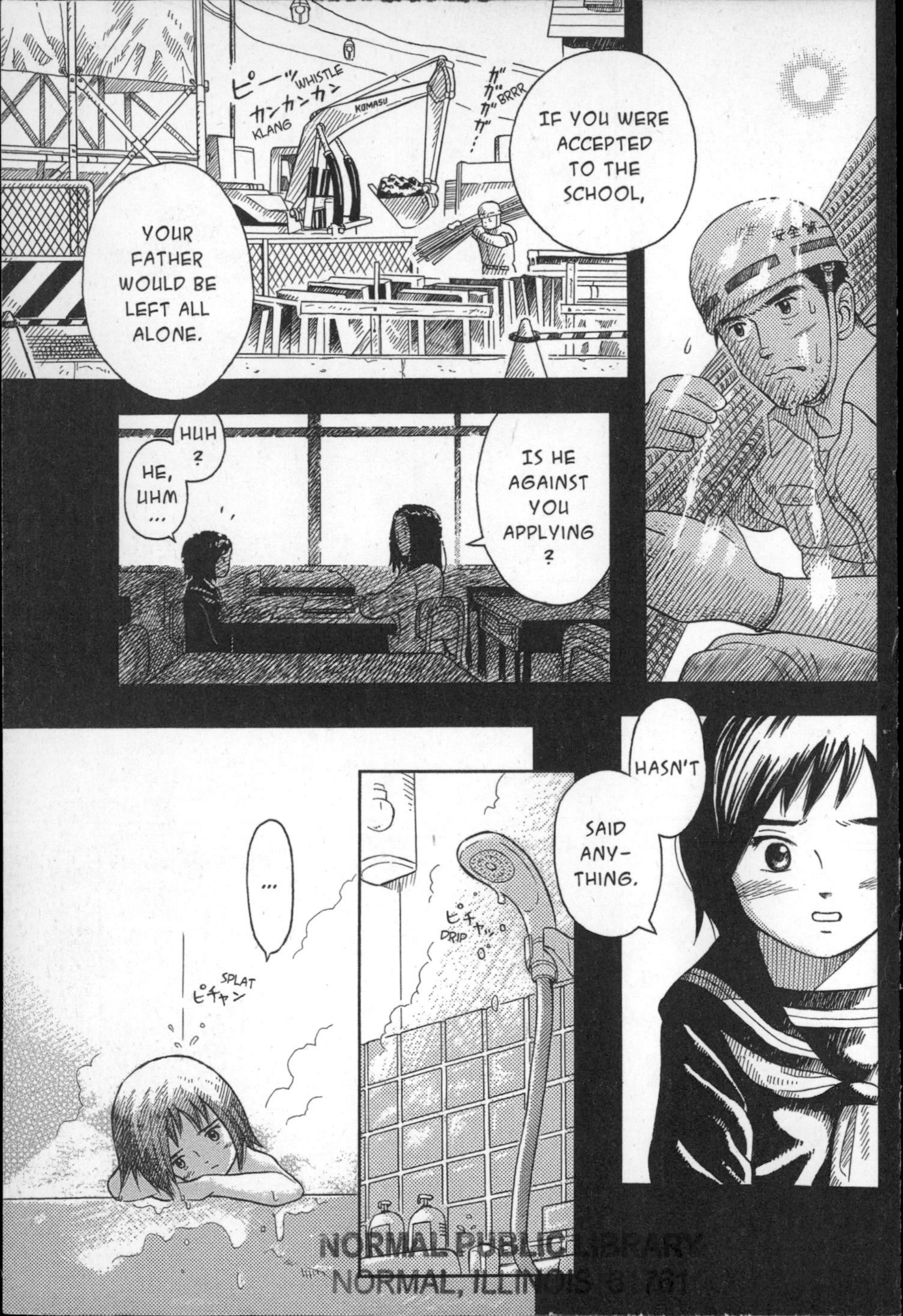
ピーッ WHISTLE
カンカンカン KLANG
ガガガガ BRRR
KOMASU
IF YOU WERE ACCEPTED TO THE SCHOOL,
YOUR FATHER WOULD BE LEFT ALL ALONE.
IS HE AGAINST YOU APPLYING?
HUH?
HE, UHM...
HASN'T
SAID ANYTHING.
ピチャッ DRIP
...
ピチャン SPLAT

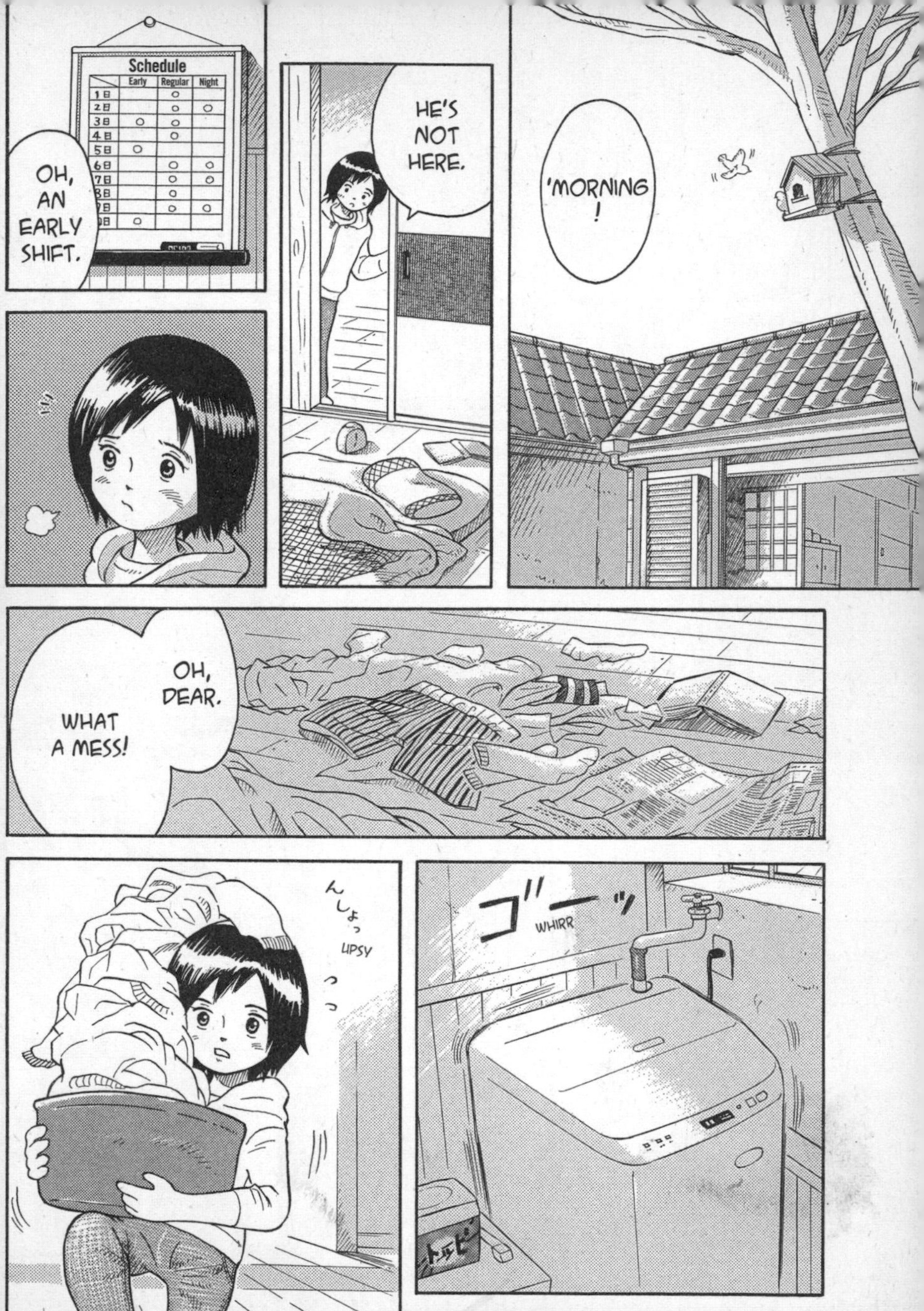
'MORNING!
HE'S NOT HERE.
Schedule
Early Regular Night
OH, AN EARLY SHIFT.
OH, DEAR.
WHAT A MESS!
ゴーッ
WHIRR
んしょっ
UPSY

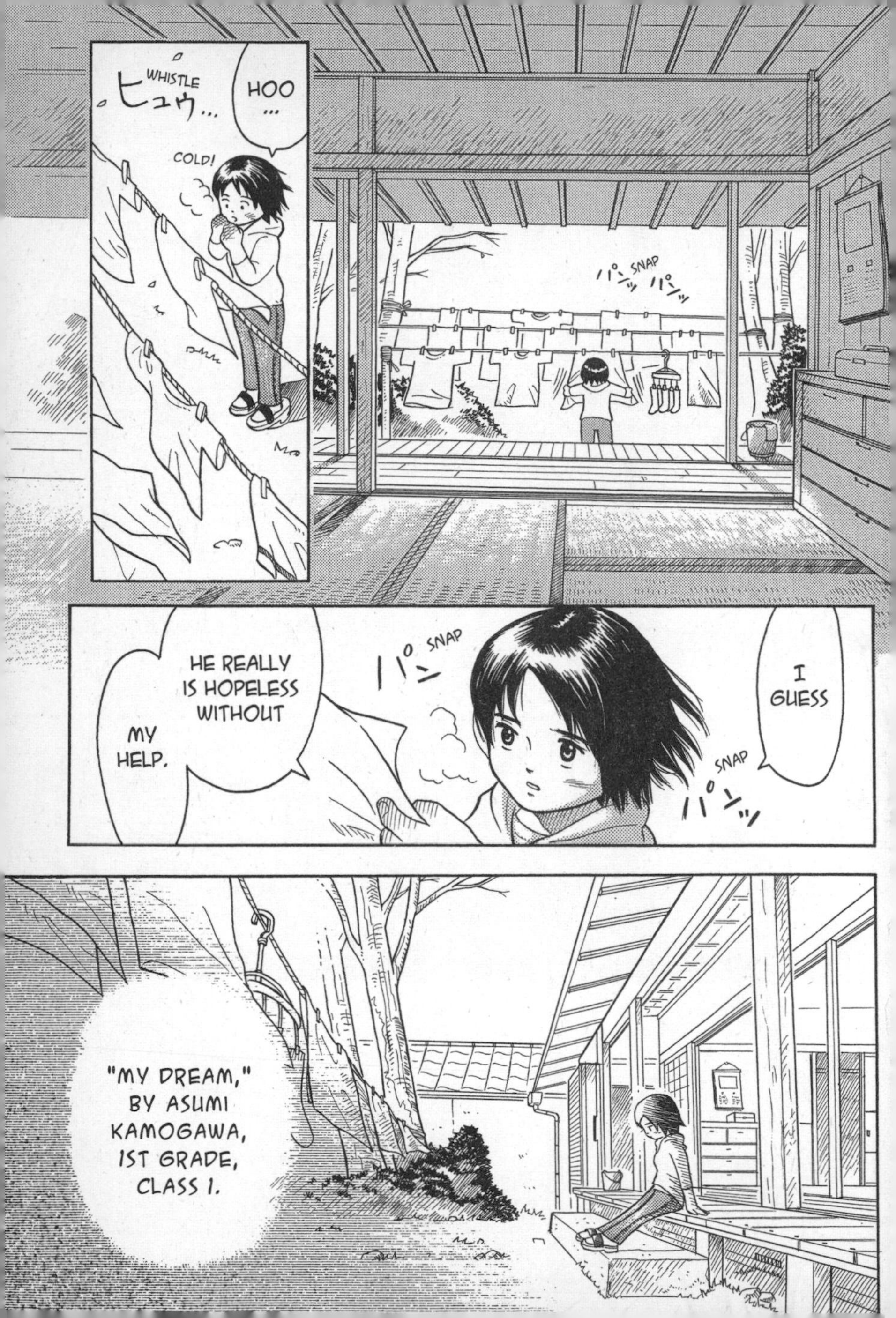

パンッ SNAP パンッ
HOO ...
WHISTLE ヒュウ...
COLD!
I GUESS
SNAP パンッ
SNAP パン
HE REALLY IS HOPELESS WITHOUT MY HELP.
"MY DREAM," BY ASUMI KAMOGAWA, 1ST GRADE, CLASS 1.

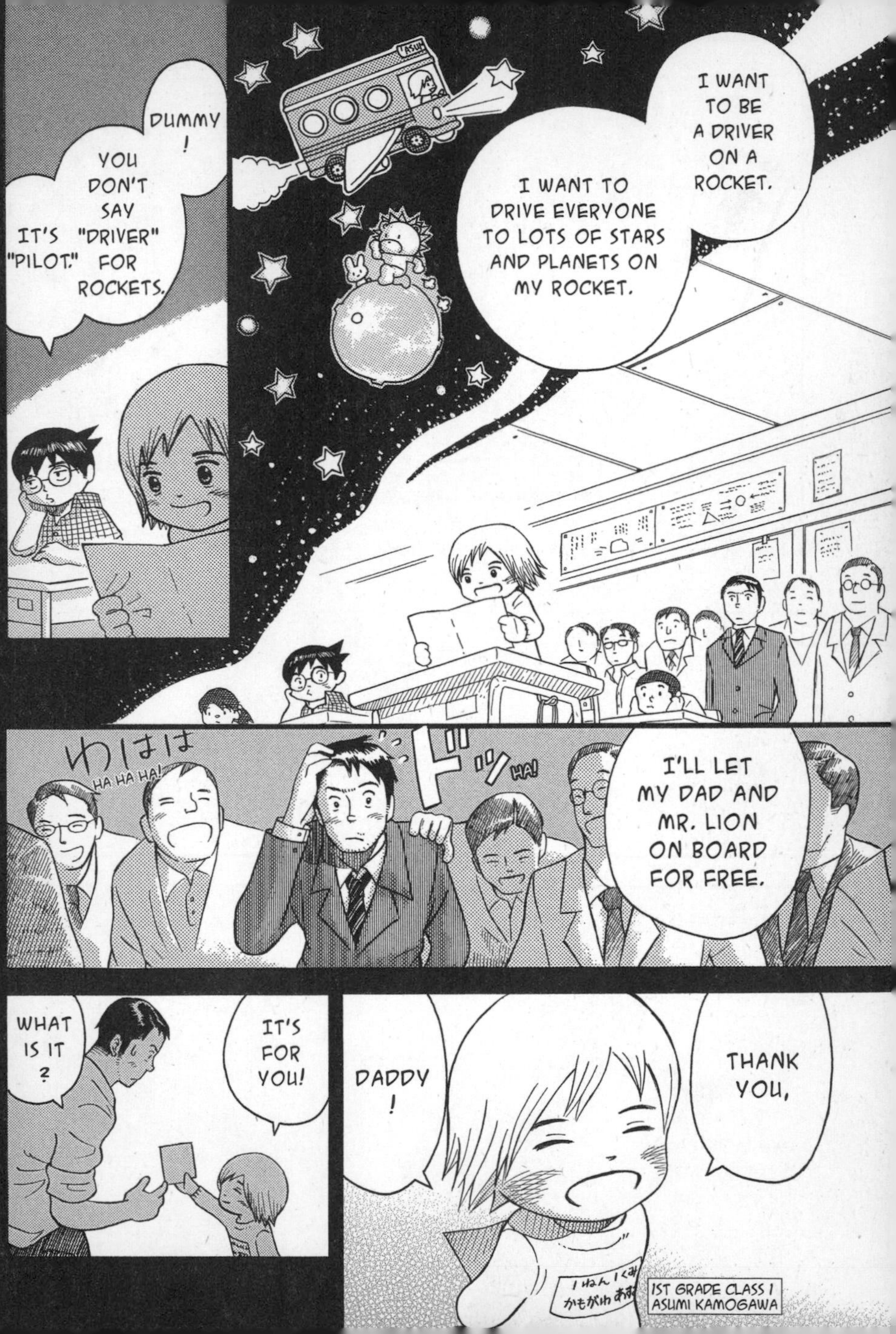
I WANT TO BE A DRIVER ON A ROCKET.
I WANT TO DRIVE EVERYONE TO LOTS OF STARS AND PLANETS ON MY ROCKET.
DUMMY!
YOU DON'T SAY "DRIVER" FOR ROCKETS.
IT'S "PILOT."
I'LL LET MY DAD AND MR. LION ON BOARD FOR FREE.
ドッ
HA!
わはは
HA HA HA!
THANK YOU,
DADDY!
1ST GRADE CLASS 1
ASUMI KAMOGAWA
IT'S FOR YOU!
WHAT IS IT?

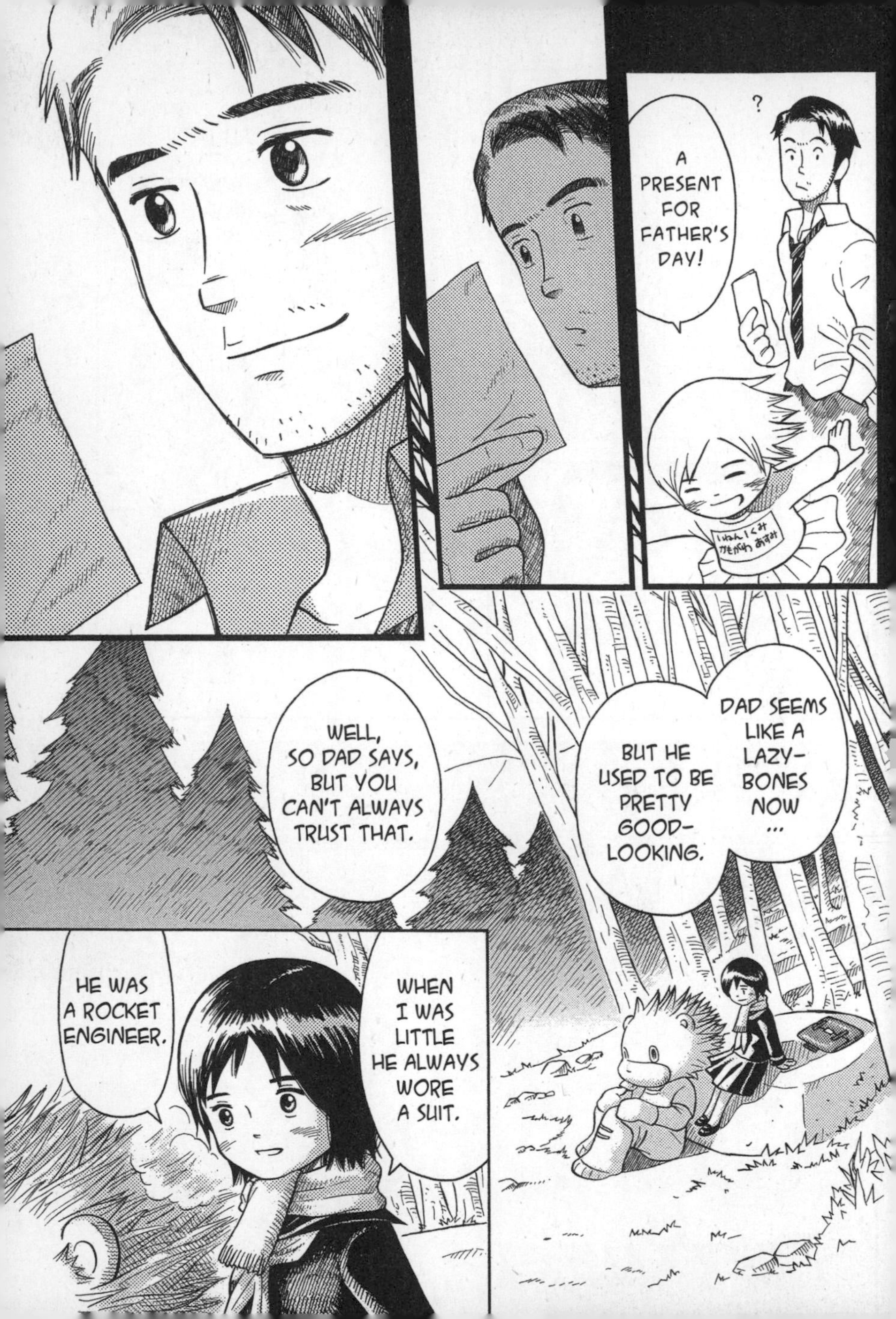
?
A PRESENT FOR FATHER'S DAY!
1ねん1くみ かもがわ あすみ
DAD SEEMS LIKE A LAZY-BONES NOW ...
BUT HE USED TO BE PRETTY GOOD-LOOKING.
WELL, SO DAD SAYS, BUT YOU CAN'T ALWAYS TRUST THAT.
WHEN I WAS LITTLE HE ALWAYS WORE A SUIT.
HE WAS A ROCKET ENGINEER.

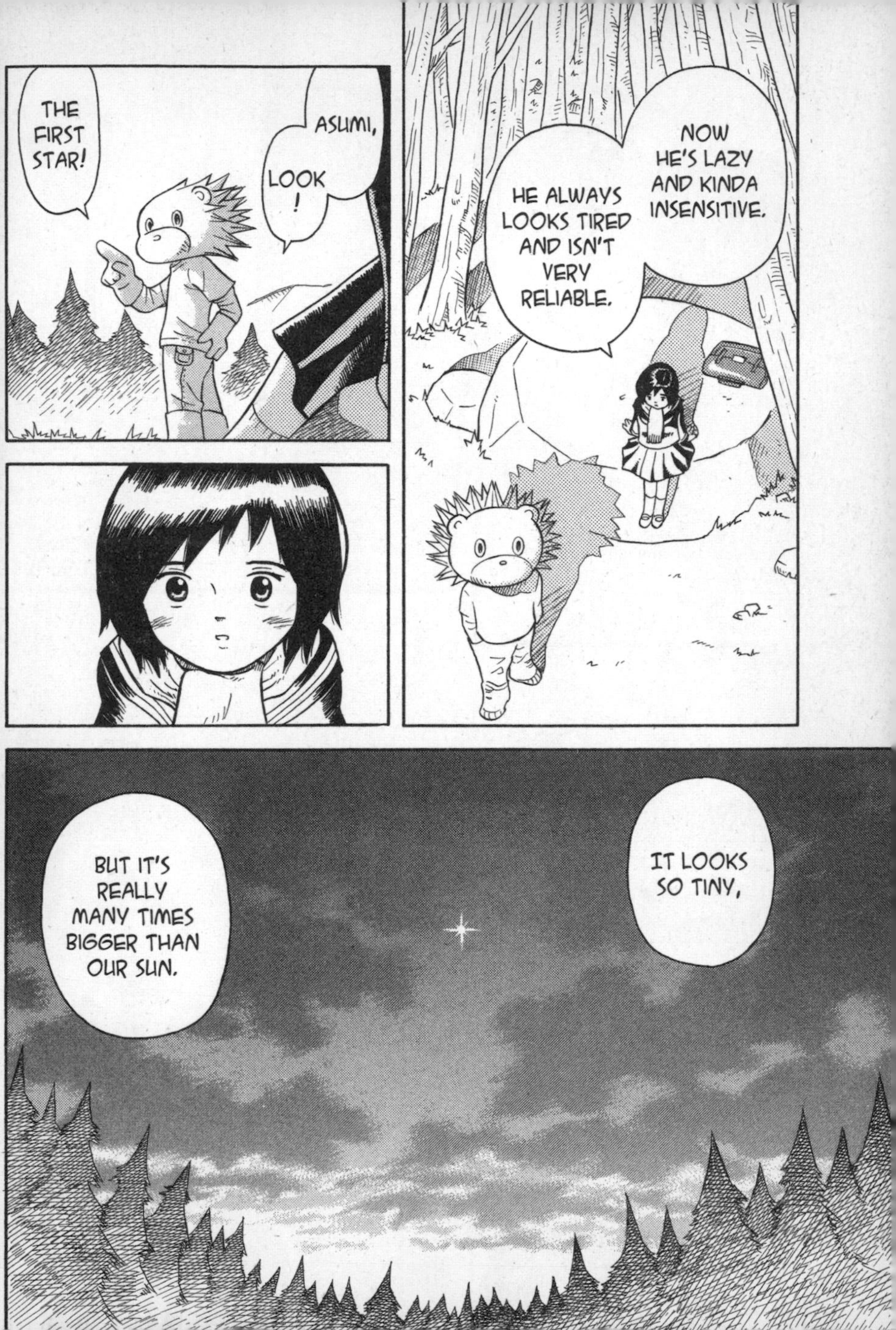
NOW HE'S LAZY AND KINDA INSENSITIVE.
HE ALWAYS LOOKS TIRED AND ISN'T VERY RELIABLE.
ASUMI,
LOOK!
THE FIRST STAR!
IT LOOKS SO TINY,
BUT IT'S REALLY MANY TIMES BIGGER THAN OUR SUN.

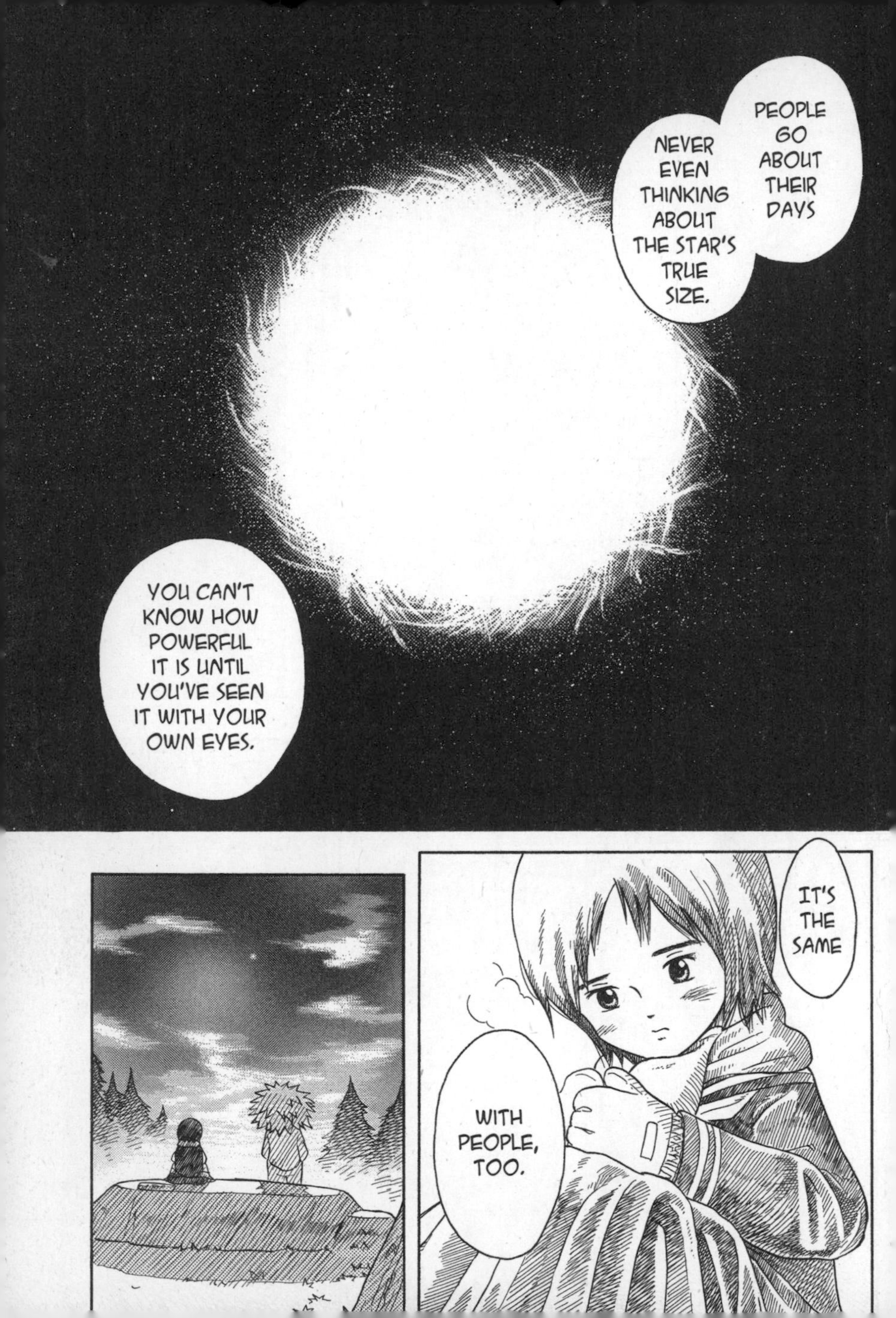
PEOPLE GO ABOUT THEIR DAYS
NEVER EVEN THINKING ABOUT THE STAR'S TRUE SIZE.
YOU CAN'T KNOW HOW POWERFUL IT IS UNTIL YOU'VE SEEN IT WITH YOUR OWN EYES.
IT'S THE SAME
WITH PEOPLE, TOO.

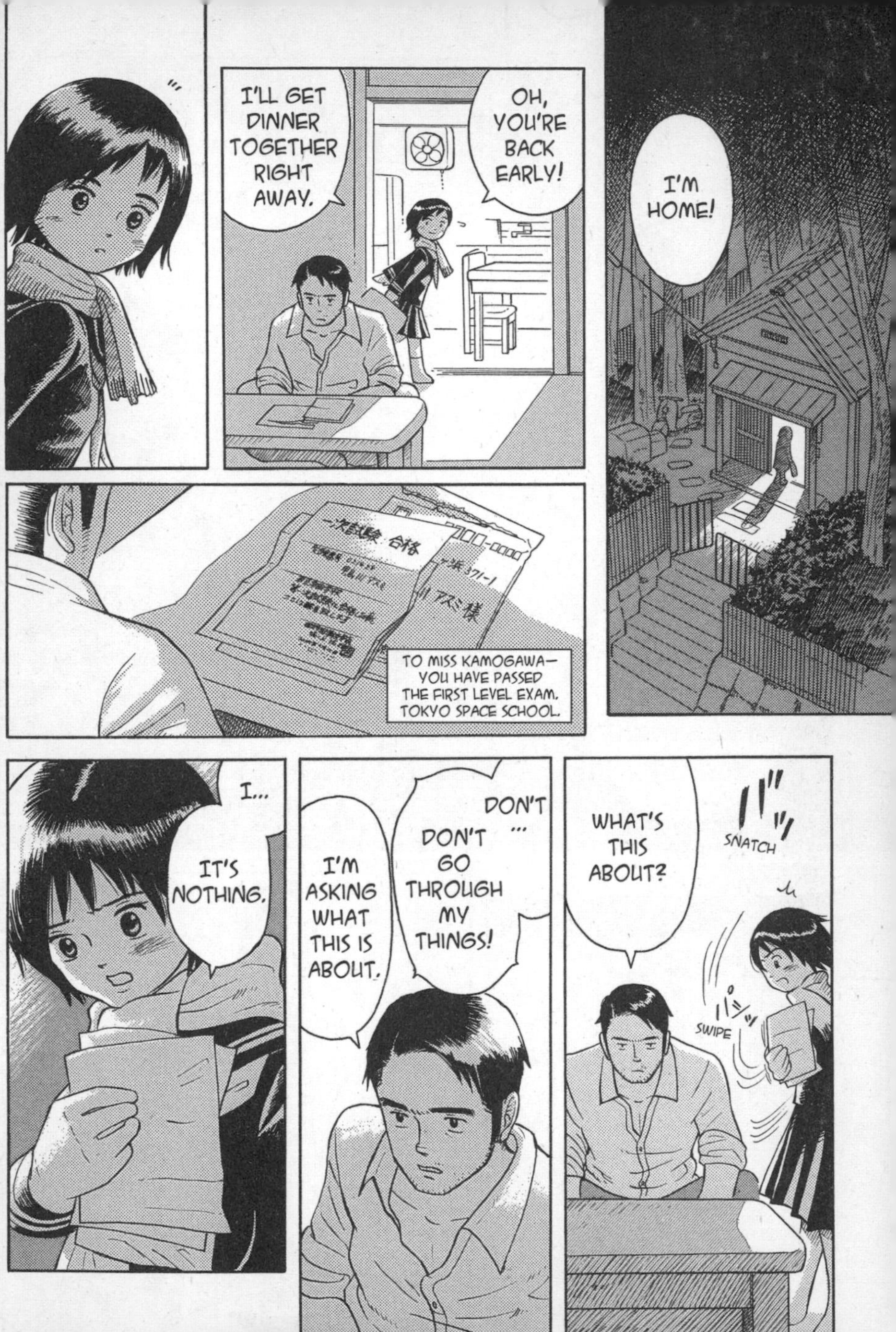
I'M HOME!
OH, YOU'RE BACK EARLY!
I'LL GET DINNER TOGETHER RIGHT AWAY.
一次試験 合格
TO MISS KAMOGAWA— YOU HAVE PASSED THE FIRST LEVEL EXAM. TOKYO SPACE SCHOOL.
WHAT'S THIS ABOUT?
SNATCH
SWIPE
DON'T ...
DON'T GO THROUGH MY THINGS!
I'M ASKING WHAT THIS IS ABOUT.
I...
IT'S NOTHING.

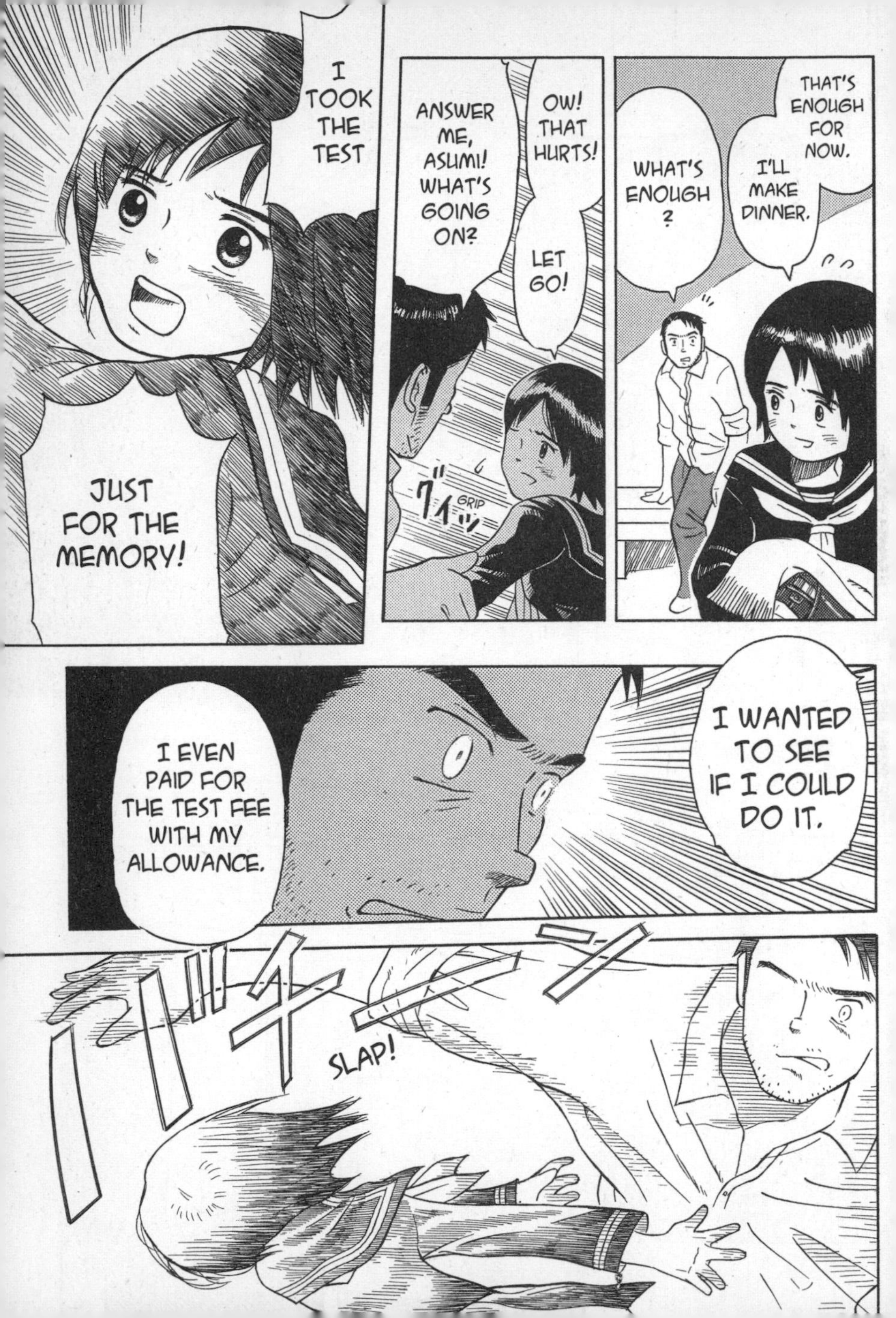
THAT'S ENOUGH FOR NOW. I'LL MAKE DINNER.
WHAT'S ENOUGH?
OW! THAT HURTS!
ANSWER ME, ASUMI! WHAT'S GOING ON?
LET GO!
GRIP
I TOOK THE TEST
JUST FOR THE MEMORY!
I WANTED TO SEE IF I COULD DO IT.
I EVEN PAID FOR THE TEST FEE WITH MY ALLOWANCE.
SLAP!

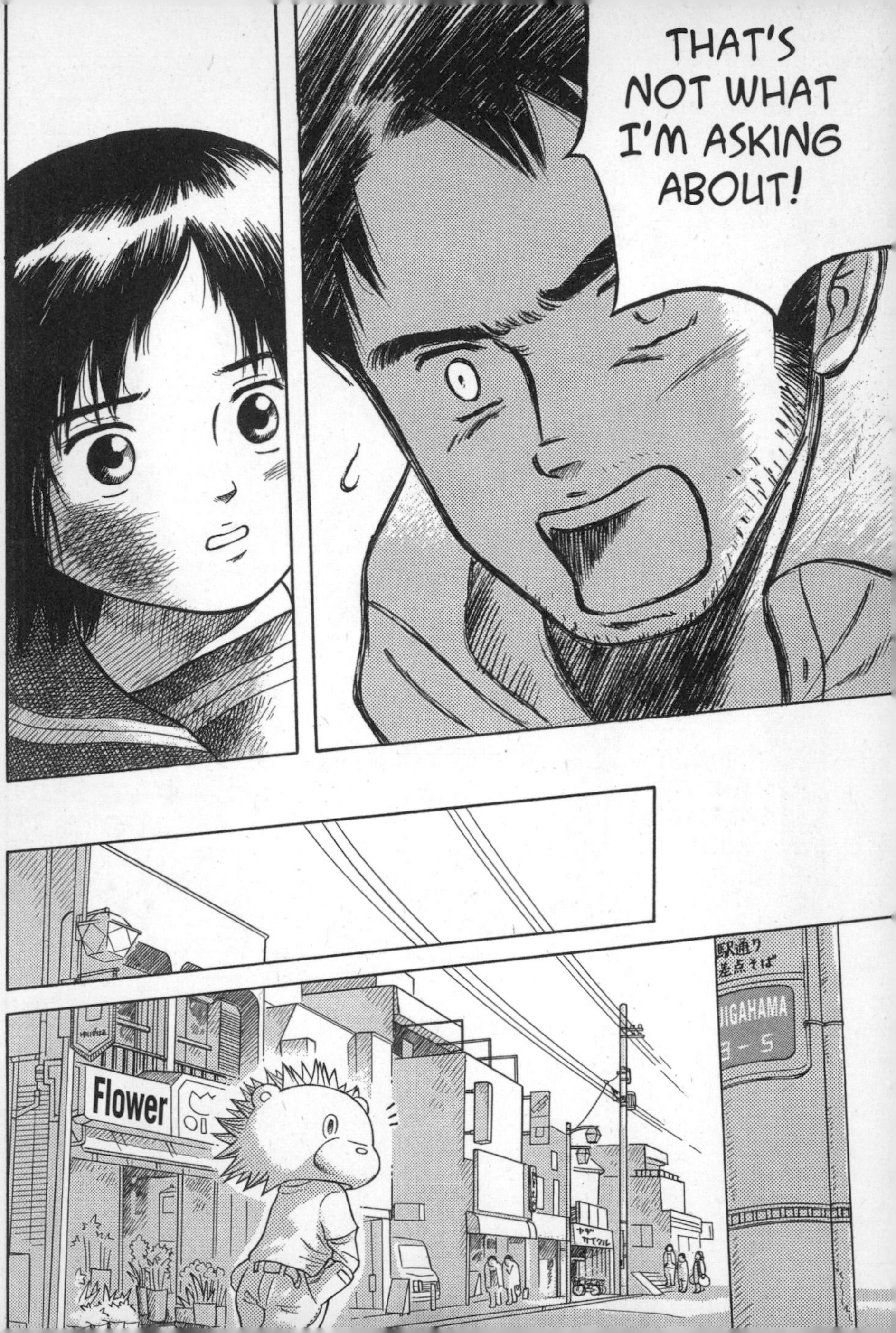
THAT'S NOT WHAT I'M ASKING ABOUT!
駅通り
差点そば
IGAHAMA
3-5
Flower

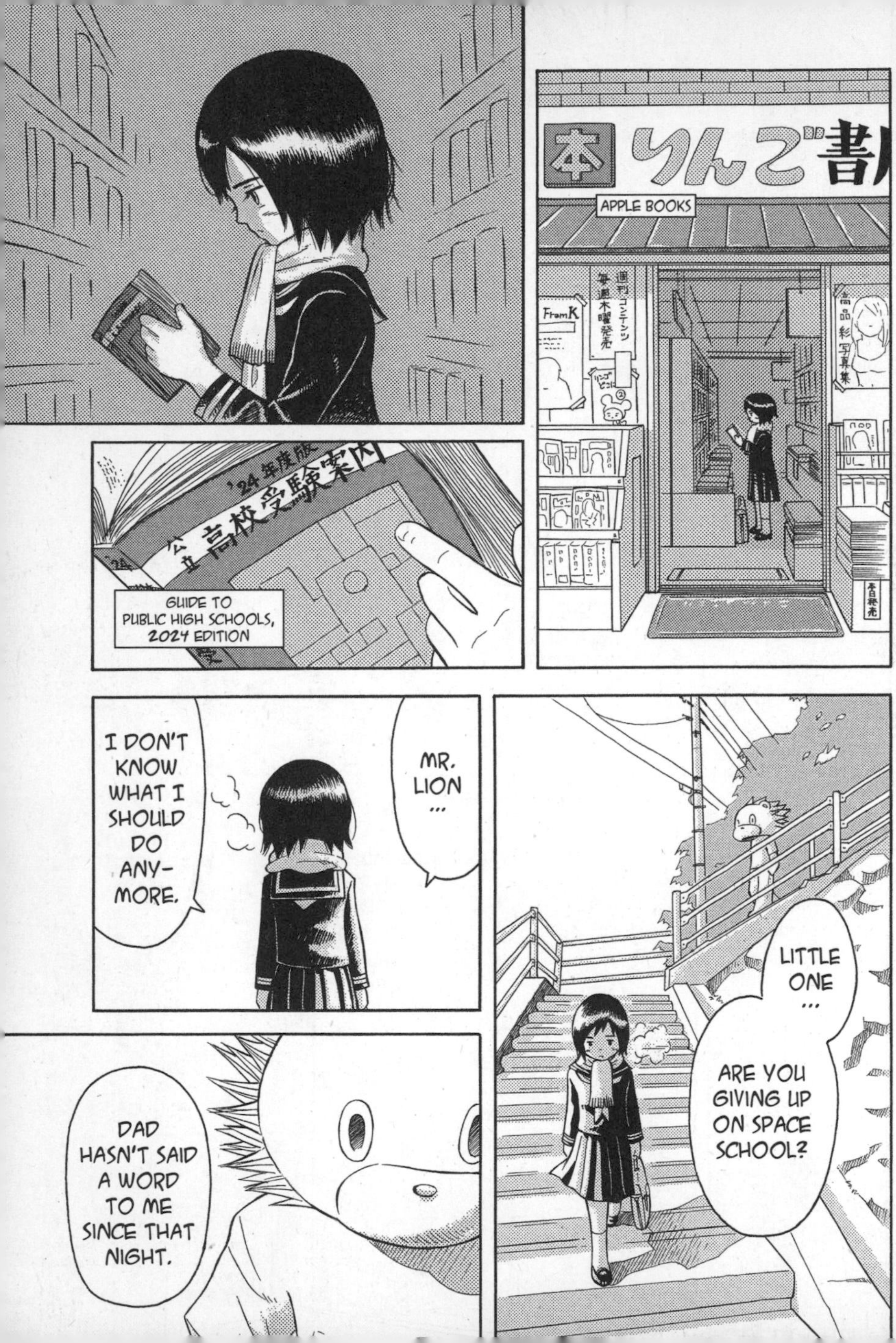

本
りんご書
APPLE BOOKS
週刊コンテンツ
毎週木曜発売
From K
高品彩写真集
'24年度版
公立高校受験案内
GUIDE TO PUBLIC HIGH SCHOOLS, 2024 EDITION
LITTLE ONE ...
ARE YOU GIVING UP ON SPACE SCHOOL?
MR. LION ...
I DON'T KNOW WHAT I SHOULD DO ANYMORE.
DAD HASN'T SAID A WORD TO ME SINCE THAT NIGHT.

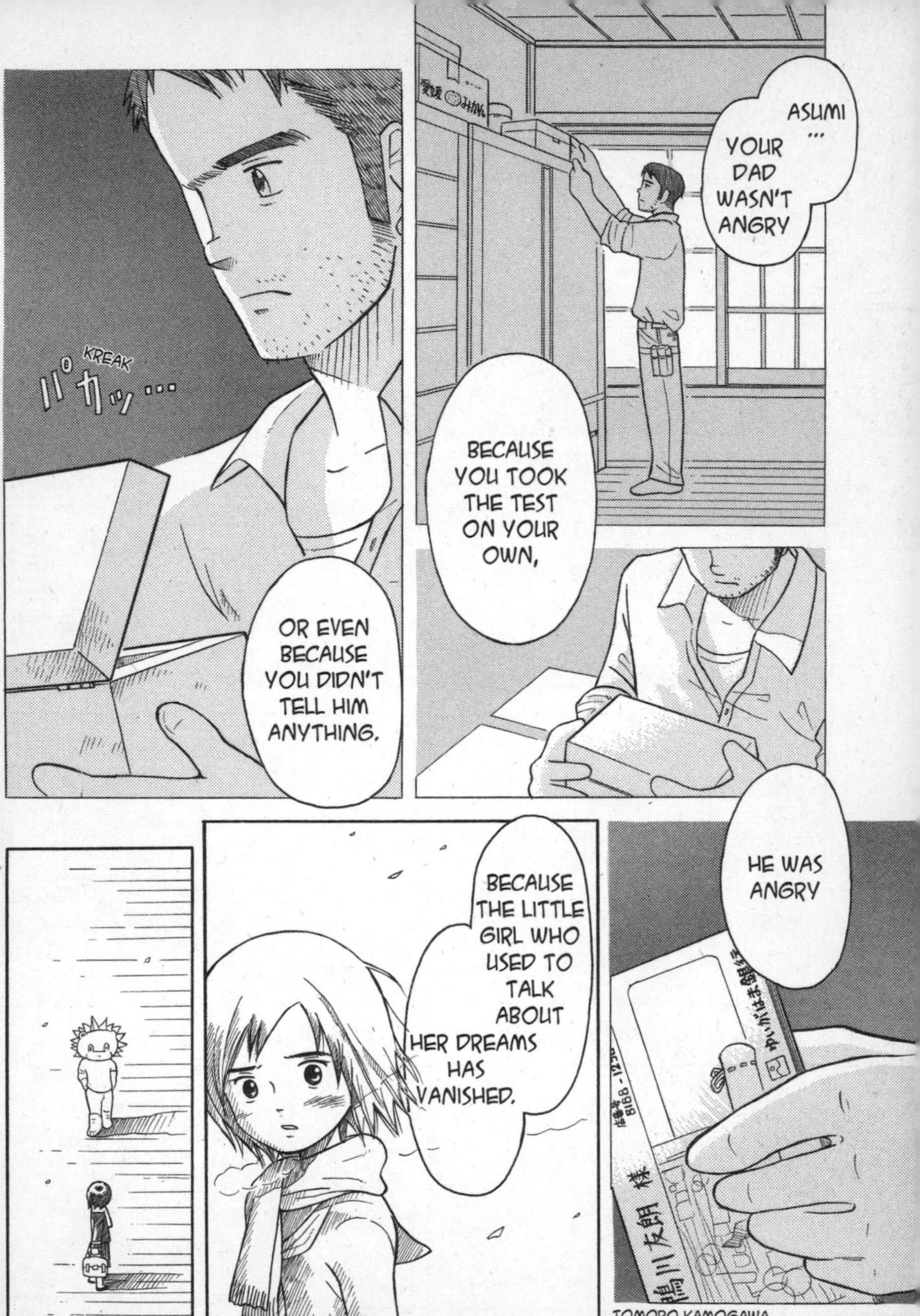
ASUMI ... YOUR DAD WASN'T ANGRY
BECAUSE YOU TOOK THE TEST ON YOUR OWN,
KREAK
パカッ...
OR EVEN BECAUSE YOU DIDN'T TELL HIM ANYTHING.
HE WAS ANGRY
鴨川友朗 様
ゆいがはま銀行
TOMORO KAMOGAWA
YUIGAHAMA BANK
BECAUSE THE LITTLE GIRL WHO USED TO TALK ABOUT HER DREAMS HAS VANISHED.

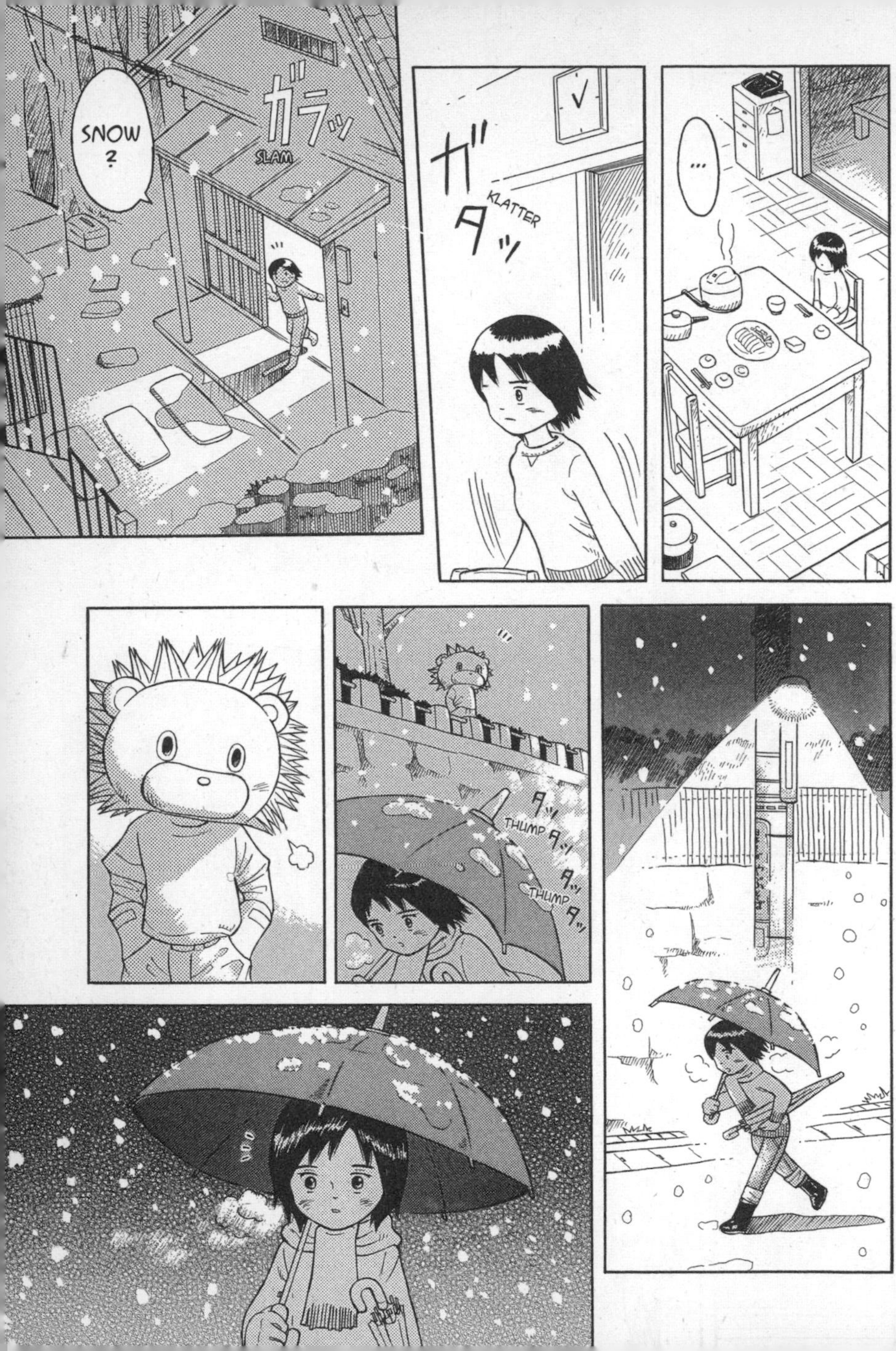
...
ガッ
タッ
KLATTER
ガラッ
SLAM
SNOW?
ダッ
THUMP
ダッ
ダッ
THUMP
ダッ

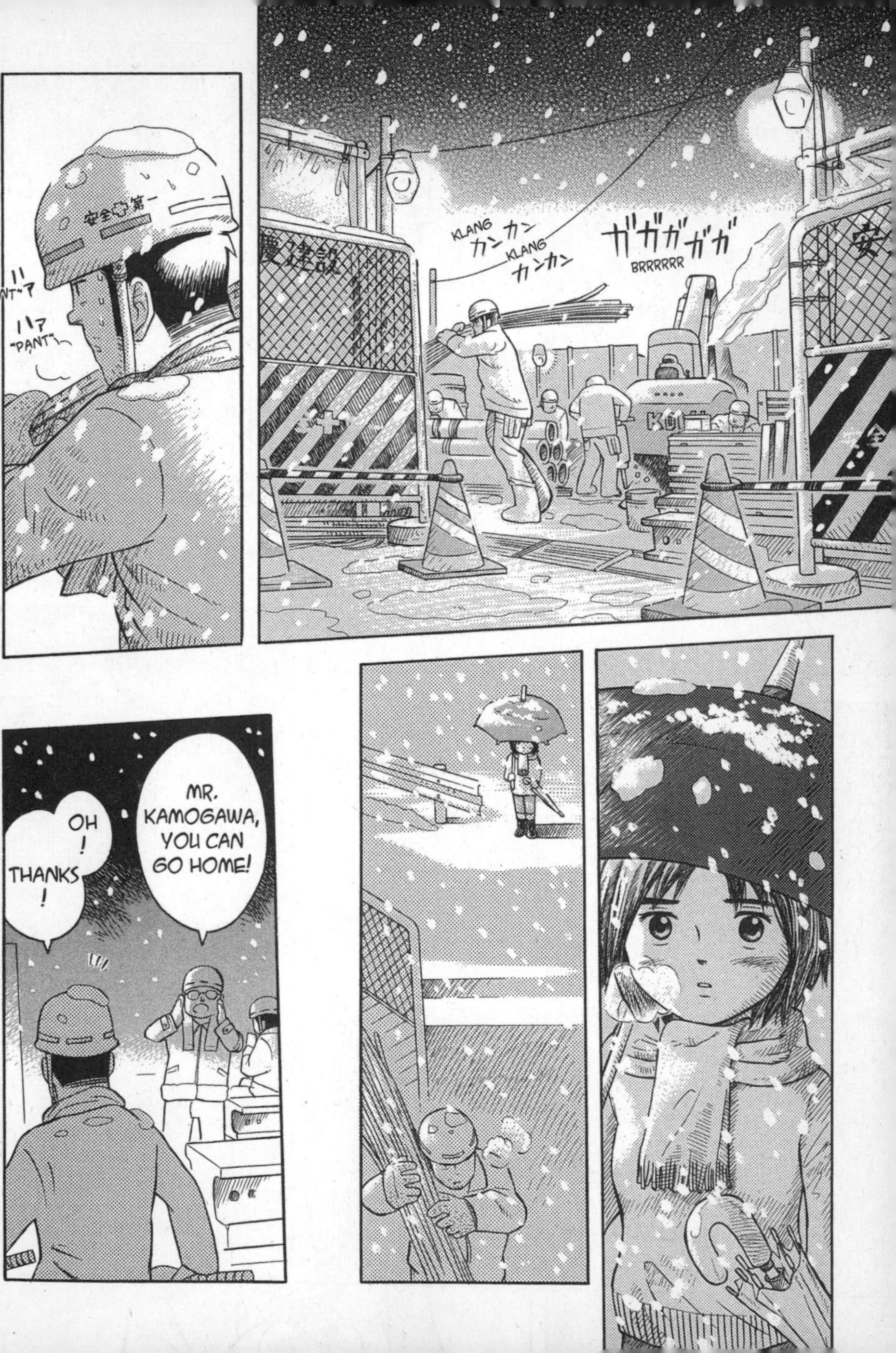
KLANG
カンカン
KLANG
カンカン
ガガガガガ
BRRRRRR
慶建設
安全第一
ハァ "PANT"
ハァ "PANT"
MR. KAMOGAWA, YOU CAN GO HOME!
OH! THANKS!

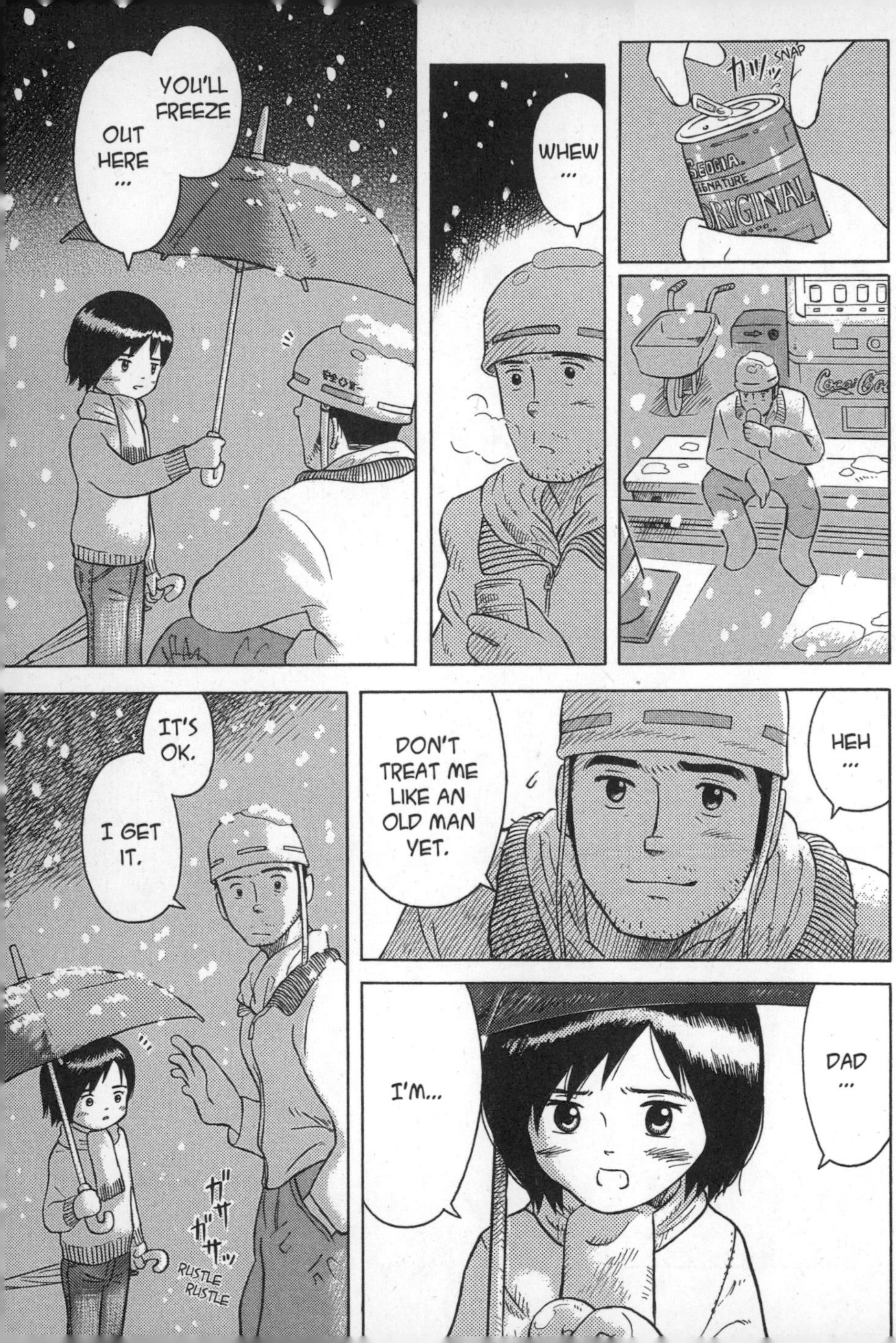
SNAP
WHEW ...
YOU'LL FREEZE OUT HERE ...
HEH ...
DON'T TREAT ME LIKE AN OLD MAN YET.
DAD ...
I'M...
IT'S OK.
I GET IT.
RUSTLE RUSTLE

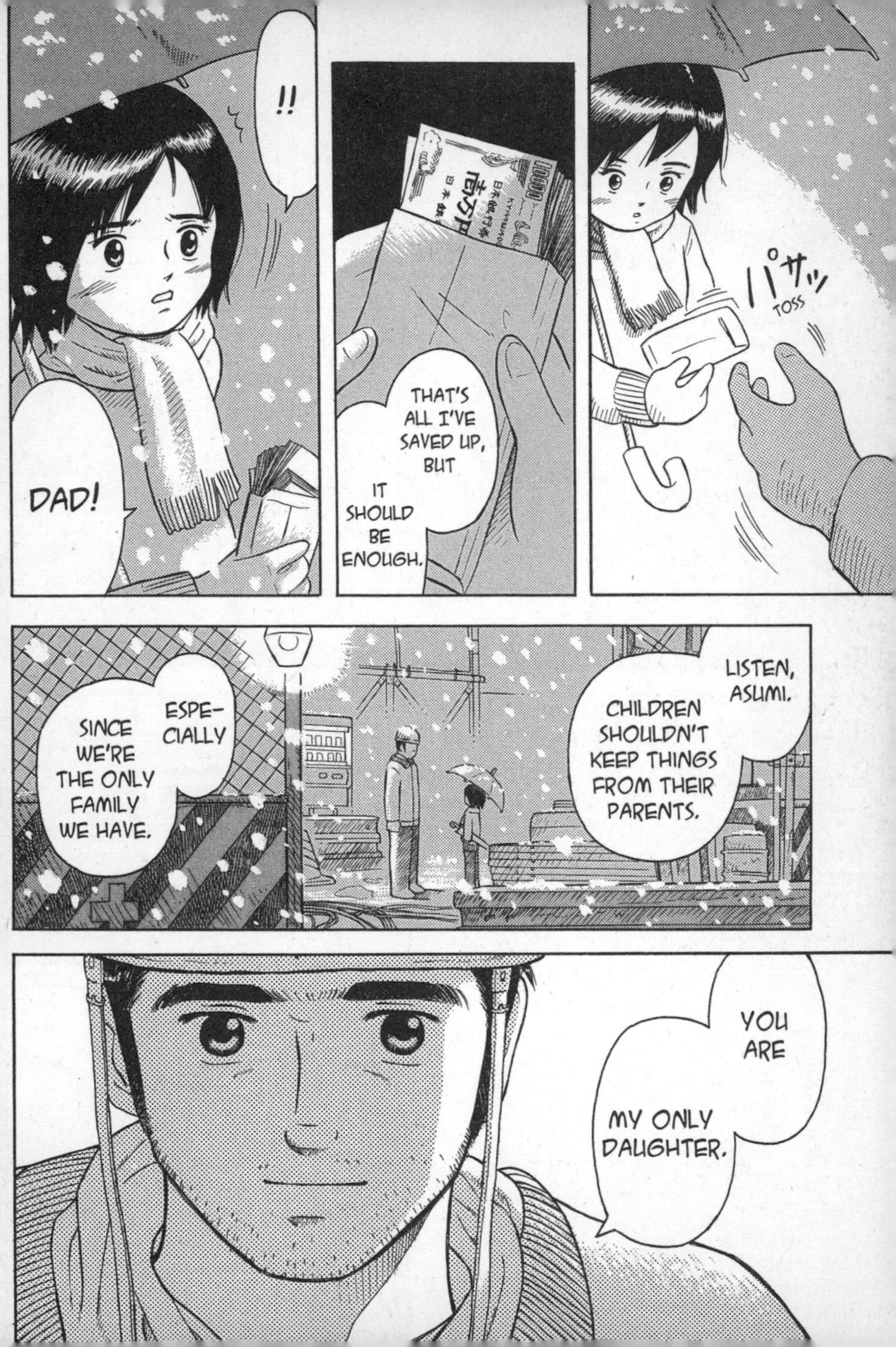

パサッ
TOSS
THAT'S ALL I'VE SAVED UP, BUT
IT SHOULD BE ENOUGH.
!!
DAD!
LISTEN, ASUMI.
CHILDREN SHOULDN'T KEEP THINGS FROM THEIR PARENTS.
ESPE-CIALLY
SINCE WE'RE THE ONLY FAMILY WE HAVE.
YOU ARE
MY ONLY DAUGHTER.

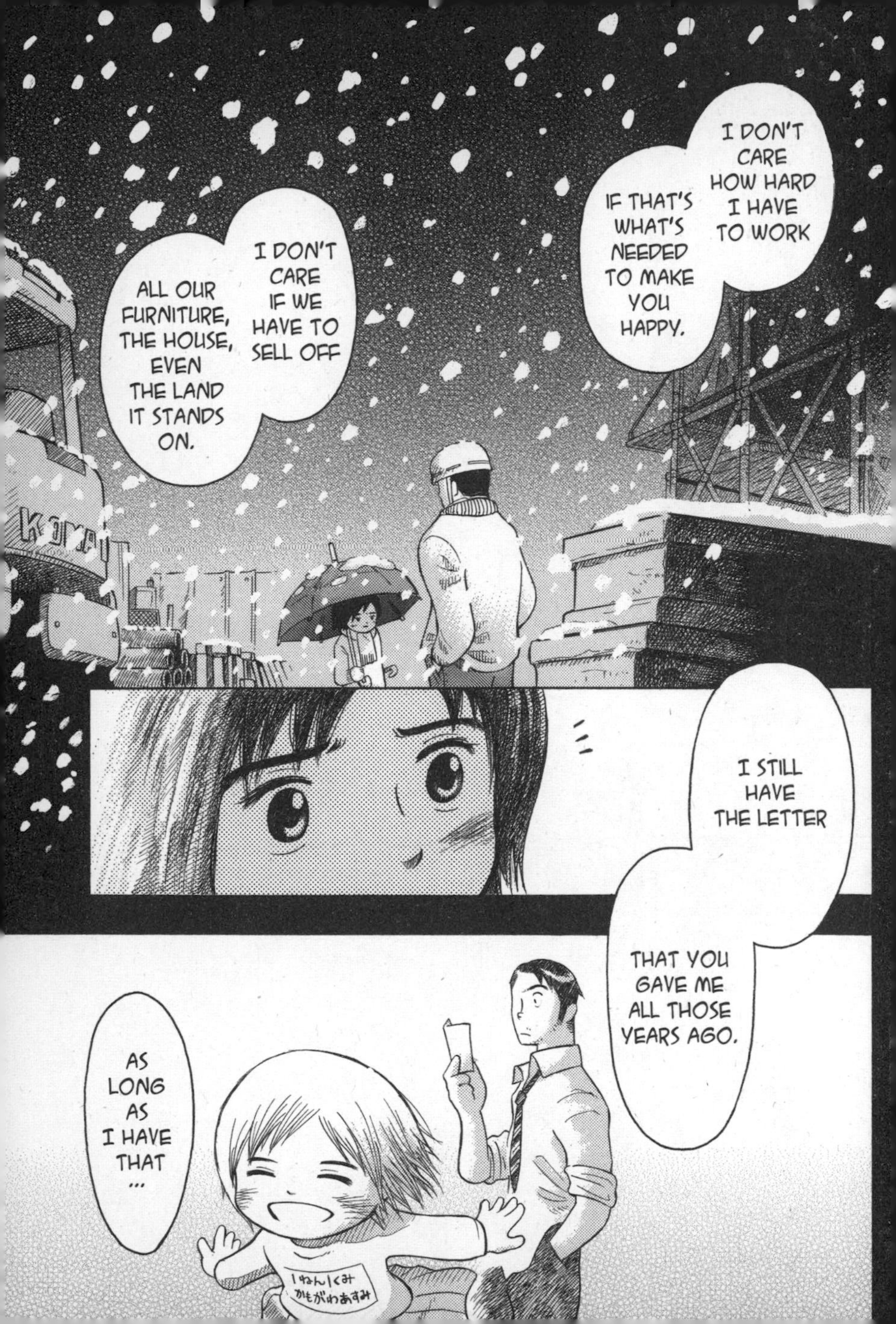
I DON'T CARE HOW HARD I HAVE TO WORK
IF THAT'S WHAT'S NEEDED TO MAKE YOU HAPPY.
I DON'T CARE IF WE HAVE TO SELL OFF
ALL OUR FURNITURE, THE HOUSE, EVEN THE LAND IT STANDS ON.
I STILL HAVE THE LETTER
THAT YOU GAVE ME ALL THOSE YEARS AGO.
AS LONG AS I HAVE THAT ...
1ねん1くみ かもがわあすみ

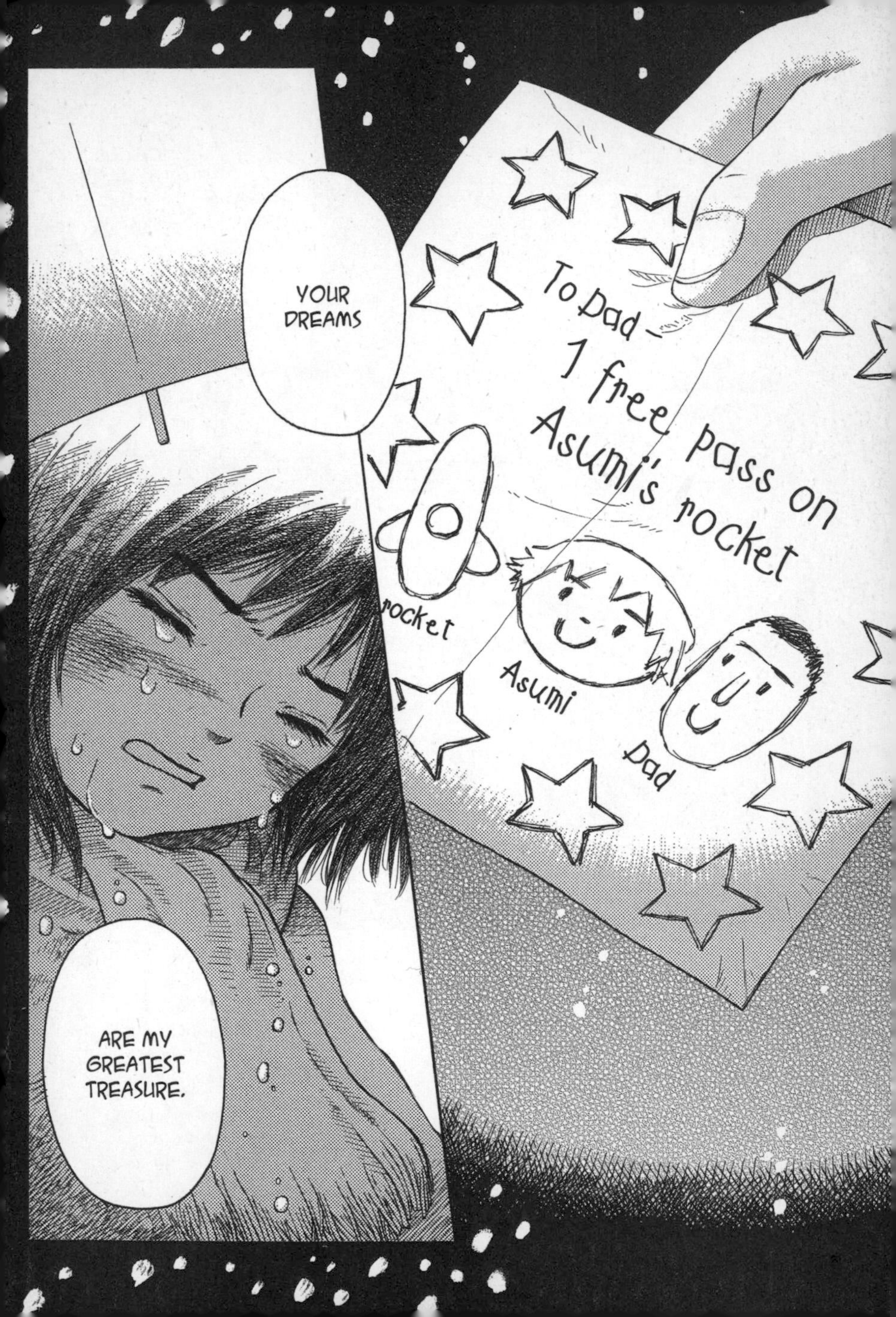
To Dad -
1 free pass on Asumi's rocket
rocket
Asumi
Dad
YOUR DREAMS
ARE MY GREATEST TREASURE.

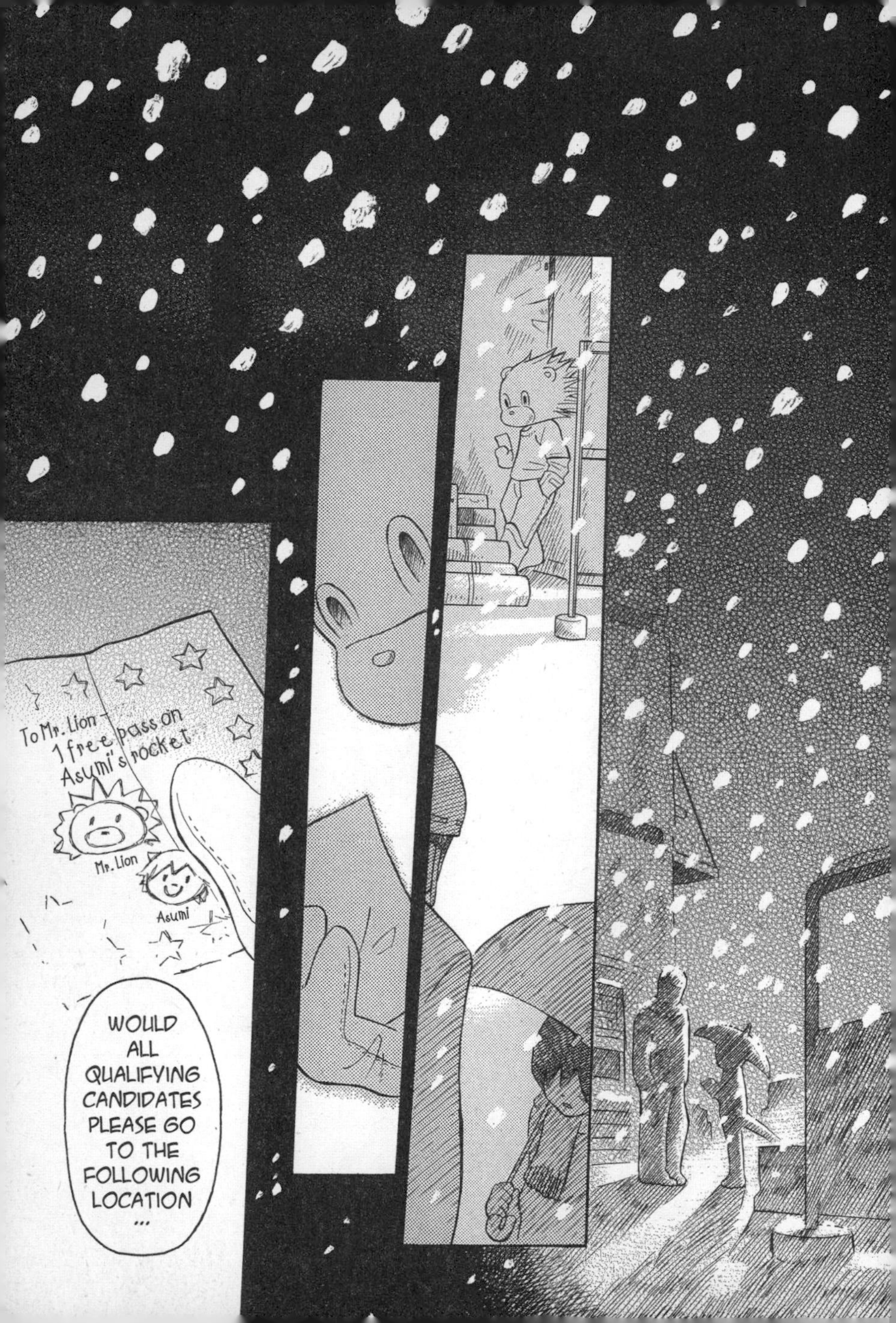
To Mr. Lion -
1 free pass on
Asumi's rocket
Mr. Lion
Asumi
WOULD ALL QUALIFYING CANDIDATES PLEASE GO TO THE FOLLOWING LOCATION ...

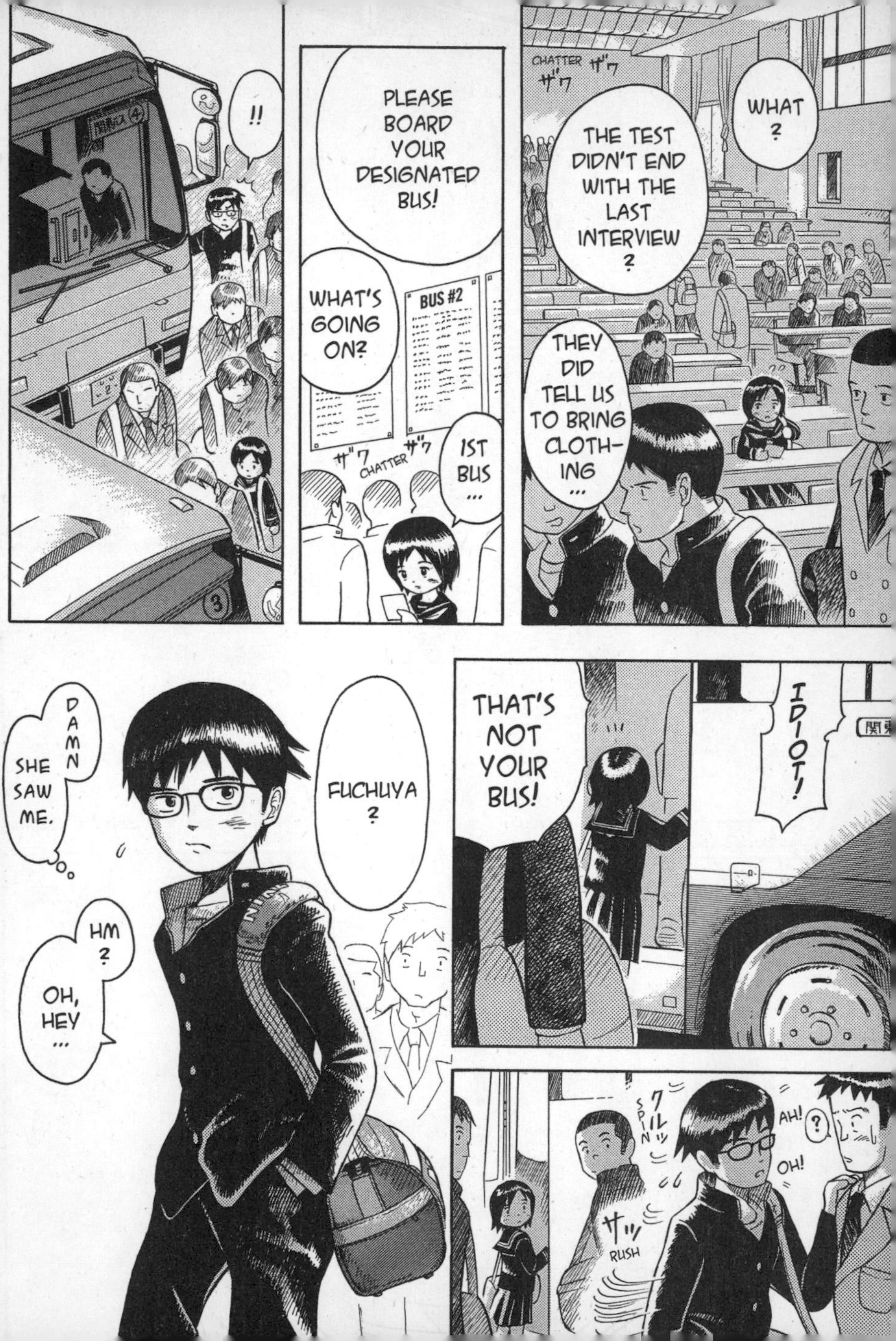 CHATTER ザワ ザワ
WHAT ?
THE TEST DIDN'T END WITH THE LAST INTERVIEW ?
THEY DID TELL US TO BRING CLOTHING ...
PLEASE BOARD YOUR DESIGNATED BUS!
BUS #2
1ST BUS ...
WHAT'S GOING ON?
ザワ CHATTER ザワ
!!
IDIOT!
THAT'S NOT YOUR BUS!
AH!
?
OH!
クルッ SPIN
サッ RUSH
FUCHUYA ?
DAMN SHE SAW ME.
HM ?
OH, HEY ...

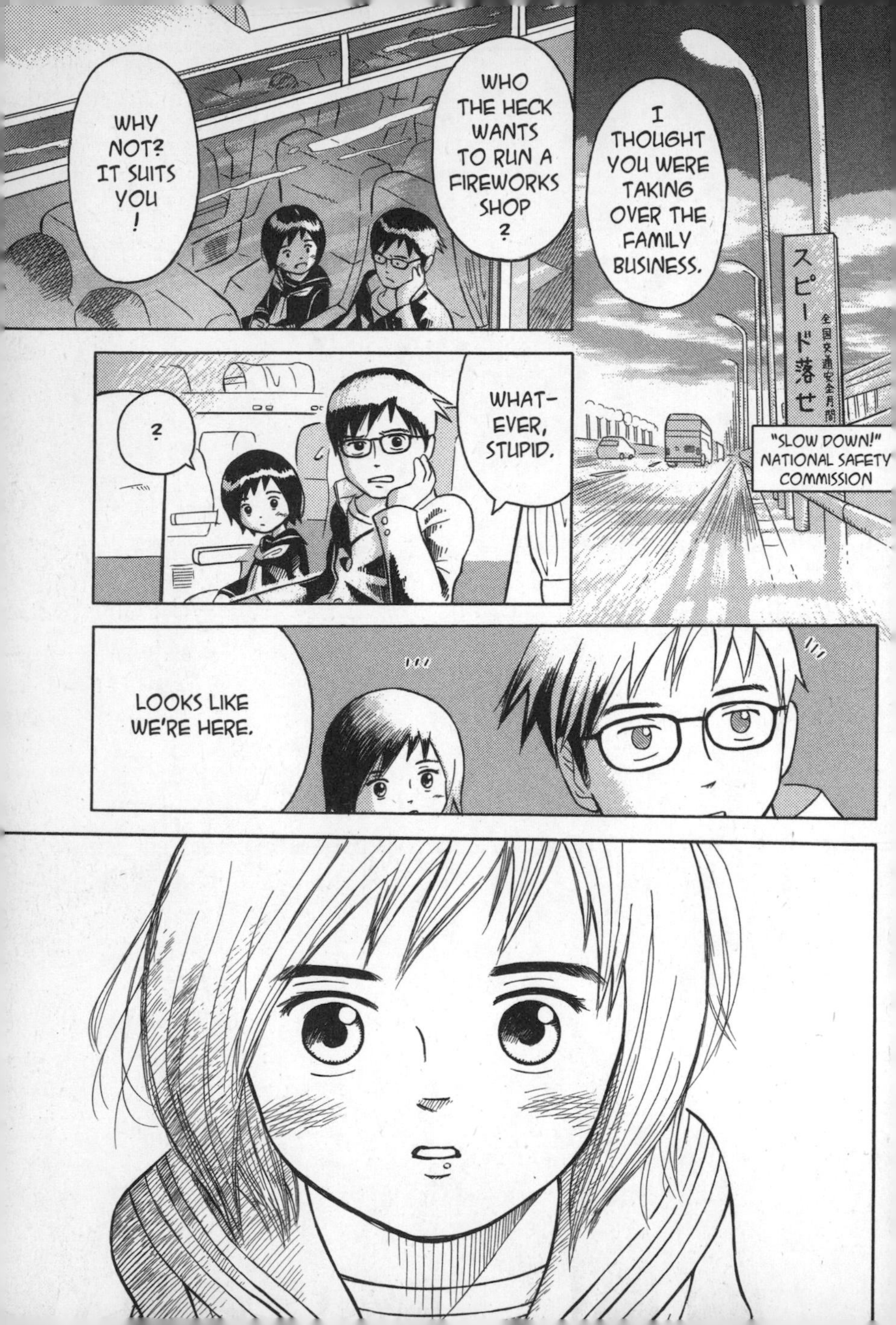
I THOUGHT YOU WERE TAKING OVER THE FAMILY BUSINESS.
スピード落せ
全国交通安全月間
"SLOW DOWN!" NATIONAL SAFETY COMMISSION
WHO THE HECK WANTS TO RUN A FIREWORKS SHOP?
WHY NOT? IT SUITS YOU!
WHAT-EVER, STUPID.
?
LOOKS LIKE WE'RE HERE.

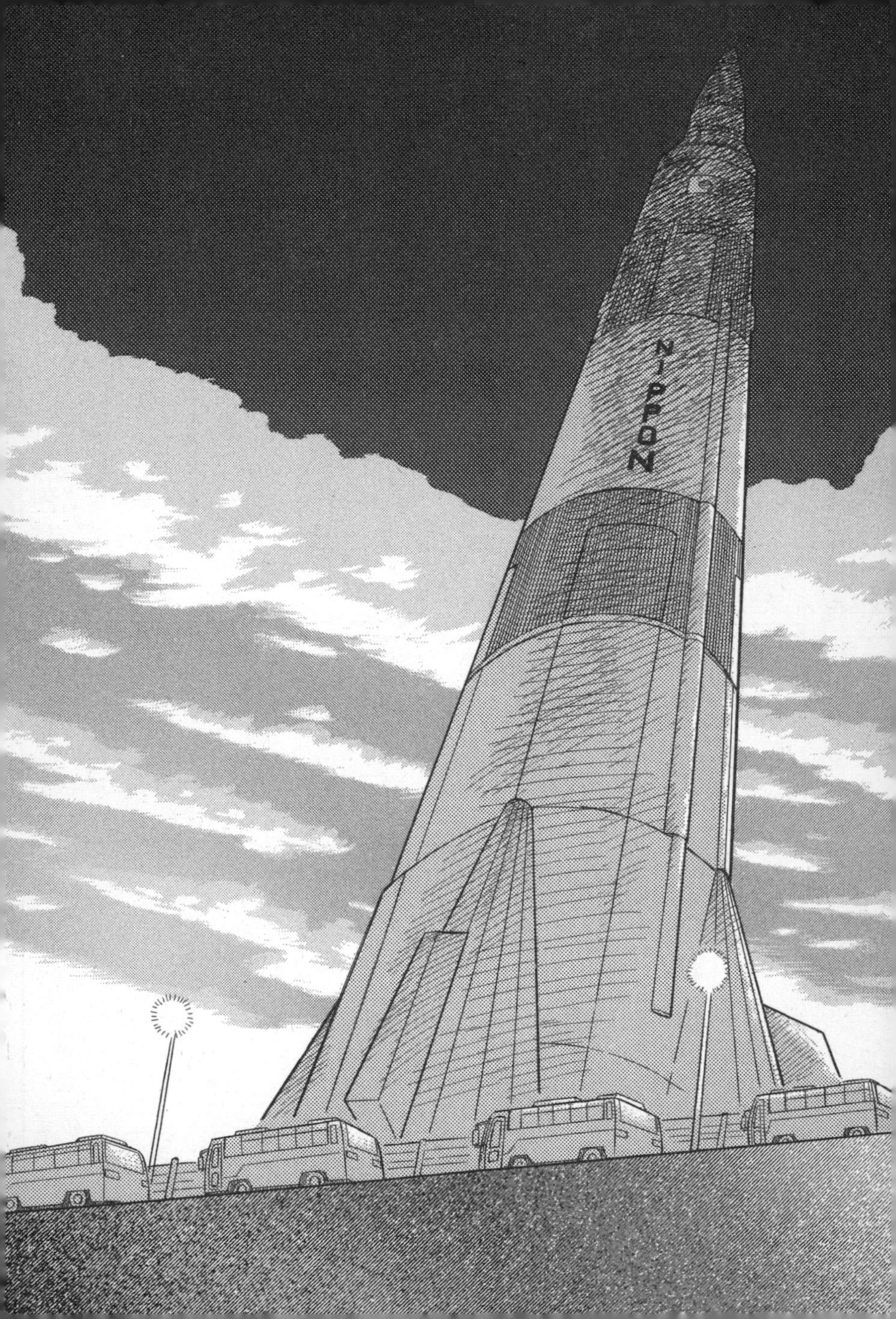
NIPPON

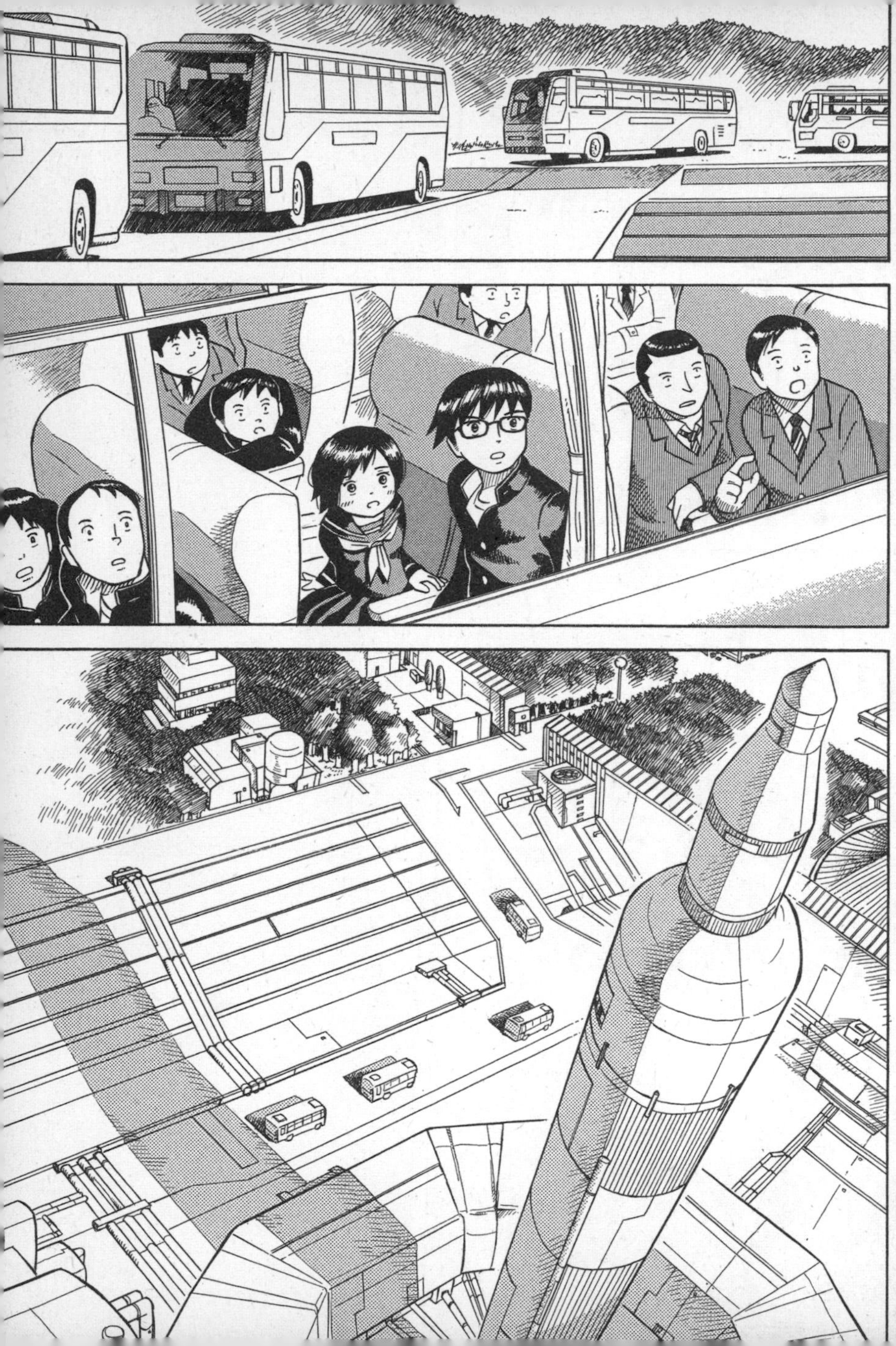

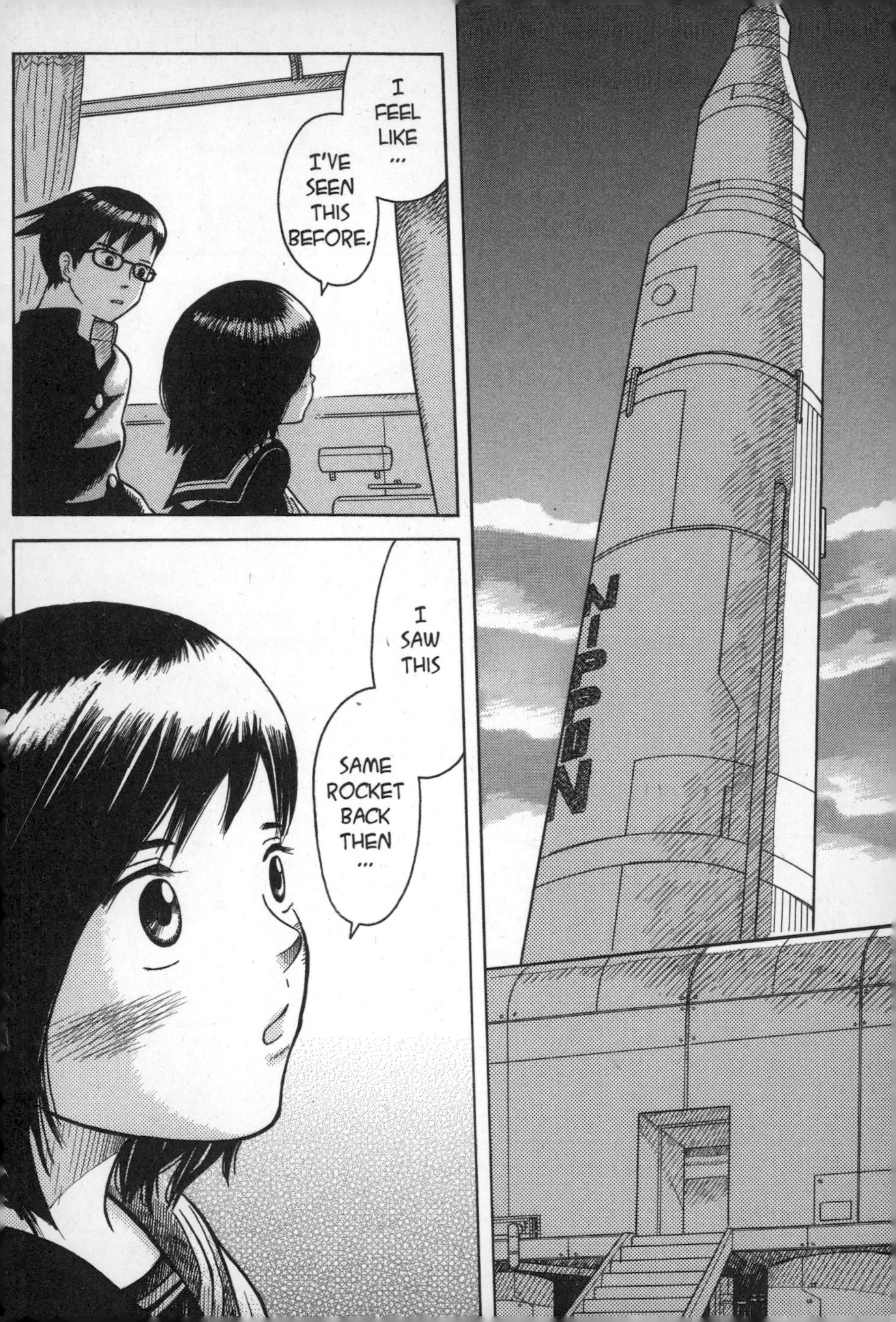
NIPPON
I FEEL LIKE ...
I'VE SEEN THIS BEFORE.
I SAW THIS
SAME ROCKET BACK THEN ...

MISSION:02

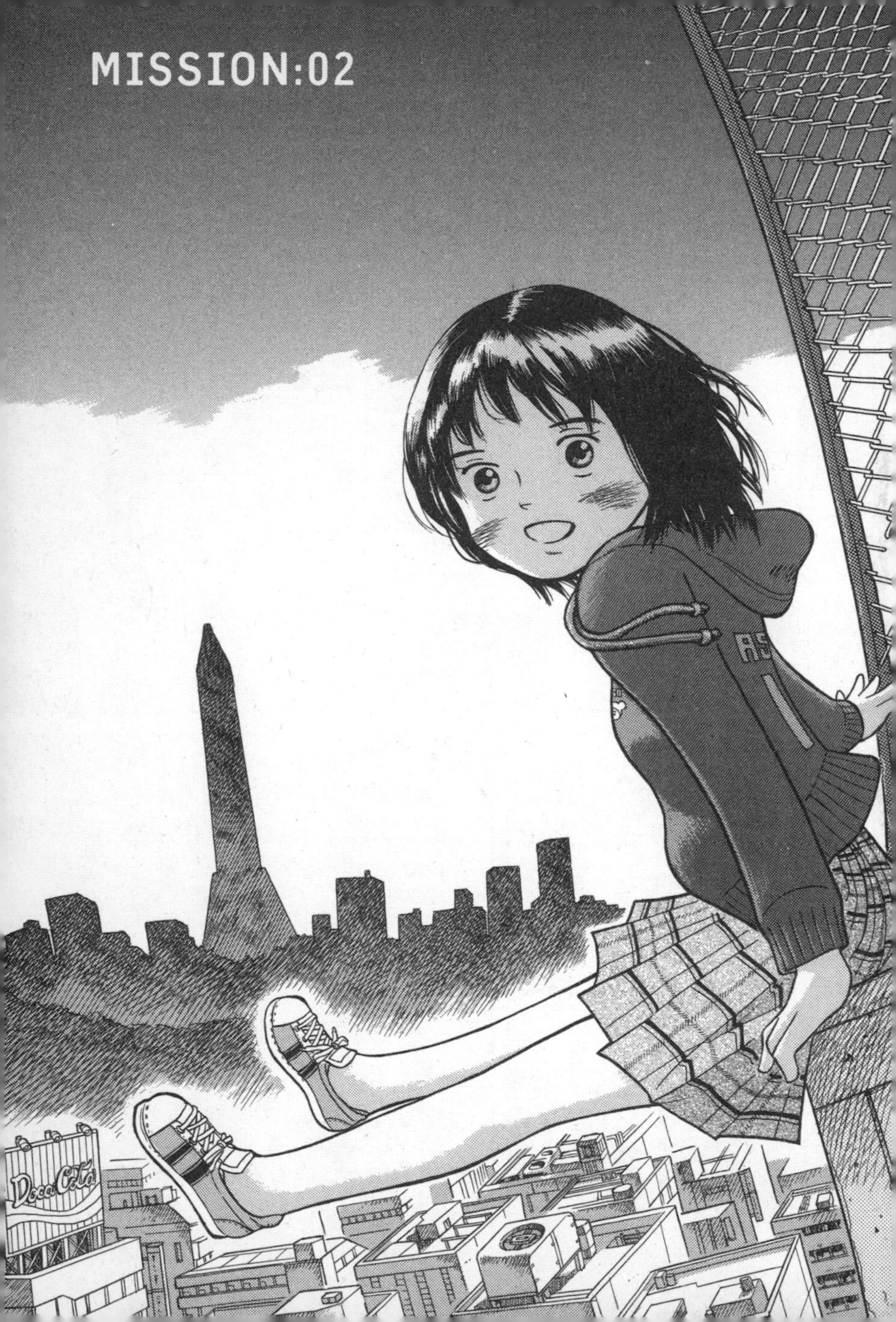

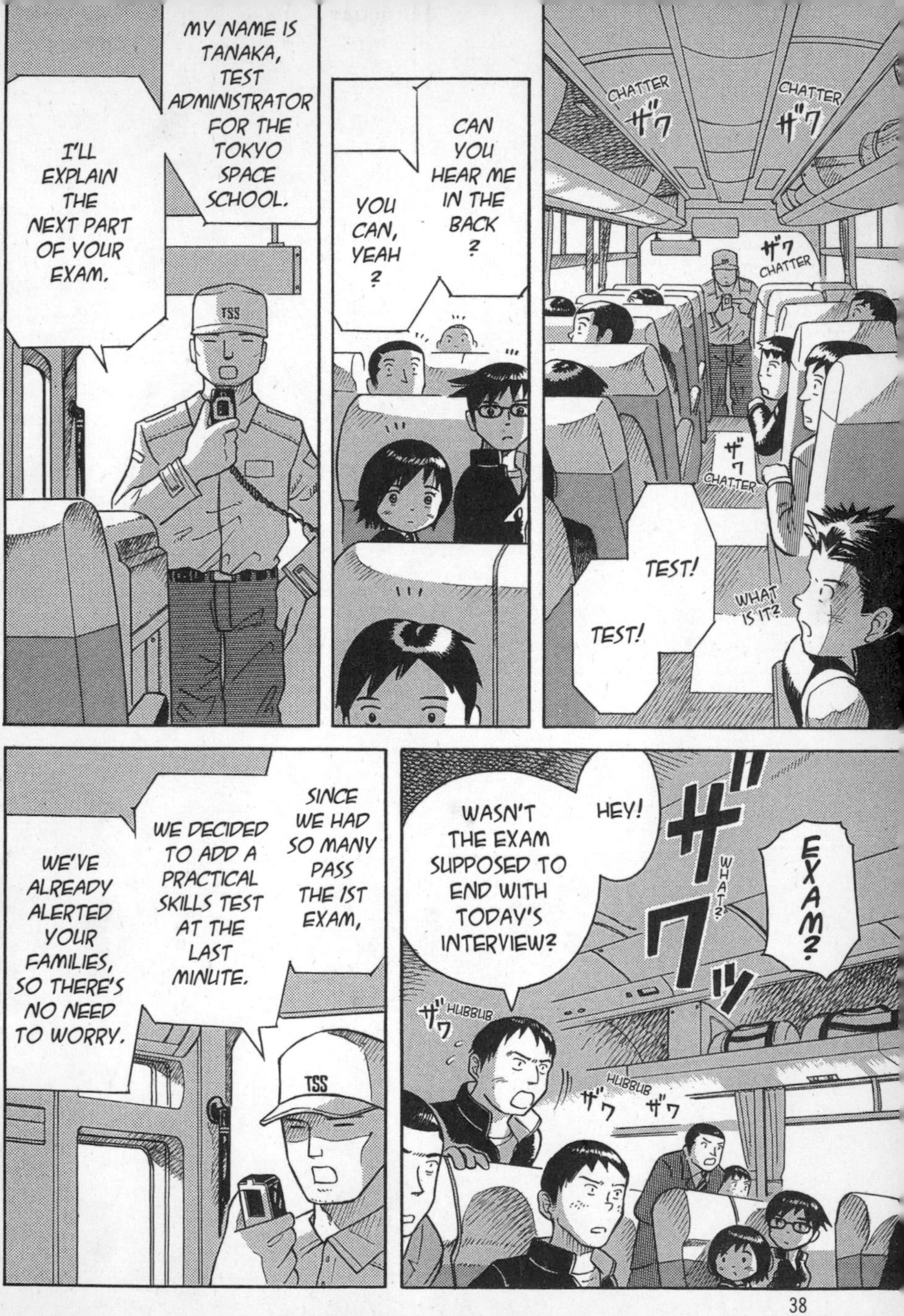
ザワ CHATTER
ザワ CHATTER
ザワ CHATTER
ザワ CHATTER
TEST! TEST!
WHAT IS IT?
CAN YOU HEAR ME IN THE BACK?
YOU CAN, YEAH?
MY NAME IS TANAKA, TEST ADMINISTRATOR FOR THE TOKYO SPACE SCHOOL.
I'LL EXPLAIN THE NEXT PART OF YOUR EXAM.
ザワッ
EXAM?
WHAT?
HEY!
WASN'T THE EXAM SUPPOSED TO END WITH TODAY'S INTERVIEW?
ザワ HUBBUB
ザワ ザワ HUBBUB
SINCE WE HAD SO MANY PASS THE 1ST EXAM,
WE DECIDED TO ADD A PRACTICAL SKILLS TEST AT THE LAST MINUTE.
WE'VE ALREADY ALERTED YOUR FAMILIES, SO THERE'S NO NEED TO WORRY.

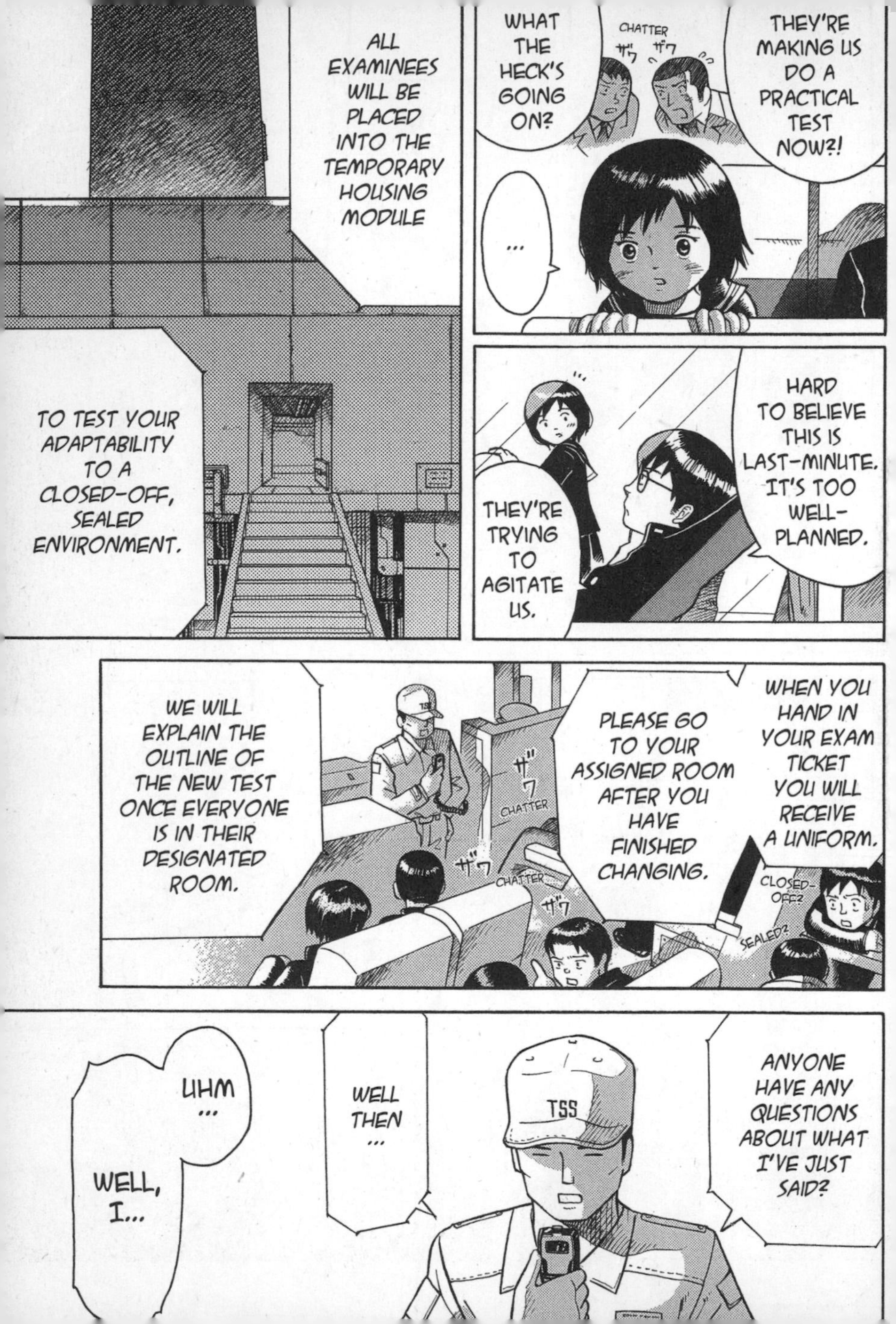
THEY'RE MAKING US DO A PRACTICAL TEST NOW?!
CHATTER
WHAT THE HECK'S GOING ON?
...
HARD TO BELIEVE THIS IS LAST-MINUTE. IT'S TOO WELL-PLANNED.
THEY'RE TRYING TO AGITATE US.
ALL EXAMINEES WILL BE PLACED INTO THE TEMPORARY HOUSING MODULE
TO TEST YOUR ADAPTABILITY TO A CLOSED-OFF, SEALED ENVIRONMENT.
WHEN YOU HAND IN YOUR EXAM TICKET YOU WILL RECEIVE A UNIFORM.
PLEASE GO TO YOUR ASSIGNED ROOM AFTER YOU HAVE FINISHED CHANGING.
CLOSED-OFF?
SEALED?
CHATTER
CHATTER
WE WILL EXPLAIN THE OUTLINE OF THE NEW TEST ONCE EVERYONE IS IN THEIR DESIGNATED ROOM.
ANYONE HAVE ANY QUESTIONS ABOUT WHAT I'VE JUST SAID?
WELL THEN ...
UHM ...
WELL, I...

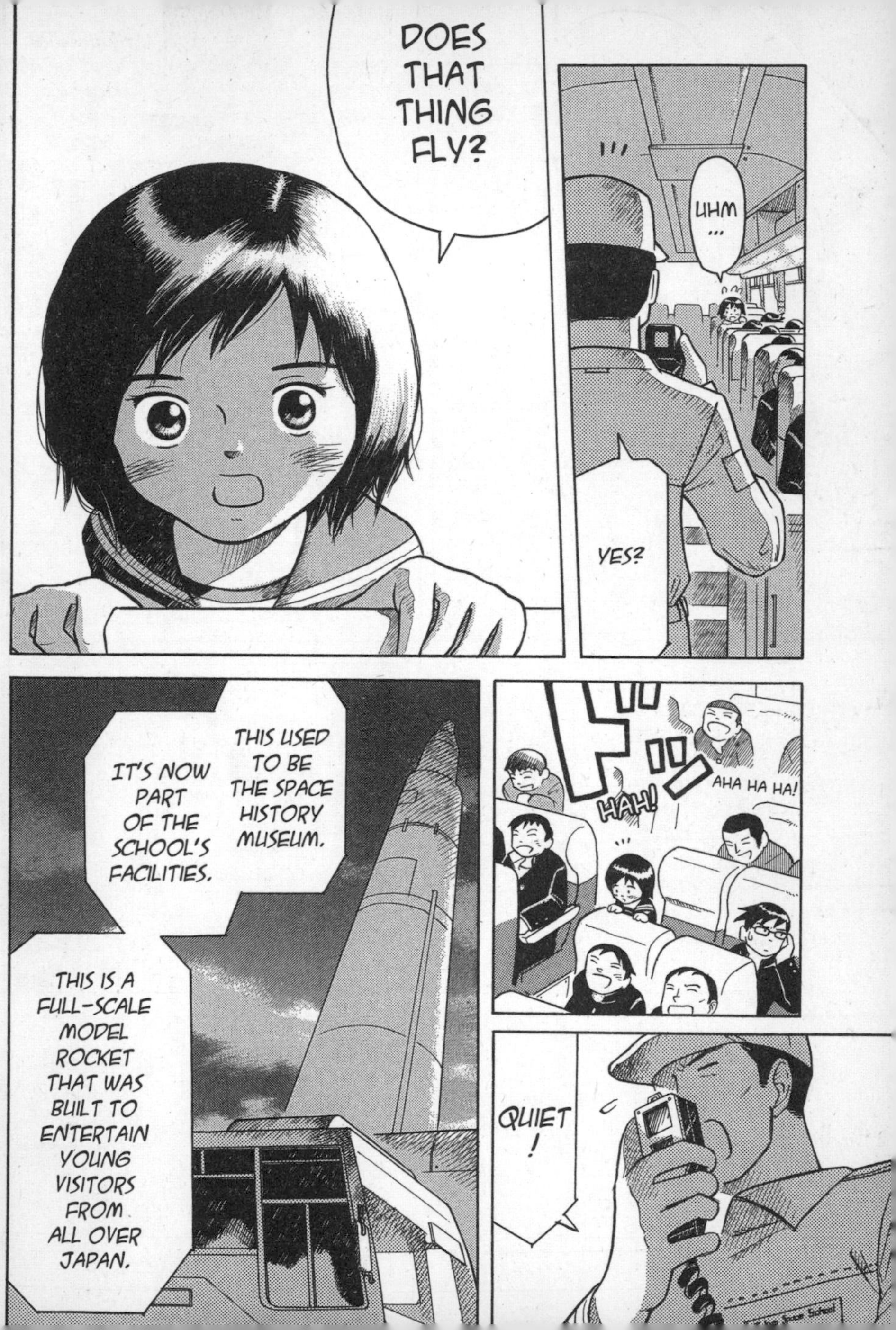
UHM ...
YES?
DOES THAT THING FLY?
AHA HA HA!
HAH!
QUIET!
THIS USED TO BE THE SPACE HISTORY MUSEUM.
IT'S NOW PART OF THE SCHOOL'S FACILITIES.
THIS IS A FULL-SCALE MODEL ROCKET THAT WAS BUILT TO ENTERTAIN YOUNG VISITORS FROM ALL OVER JAPAN.

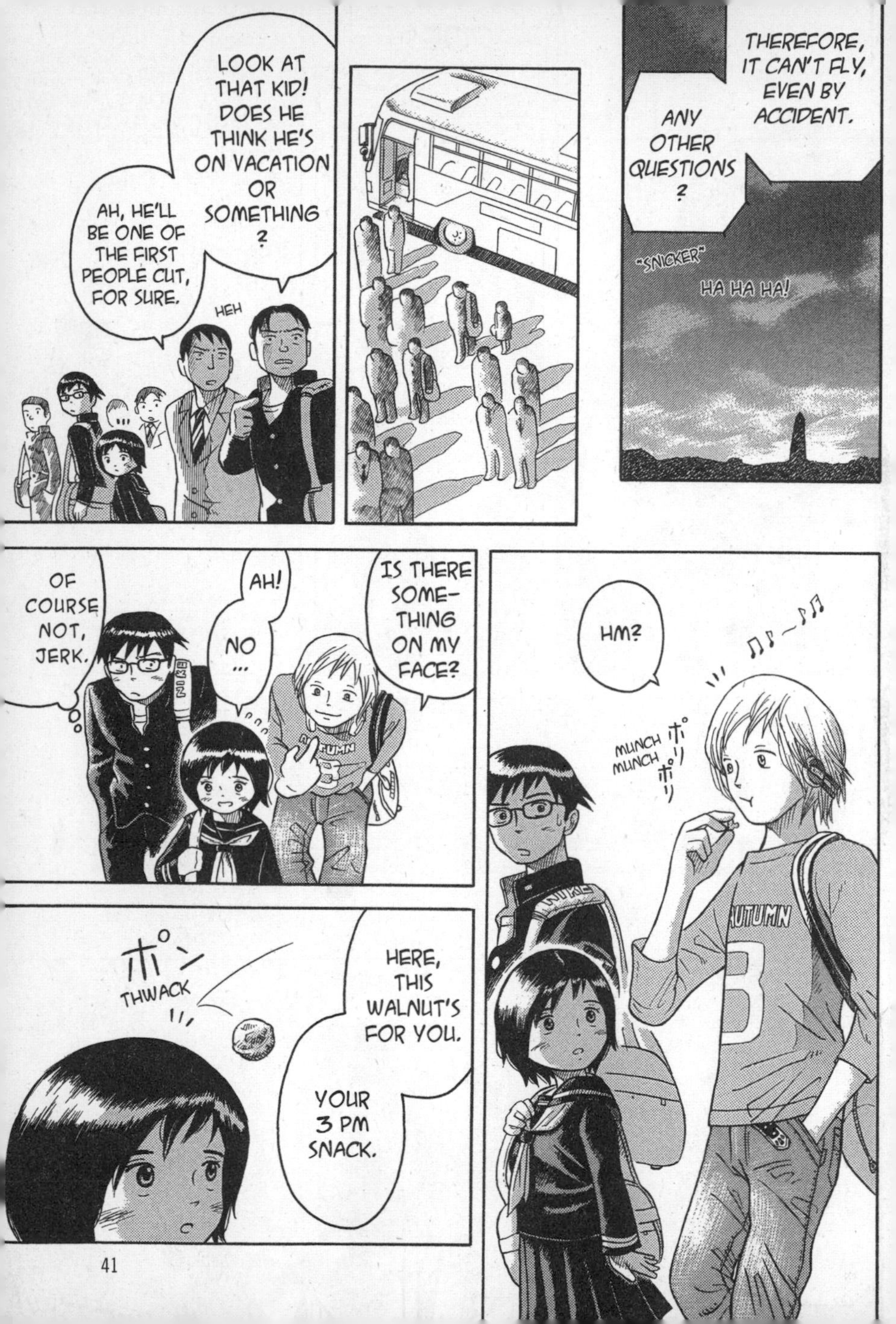
THEREFORE, IT CAN'T FLY, EVEN BY ACCIDENT.
ANY OTHER QUESTIONS?
"SNICKER"
HA HA HA!
LOOK AT THAT KID! DOES HE THINK HE'S ON VACATION OR SOMETHING?
AH, HE'LL BE ONE OF THE FIRST PEOPLE CUT, FOR SURE.
HEH
HM?
MUNCH MUNCH ポリポリ
IS THERE SOMETHING ON MY FACE?
AH!
NO ...
OF COURSE NOT, JERK.
HERE, THIS WALNUT'S FOR YOU.
YOUR 3 PM SNACK.
ポン THWACK

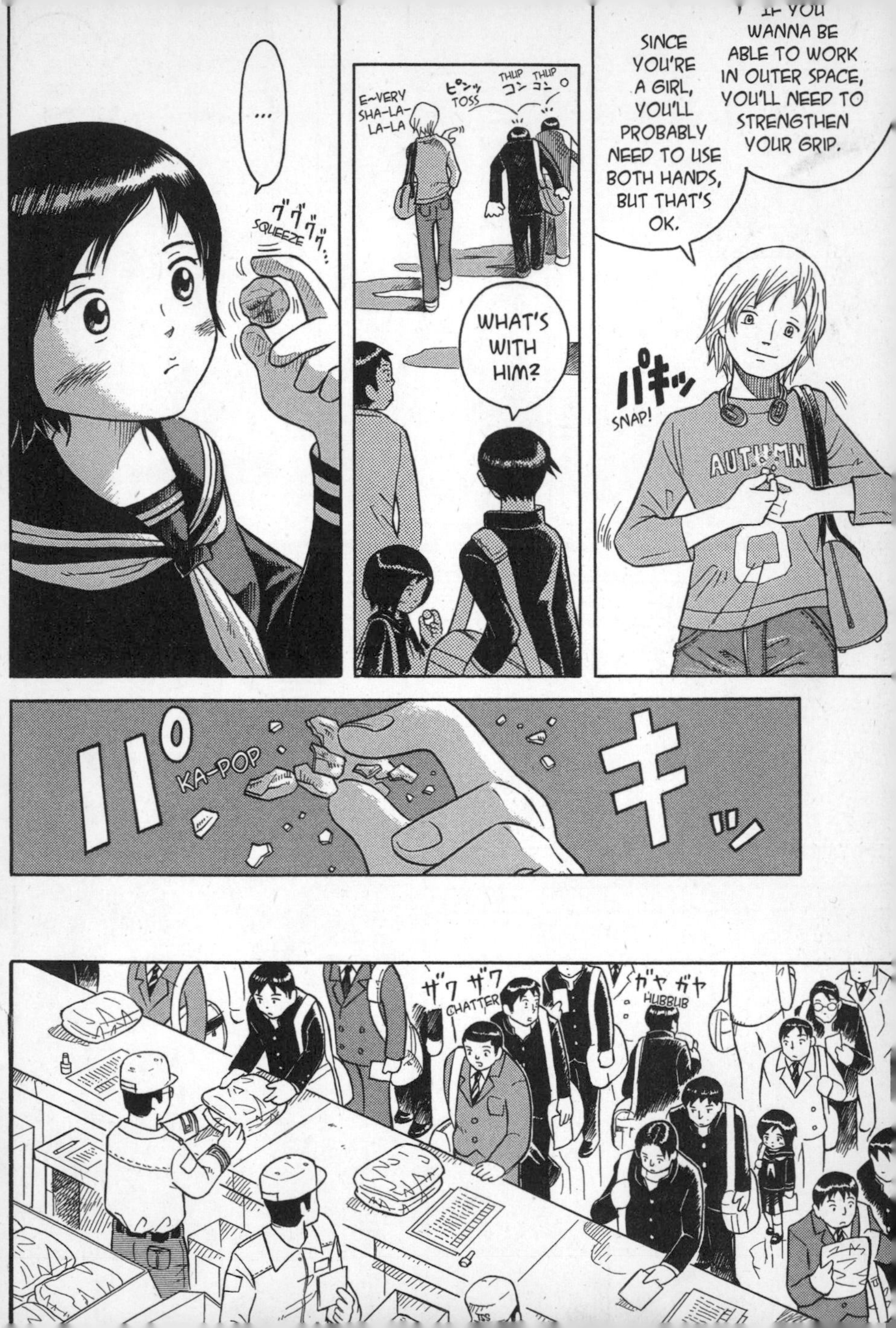
IF YOU WANNA BE ABLE TO WORK IN OUTER SPACE, YOU'LL NEED TO STRENGTHEN YOUR GRIP.
SINCE YOU'RE A GIRL, YOU'LL PROBABLY NEED TO USE BOTH HANDS, BUT THAT'S OK.
パキッ
SNAP!
コン コン
THUP THUP
ピンッ
TOSS
E~VERY SHA-LA-LA-LA
WHAT'S WITH HIM?
...
ググググ...
SQUEEZE
パキッ
KA-POP
ガヤ ガヤ
HUBBUB
ザワ ザワ
CHATTER

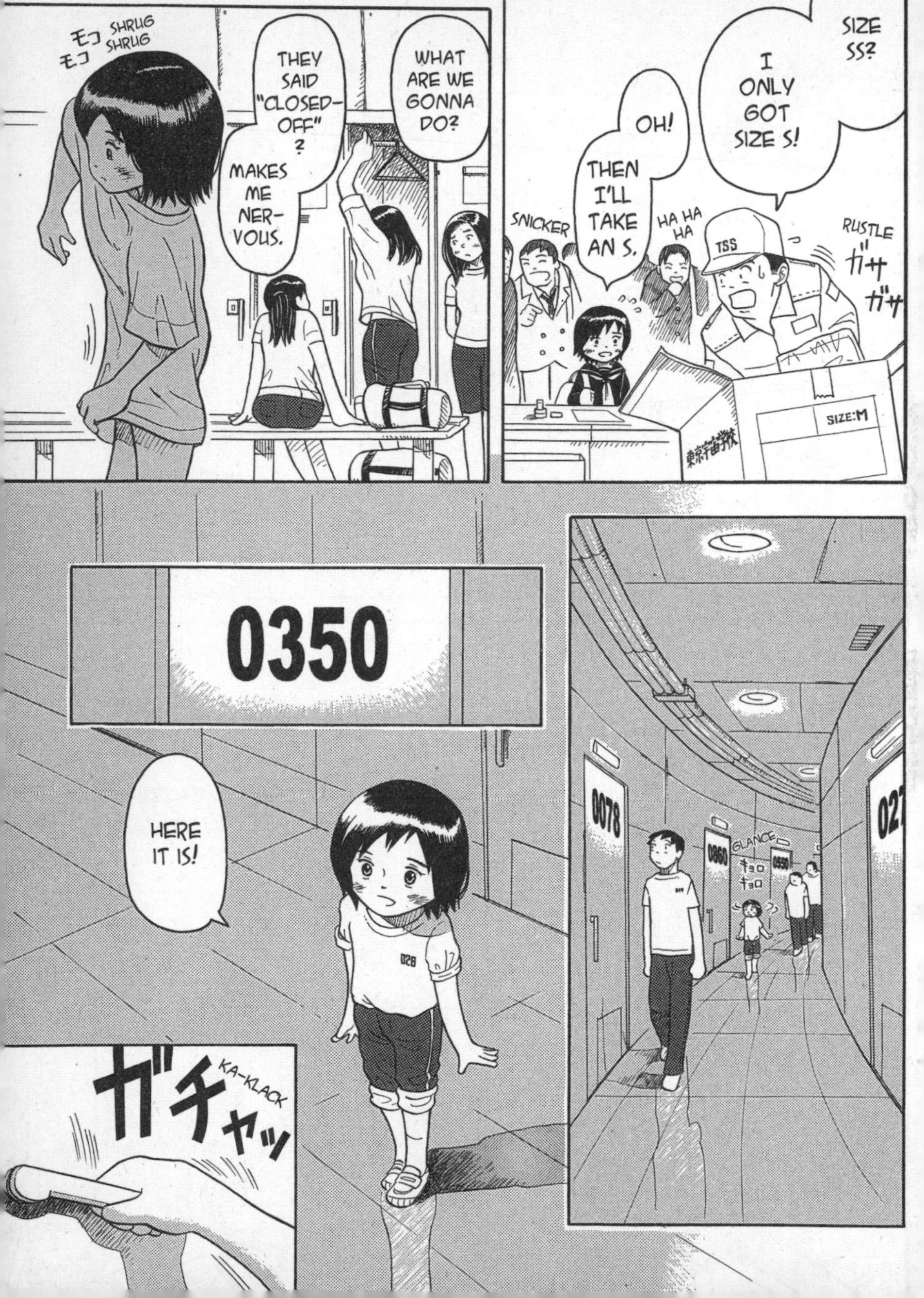
SIZE SS?
I ONLY GOT SIZE S!
TSS
RUSTLE
ガサ ガサ
OH!
THEN I'LL TAKE AN S.
HA HA HA
SNICKER
SIZE:M
WHAT ARE WE GONNA DO?
THEY SAID "CLOSED-OFF"?
MAKES ME NERVOUS.
モコ SHRUG
モコ SHRUG
0078
027
GLANCE
キョロ キョロ
0860
0350
0350
HERE IT IS!
028
ガチャッ
KA-KLACK

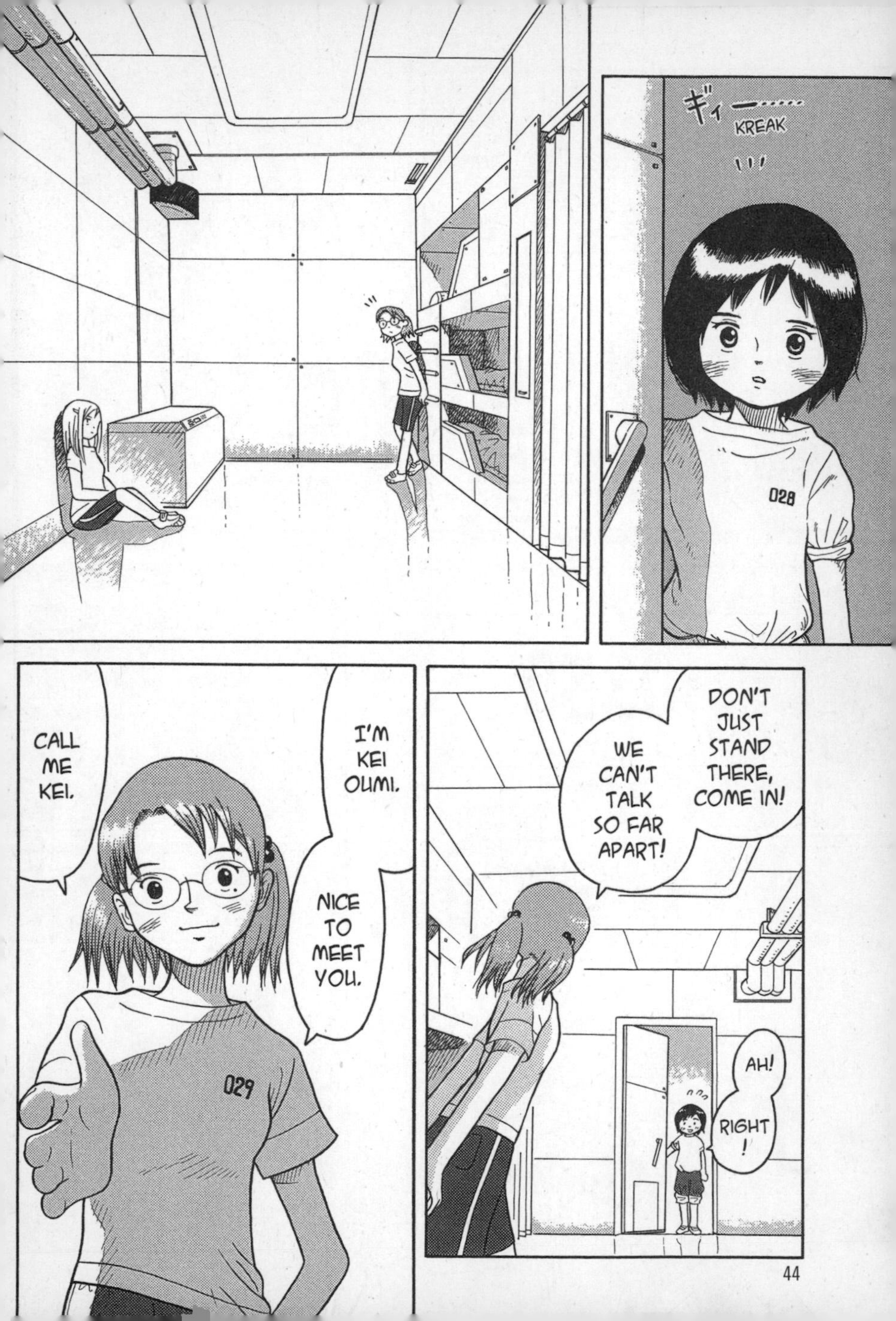
ギィー……
KREAK
!!!
DON'T JUST STAND THERE, COME IN!
WE CAN'T TALK SO FAR APART!
AH!
RIGHT!
I'M KEI OUMI.
NICE TO MEET YOU.
CALL ME KEI.

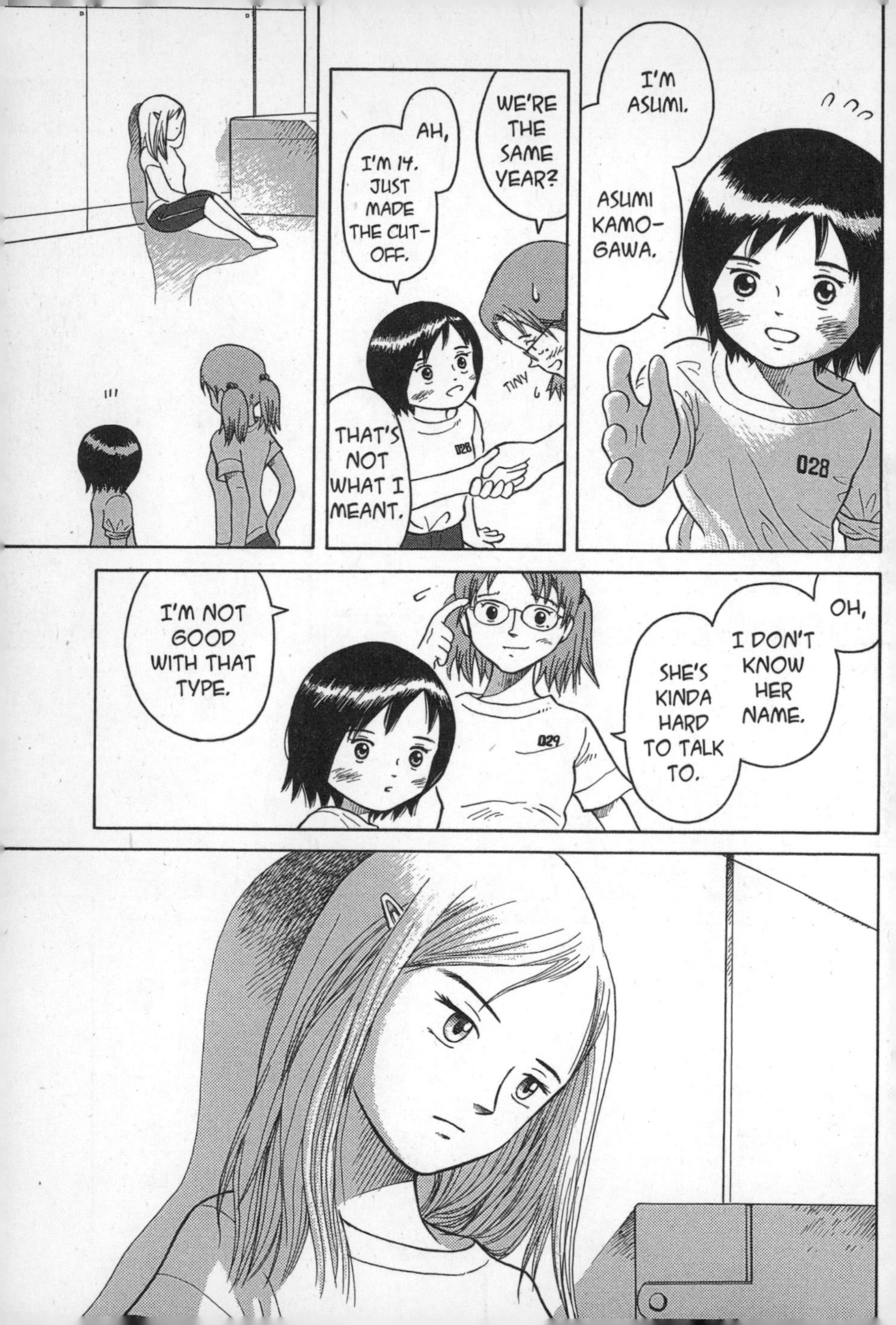
I'M ASUMI.
ASUMI KAMO-GAWA.
WE'RE THE SAME YEAR?
AH, I'M 14. JUST MADE THE CUT-OFF.
TINY
THAT'S NOT WHAT I MEANT.
OH, I DON'T KNOW HER NAME.
SHE'S KINDA HARD TO TALK TO.
I'M NOT GOOD WITH THAT TYPE.

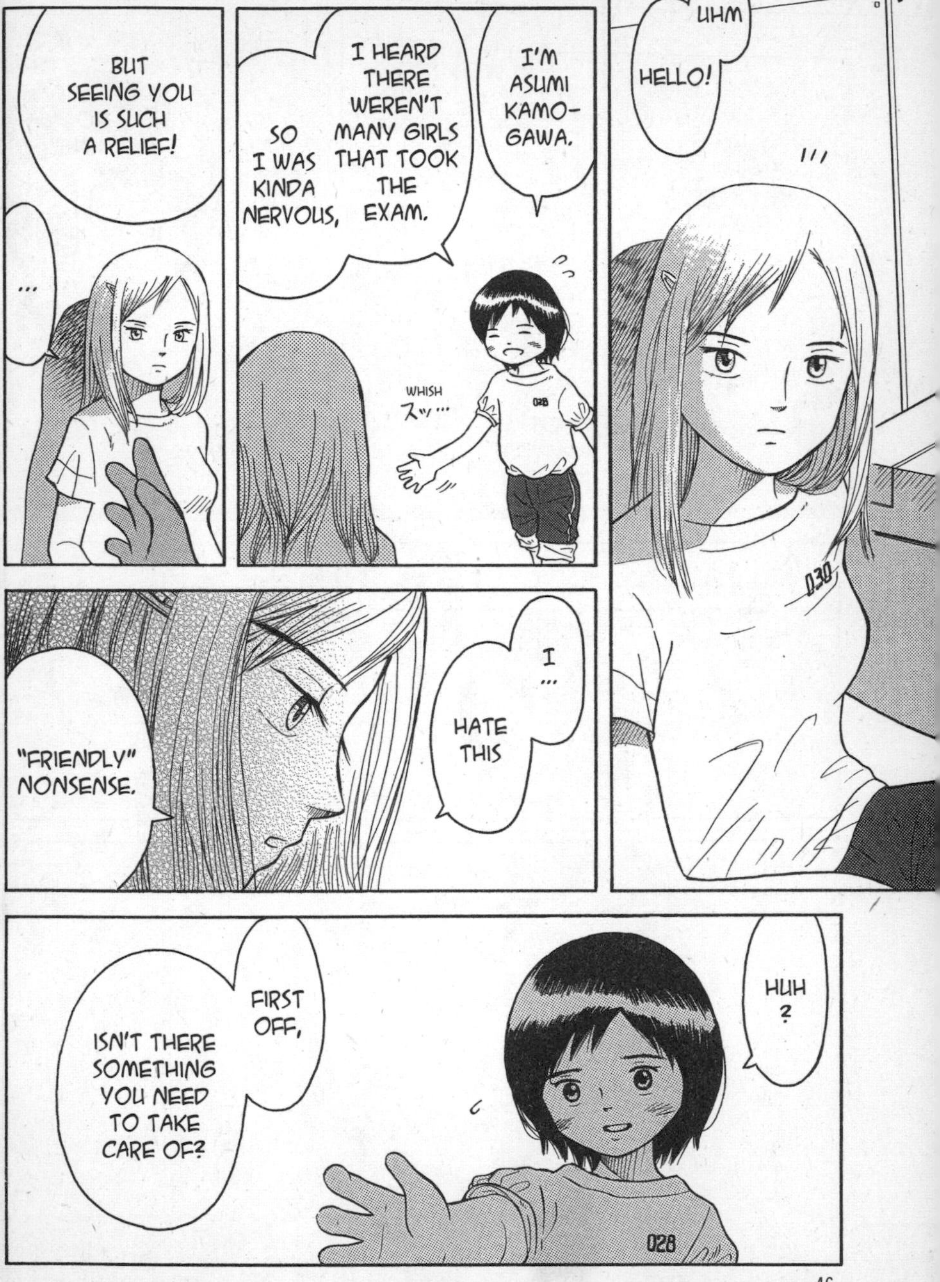
UHM
HELLO!
I'M ASUMI KAMOGAWA.
I HEARD THERE WEREN'T MANY GIRLS THAT TOOK THE EXAM.
SO I WAS KINDA NERVOUS,
WHISH
スッ…
BUT SEEING YOU IS SUCH A RELIEF!
...
I ...
HATE THIS
"FRIENDLY" NONSENSE.
HUH ?
FIRST OFF,
ISN'T THERE SOMETHING YOU NEED TO TAKE CARE OF?

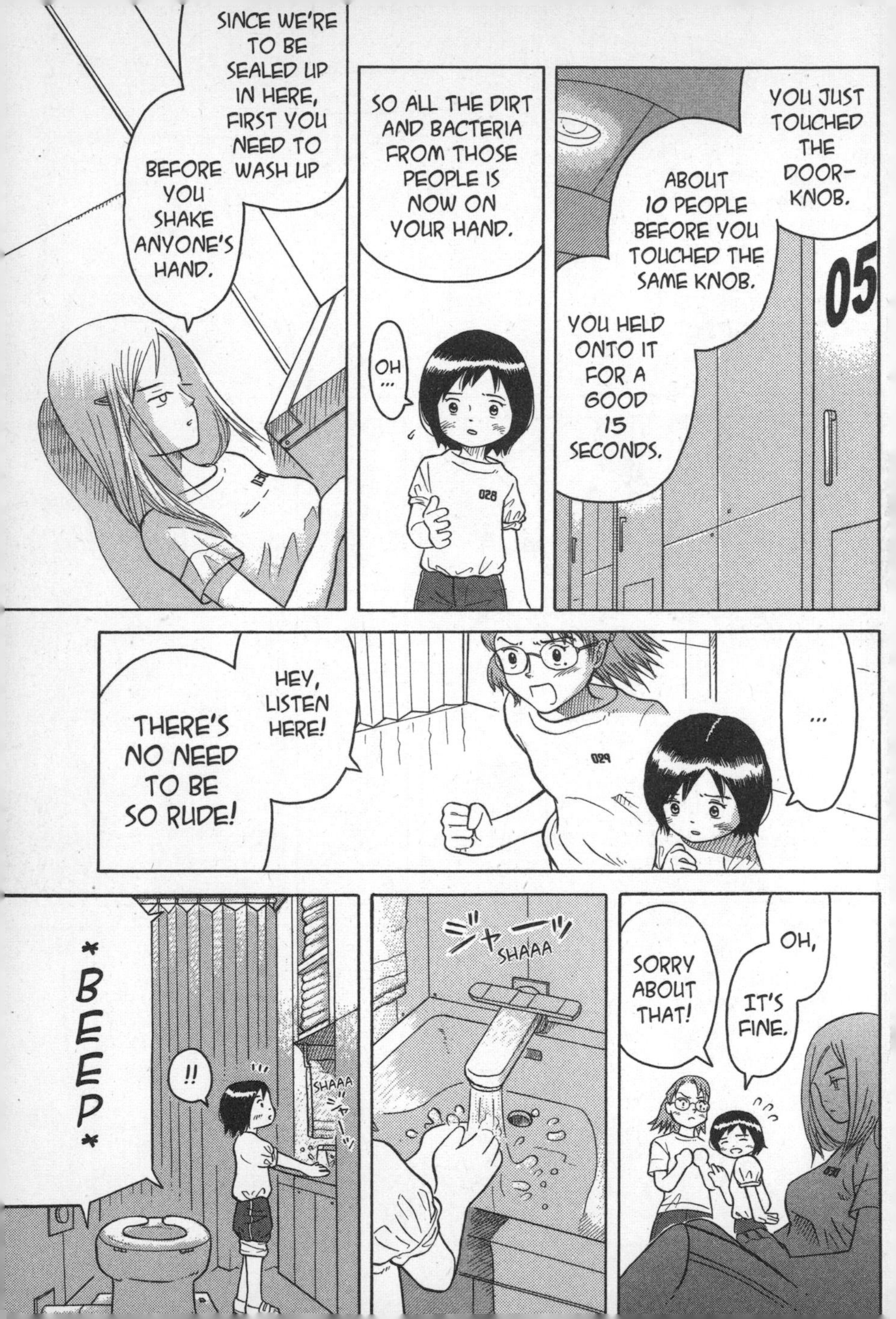
YOU JUST TOUCHED THE DOOR-KNOB.
ABOUT 10 PEOPLE BEFORE YOU TOUCHED THE SAME KNOB.
YOU HELD ONTO IT FOR A GOOD 15 SECONDS.
05
SO ALL THE DIRT AND BACTERIA FROM THOSE PEOPLE IS NOW ON YOUR HAND.
OH ...
028
SINCE WE'RE TO BE SEALED UP IN HERE, FIRST YOU NEED TO WASH UP
BEFORE YOU SHAKE ANYONE'S HAND.
...
HEY, LISTEN HERE!
THERE'S NO NEED TO BE SO RUDE!
029
OH,
IT'S FINE.
SORRY ABOUT THAT!
SHAAA
!!
SHAAA
BEEP

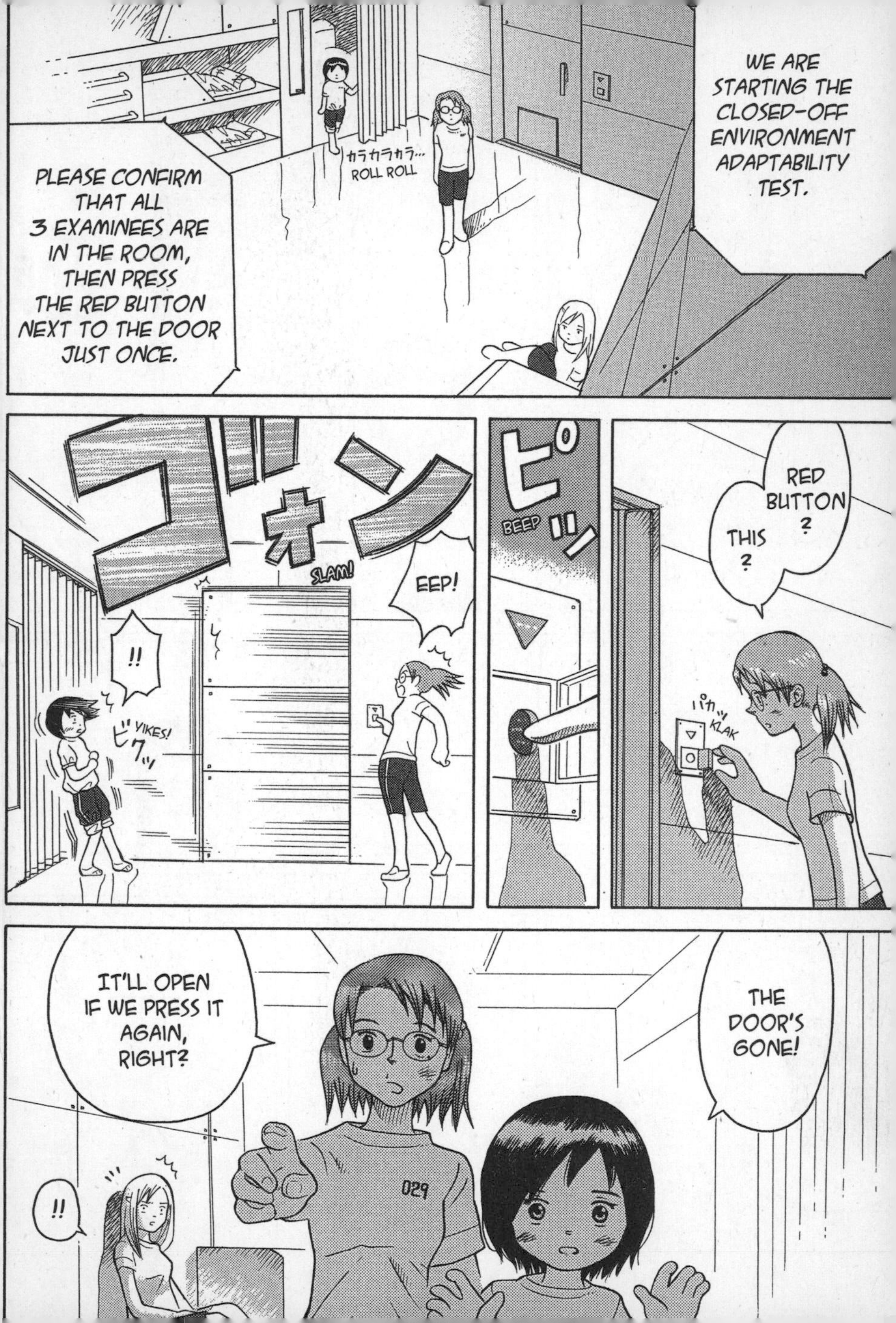
WE ARE STARTING THE CLOSED-OFF ENVIRONMENT ADAPTABILITY TEST.
PLEASE CONFIRM THAT ALL 3 EXAMINEES ARE IN THE ROOM, THEN PRESS THE RED BUTTON NEXT TO THE DOOR JUST ONCE.
カラカラカラ… ROLL ROLL
RED BUTTON?
THIS?
パカッ KLAK
ピッ BEEP
SLAM!
EEP!
!!
ビクッ YIKES!
THE DOOR'S GONE!
IT'LL OPEN IF WE PRESS IT AGAIN, RIGHT?
!!
029

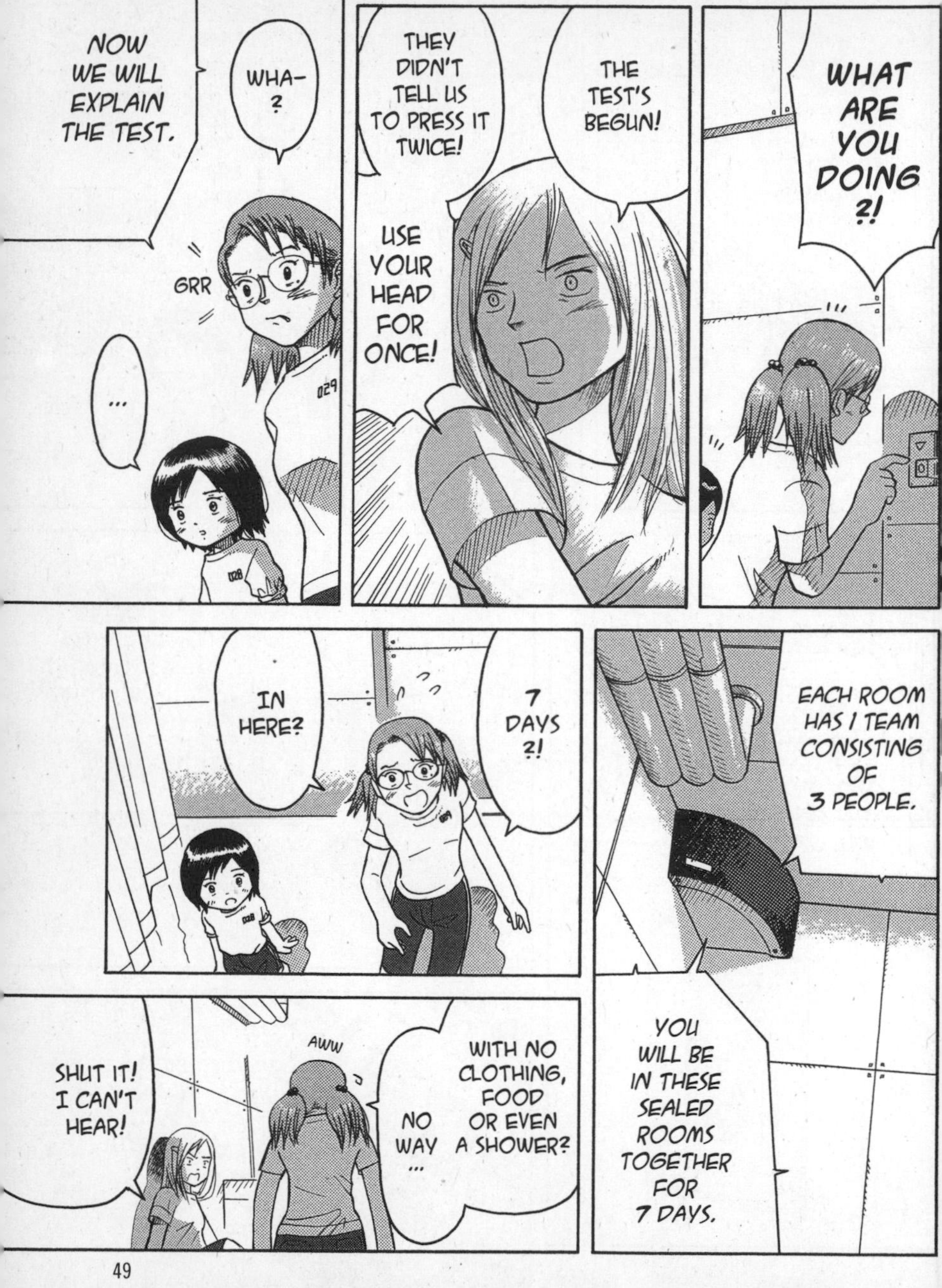
WHAT ARE YOU DOING?!
THE TEST'S BEGUN!
THEY DIDN'T TELL US TO PRESS IT TWICE!
USE YOUR HEAD FOR ONCE!
WHA-?
NOW WE WILL EXPLAIN THE TEST.
GRR
...
EACH ROOM HAS 1 TEAM CONSISTING OF 3 PEOPLE.
YOU WILL BE IN THESE SEALED ROOMS TOGETHER FOR 7 DAYS.
7 DAYS?!
IN HERE?
WITH NO CLOTHING, FOOD OR EVEN A SHOWER?
NO WAY ...
AWW
SHUT IT! I CAN'T HEAR!

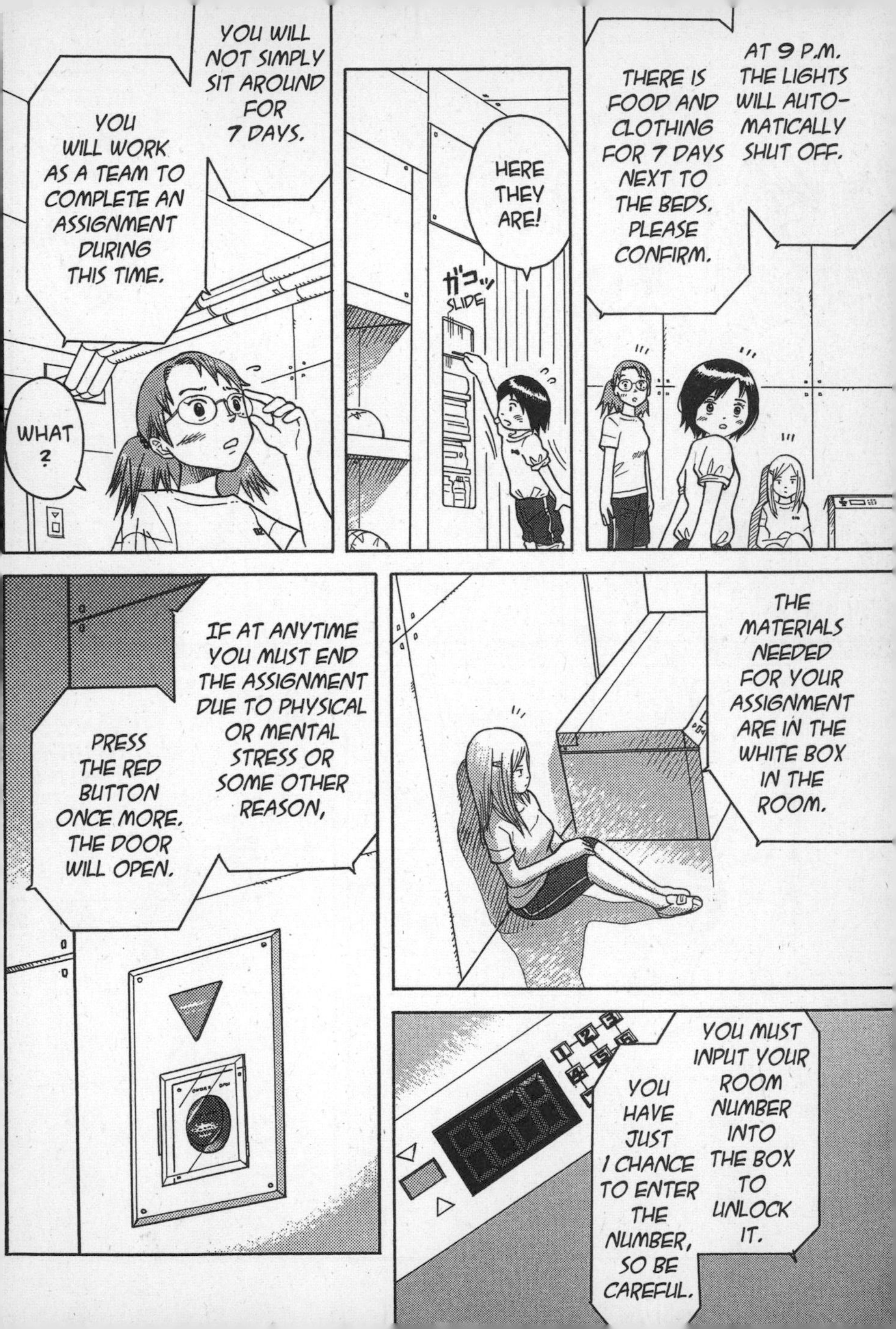
THERE IS FOOD AND CLOTHING FOR 7 DAYS NEXT TO THE BEDS. PLEASE CONFIRM.
AT 9 P.M. THE LIGHTS WILL AUTO-MATICALLY SHUT OFF.
HERE THEY ARE!
ガコッ SLIDE
YOU WILL NOT SIMPLY SIT AROUND FOR 7 DAYS.
YOU WILL WORK AS A TEAM TO COMPLETE AN ASSIGNMENT DURING THIS TIME.
WHAT?
THE MATERIALS NEEDED FOR YOUR ASSIGNMENT ARE IN THE WHITE BOX IN THE ROOM.
IF AT ANYTIME YOU MUST END THE ASSIGNMENT DUE TO PHYSICAL OR MENTAL STRESS OR SOME OTHER REASON,
PRESS THE RED BUTTON ONCE MORE. THE DOOR WILL OPEN.
YOU MUST INPUT YOUR ROOM NUMBER INTO THE BOX TO UNLOCK IT.
YOU HAVE JUST 1 CHANCE TO ENTER THE NUMBER, SO BE CAREFUL.

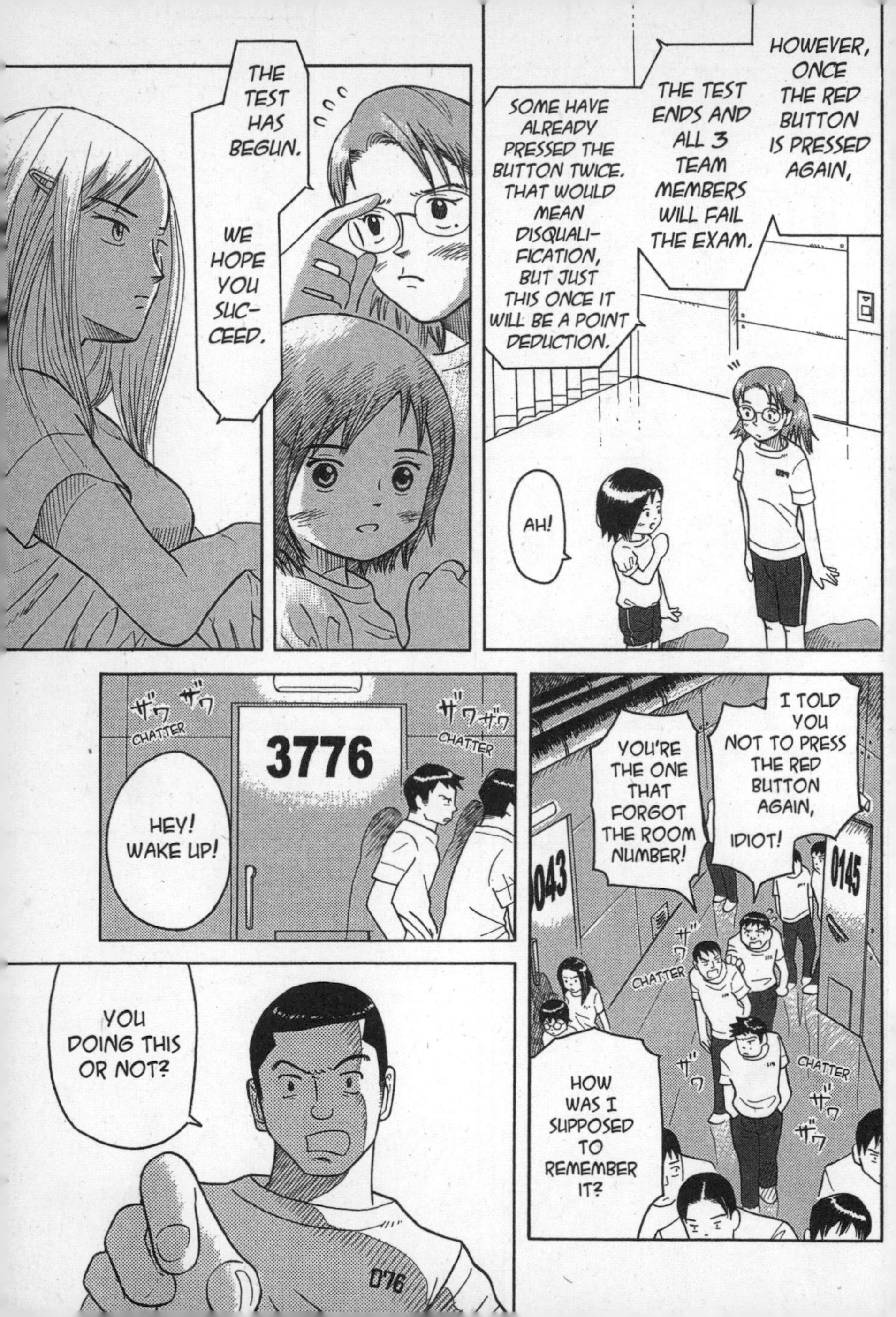
HOWEVER, ONCE THE RED BUTTON IS PRESSED AGAIN,
THE TEST ENDS AND ALL 3 TEAM MEMBERS WILL FAIL THE EXAM.
SOME HAVE ALREADY PRESSED THE BUTTON TWICE. THAT WOULD MEAN DISQUALIFICATION, BUT JUST THIS ONCE IT WILL BE A POINT DEDUCTION.
AH!
THE TEST HAS BEGUN.
WE HOPE YOU SUCCEED.
I TOLD YOU NOT TO PRESS THE RED BUTTON AGAIN,
IDIOT!
YOU'RE THE ONE THAT FORGOT THE ROOM NUMBER!
0145
0043
ザワ
CHATTER
CHATTER
ザワ
ザワ
HOW WAS I SUPPOSED TO REMEMBER IT?
ザワザワ
CHATTER
3776
ザワ ザワ
CHATTER
HEY! WAKE UP!
YOU DOING THIS OR NOT?
0'76

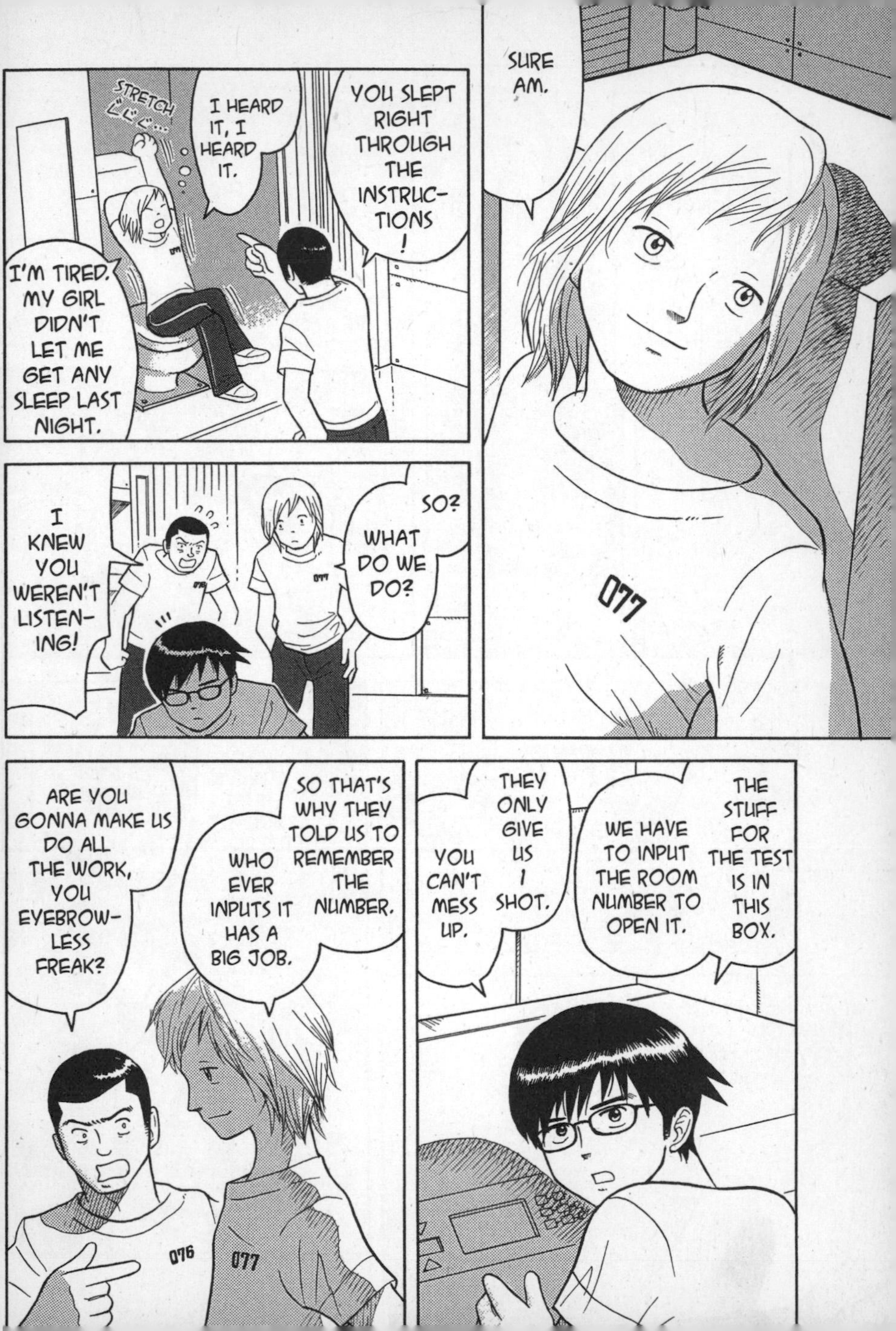
SURE AM.
YOU SLEPT RIGHT THROUGH THE INSTRUCTIONS!
I HEARD IT, I HEARD IT.
STRETCH
I'M TIRED. MY GIRL DIDN'T LET ME GET ANY SLEEP LAST NIGHT.
SO? WHAT DO WE DO?
I KNEW YOU WEREN'T LISTENING!
THE STUFF FOR THE TEST IS IN THIS BOX.
WE HAVE TO INPUT THE ROOM NUMBER TO OPEN IT.
THEY ONLY GIVE US 1 SHOT.
YOU CAN'T MESS UP.
SO THAT'S WHY THEY TOLD US TO REMEMBER THE NUMBER.
WHO EVER INPUTS IT HAS A BIG JOB.
ARE YOU GONNA MAKE US DO ALL THE WORK, YOU EYEBROW-LESS FREAK?

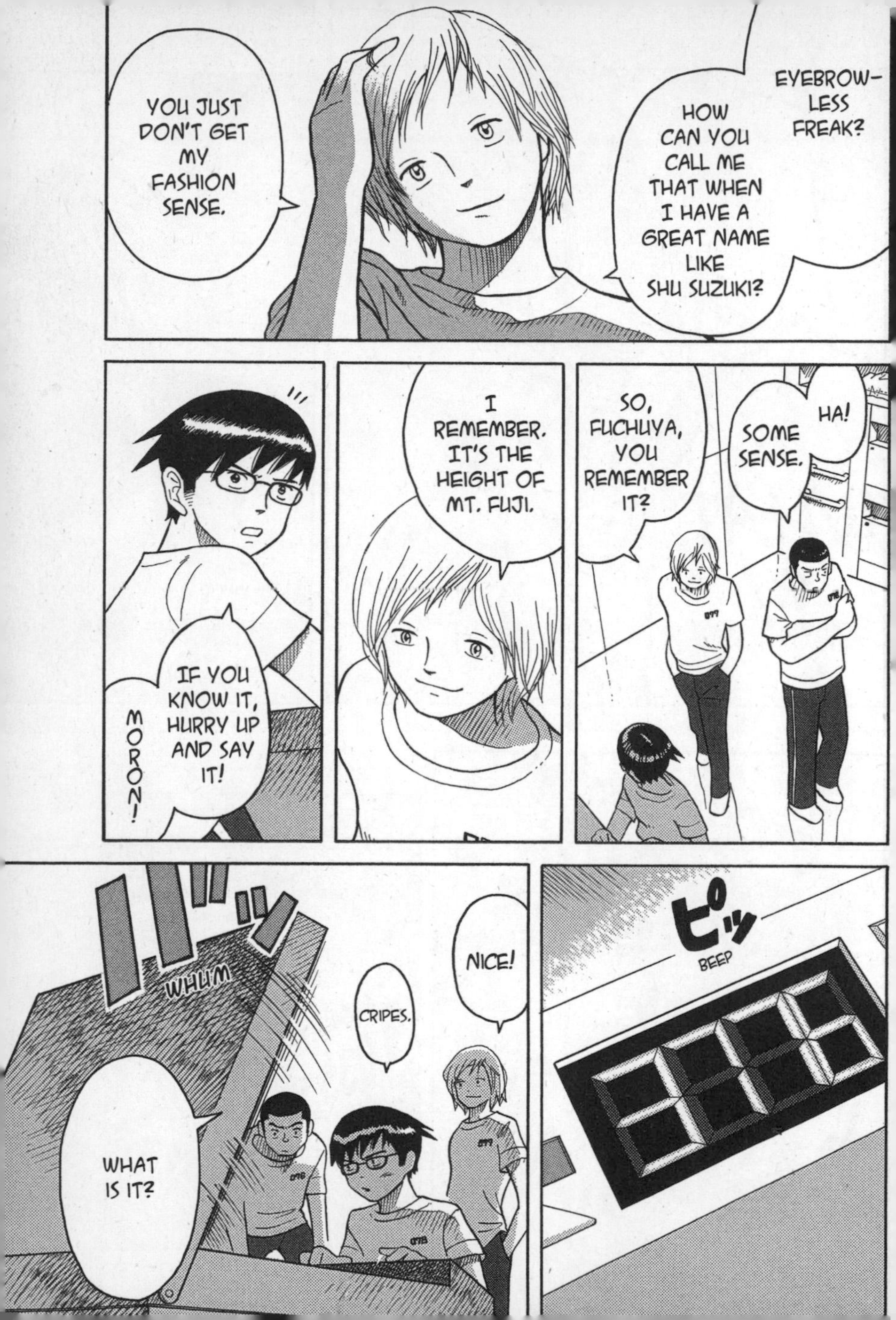
EYEBROW-LESS FREAK?
HOW CAN YOU CALL ME THAT WHEN I HAVE A GREAT NAME LIKE SHU SUZUKI?
YOU JUST DON'T GET MY FASHION SENSE.
HA!
SOME SENSE.
SO, FUCHUYA, YOU REMEMBER IT?
I REMEMBER. IT'S THE HEIGHT OF MT. FUJI.
IF YOU KNOW IT, HURRY UP AND SAY IT!
MORON!
ピッ
BEEP
NICE!
CRIPES.
WHUM
WHAT IS IT?

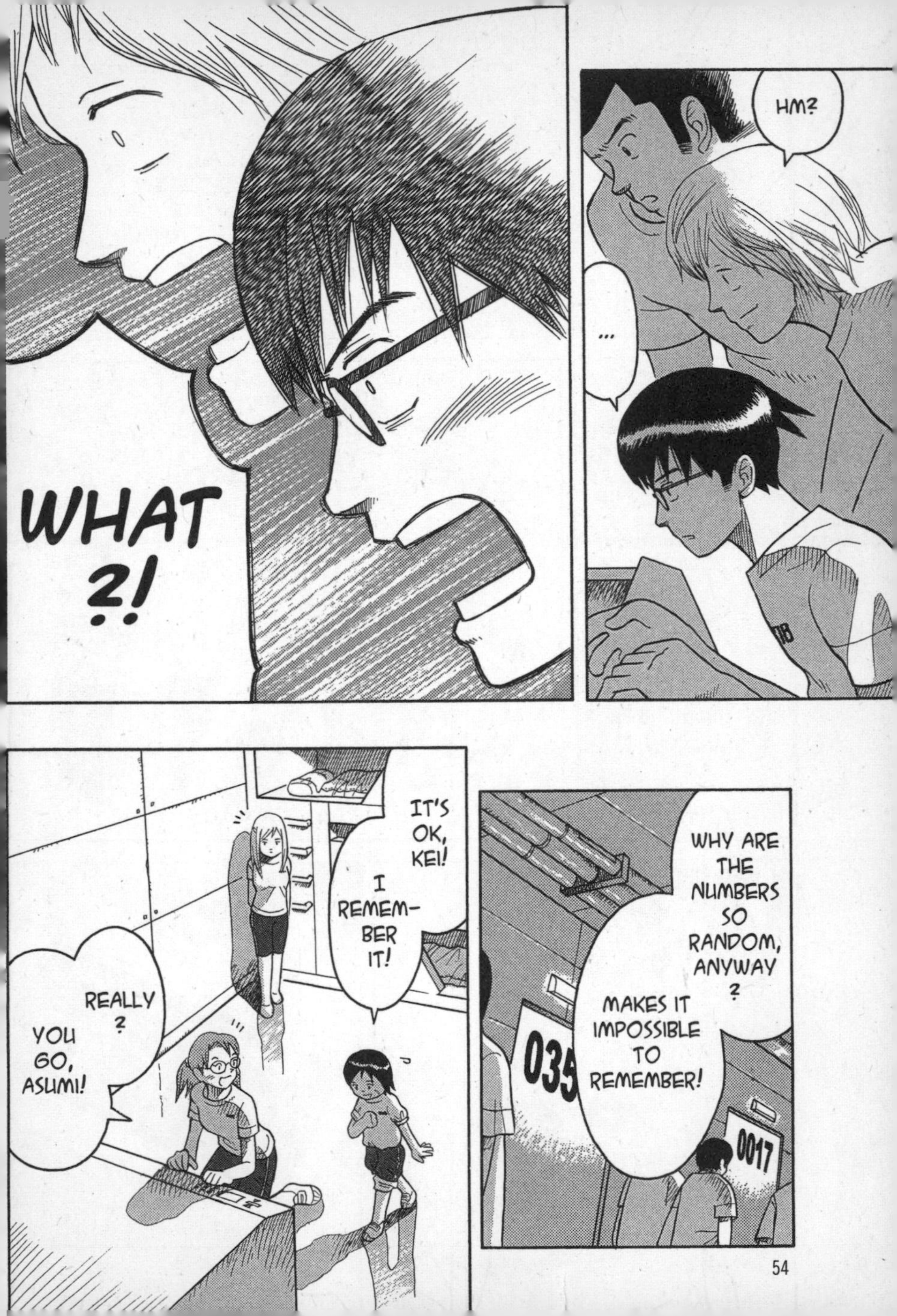
HM?
...
WHAT?!
WHY ARE THE NUMBERS SO RANDOM, ANYWAY?
MAKES IT IMPOSSIBLE TO REMEMBER!
035
0017
IT'S OK, KEI!
I REMEMBER IT!
REALLY? YOU GO, ASUMI!

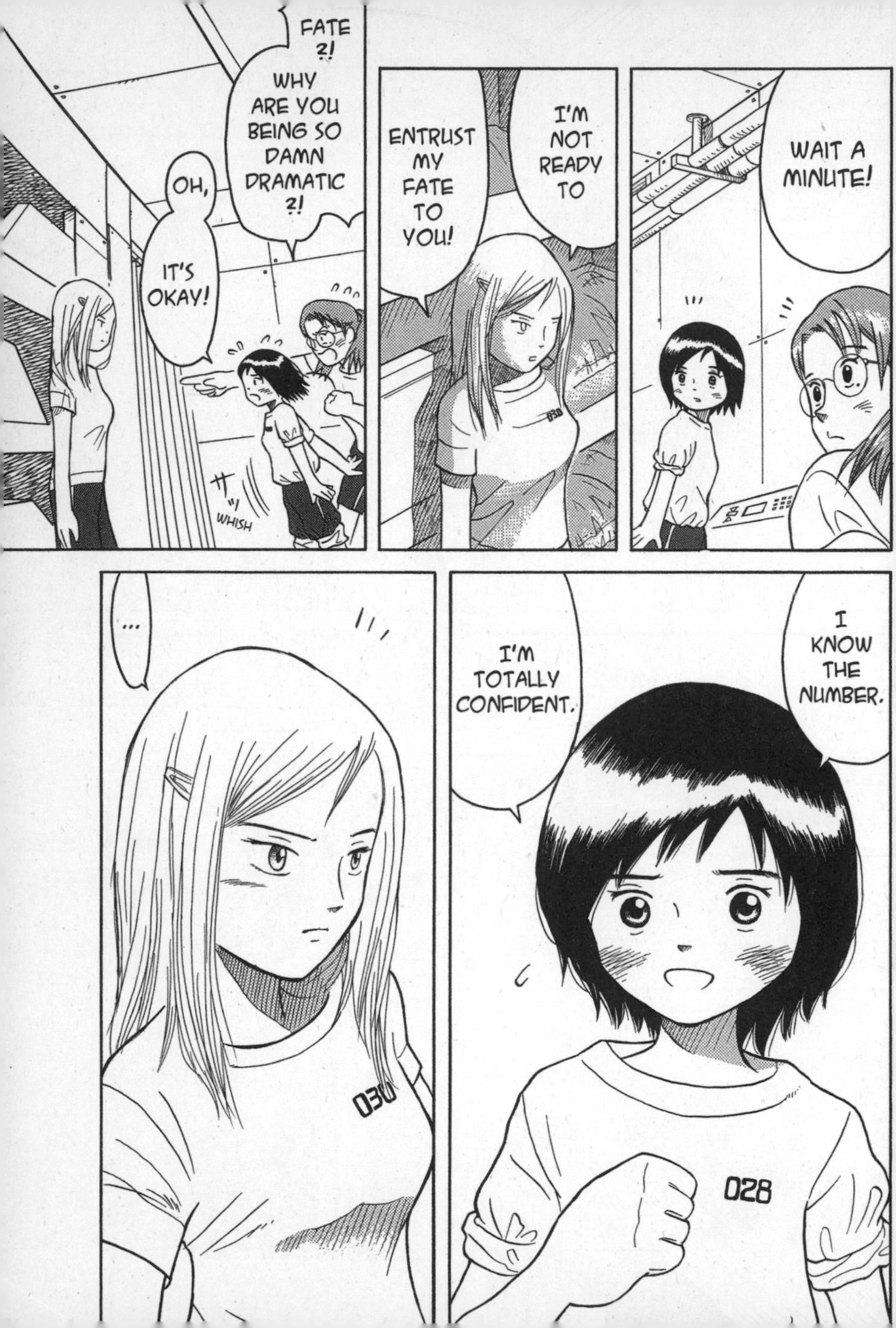
WAIT A MINUTE!
I'M NOT READY TO
ENTRUST MY FATE TO YOU!
FATE ?!
WHY ARE YOU BEING SO DAMN DRAMATIC ?!
OH,
IT'S OKAY!
WHISH
I KNOW THE NUMBER.
I'M TOTALLY CONFIDENT.
...

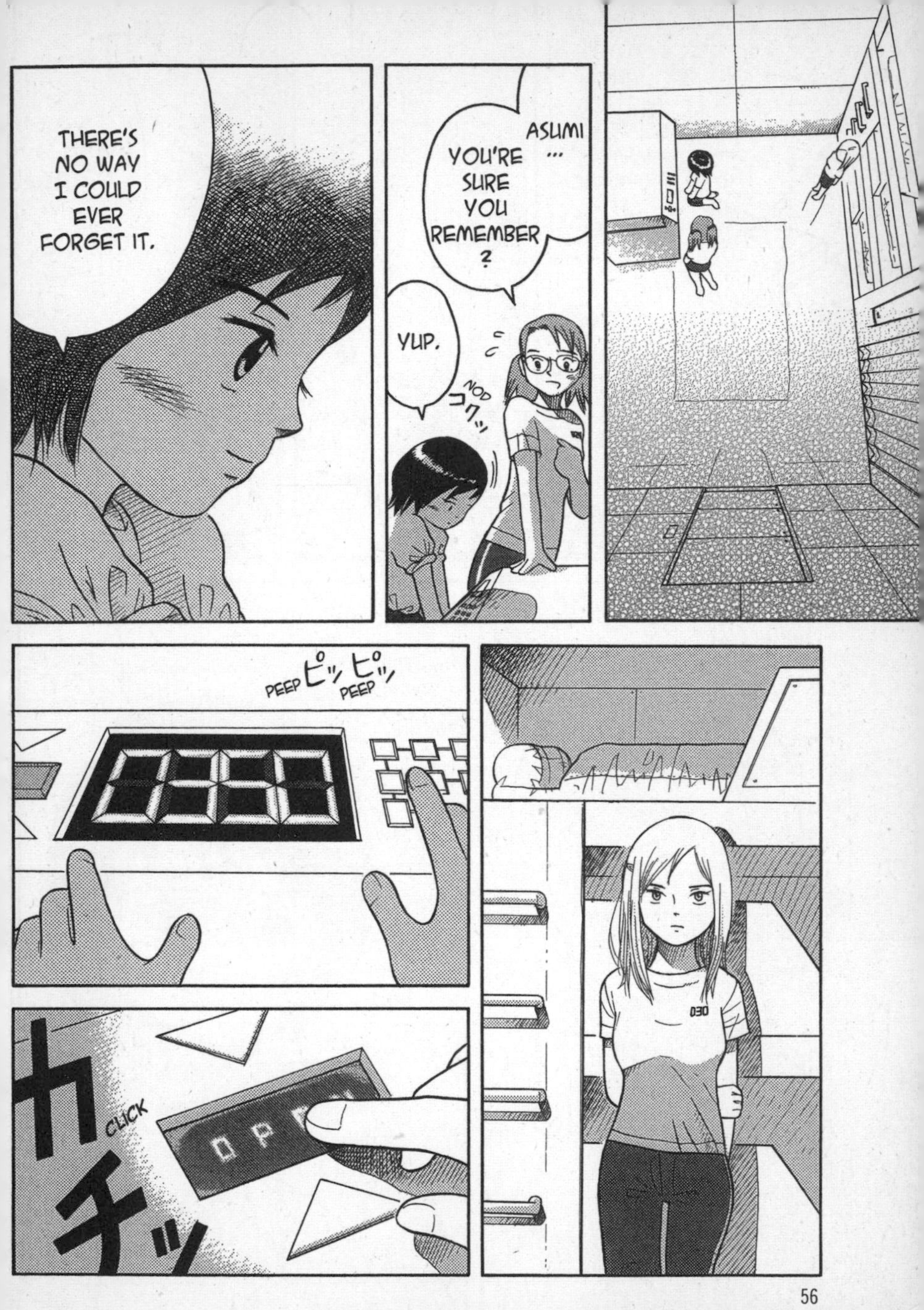
ASUMI ... YOU'RE SURE YOU REMEMBER?
YUP.
NOD コクッ
THERE'S NO WAY I COULD EVER FORGET IT.
PEEP ピッ ピッ PEEP
CLICK カチッ

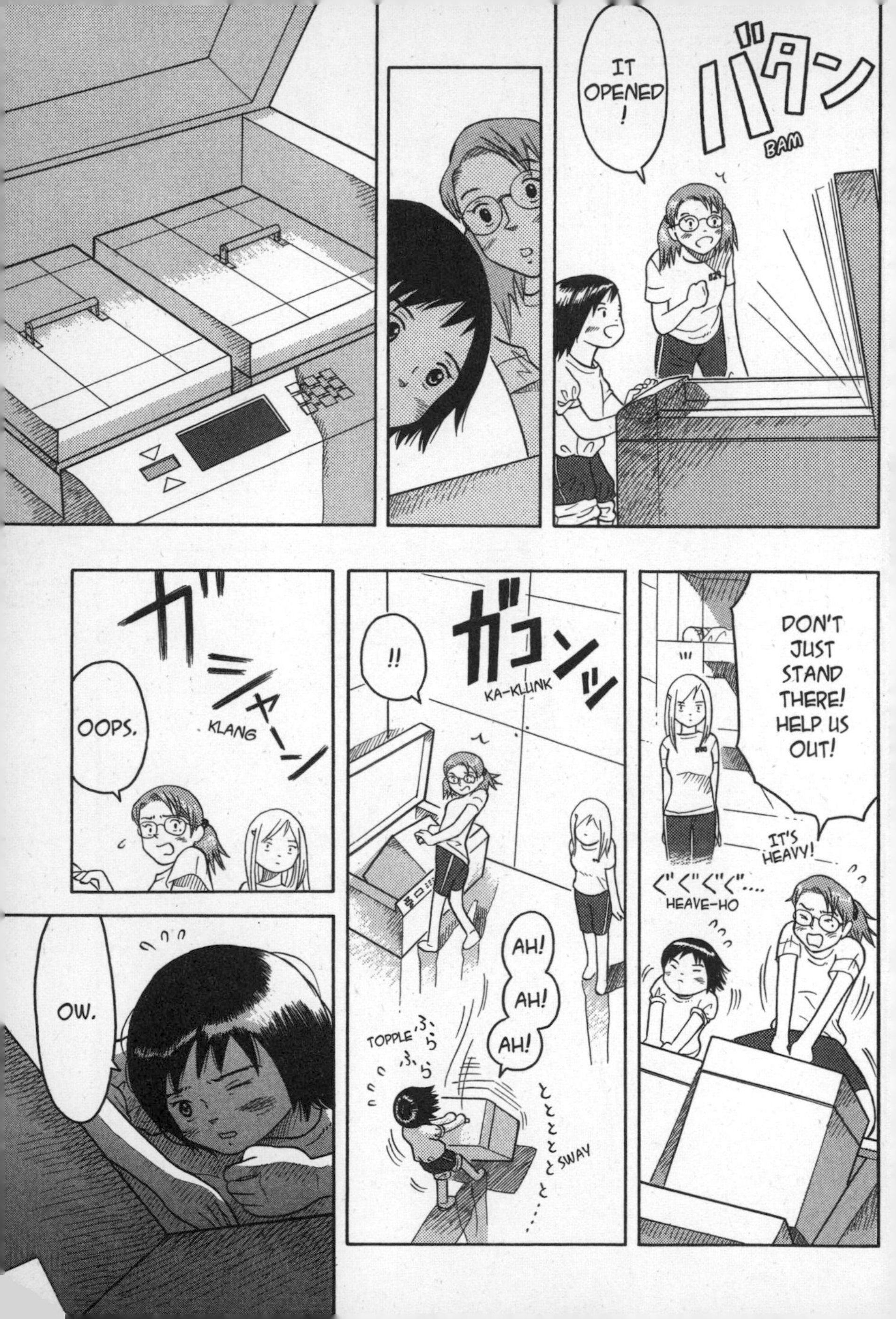
バタン
BAM
IT OPENED!
DON'T JUST STAND THERE! HELP US OUT!
IT'S HEAVY!
ぐぐぐぐ....
HEAVE-HO
ガコンッ
KA-KLUNK
!!
AH!
AH!
AH!
ふらふら
TOPPLE
とととと
SWAY
ガシャーン
KLANG
OOPS.
OW.

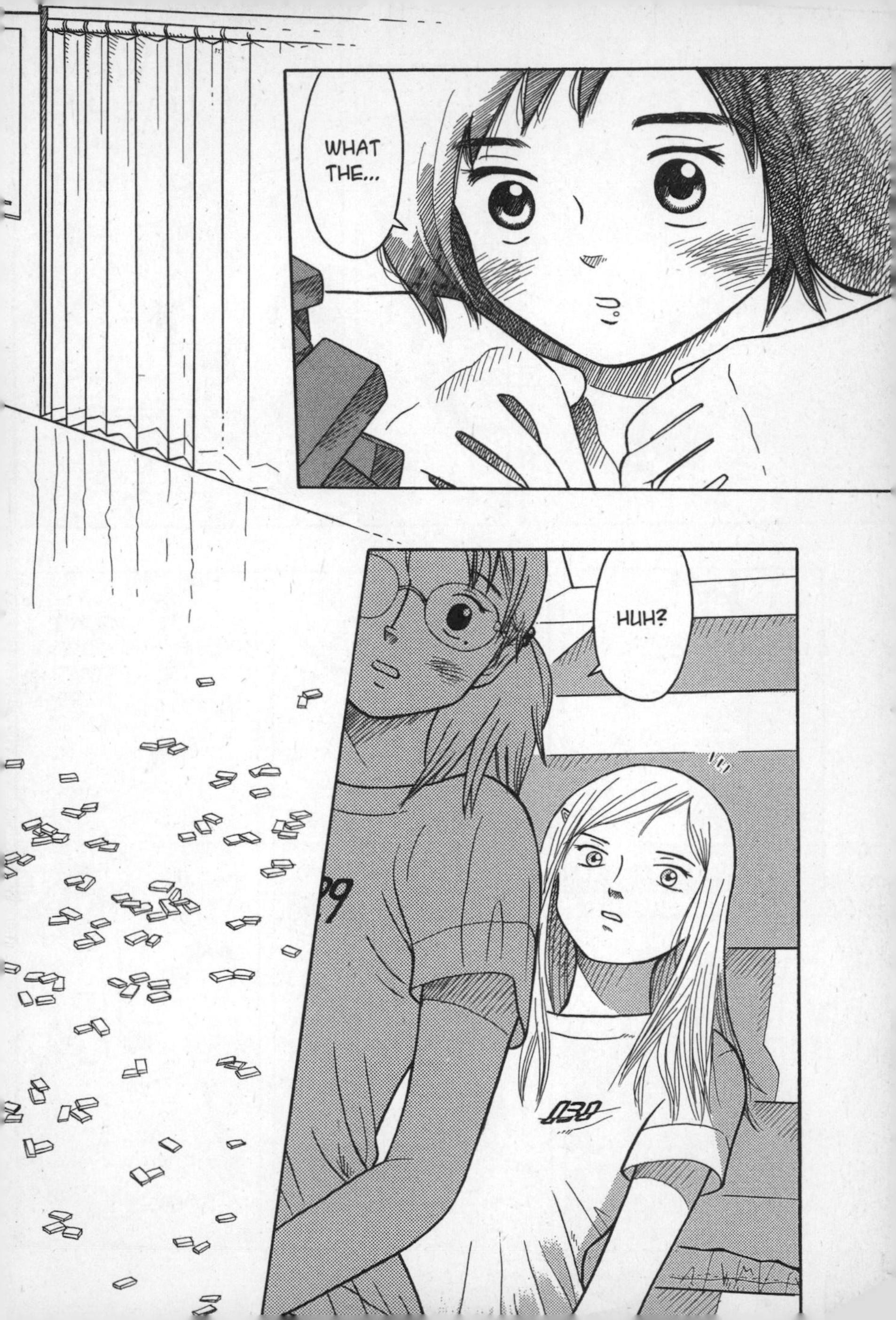
WHAT THE...
HUH?

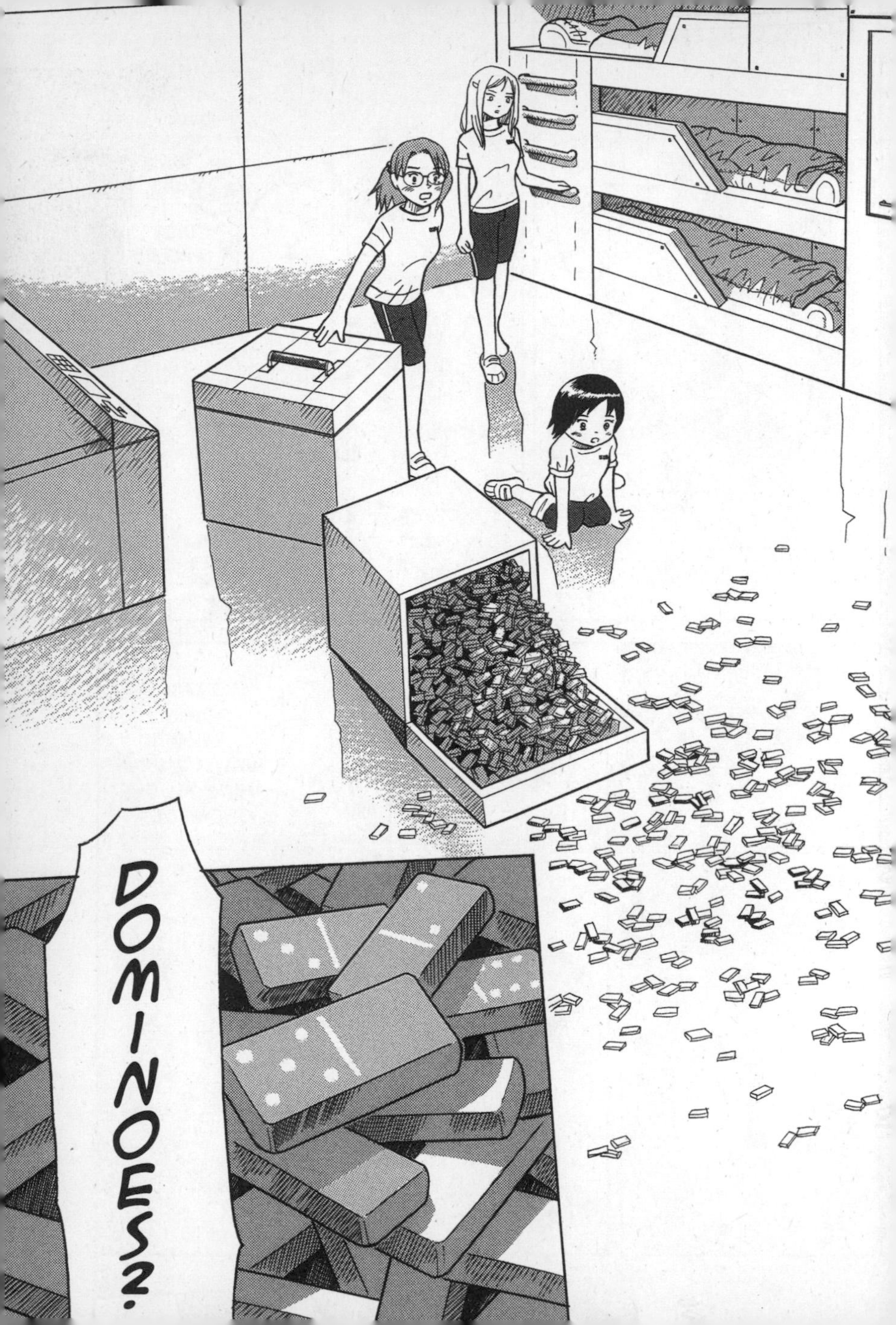
DOMINOES?.

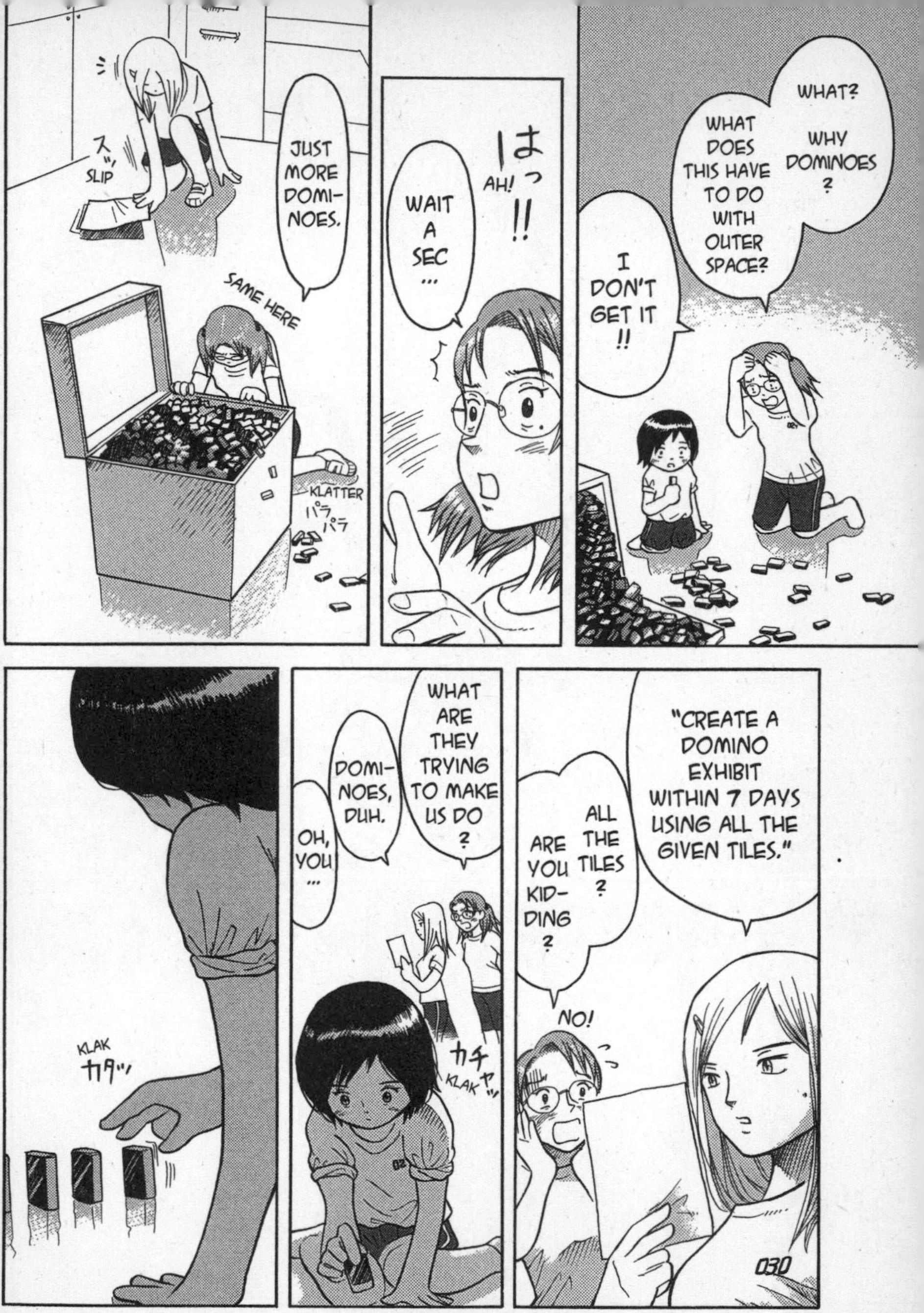
WHAT?
WHY DOMINOES?
WHAT DOES THIS HAVE TO DO WITH OUTER SPACE?
I DON'T GET IT!!
はっ!!
AH!
WAIT A SEC...
JUST MORE DOMINOES.
スッ
SLIP
SAME HERE
KLATTER
パラパラ
"CREATE A DOMINO EXHIBIT WITHIN 7 DAYS USING ALL THE GIVEN TILES."
ALL THE TILES?
ARE YOU KIDDING?
NO!
WHAT ARE THEY TRYING TO MAKE US DO?
DOMINOES, DUH.
OH, YOU...
カチャッ
KLAK
030
KLAK
カタッ

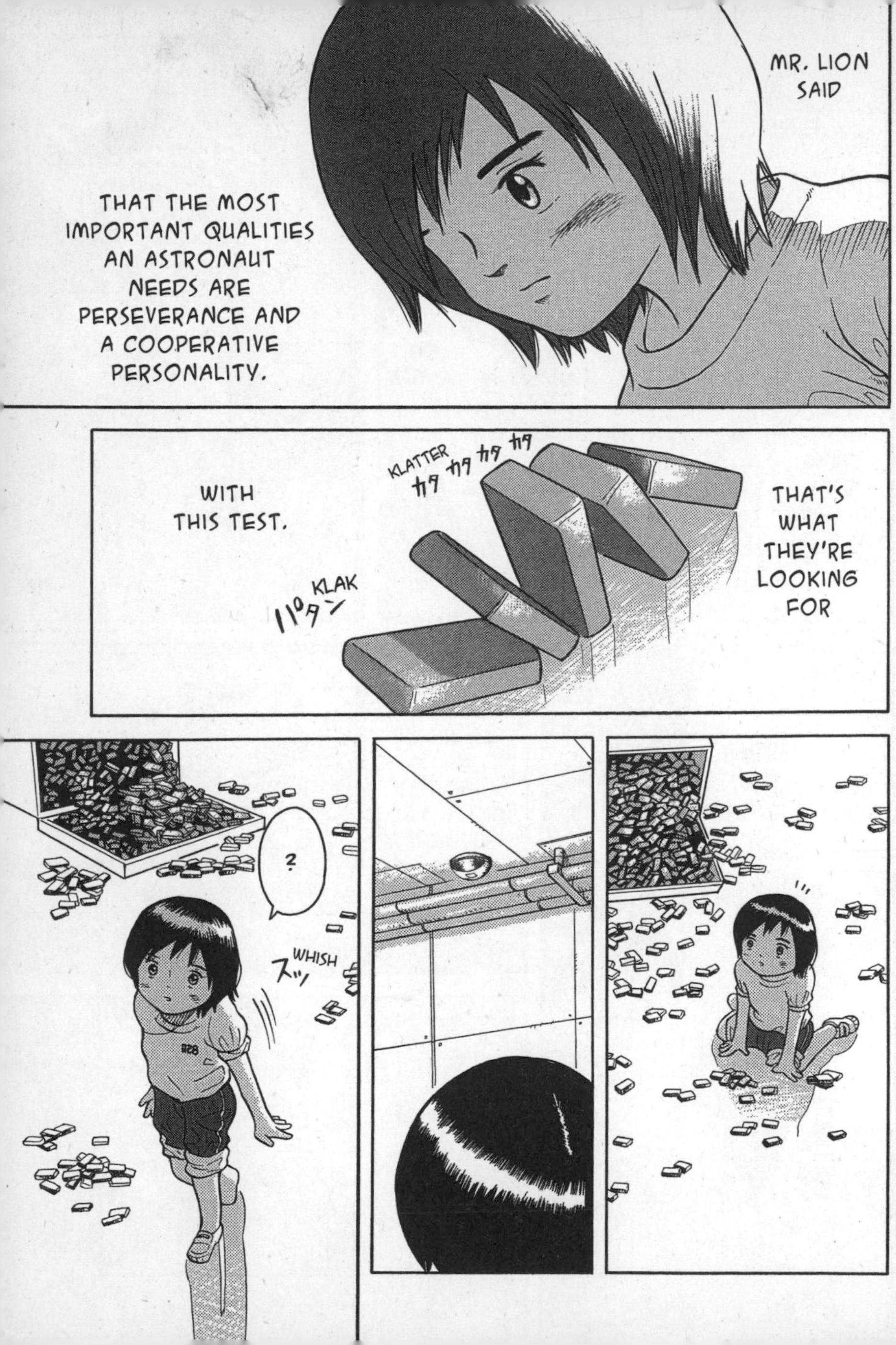
MR. LION SAID
THAT THE MOST IMPORTANT QUALITIES AN ASTRONAUT NEEDS ARE PERSEVERANCE AND A COOPERATIVE PERSONALITY.
THAT'S WHAT THEY'RE LOOKING FOR
KLATTER
カタ カタ カタ カタ
KLAK
パタン
WITH THIS TEST.
?
WHISH
ズッ

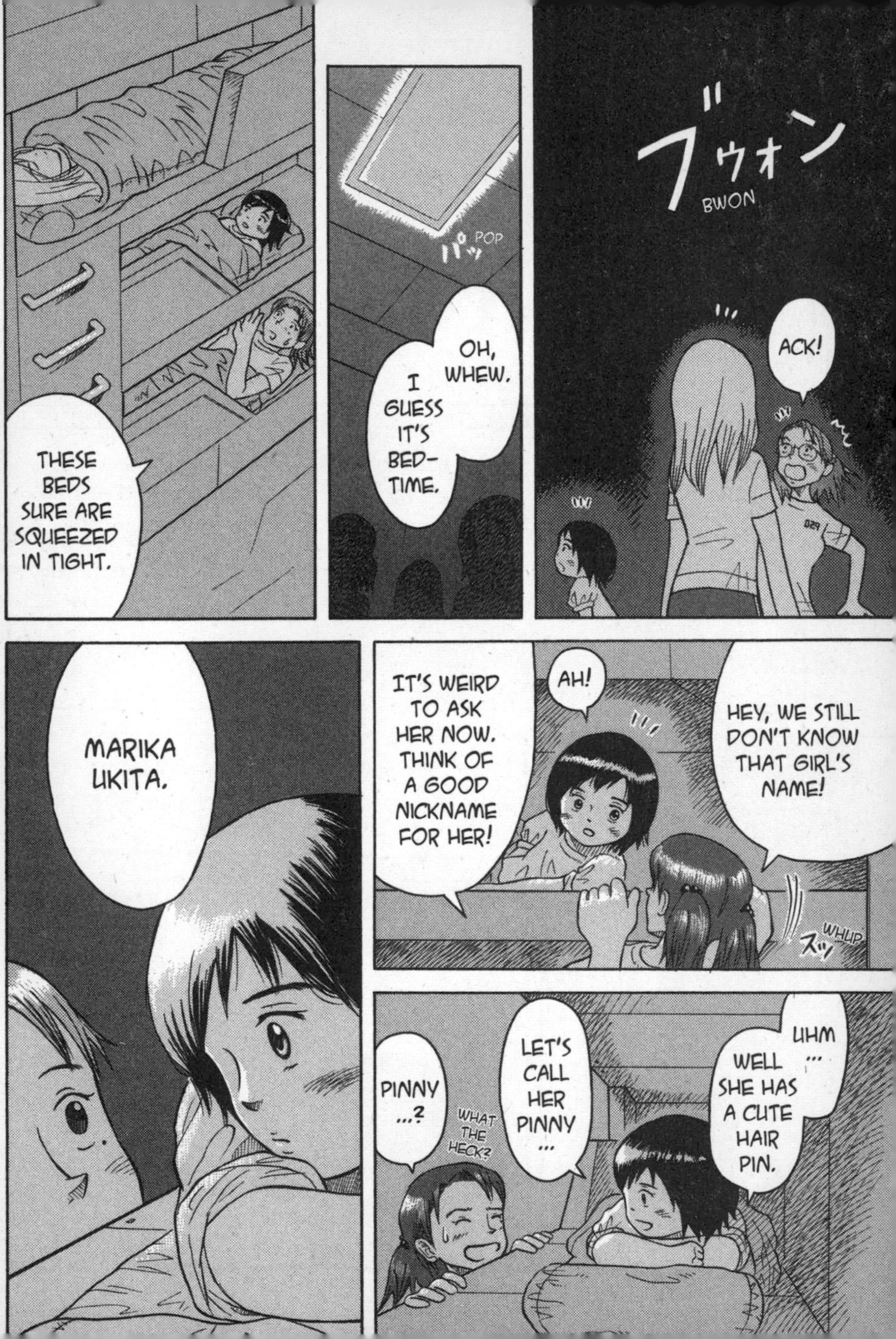
ブウォン
BWON
ACK!
パッ
POP
OH, WHEW.
I GUESS IT'S BED-TIME.
THESE BEDS SURE ARE SQUEEZED IN TIGHT.
HEY, WE STILL DON'T KNOW THAT GIRL'S NAME!
AH!
IT'S WEIRD TO ASK HER NOW. THINK OF A GOOD NICKNAME FOR HER!
ズッ
WHUP
UHM ...
WELL SHE HAS A CUTE HAIR PIN.
LET'S CALL HER PINNY ...
PINNY ...?
WHAT THE HECK?
MARIKA UKITA.

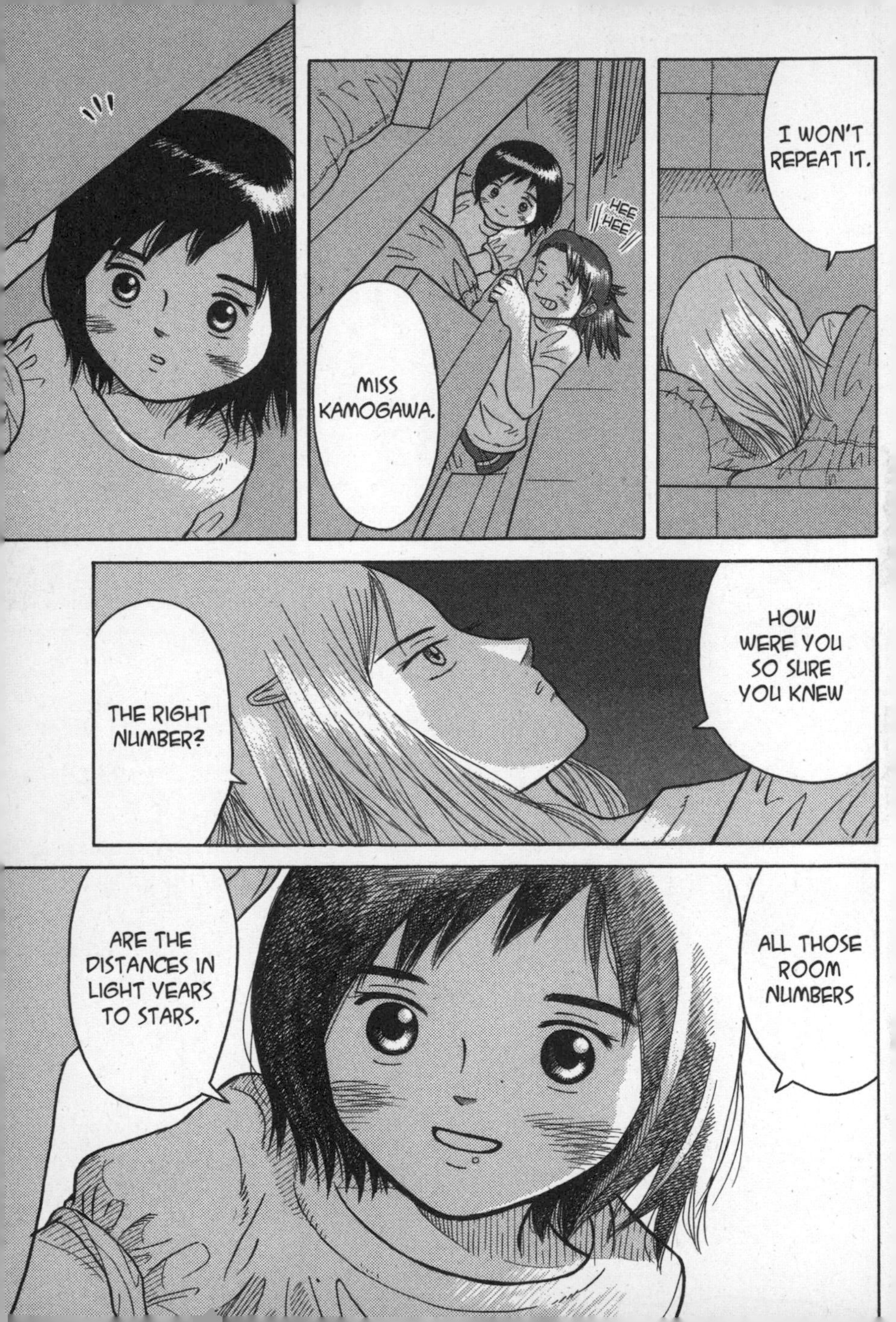
I WON'T REPEAT IT.
HEE HEE
MISS KAMOGAWA.
HOW WERE YOU SO SURE YOU KNEW
THE RIGHT NUMBER?
ALL THOSE ROOM NUMBERS
ARE THE DISTANCES IN LIGHT YEARS TO STARS.

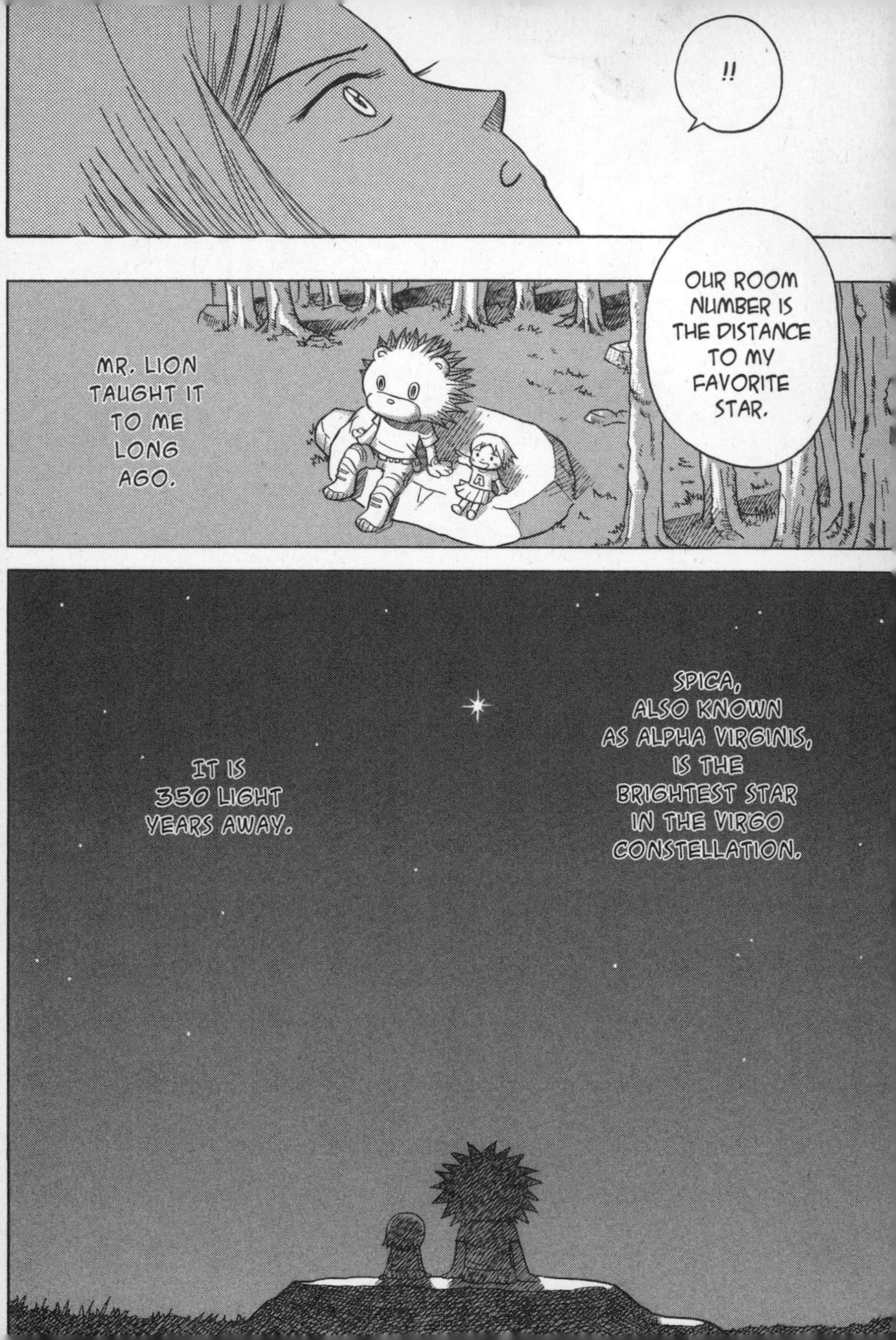
!!
OUR ROOM NUMBER IS THE DISTANCE TO MY FAVORITE STAR.
MR. LION TAUGHT IT TO ME LONG AGO.
SPICA, ALSO KNOWN AS ALPHA VIRGINIS, IS THE BRIGHTEST STAR IN THE VIRGO CONSTELLATION.
IT IS 350 LIGHT YEARS AWAY.

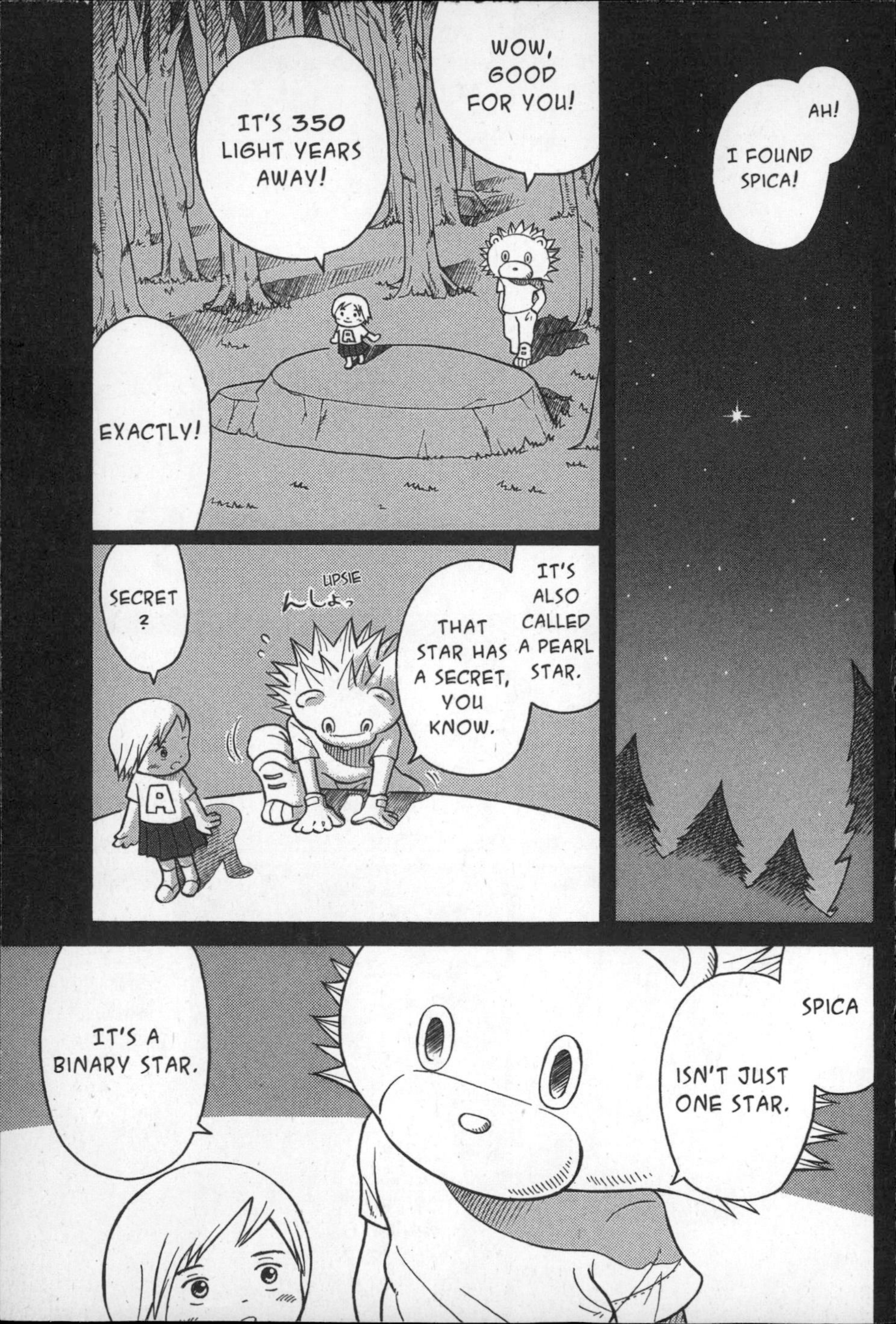
AH!
I FOUND SPICA!
WOW, GOOD FOR YOU!
IT'S 350 LIGHT YEARS AWAY!
EXACTLY!
IT'S ALSO CALLED A PEARL STAR.
THAT STAR HAS A SECRET, YOU KNOW.
LIPSIE
んしょっ
SECRET?
SPICA
ISN'T JUST ONE STAR.
IT'S A BINARY STAR.

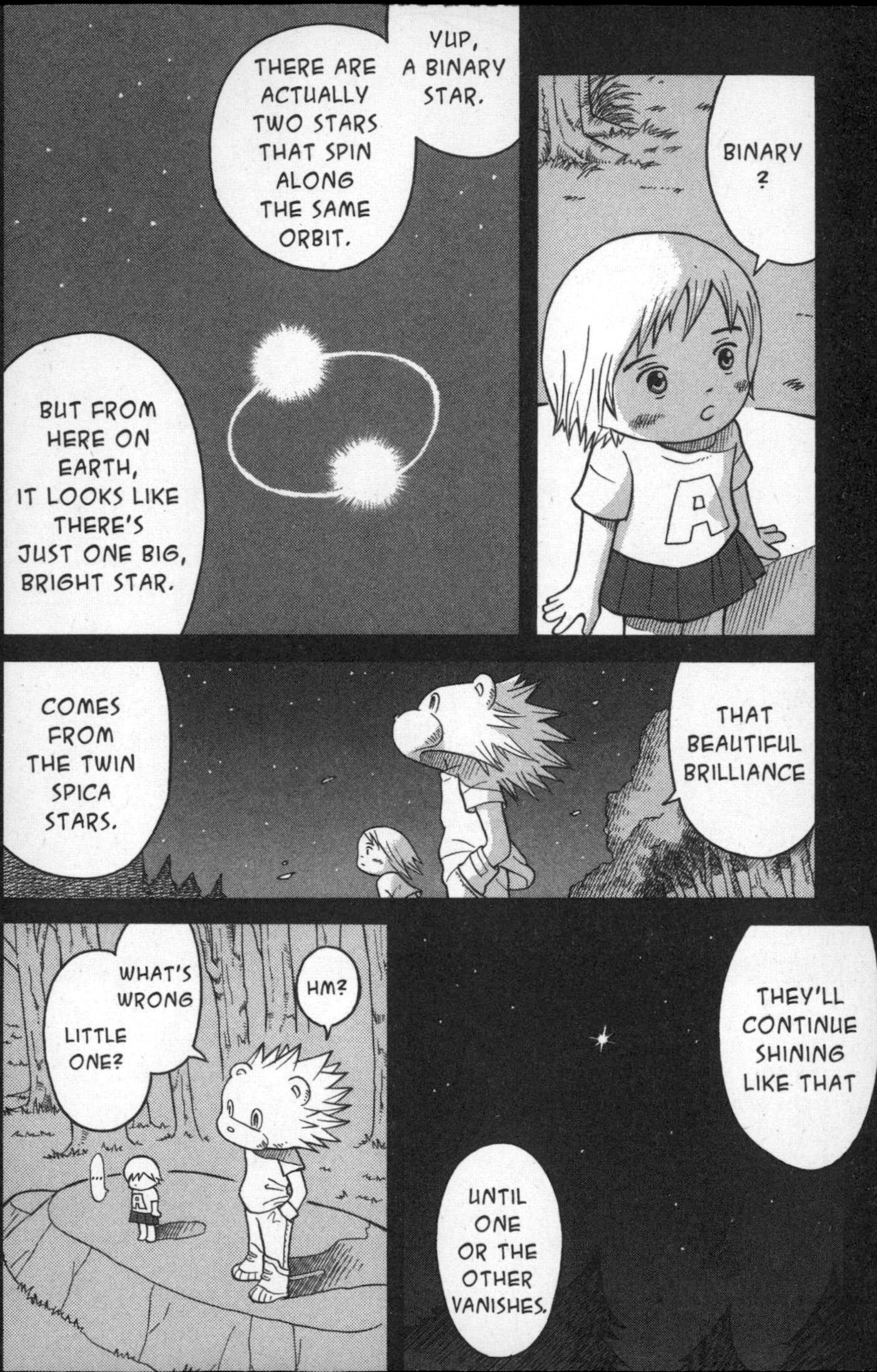
BINARY?
YUP, A BINARY STAR.
THERE ARE ACTUALLY TWO STARS THAT SPIN ALONG THE SAME ORBIT.
BUT FROM HERE ON EARTH, IT LOOKS LIKE THERE'S JUST ONE BIG, BRIGHT STAR.
THAT BEAUTIFUL BRILLIANCE
COMES FROM THE TWIN SPICA STARS.
THEY'LL CONTINUE SHINING LIKE THAT
UNTIL ONE OR THE OTHER VANISHES.
HM?
WHAT'S WRONG LITTLE ONE?
...

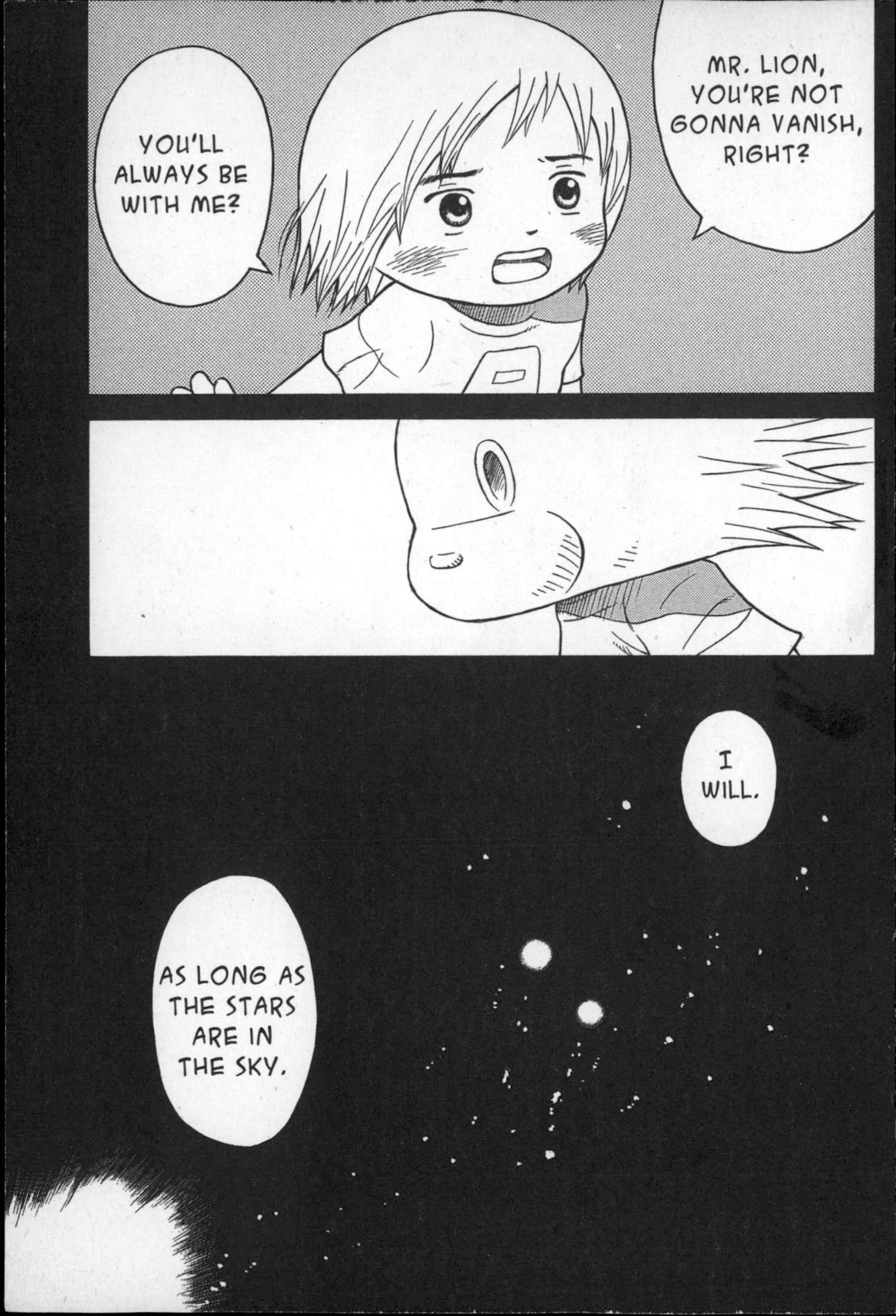
MR. LION, YOU'RE NOT GONNA VANISH, RIGHT?
YOU'LL ALWAYS BE WITH ME?
I WILL.
AS LONG AS THE STARS ARE IN THE SKY.

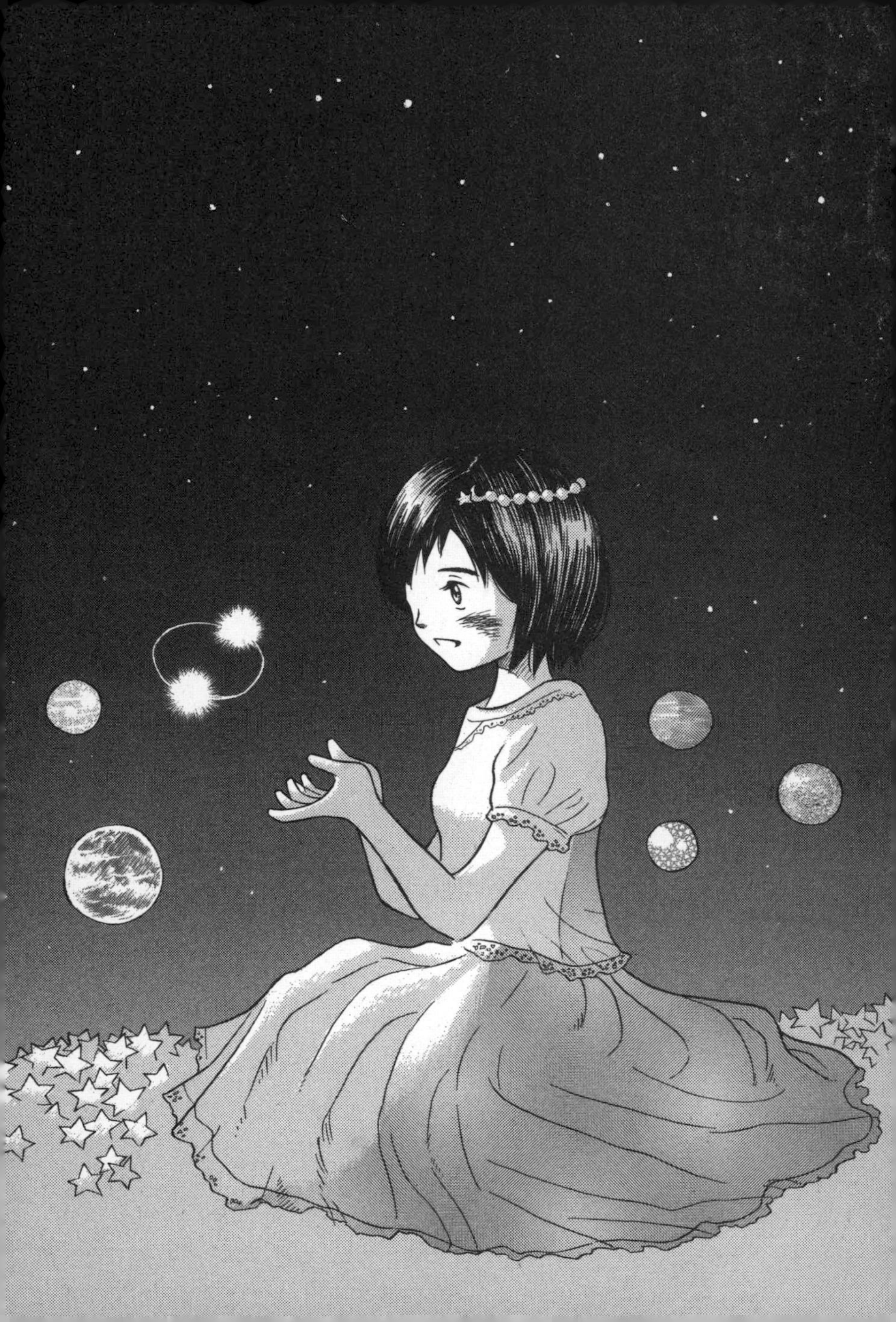

MISSION:03

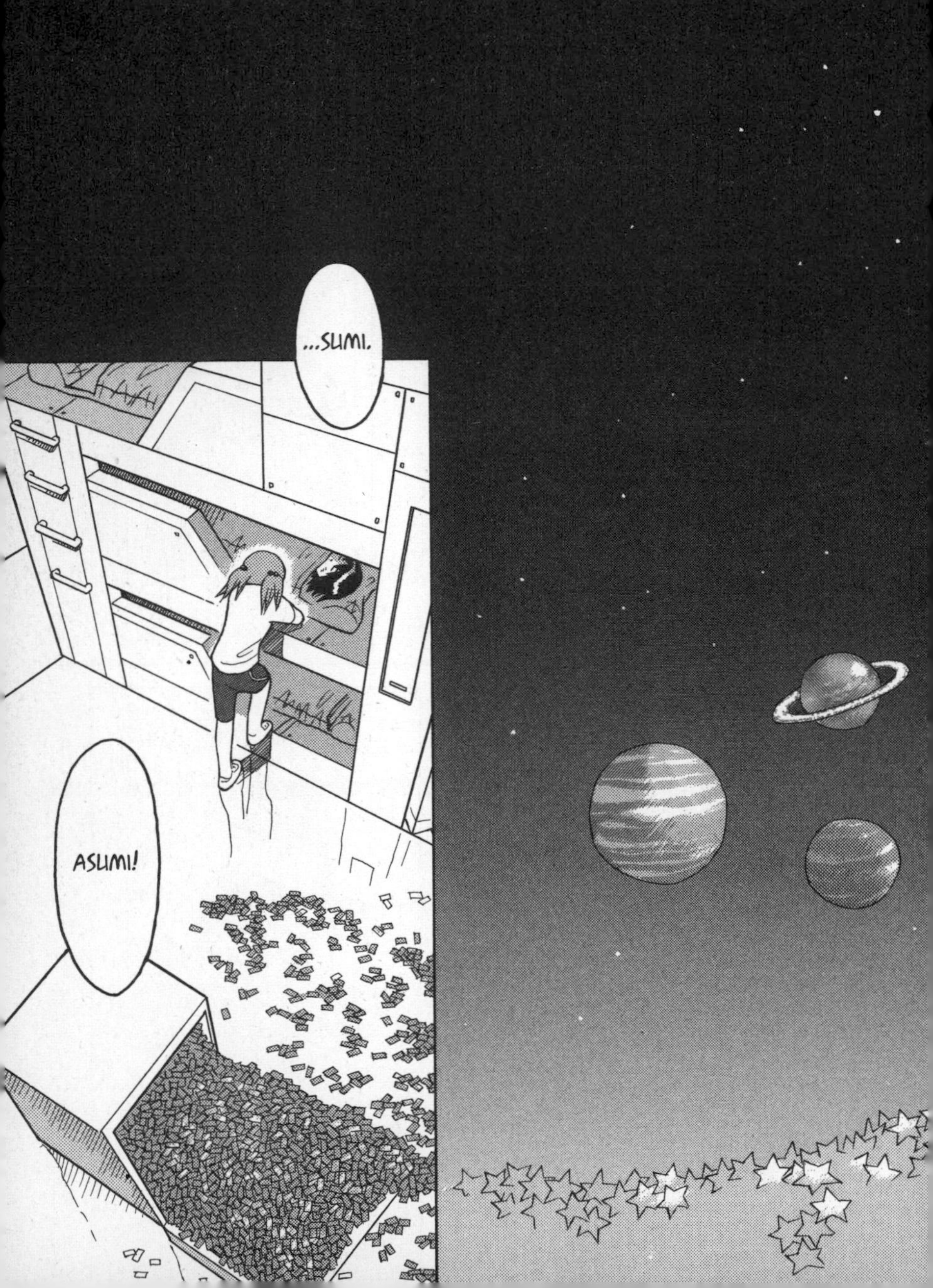

...SUMI.
ASUMI!

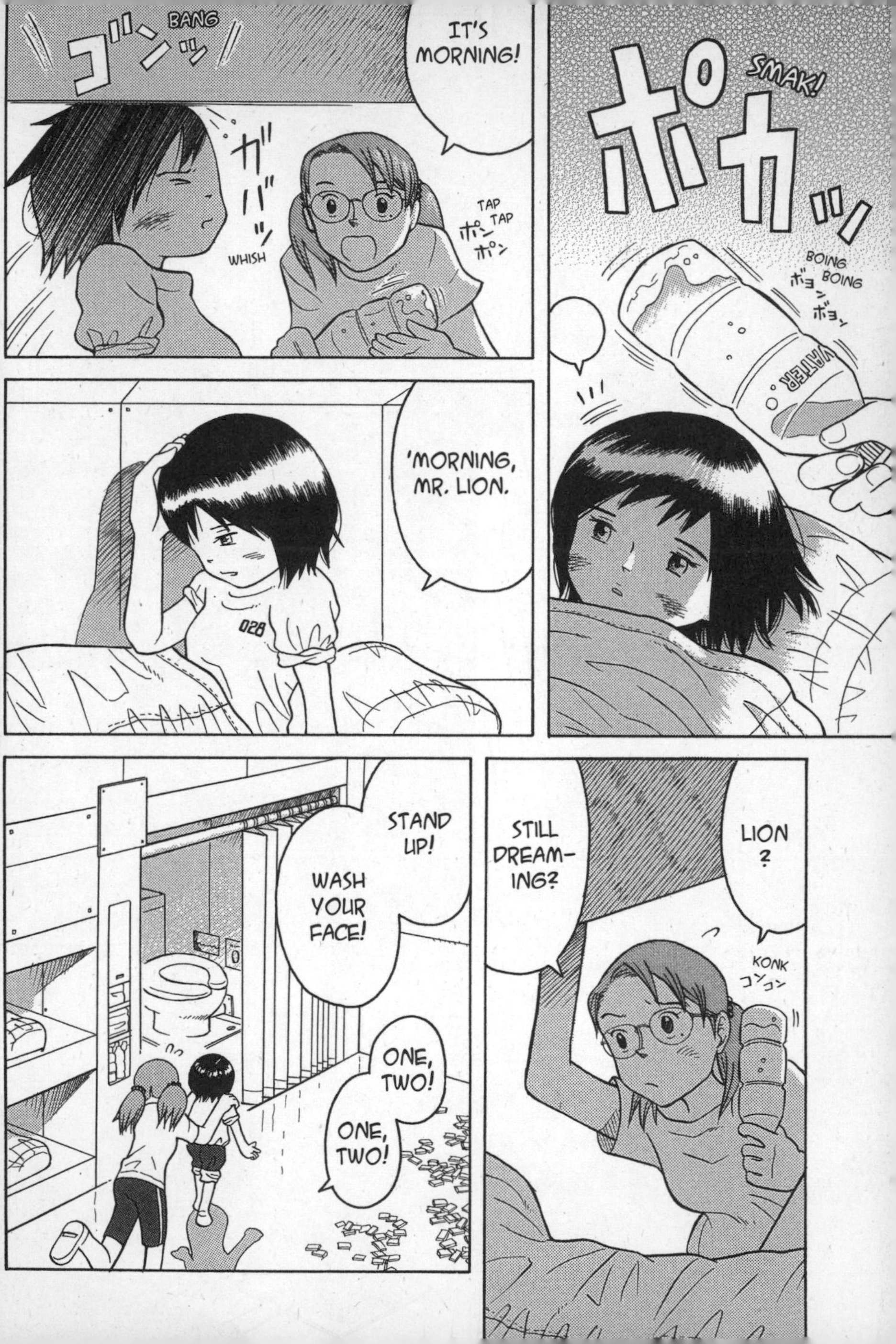
SMAK!
BOING BOING
IT'S MORNING!
TAP TAP
WHISH
BANG
'MORNING, MR. LION.
LION?
STILL DREAMING-ING?
KONK
STAND UP!
WASH YOUR FACE!
ONE, TWO!
ONE, TWO!

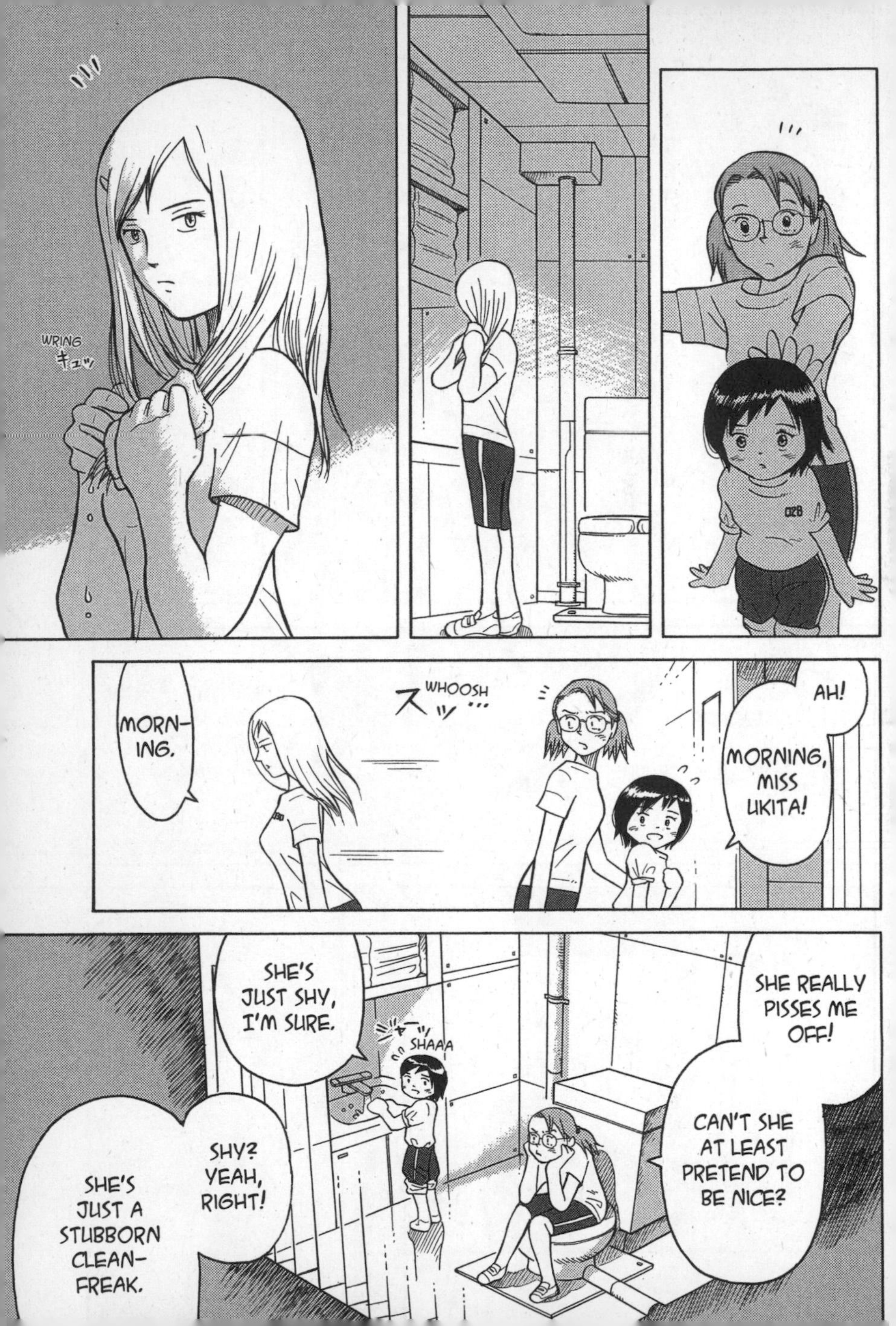
WRING
キュッ
AH!
MORNING, MISS UKITA!
WHOOSH
スッ
MORN-ING.
SHE REALLY PISSES ME OFF!
CAN'T SHE AT LEAST PRETEND TO BE NICE?
SHAAA
SHE'S JUST SHY, I'M SURE.
SHY? YEAH, RIGHT!
SHE'S JUST A STUBBORN CLEAN-FREAK.

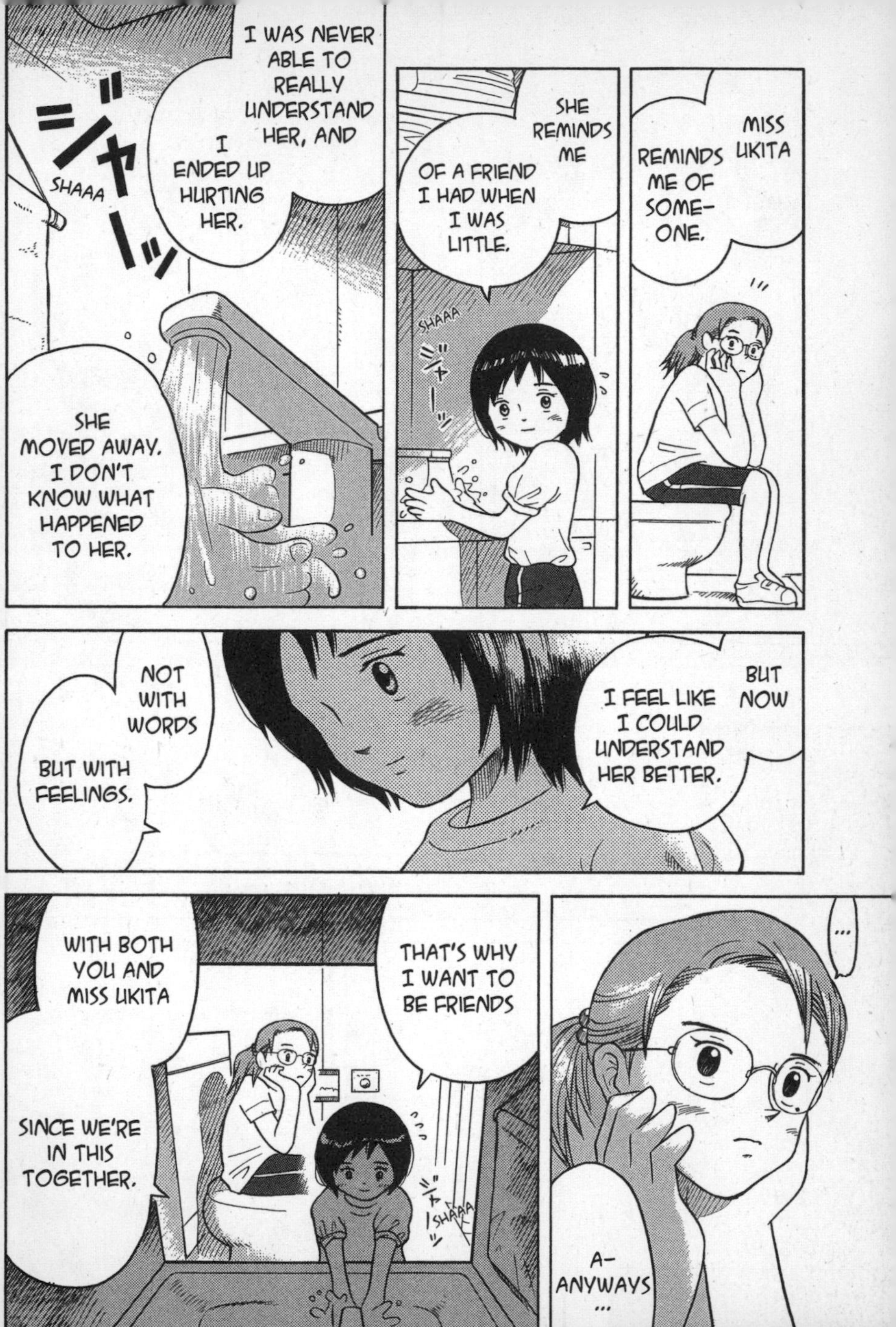
MISS UKITA
REMINDS ME OF SOME-ONE.
SHE REMINDS ME
OF A FRIEND I HAD WHEN I WAS LITTLE.
SHAAA
I WAS NEVER ABLE TO REALLY UNDERSTAND HER, AND
I ENDED UP HURTING HER.
SHAAA
SHE MOVED AWAY. I DON'T KNOW WHAT HAPPENED TO HER.
BUT NOW
I FEEL LIKE I COULD UNDERSTAND HER BETTER.
NOT WITH WORDS
BUT WITH FEELINGS.
...
A- ANYWAYS ...
THAT'S WHY I WANT TO BE FRIENDS
WITH BOTH YOU AND MISS UKITA
SINCE WE'RE IN THIS TOGETHER.
SHAAA

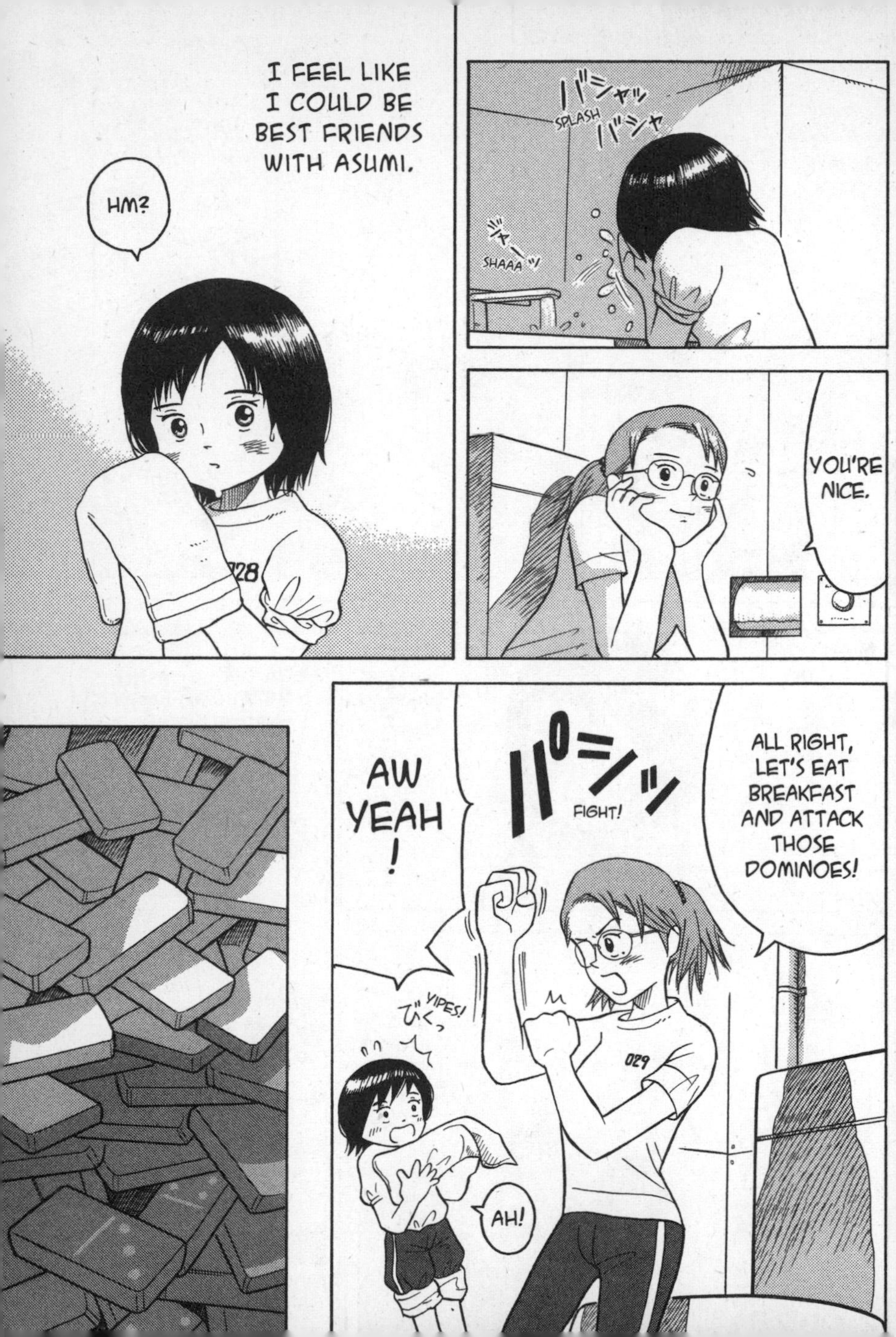

バシャッ
SPLASH
バシャ
ジャーッ
SHAAA
YOU'RE NICE.
I FEEL LIKE I COULD BE BEST FRIENDS WITH ASUMI.
HM?
ALL RIGHT, LET'S EAT BREAKFAST AND ATTACK THOSE DOMINOES!
パシッ
FIGHT!
AW YEAH!
YIPES!
びくっ
AH!

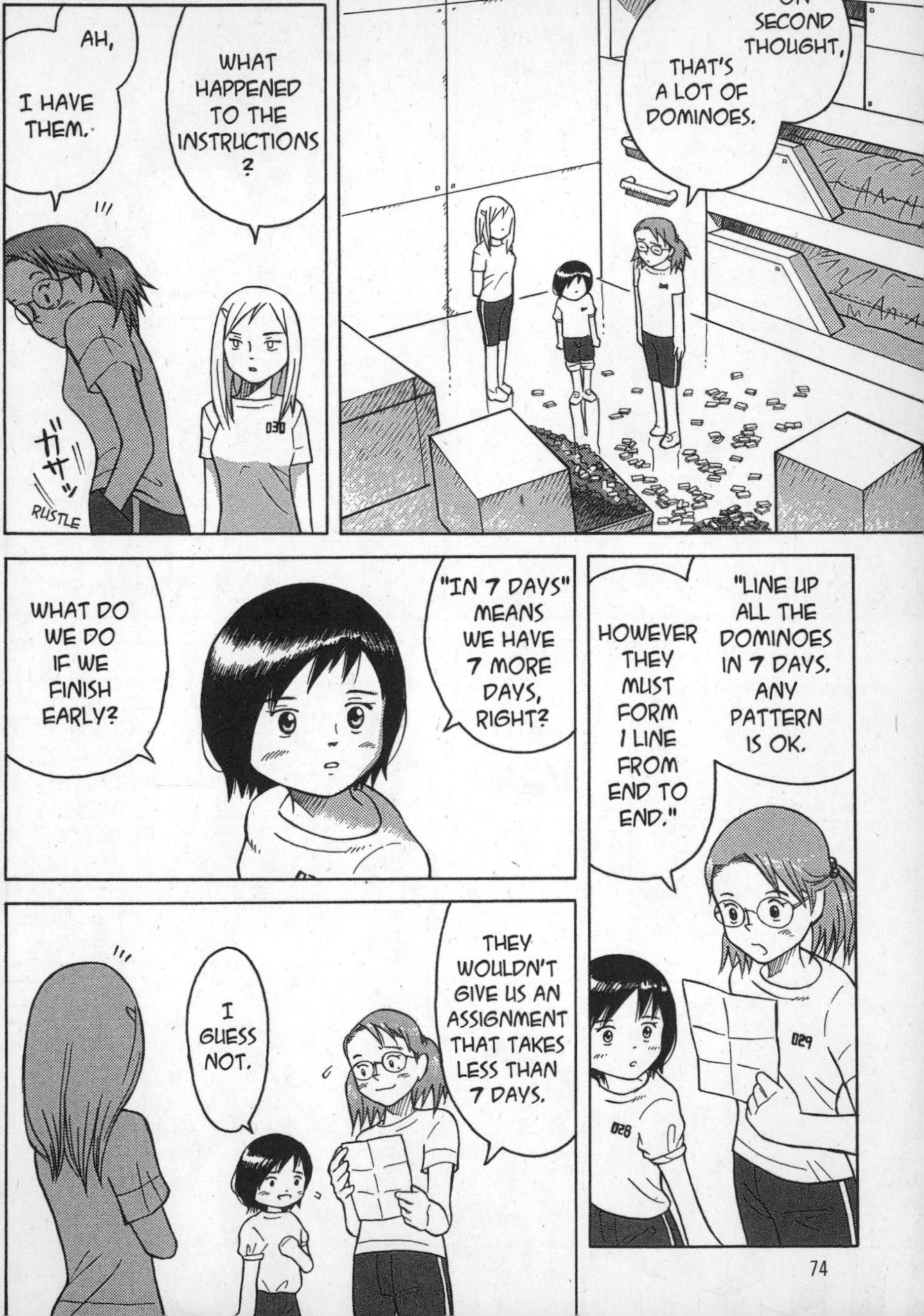
ON SECOND THOUGHT,
THAT'S A LOT OF DOMINOES.
WHAT HAPPENED TO THE INSTRUCTIONS?
AH,
I HAVE THEM.
ガサッ
RUSTLE
"LINE UP ALL THE DOMINOES IN 7 DAYS. ANY PATTERN IS OK.
HOWEVER THEY MUST FORM 1 LINE FROM END TO END."
"IN 7 DAYS" MEANS WE HAVE 7 MORE DAYS, RIGHT?
WHAT DO WE DO IF WE FINISH EARLY?
THEY WOULDN'T GIVE US AN ASSIGNMENT THAT TAKES LESS THAN 7 DAYS.
I GUESS NOT.

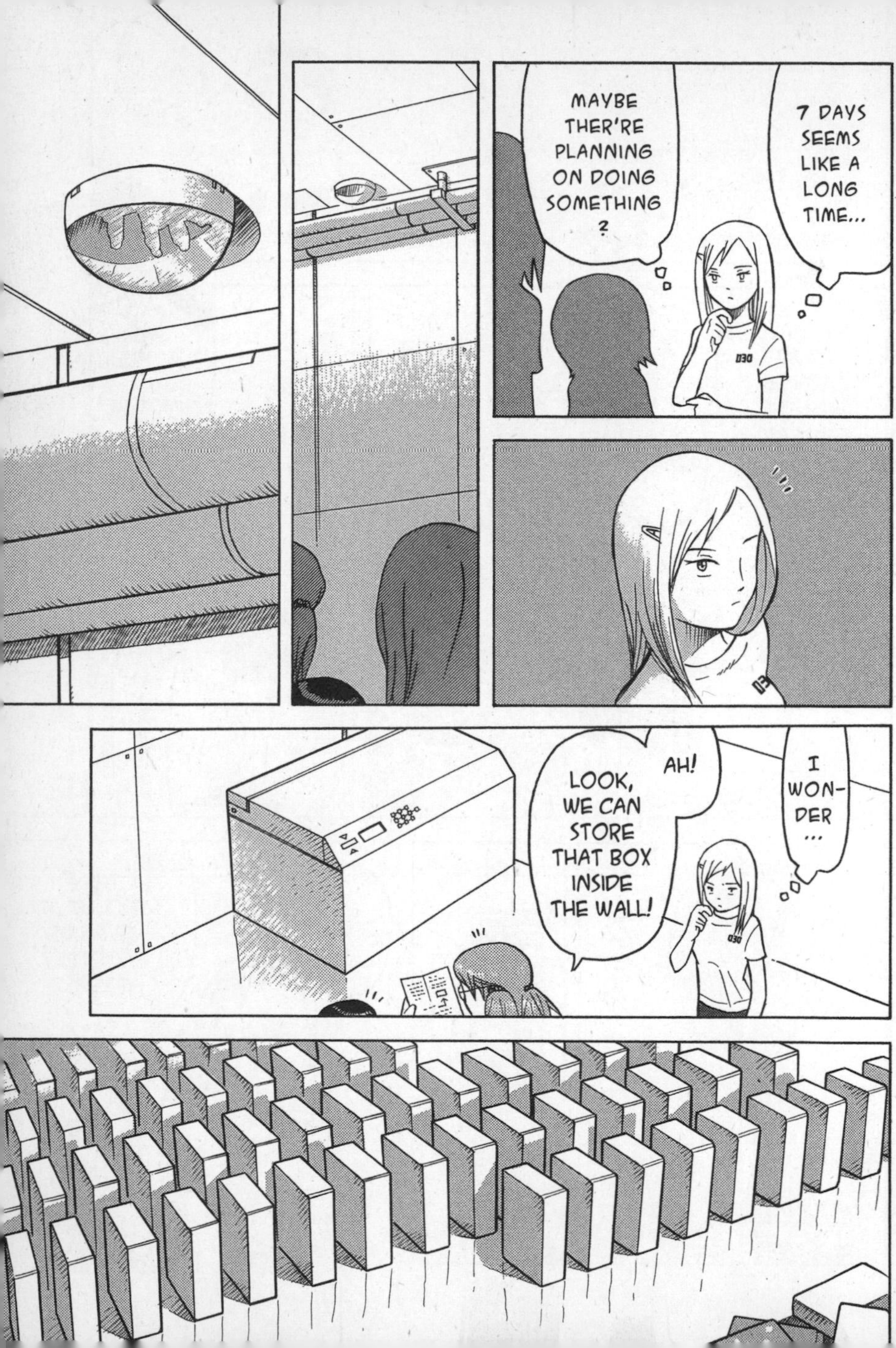
7 DAYS SEEMS LIKE A LONG TIME...
MAYBE THER'RE PLANNING ON DOING SOMETHING ?
I WON-DER ...
AH!
LOOK, WE CAN STORE THAT BOX INSIDE THE WALL!

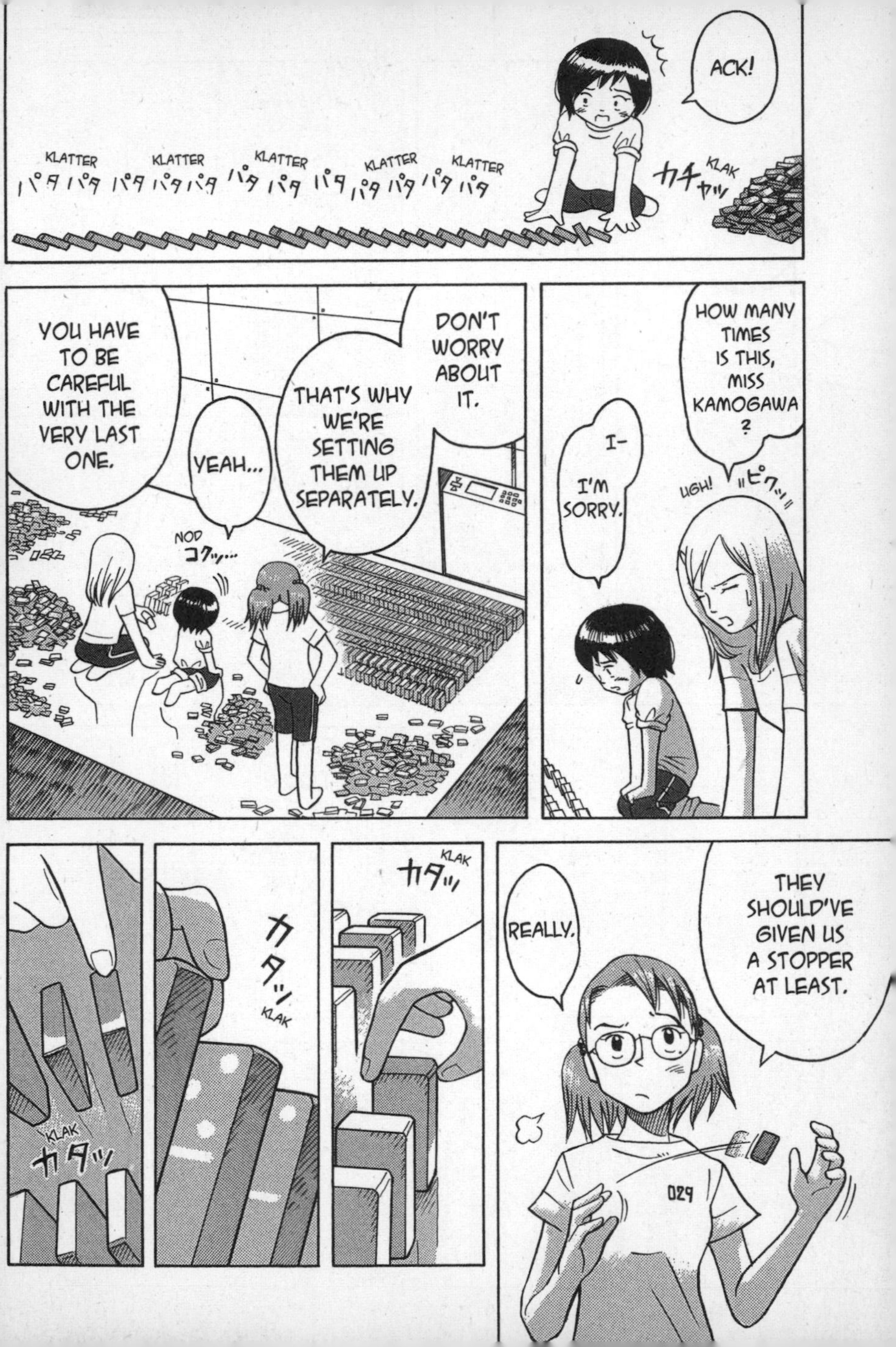
ACK!
KLAK カチャッ
KLATTER パタ パタ
KLATTER パタ パタ
KLATTER パタ パタ
KLATTER パタ パタ パタ
KLATTER パタ パタ パタ
HOW MANY TIMES IS THIS, MISS KAMOGAWA?
UGH! ピクッ
I- I'M SORRY.
DON'T WORRY ABOUT IT.
THAT'S WHY WE'RE SETTING THEM UP SEPARATELY.
YEAH...
NOD コクッ…
YOU HAVE TO BE CAREFUL WITH THE VERY LAST ONE.
THEY SHOULD'VE GIVEN US A STOPPER AT LEAST.
REALLY.
029
KLAK カタッ
KLAK カタッ
KLAK カタッ

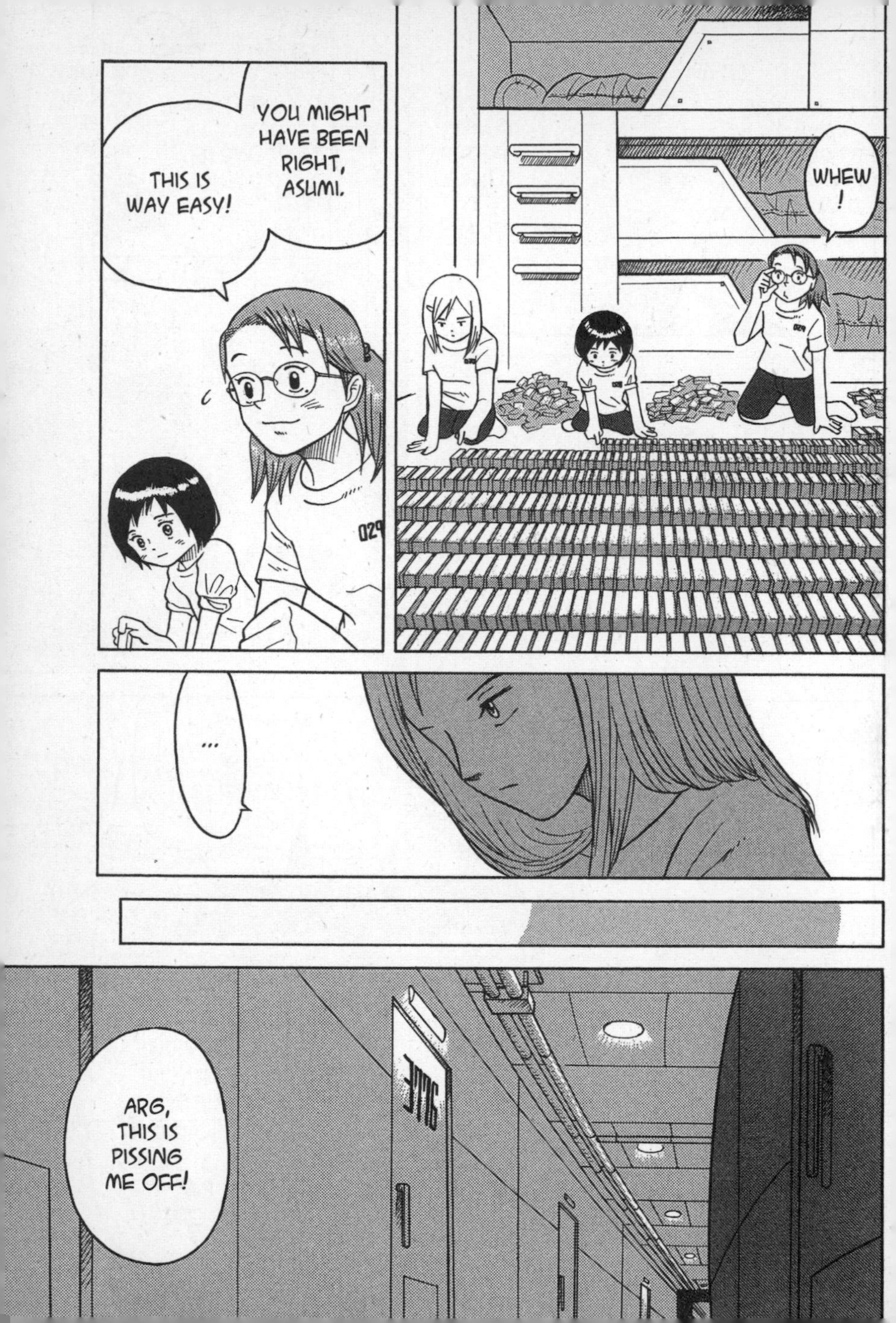
WHEW!
YOU MIGHT HAVE BEEN RIGHT, ASUMI.
THIS IS WAY EASY!
...
ARG, THIS IS PISSING ME OFF!

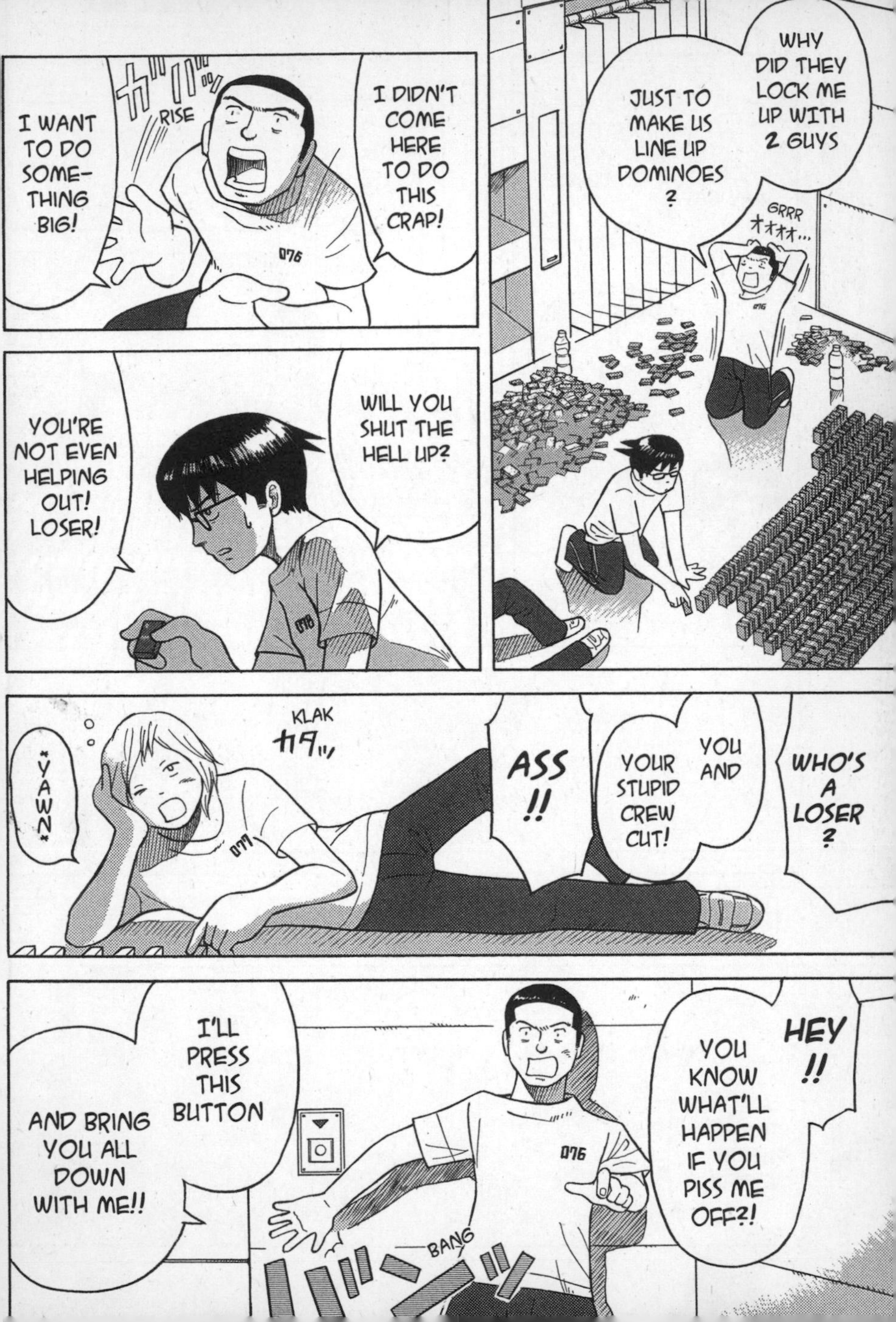
WHY DID THEY LOCK ME UP WITH 2 GUYS
JUST TO MAKE US LINE UP DOMINOES?
GRRR
オオオオ...
RISE
ガバッ
I DIDN'T COME HERE TO DO THIS CRAP!
I WANT TO DO SOMETHING BIG!
WILL YOU SHUT THE HELL UP?
YOU'RE NOT EVEN HELPING OUT! LOSER!
WHO'S A LOSER?
YOU AND YOUR STUPID CREW CUT!
ASS!!
KLAK
カタッ
YAWN
HEY!!
YOU KNOW WHAT'LL HAPPEN IF YOU PISS ME OFF?!
I'LL PRESS THIS BUTTON
AND BRING YOU ALL DOWN WITH ME!!
BANG

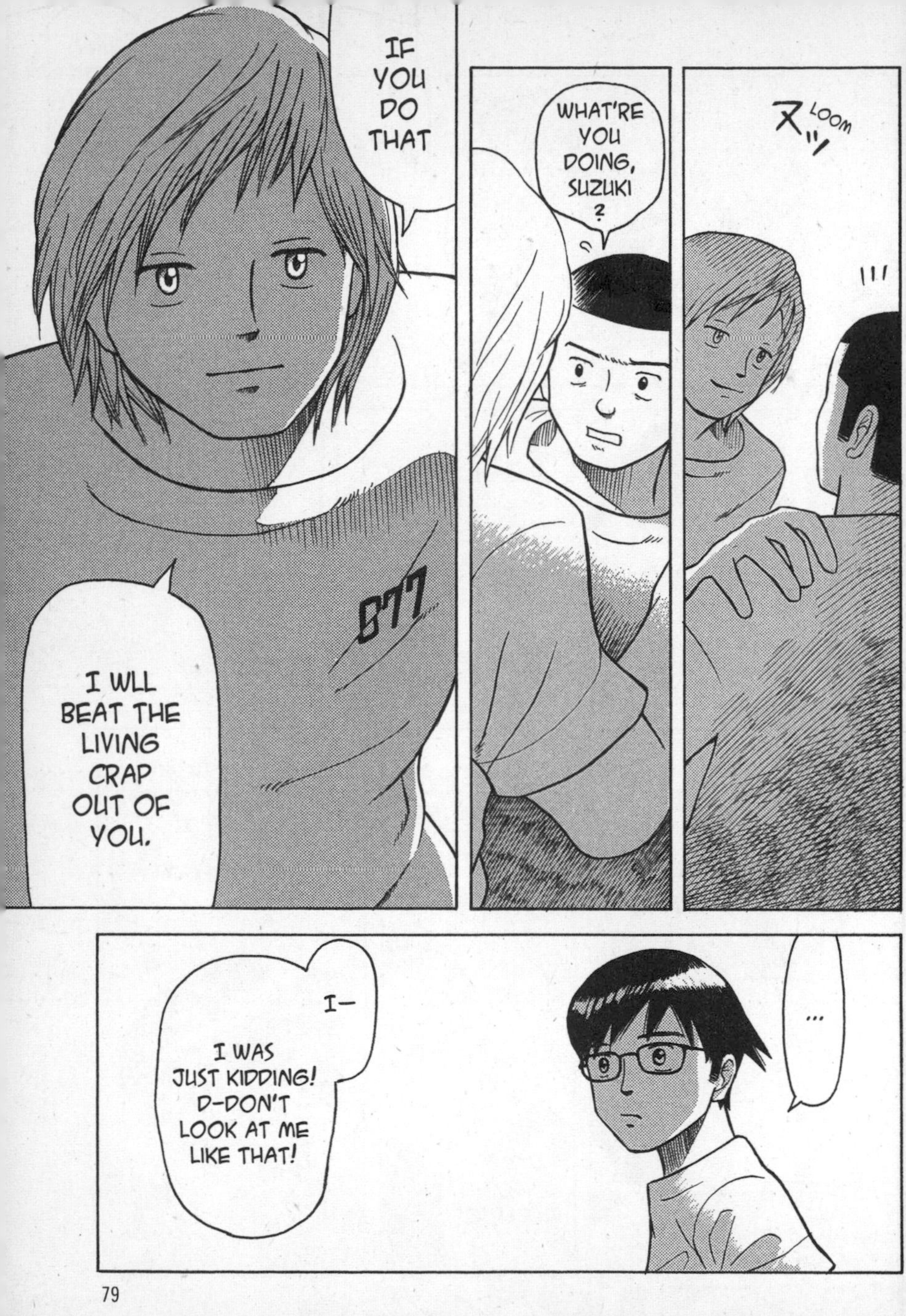
ヌッ LOOM
!!!
WHAT'RE YOU DOING, SUZUKI?
IF YOU DO THAT
I WLL BEAT THE LIVING CRAP OUT OF YOU.
...
I—
I WAS JUST KIDDING! D-DON'T LOOK AT ME LIKE THAT!

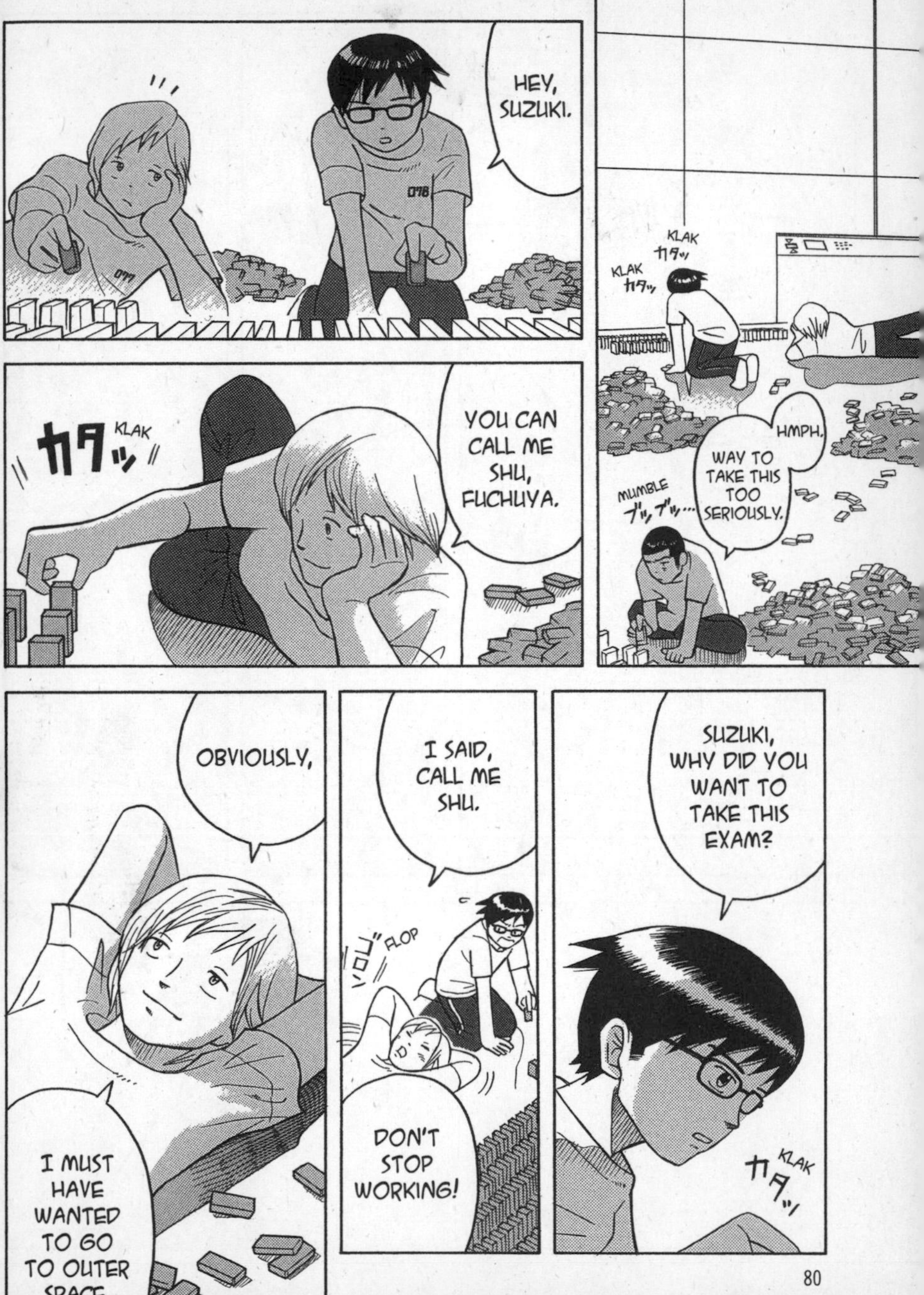
KLAK
カタッ
KLAK
カタッ
HMPH.
WAY TO TAKE THIS TOO SERIOUSLY.
MUMBLE
ブツ,ブツ…
HEY, SUZUKI.
YOU CAN CALL ME SHU, FUCHUYA.
KLAK
カタッ
SUZUKI, WHY DID YOU WANT TO TAKE THIS EXAM?
KLAK
カタッ
I SAID, CALL ME SHU.
FLOP
DON'T STOP WORKING!
OBVIOUSLY,
I MUST HAVE WANTED TO GO TO OUTER SPACE.

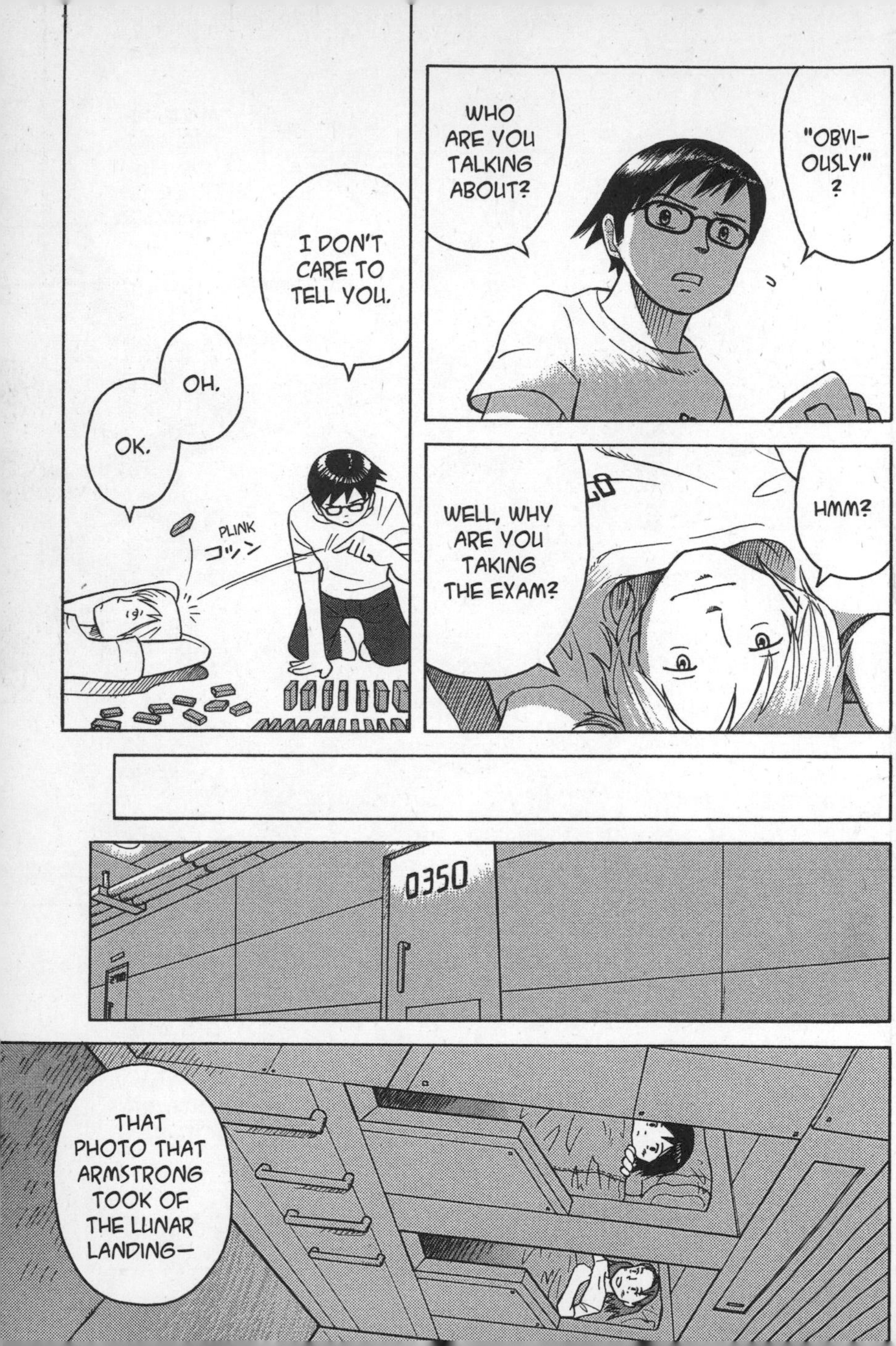
"OBVI-OUSLY"?
WHO ARE YOU TALKING ABOUT?
HMM?
WELL, WHY ARE YOU TAKING THE EXAM?
I DON'T CARE TO TELL YOU.
OH. OK.
PLINK
コツン
0350
THAT PHOTO THAT ARMSTRONG TOOK OF THE LUNAR LANDING—

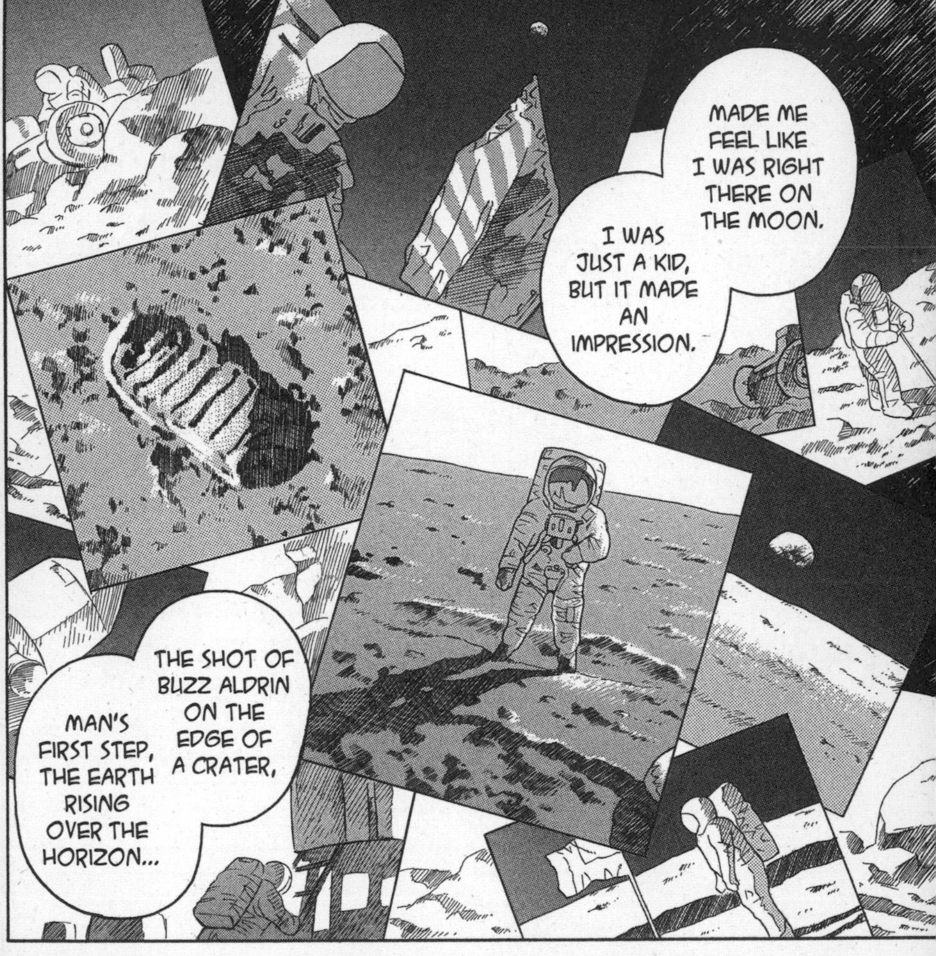
MADE ME FEEL LIKE I WAS RIGHT THERE ON THE MOON.
I WAS JUST A KID, BUT IT MADE AN IMPRESSION.
THE SHOT OF BUZZ ALDRIN ON THE EDGE OF A CRATER,
MAN'S FIRST STEP, THE EARTH RISING OVER THE HORIZON...

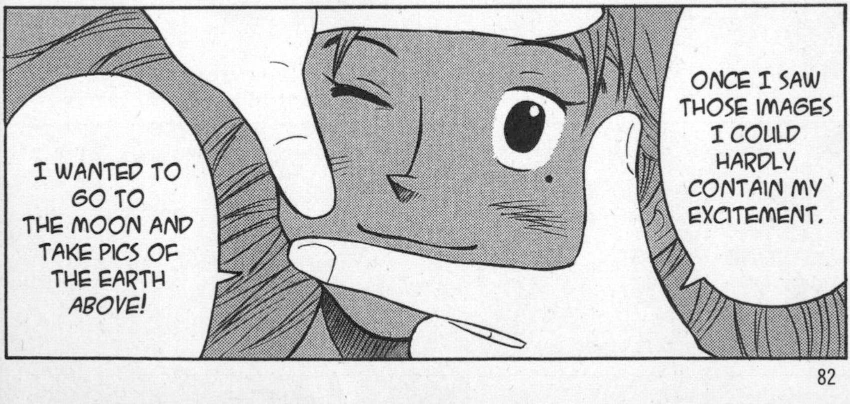
ONCE I SAW THOSE IMAGES I COULD HARDLY CONTAIN MY EXCITEMENT.
I WANTED TO GO TO THE MOON AND TAKE PICS OF THE EARTH *ABOVE*!

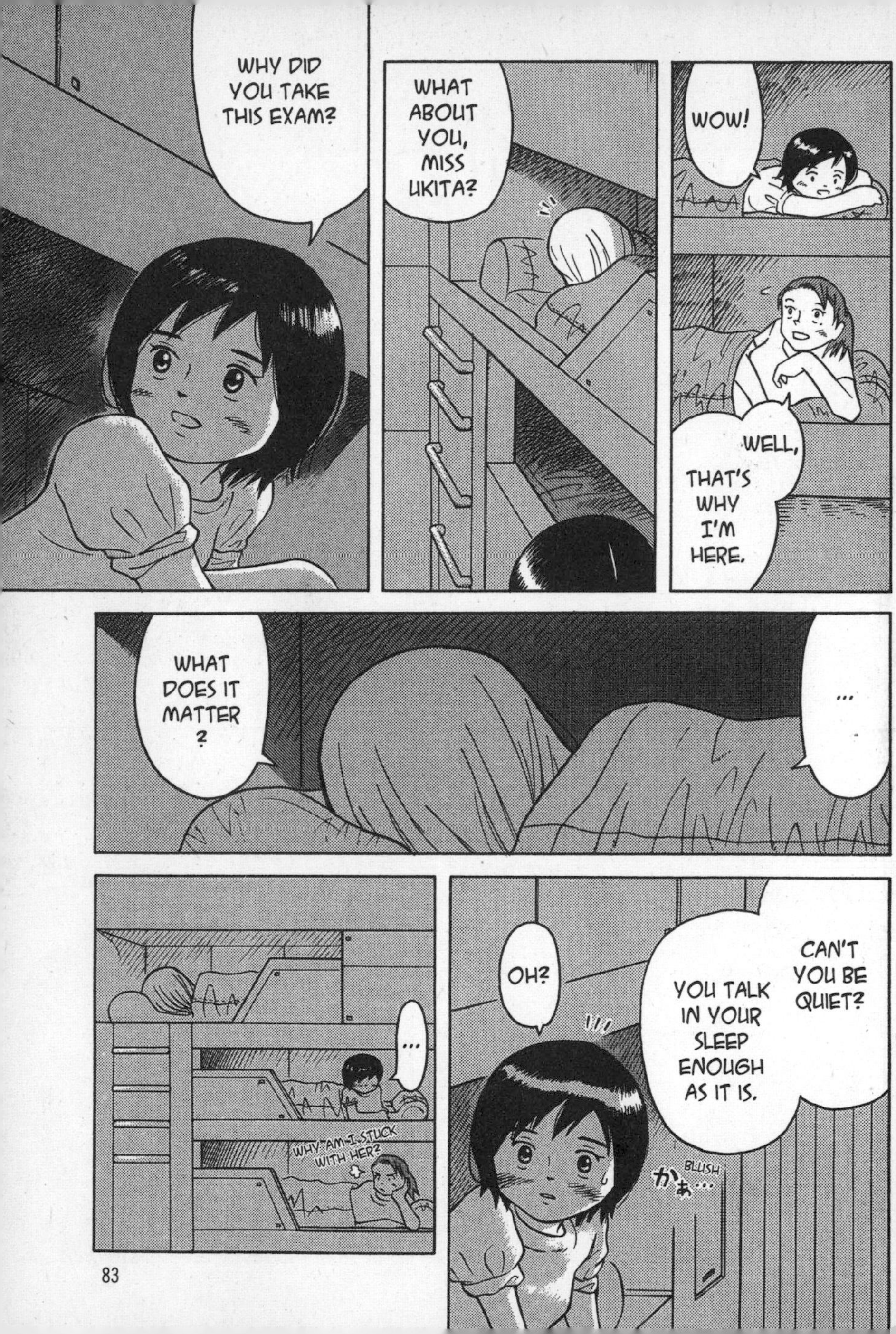
WOW!
WELL, THAT'S WHY I'M HERE.
WHAT ABOUT YOU, MISS UKITA?
WHY DID YOU TAKE THIS EXAM?
...
WHAT DOES IT MATTER?
CAN'T YOU BE QUIET?
YOU TALK IN YOUR SLEEP ENOUGH AS IT IS.
OH?
BLUSH
かぁ…
...
WHY AM I STUCK WITH HER?

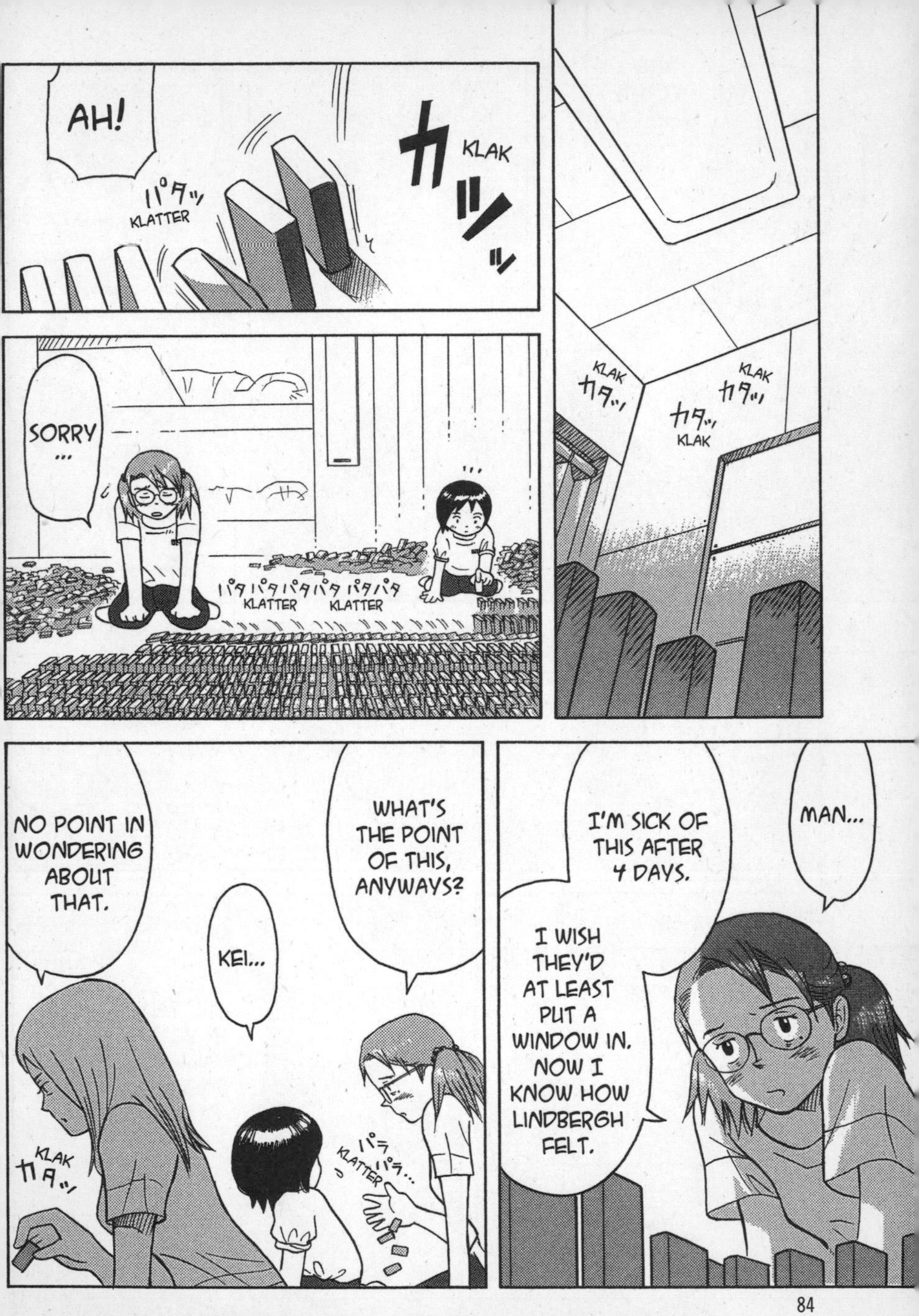
KLAK
カタッ
カタッ
KLAK
KLAK
カタッ
KLAK
カッツ
AH!
パタッ
KLATTER
SORRY ...
パタパタパタパタ パタパタ
KLATTER KLATTER
MAN...
I'M SICK OF THIS AFTER 4 DAYS.
I WISH THEY'D AT LEAST PUT A WINDOW IN. NOW I KNOW HOW LINDBERGH FELT.
WHAT'S THE POINT OF THIS, ANYWAYS?
KEI...
NO POINT IN WONDERING ABOUT THAT.
パラパラ...
KLATTER
KLAK
カタッ

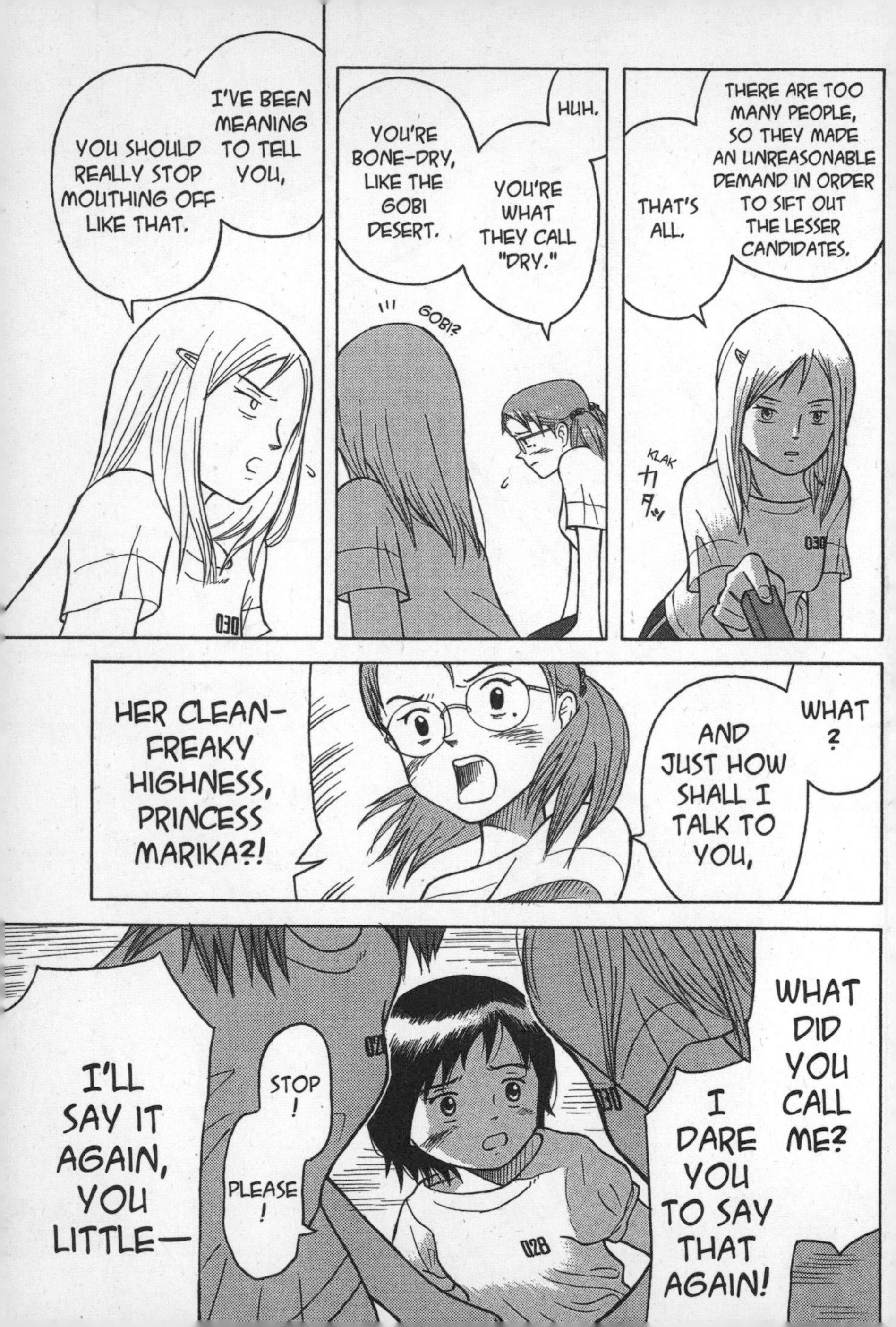
THERE ARE TOO MANY PEOPLE, SO THEY MADE AN UNREASONABLE DEMAND IN ORDER TO SIFT OUT THE LESSER CANDIDATES.
THAT'S ALL.
KLAK
カタッ
HUH.
YOU'RE WHAT THEY CALL "DRY."
YOU'RE BONE-DRY, LIKE THE GOBI DESERT.
GOBI?
I'VE BEEN MEANING TO TELL YOU,
YOU SHOULD REALLY STOP MOUTHING OFF LIKE THAT.
WHAT?
AND JUST HOW SHALL I TALK TO YOU,
HER CLEAN-FREAKY HIGHNESS, PRINCESS MARIKA?!
WHAT DID YOU CALL ME?
I DARE YOU TO SAY THAT AGAIN!
STOP!
PLEASE!
I'LL SAY IT AGAIN, YOU LITTLE—

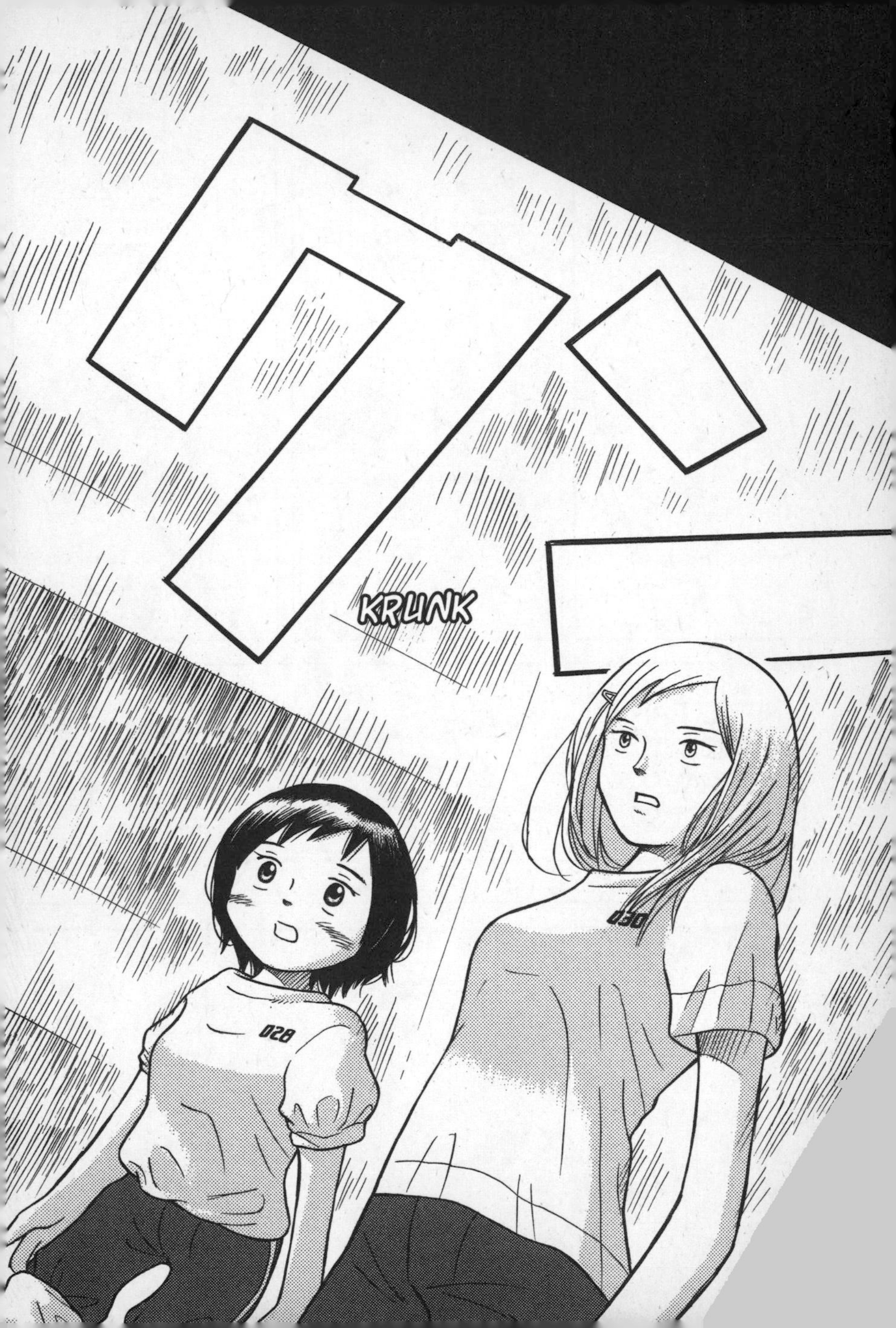
KRUNK
028
030

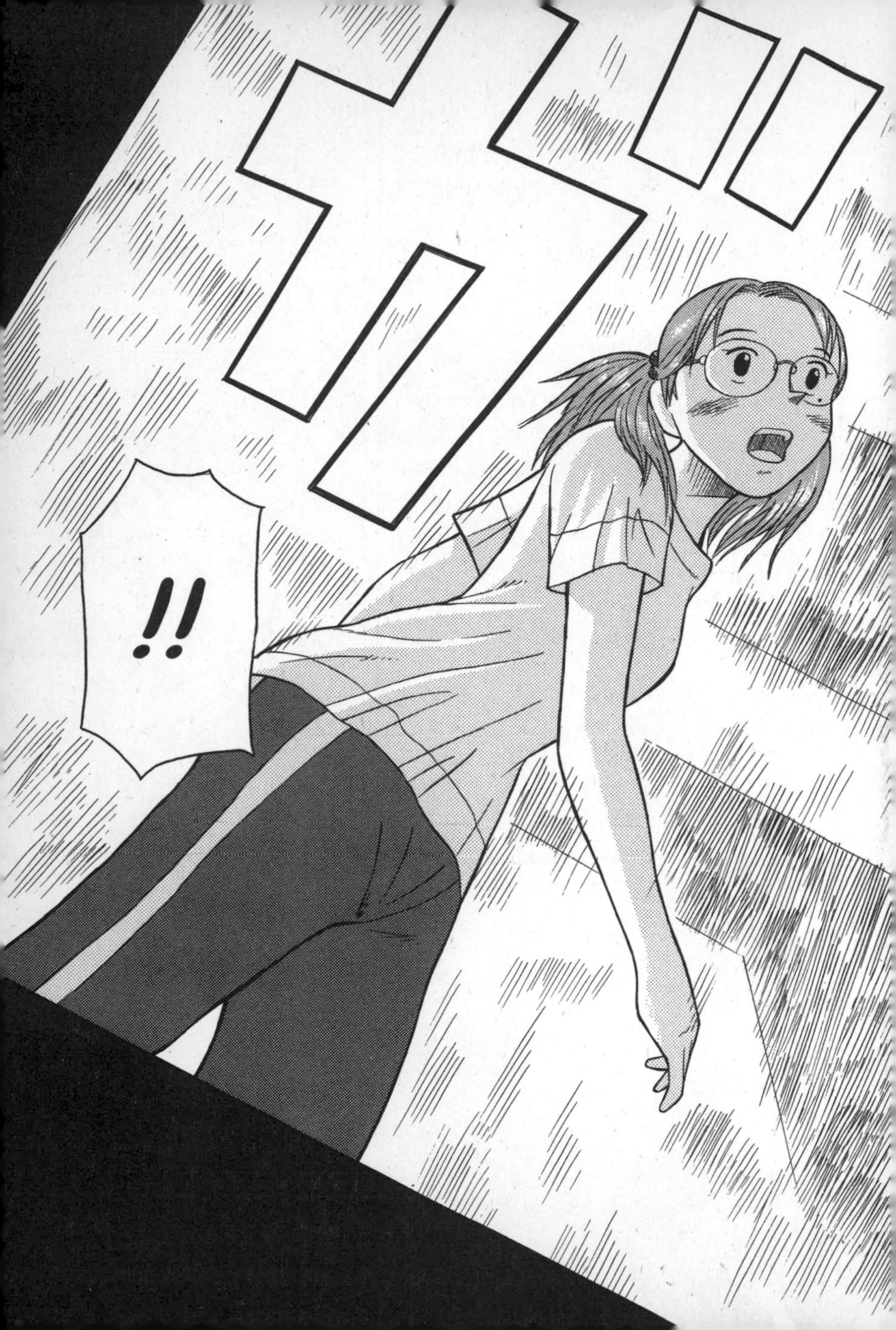
!!

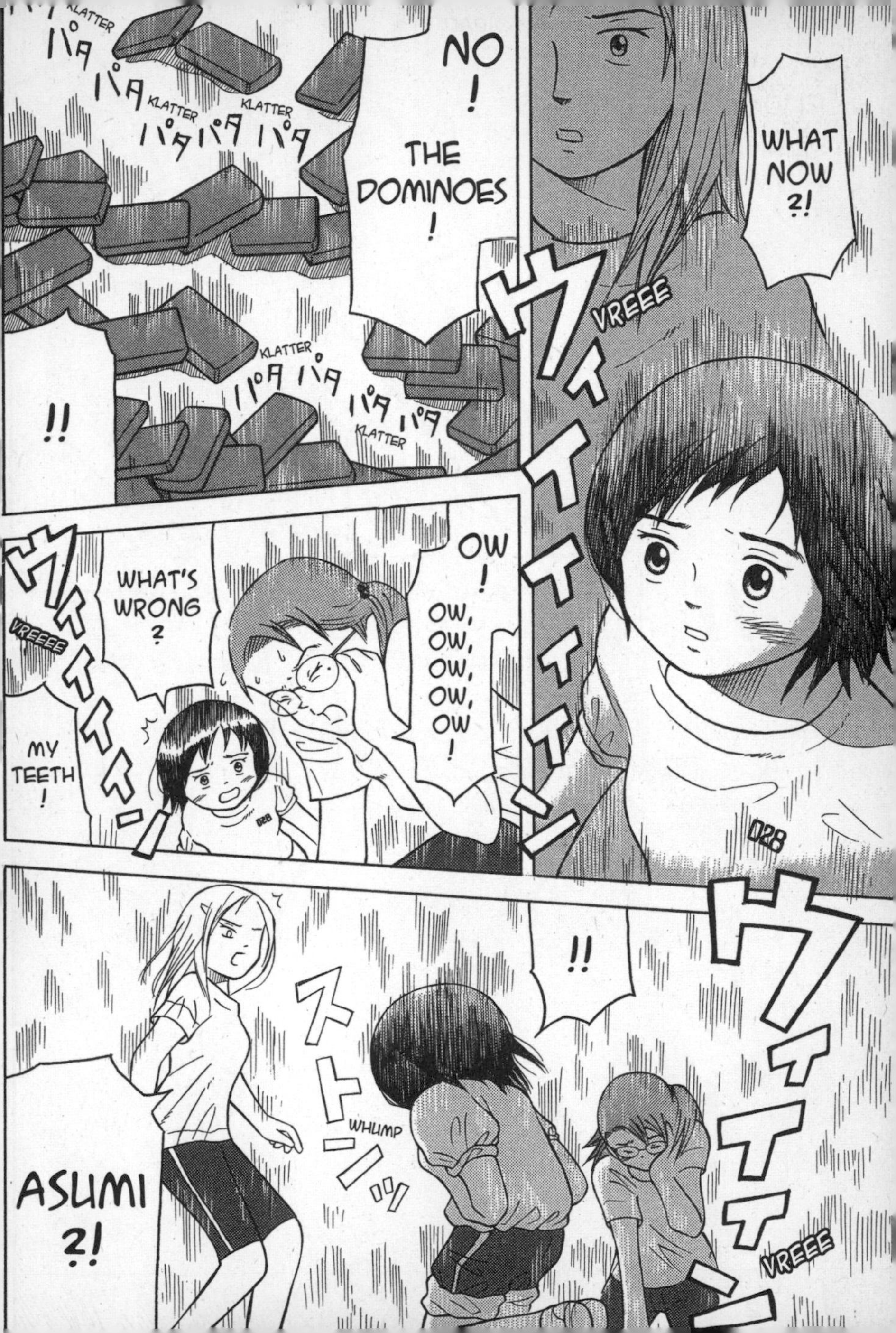
WHAT NOW ?!
VREEE
NO!
THE DOMINOES!
KLATTER
KLATTER
KLATTER
KLATTER
KLATTER
!!
OW!
OW, OW, OW, OW, OW!
WHAT'S WRONG?
VREEEE
MY TEETH!
!!
VREEE
WHUMP
ASUMI ?!

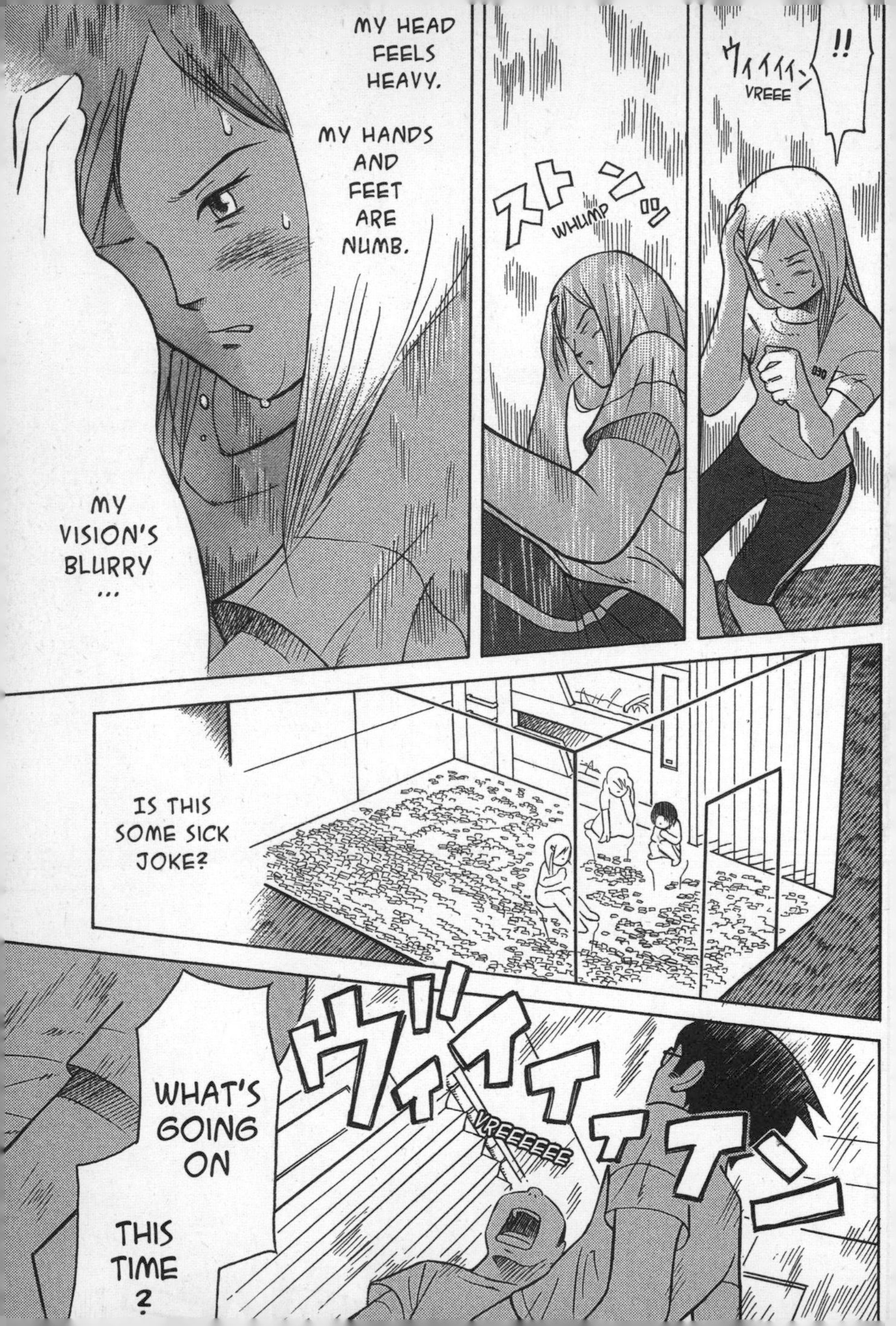
!!
VREEE
WHUMP
MY HEAD FEELS HEAVY.
MY HANDS AND FEET ARE NUMB.
MY VISION'S BLURRY ...
IS THIS SOME SICK JOKE?
VREEEEEE
WHAT'S GOING ON THIS TIME?

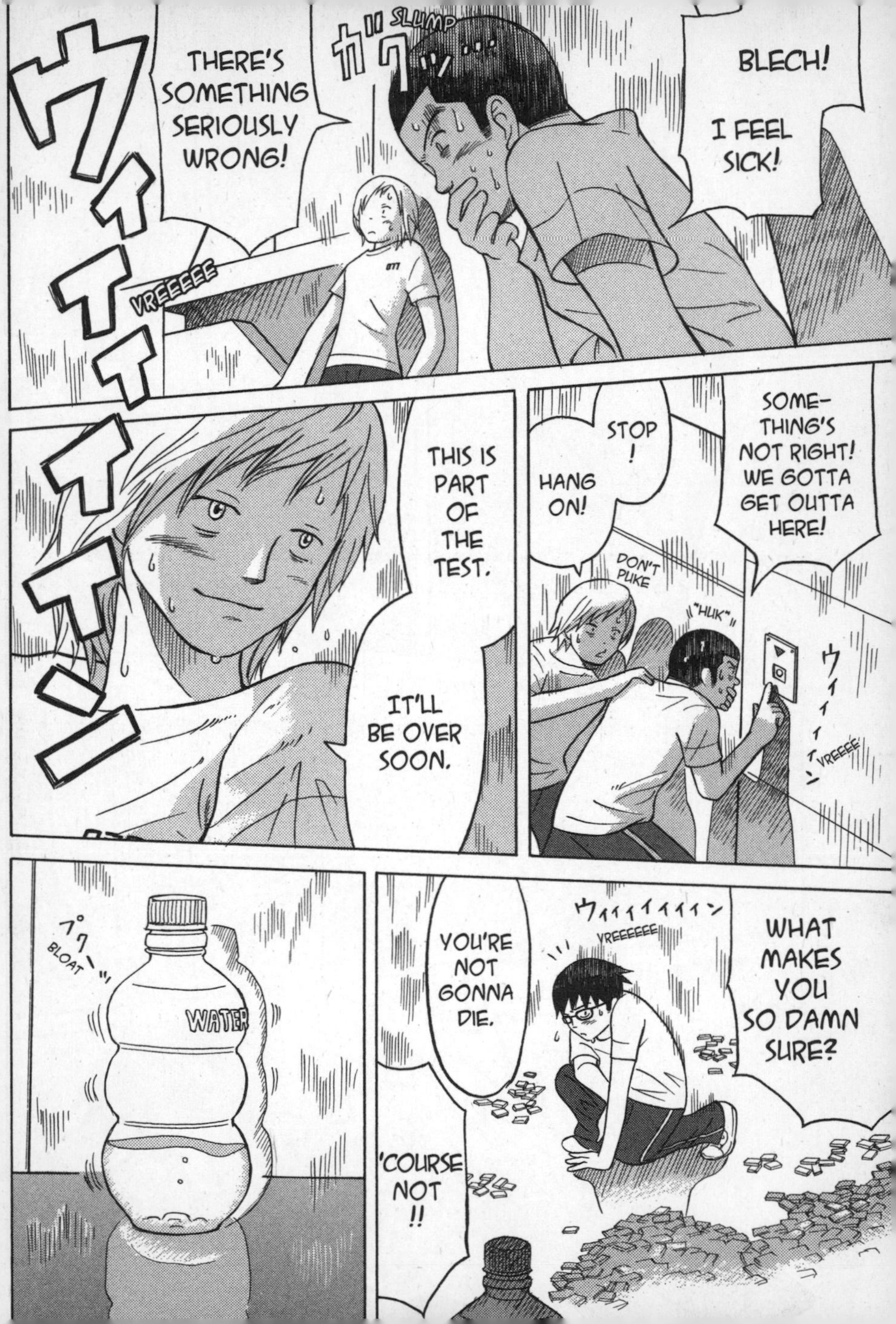
BLECH!
I FEEL SICK!
ガク SLUMP
THERE'S SOMETHING SERIOUSLY WRONG!
ウィィィィィン
VREEEEEE
SOME-THING'S NOT RIGHT! WE GOTTA GET OUTTA HERE!
STOP!
HANG ON!
DON'T PUKE
"HUK"
ウィィィン
VREEEE
THIS IS PART OF THE TEST.
IT'LL BE OVER SOON.
WHAT MAKES YOU SO DAMN SURE?
ウィィィイイイン
VREEEEEE
YOU'RE NOT GONNA DIE.
'COURSE NOT !!
パク
BLOAT
WATER

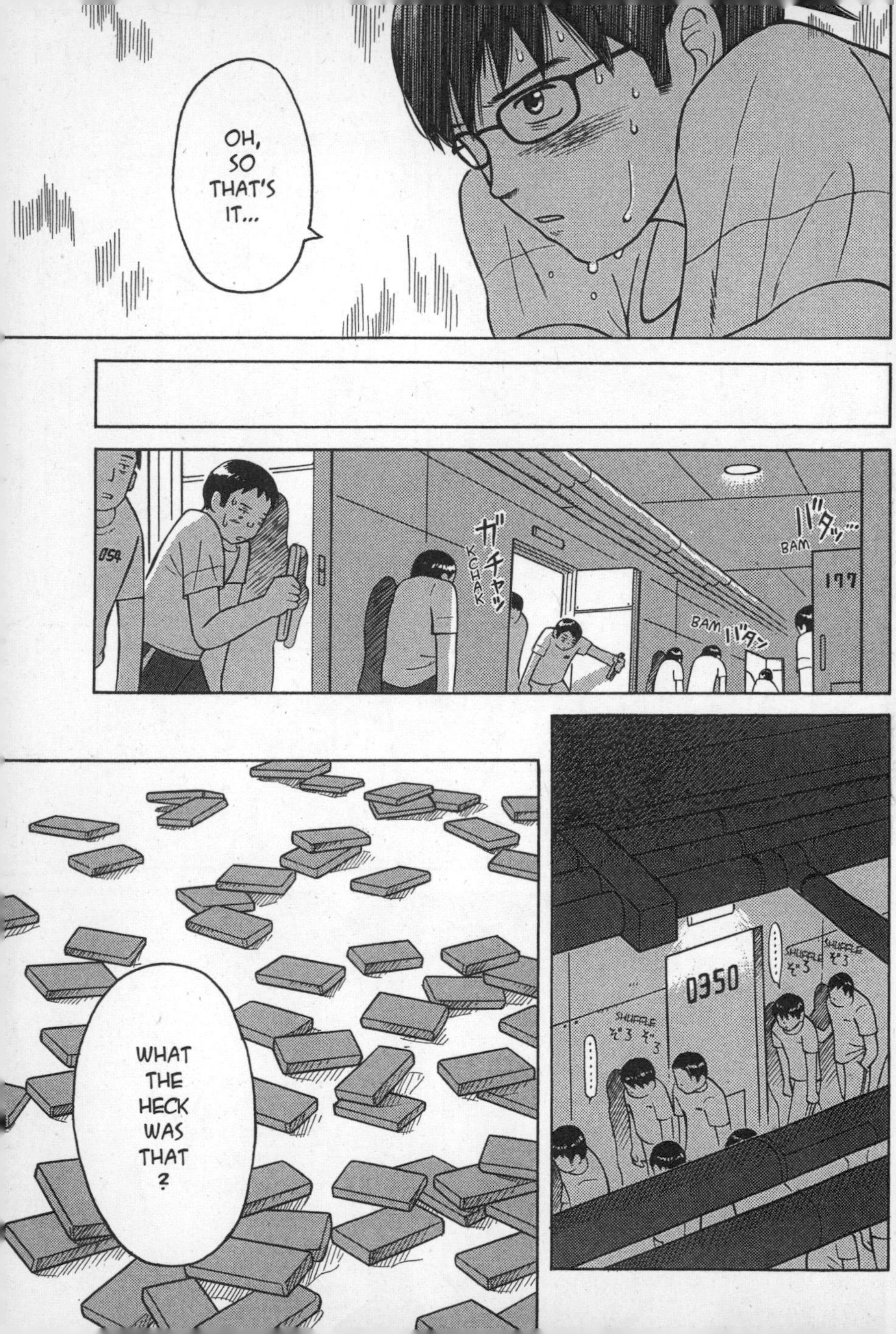
OH, SO THAT'S IT...
バタッ…
BAM
177
ガチャッ
KCHAK
BAM バタン
054
……
SHUFFLE ぞろ
SHUFFLE ぞろ
0350
……
SHUFFLE ぞろ ぞろ
WHAT THE HECK WAS THAT?

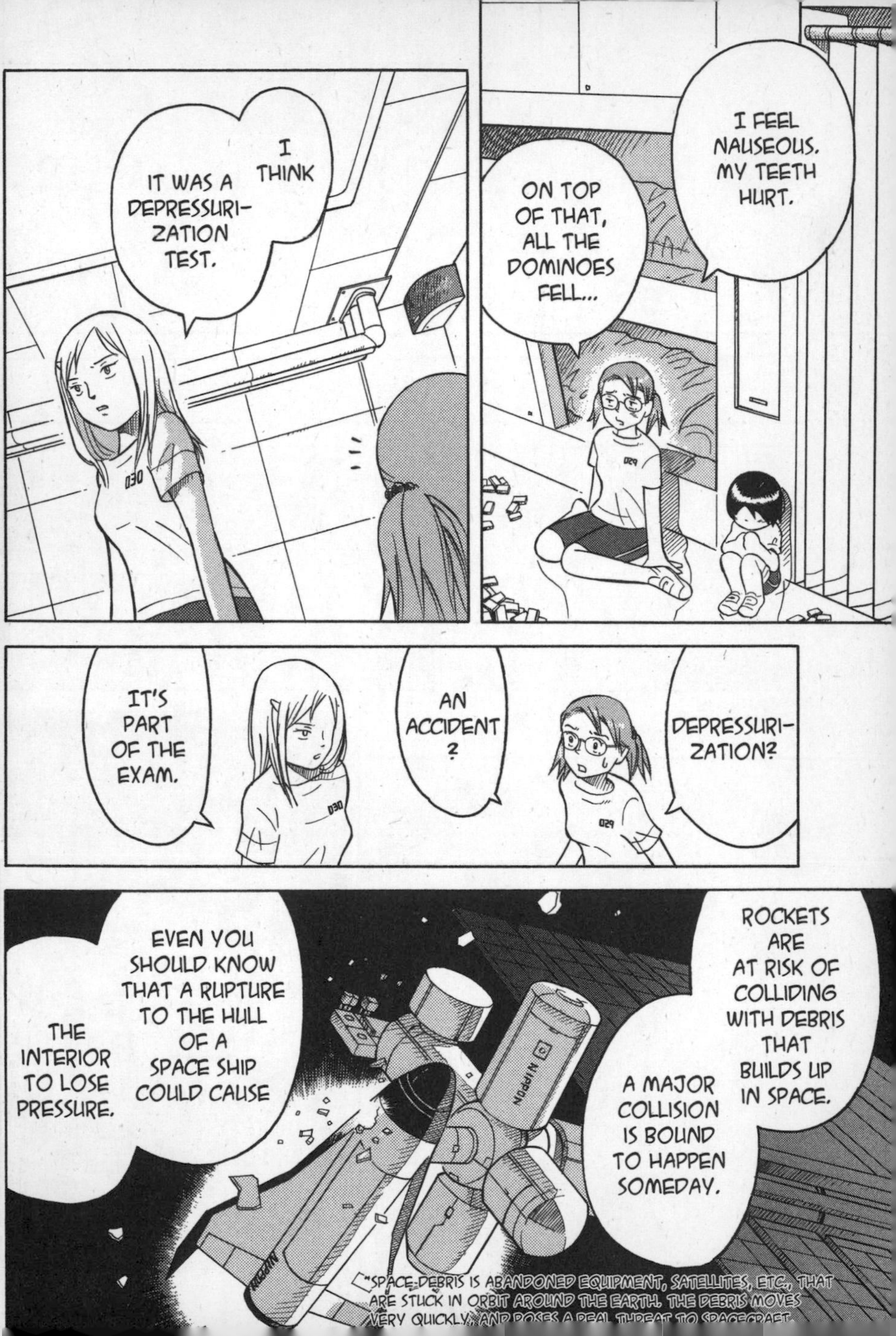
I FEEL NAUSEOUS. MY TEETH HURT.
ON TOP OF THAT, ALL THE DOMINOES FELL...
I THINK
IT WAS A DEPRESSURI-ZATION TEST.
DEPRESSURI-ZATION?
AN ACCIDENT?
IT'S PART OF THE EXAM.
ROCKETS ARE AT RISK OF COLLIDING WITH DEBRIS THAT BUILDS UP IN SPACE.
A MAJOR COLLISION IS BOUND TO HAPPEN SOMEDAY.
EVEN YOU SHOULD KNOW THAT A RUPTURE TO THE HULL OF A SPACE SHIP COULD CAUSE
THE INTERIOR TO LOSE PRESSURE.
NIPPON
*SPACE-DEBRIS IS ABANDONED EQUIPMENT, SATELLITES, ETC., THAT ARE STUCK IN ORBIT AROUND THE EARTH. THE DEBRIS MOVES VERY QUICKLY, AND POSES A REAL THREAT TO SPACECRAFT.

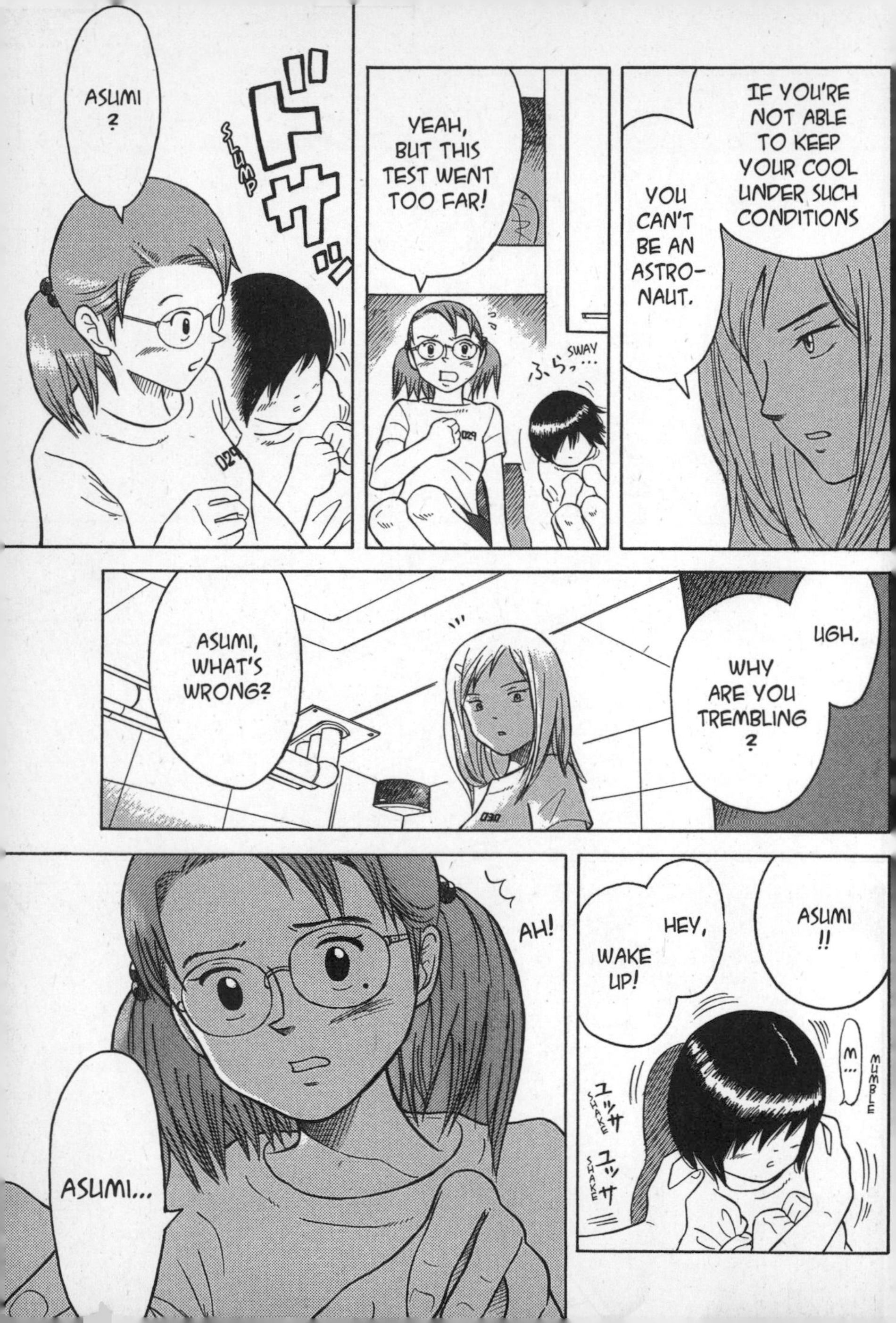
IF YOU'RE NOT ABLE TO KEEP YOUR COOL UNDER SUCH CONDITIONS
YOU CAN'T BE AN ASTRO- NAUT.
YEAH, BUT THIS TEST WENT TOO FAR!
SWAY
ふらっ…
ドサッ
SLUMP
ASUMI?
UGH.
WHY ARE YOU TREMBLING?
ASUMI, WHAT'S WRONG?
ASUMI!!
HEY, WAKE UP!
M...
MUMBLE
ユッサ
SHAKE
ユッサ
SHAKE
AH!
ASUMI...

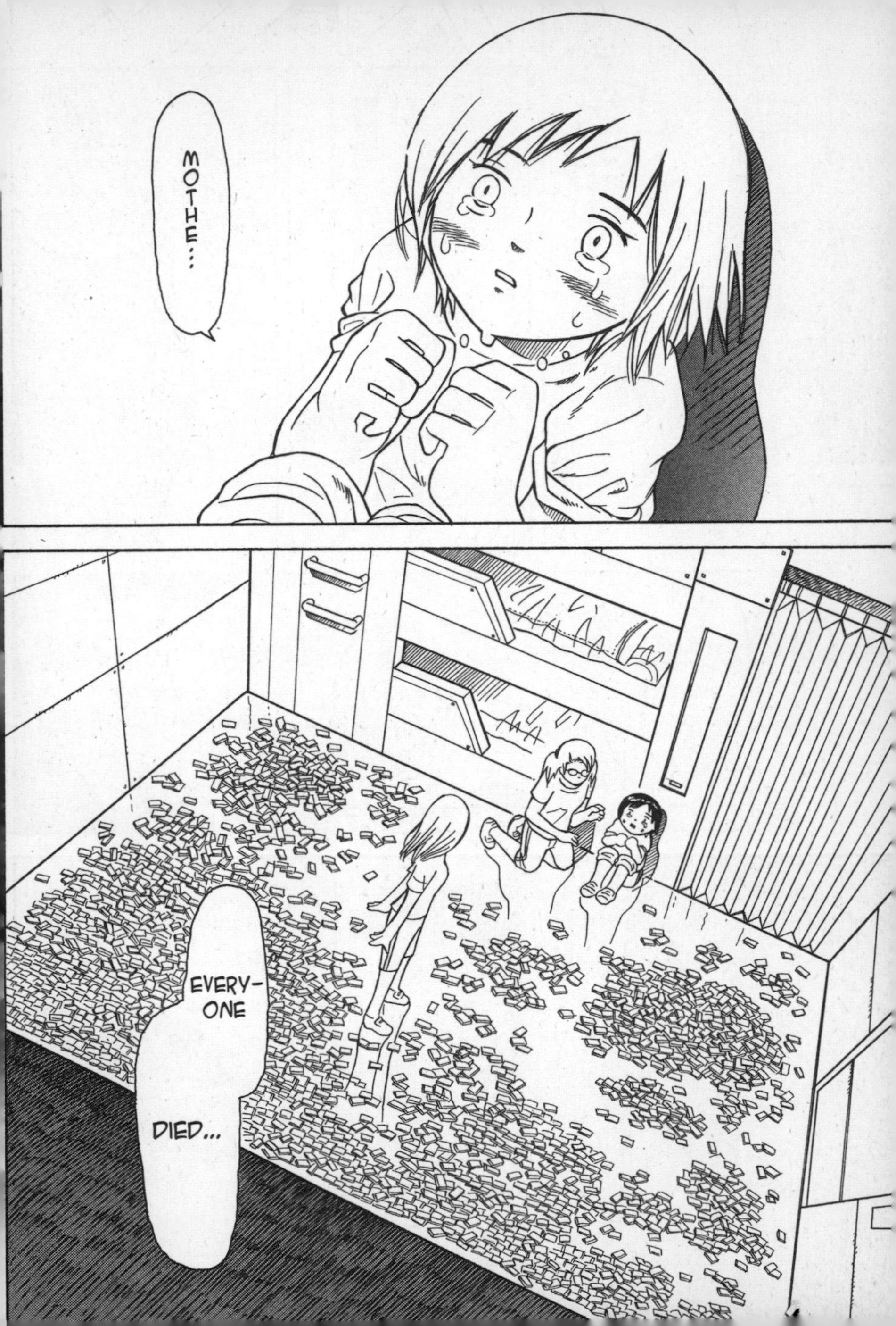
MOTHE...
EVERY-ONE
DIED...

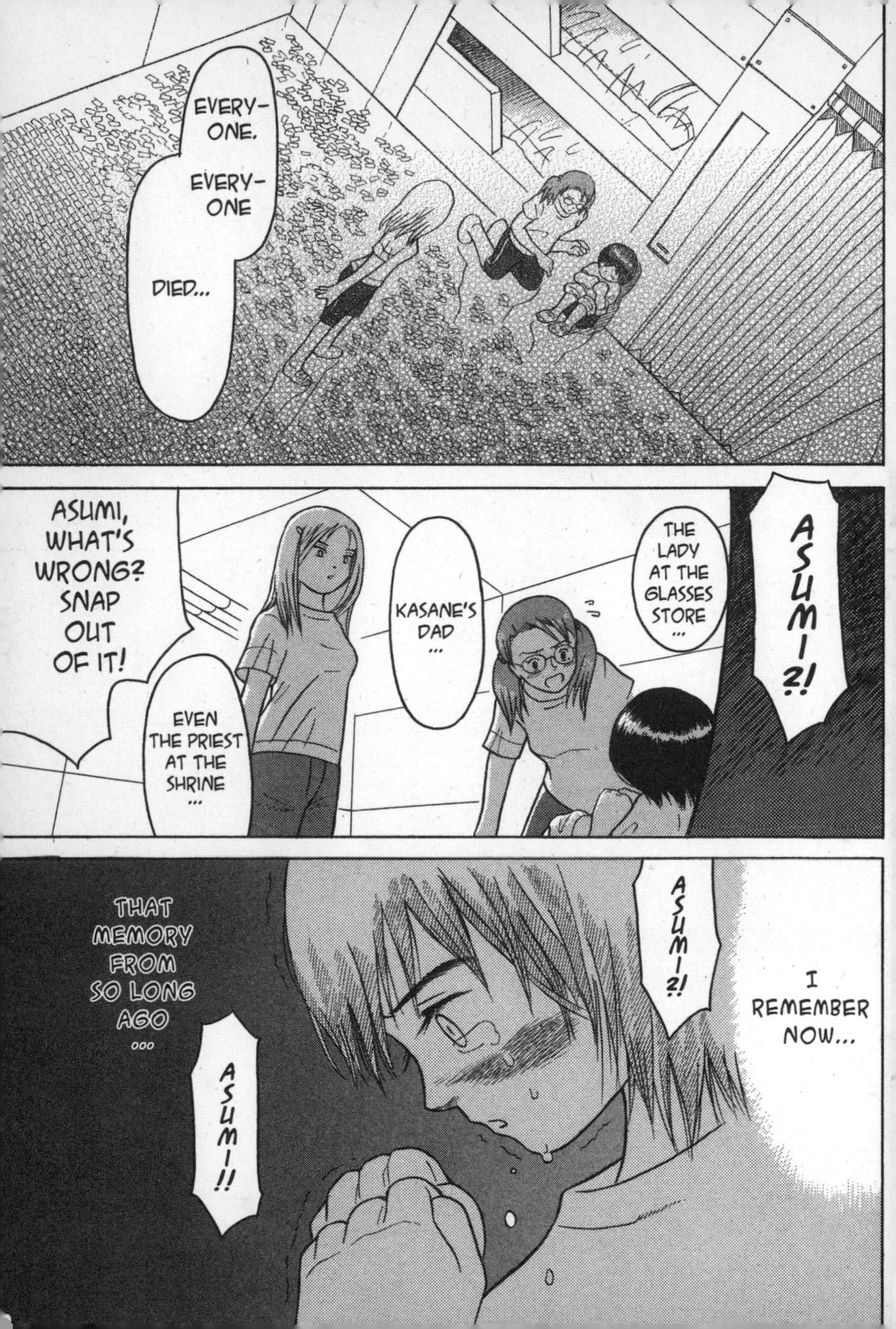
EVERY-ONE.
EVERY-ONE
DIED...
ASUMI?!
THE LADY AT THE GLASSES STORE...
KASANE'S DAD...
EVEN THE PRIEST AT THE SHRINE...
ASUMI, WHAT'S WRONG? SNAP OUT OF IT!
I REMEMBER NOW...
ASUMI?!
ASUMI!!
THAT MEMORY FROM SO LONG AGO...

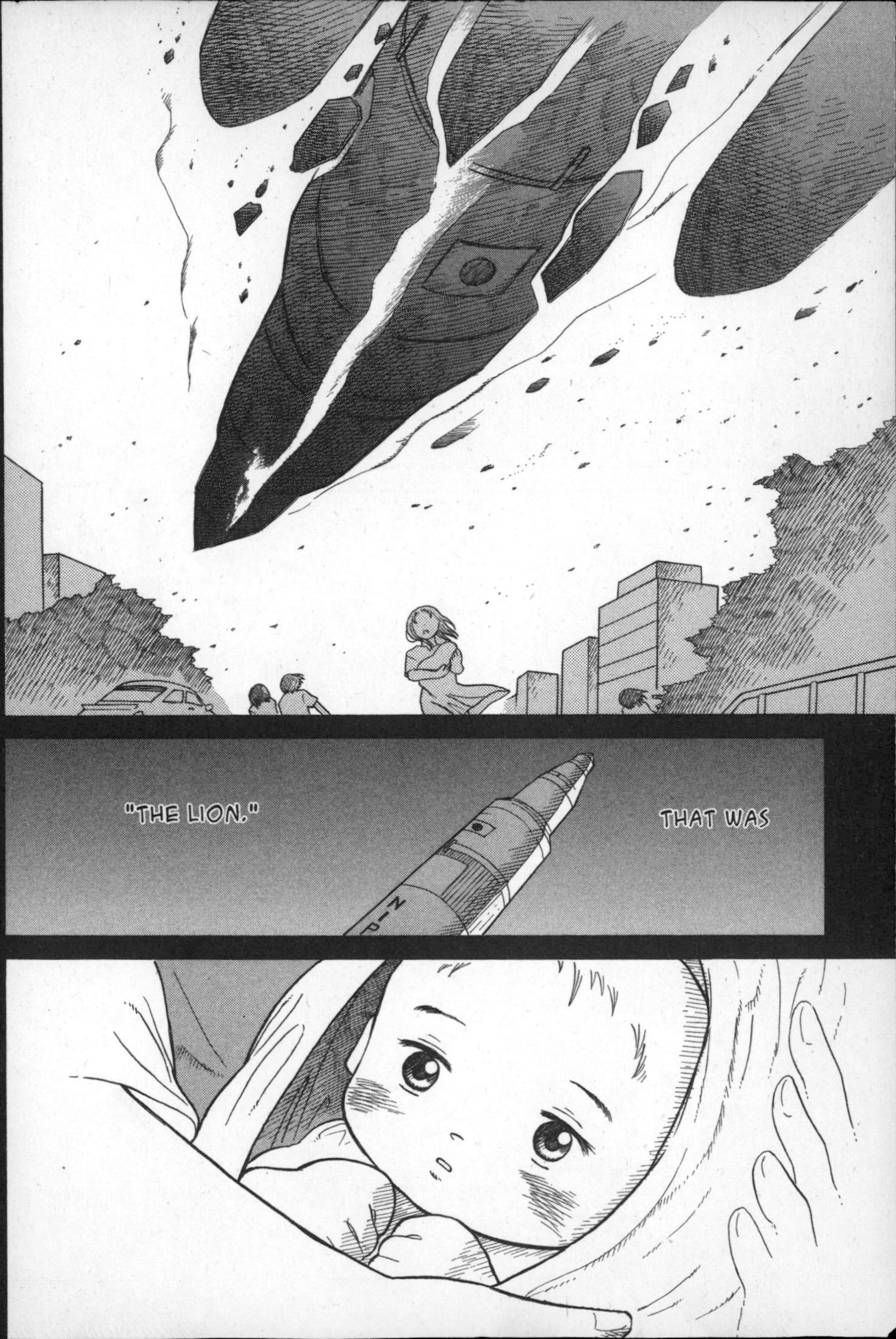
THAT WAS
"THE LION."

MISSION:04

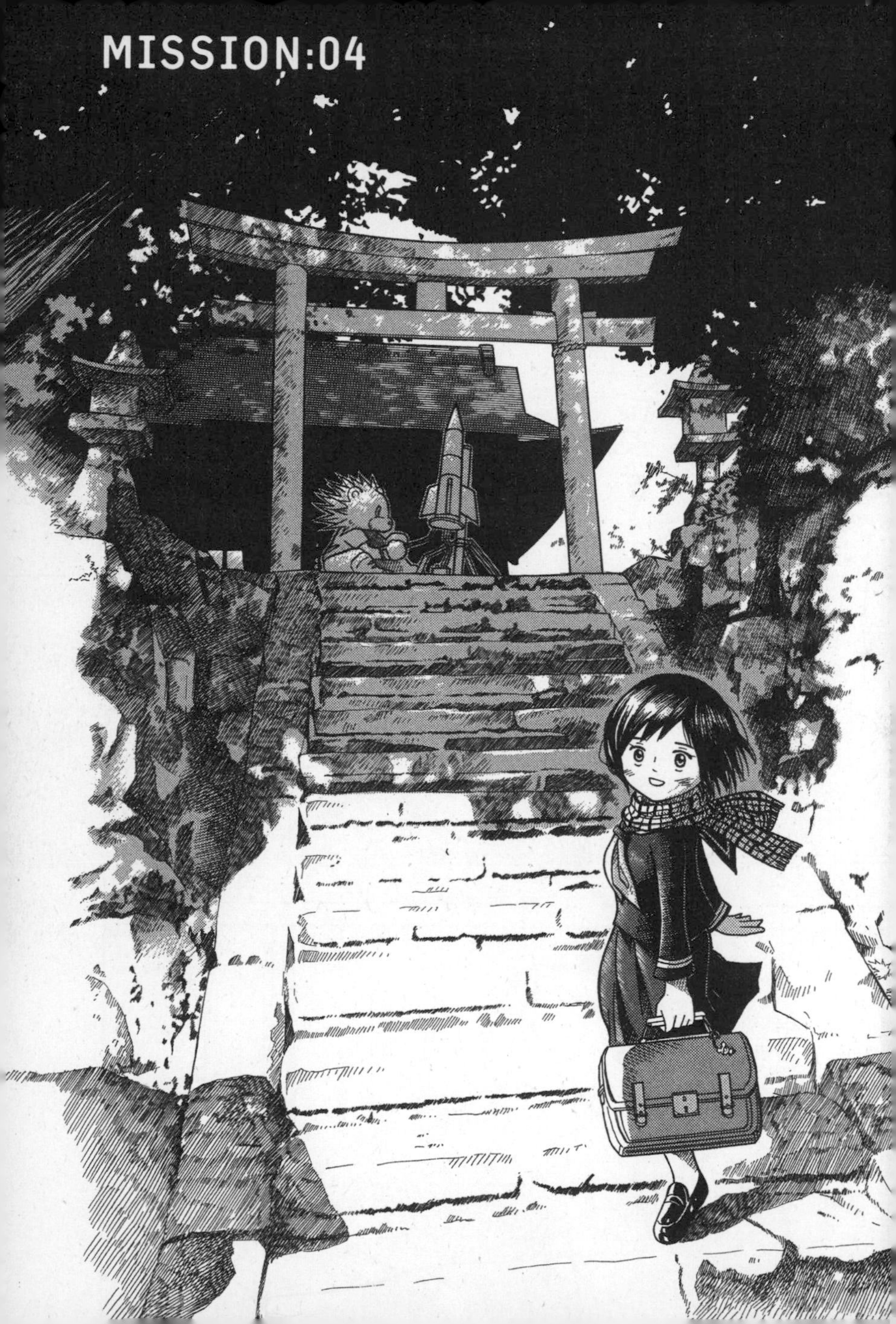

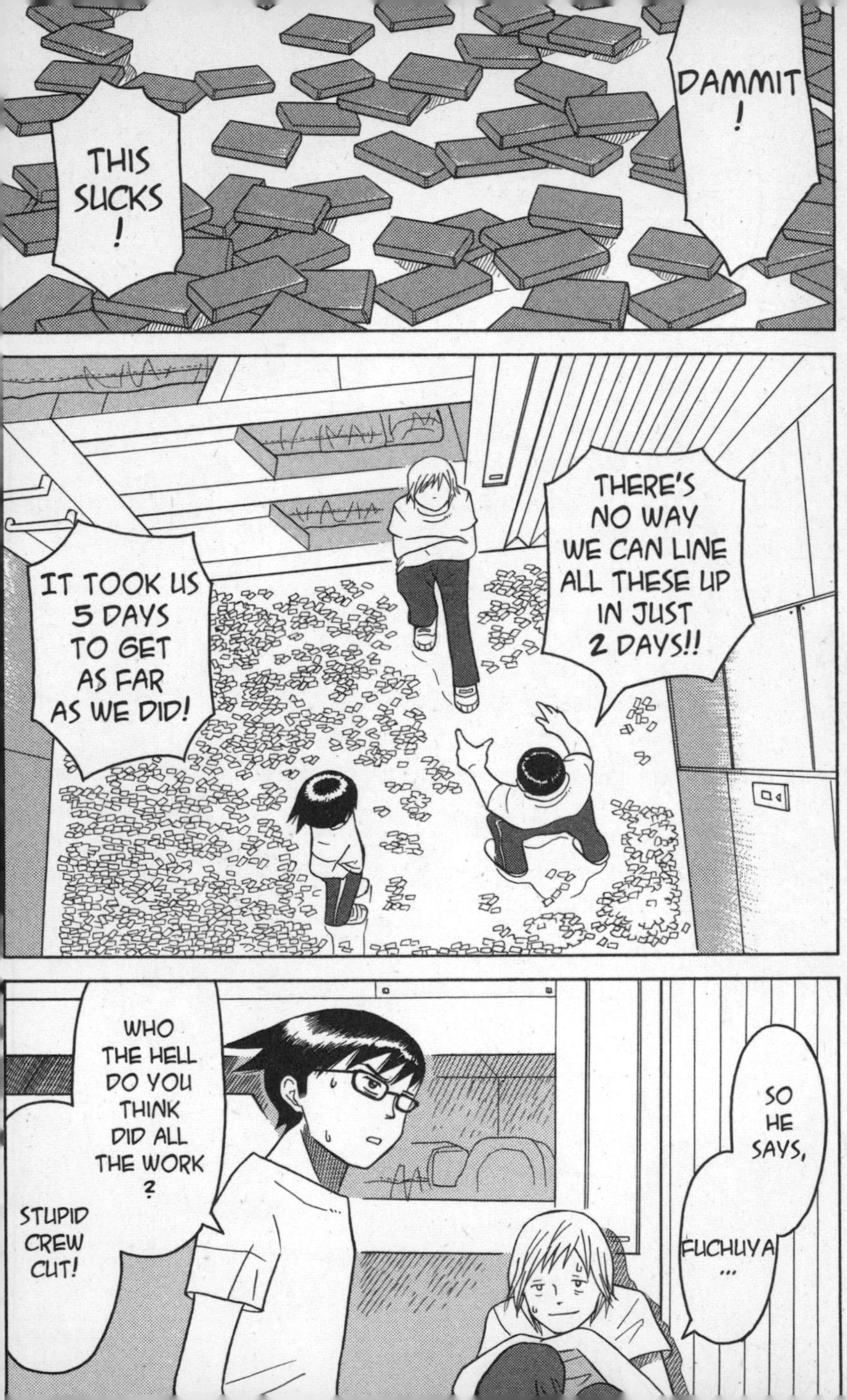
DAMMIT!
THIS SUCKS!
THERE'S NO WAY WE CAN LINE ALL THESE UP IN JUST 2 DAYS!!
IT TOOK US 5 DAYS TO GET AS FAR AS WE DID!
SO HE SAYS,
FUCHUYA...
WHO THE HELL DO YOU THINK DID ALL THE WORK?
STUPID CREW CUT!

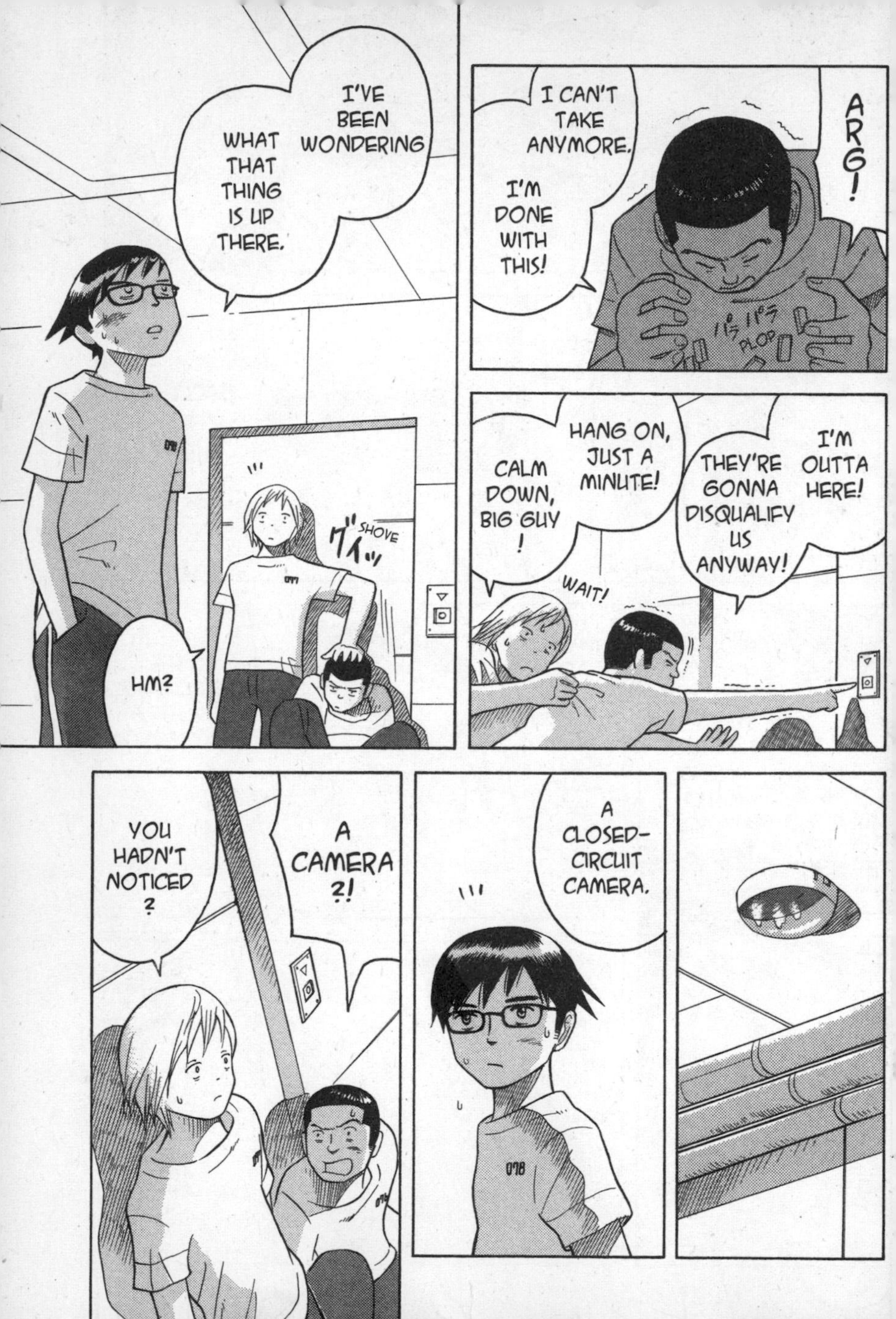
ARG!
I CAN'T TAKE ANYMORE.
I'M DONE WITH THIS!
パラパラ PLOP
I'M OUTTA HERE!
THEY'RE GONNA DISQUALIFY US ANYWAY!
HANG ON, JUST A MINUTE!
CALM DOWN, BIG GUY!
WAIT!
I'VE BEEN WONDERING
WHAT THAT THING IS UP THERE.
グイッ SHOVE
HM?
A CLOSED-CIRCUIT CAMERA.
A CAMERA?!
YOU HADN'T NOTICED?

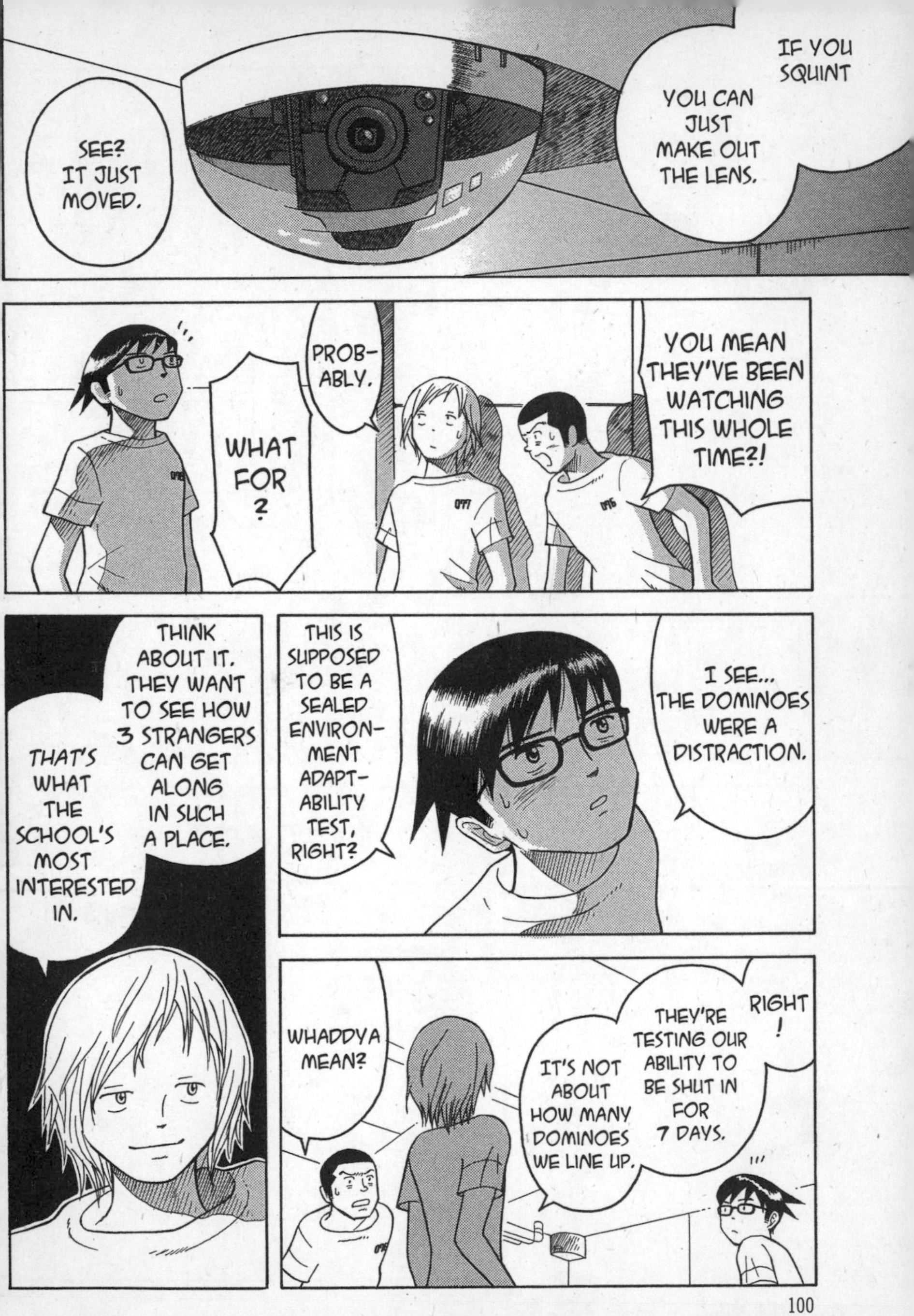
IF YOU SQUINT
YOU CAN JUST MAKE OUT THE LENS.
SEE? IT JUST MOVED.
YOU MEAN THEY'VE BEEN WATCHING THIS WHOLE TIME?!
PROB-ABLY.
WHAT FOR ?
I SEE... THE DOMINOES WERE A DISTRACTION.
THIS IS SUPPOSED TO BE A SEALED ENVIRON-MENT ADAPT-ABILITY TEST, RIGHT?
RIGHT !
THEY'RE TESTING OUR ABILITY TO BE SHUT IN FOR 7 DAYS.
IT'S NOT ABOUT HOW MANY DOMINOES WE LINE UP.
WHADDYA MEAN?
THINK ABOUT IT. THEY WANT TO SEE HOW 3 STRANGERS CAN GET ALONG IN SUCH A PLACE.
THAT'S WHAT THE SCHOOL'S MOST INTERESTED IN.

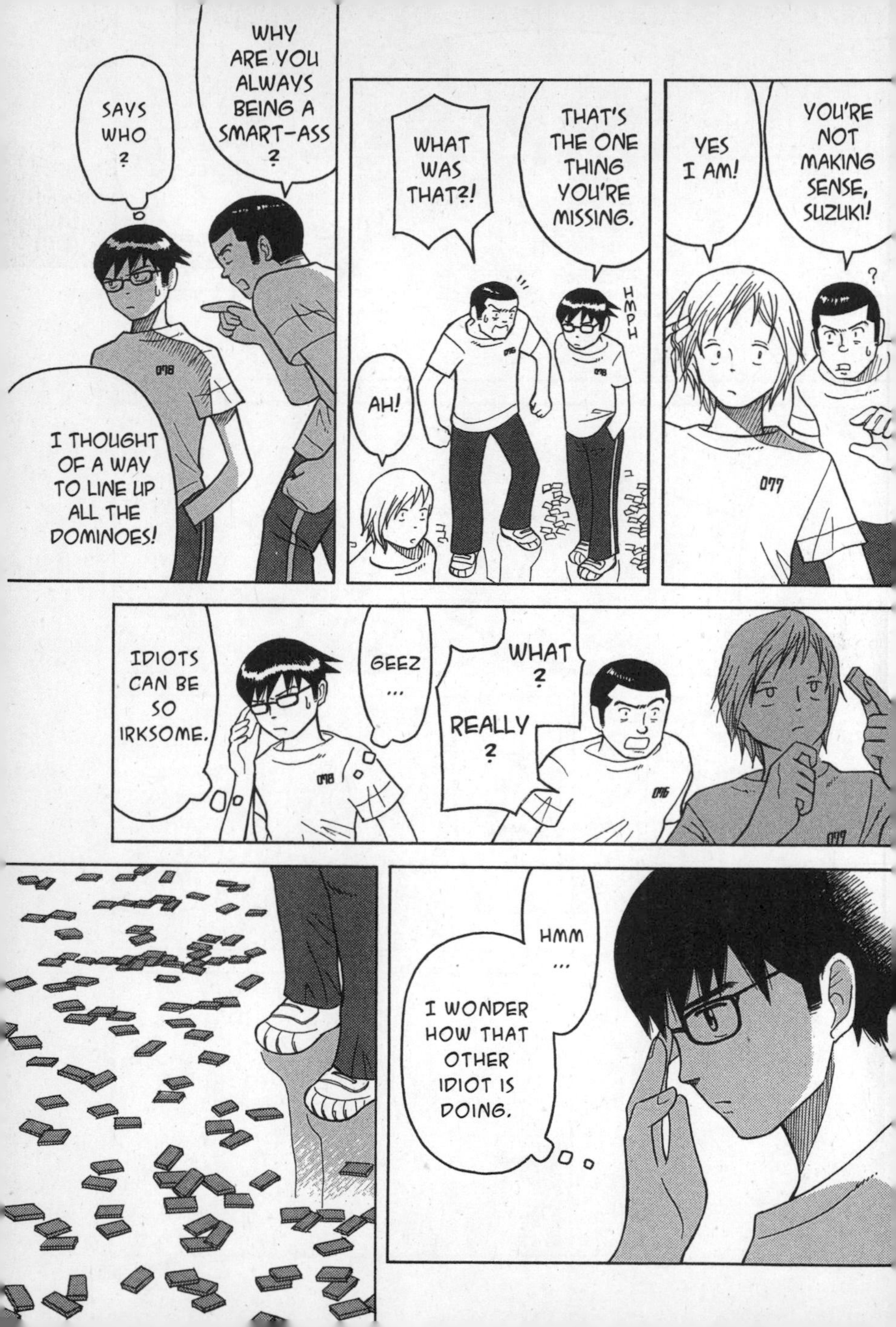
YOU'RE NOT MAKING SENSE, SUZUKI!
YES I AM!
THAT'S THE ONE THING YOU'RE MISSING.
WHAT WAS THAT?!
HMPH
AH!
WHY ARE YOU ALWAYS BEING A SMART-ASS?
SAYS WHO?
I THOUGHT OF A WAY TO LINE UP ALL THE DOMINOES!
WHAT?
REALLY?
GEEZ ...
IDIOTS CAN BE SO IRKSOME.
HMM ...
I WONDER HOW THAT OTHER IDIOT IS DOING.

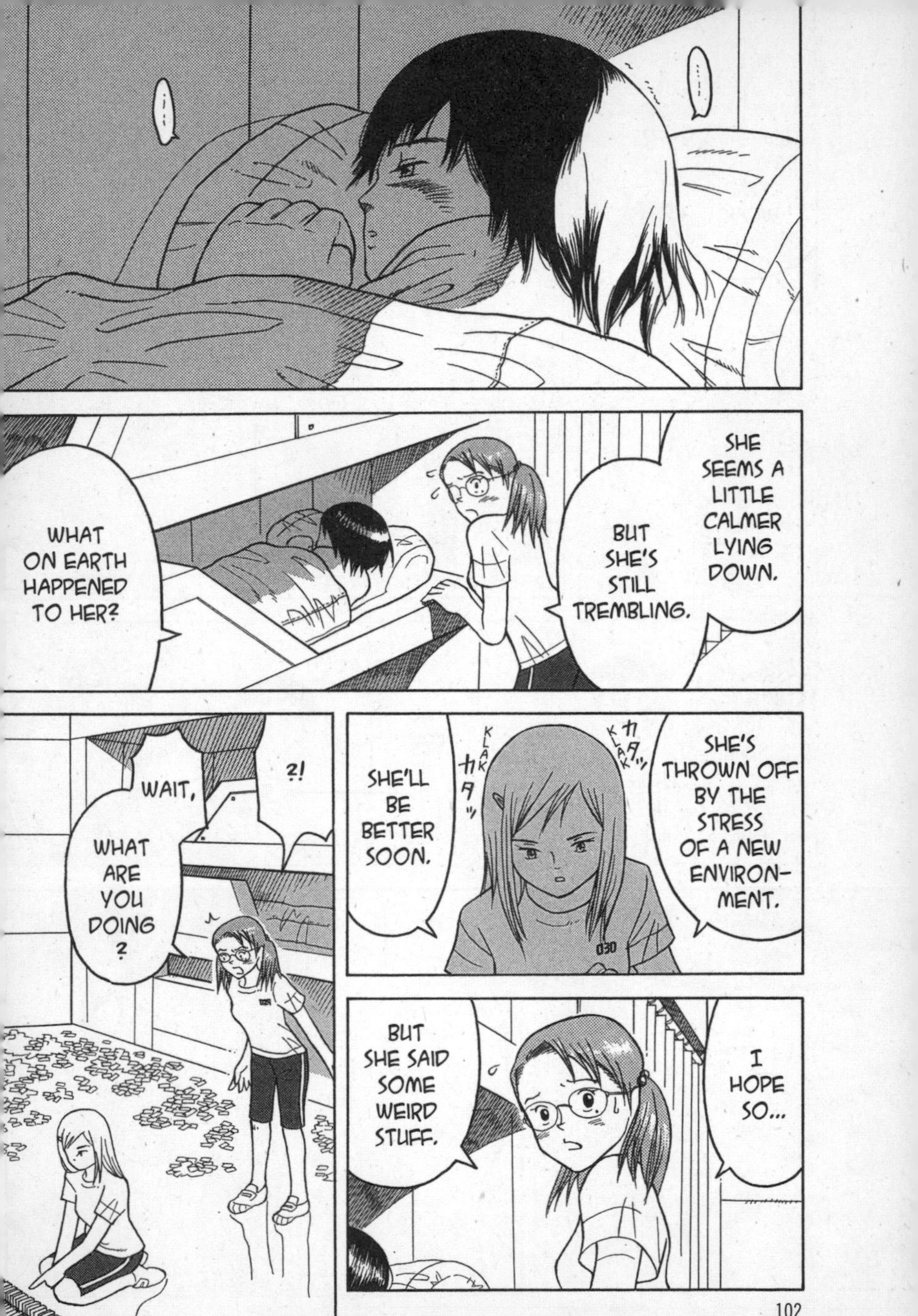
...!
...!
SHE SEEMS A LITTLE CALMER LYING DOWN.
BUT SHE'S STILL TREMBLING.
WHAT ON EARTH HAPPENED TO HER?
SHE'S THROWN OFF BY THE STRESS OF A NEW ENVIRONMENT.
KLAK カタッ
SHE'LL BE BETTER SOON.
KLAK カタッ
I HOPE SO...
BUT SHE SAID SOME WEIRD STUFF.
?!
WAIT,
WHAT ARE YOU DOING?

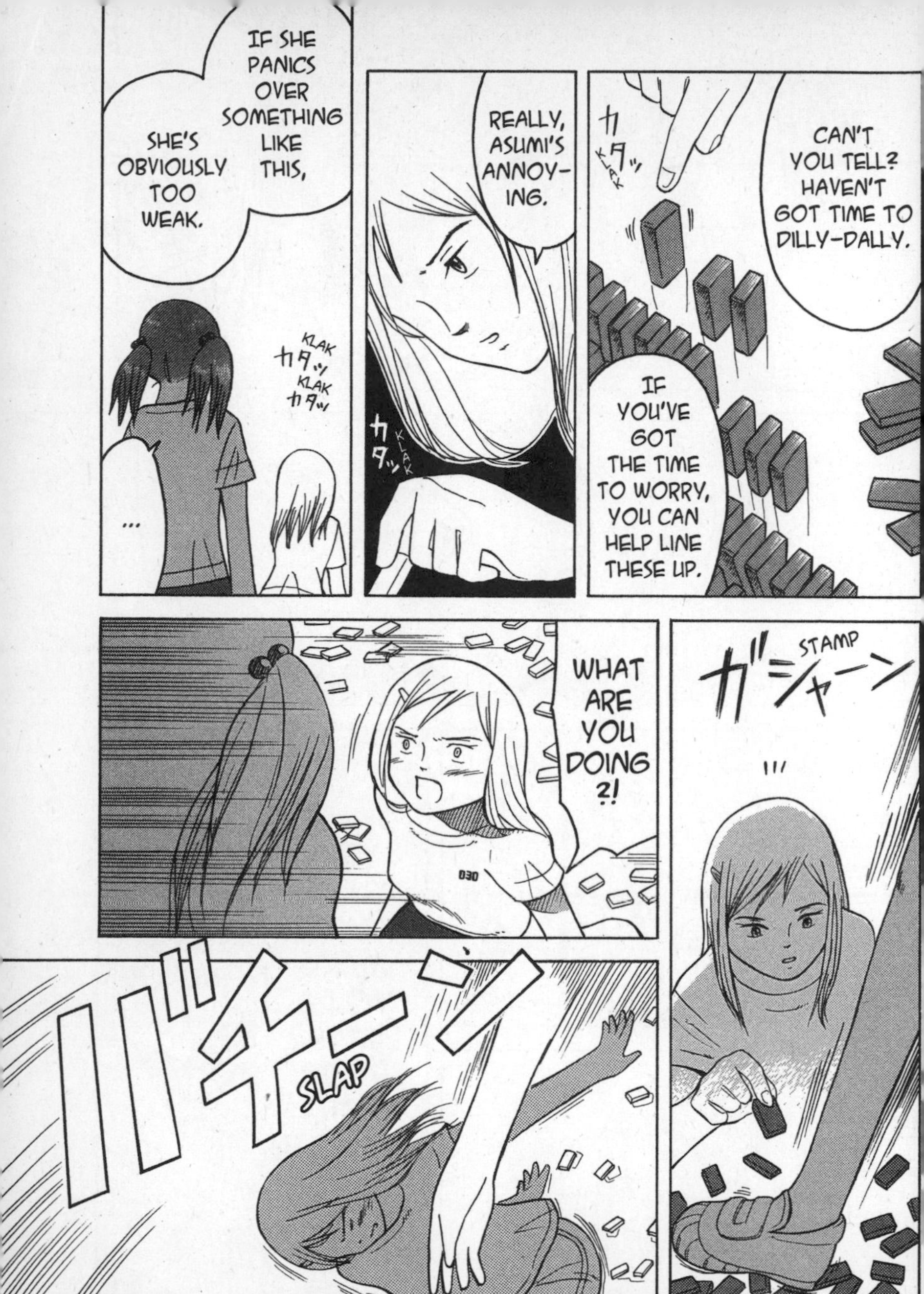

カタッ
KLAK
CAN'T YOU TELL? HAVEN'T GOT TIME TO DILLY-DALLY.
IF YOU'VE GOT THE TIME TO WORRY, YOU CAN HELP LINE THESE UP.
REALLY, ASUMI'S ANNOY-ING.
カタッ
KLAK
IF SHE PANICS OVER SOMETHING LIKE THIS,
SHE'S OBVIOUSLY TOO WEAK.
カタッ
KLAK
カタッ
KLAK
...
ガシャーン
STAMP
WHAT ARE YOU DOING?!
バチーン
SLAP

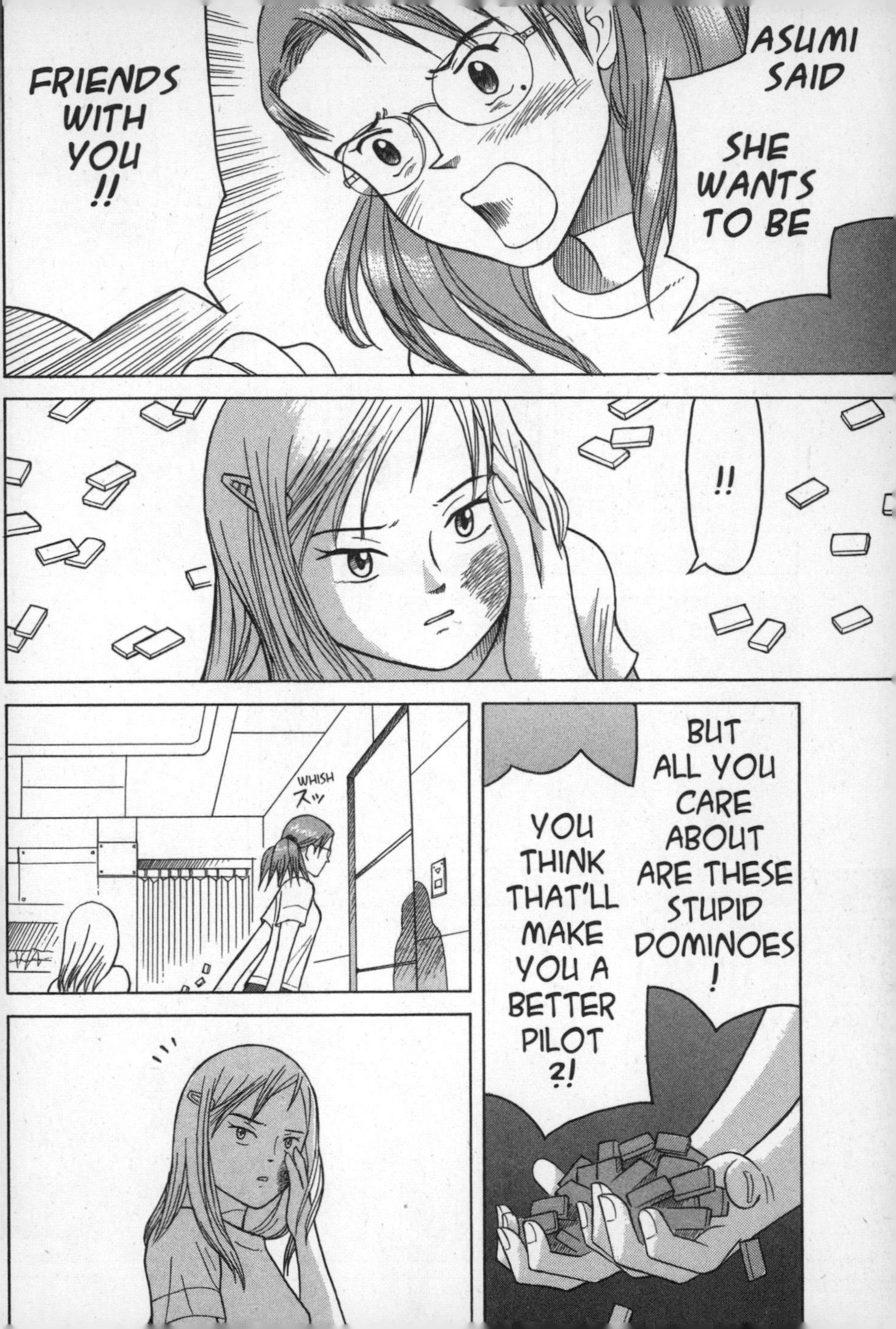
ASUMI SAID
SHE WANTS TO BE
FRIENDS WITH YOU !!
!!
BUT ALL YOU CARE ABOUT ARE THESE STUPID DOMINOES !
YOU THINK THAT'LL MAKE YOU A BETTER PILOT ?!
WHISH
スッ

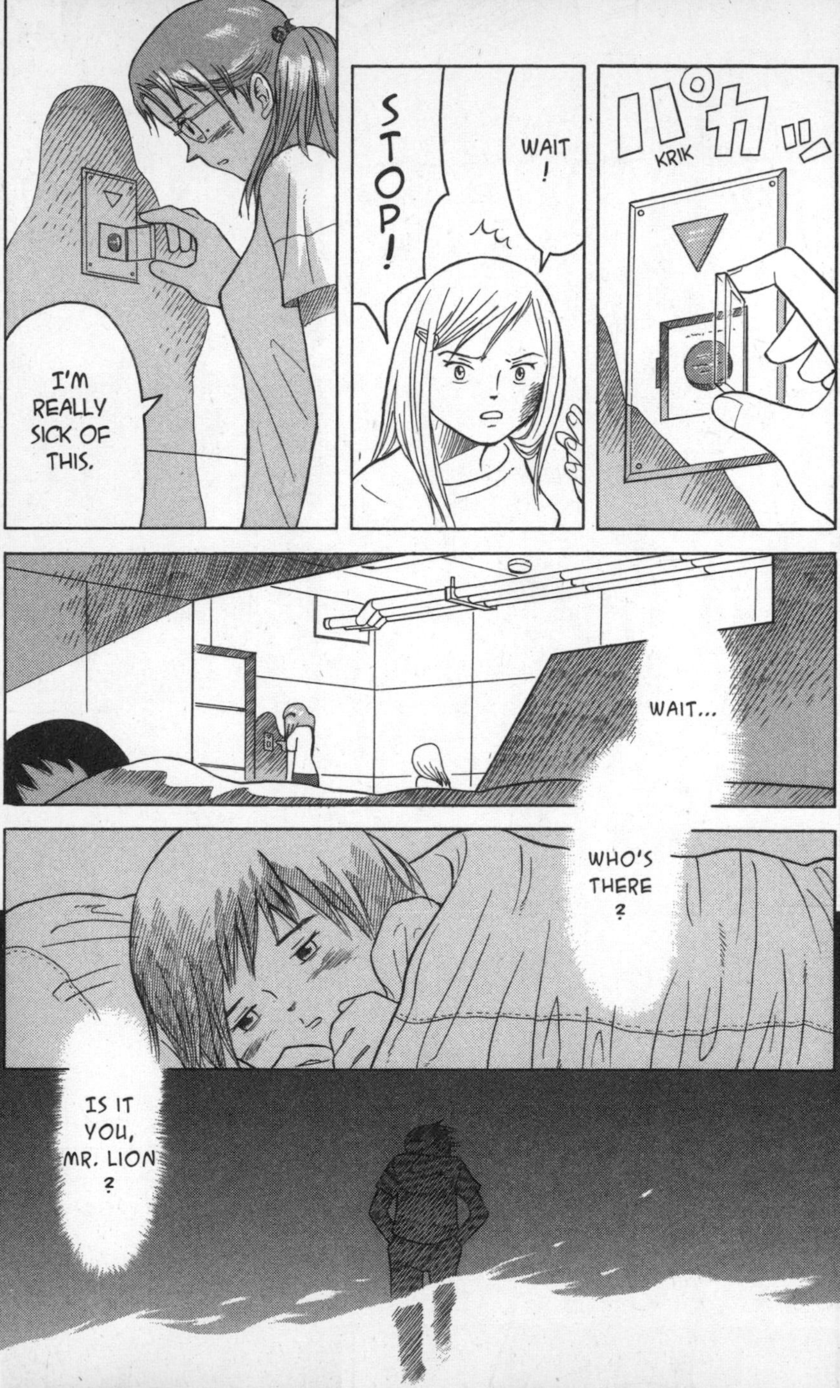
パカッ
KRIK
WAIT!
STOP!
I'M REALLY SICK OF THIS.
WAIT...
WHO'S THERE?
IS IT YOU, MR. LION?

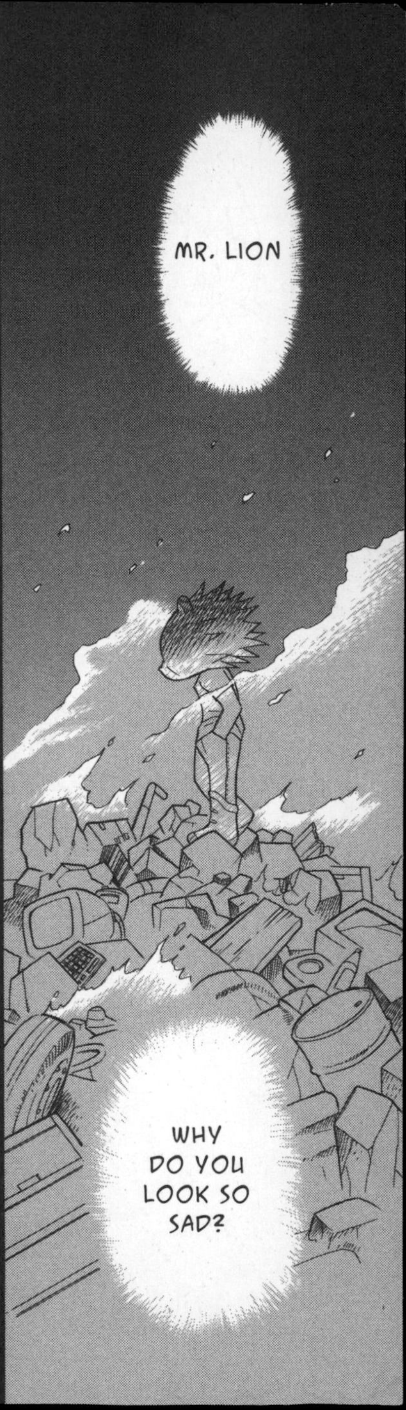
MR. LION
WHY DO YOU LOOK SO SAD?
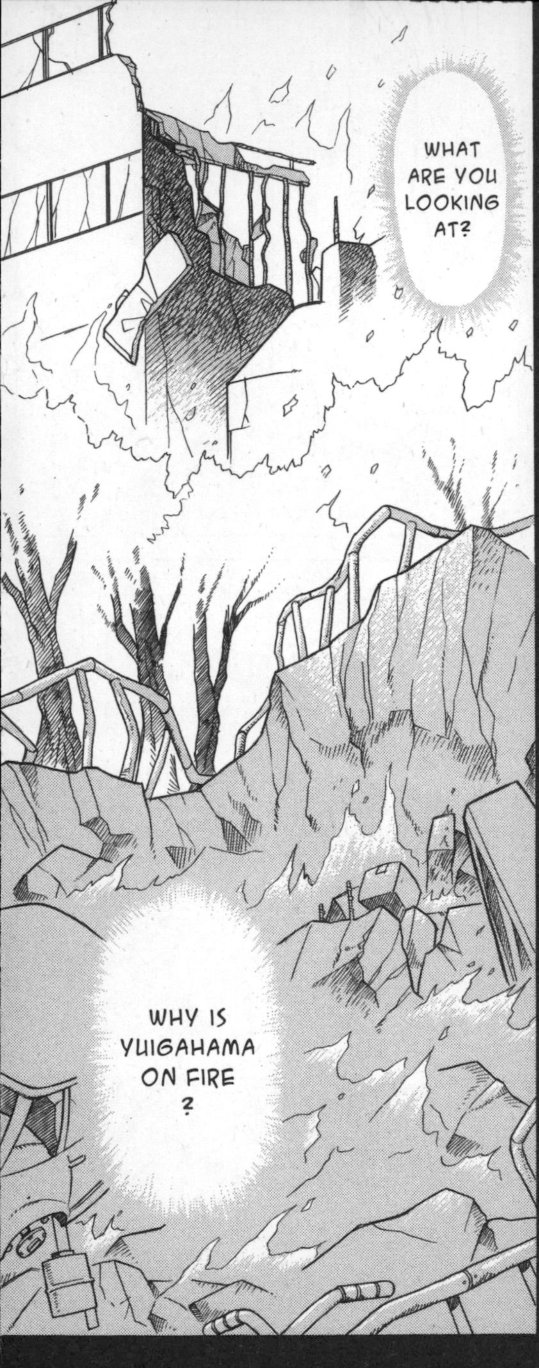
WHAT ARE YOU LOOKING AT?
WHY IS YUIGAHAMA ON FIRE ?

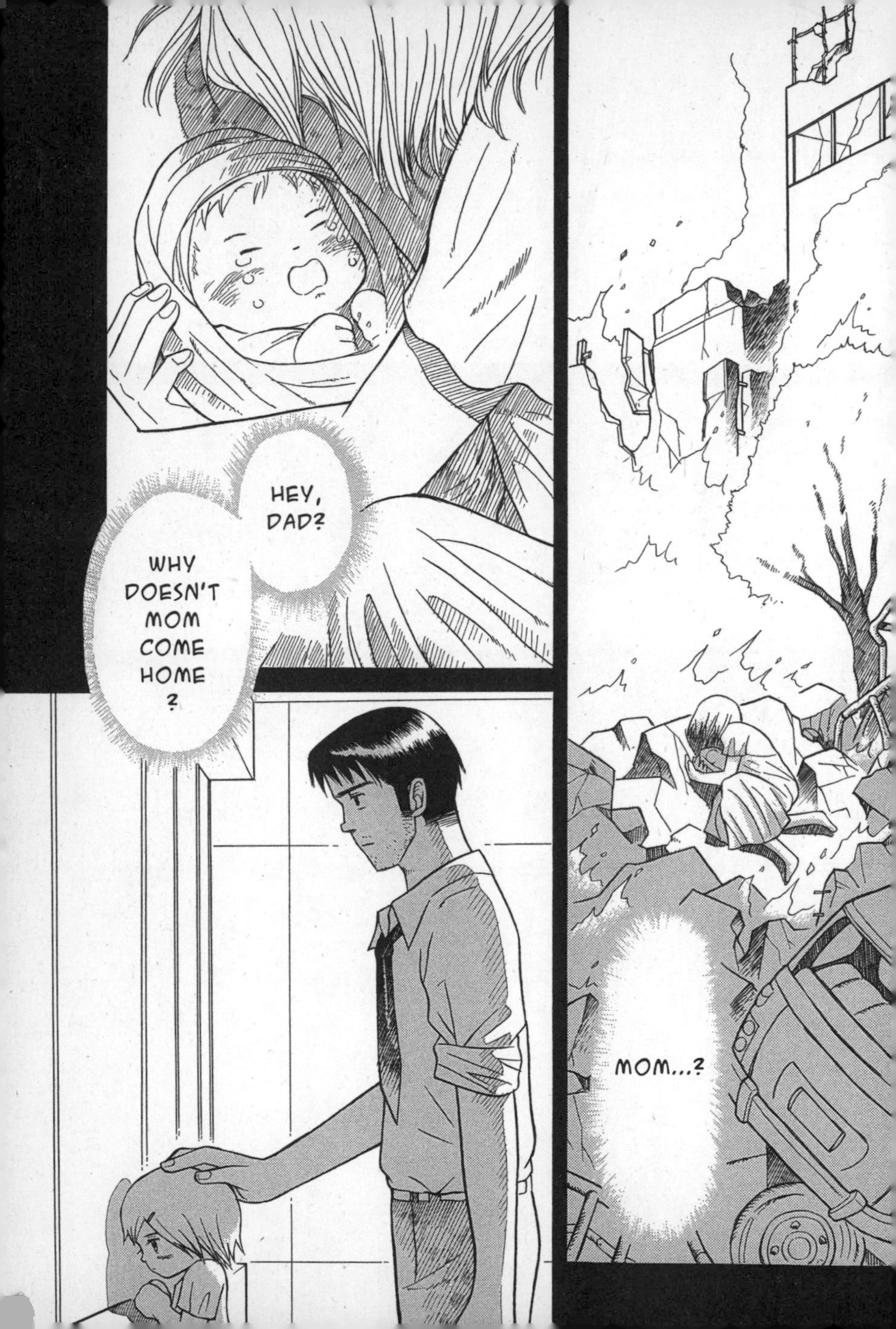
MOM...?
HEY, DAD?
WHY DOESN'T MOM COME HOME?

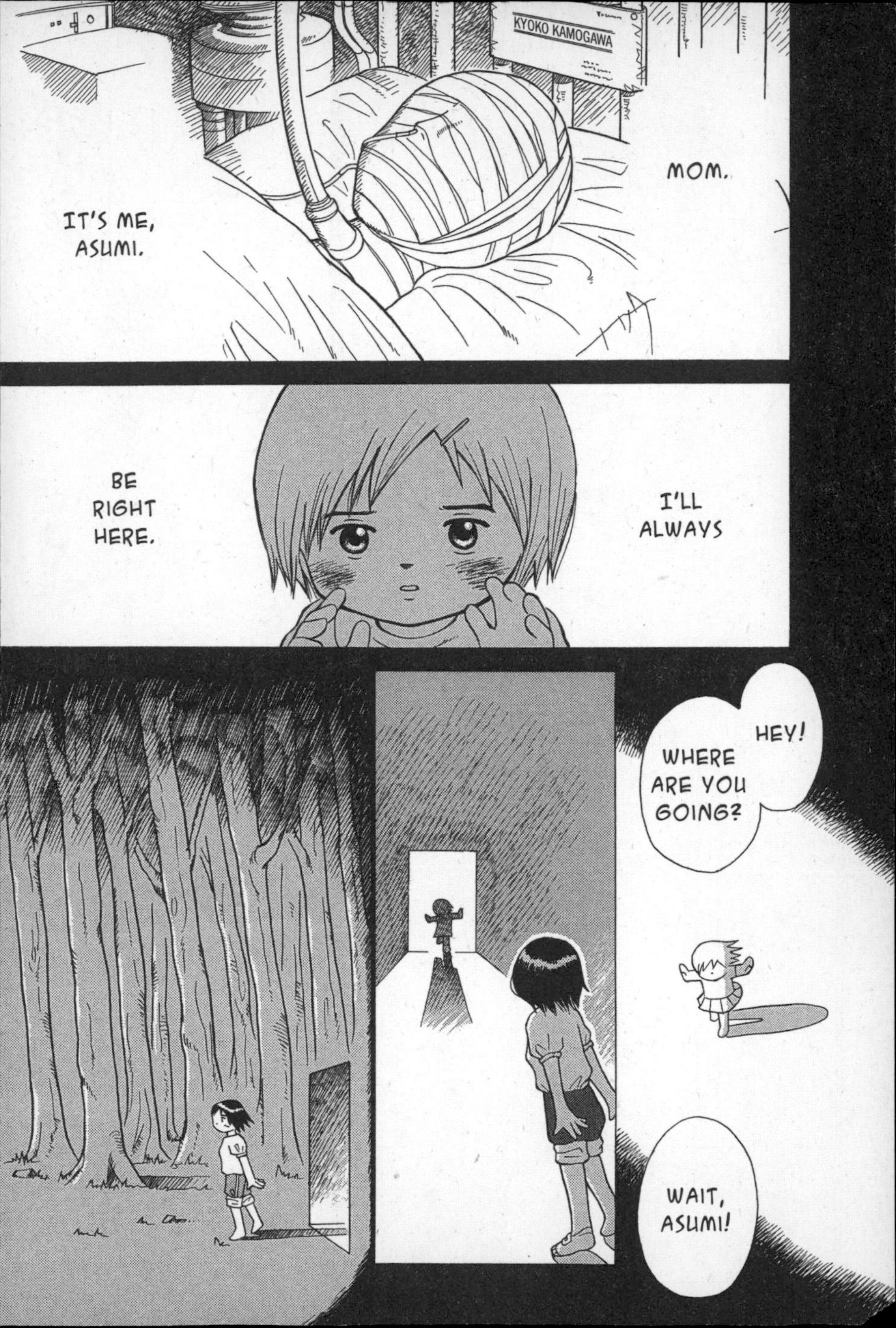
KYOKO KAMOGAWA
MOM.
IT'S ME, ASUMI.
I'LL ALWAYS
BE RIGHT HERE.
HEY! WHERE ARE YOU GOING?
WAIT, ASUMI!

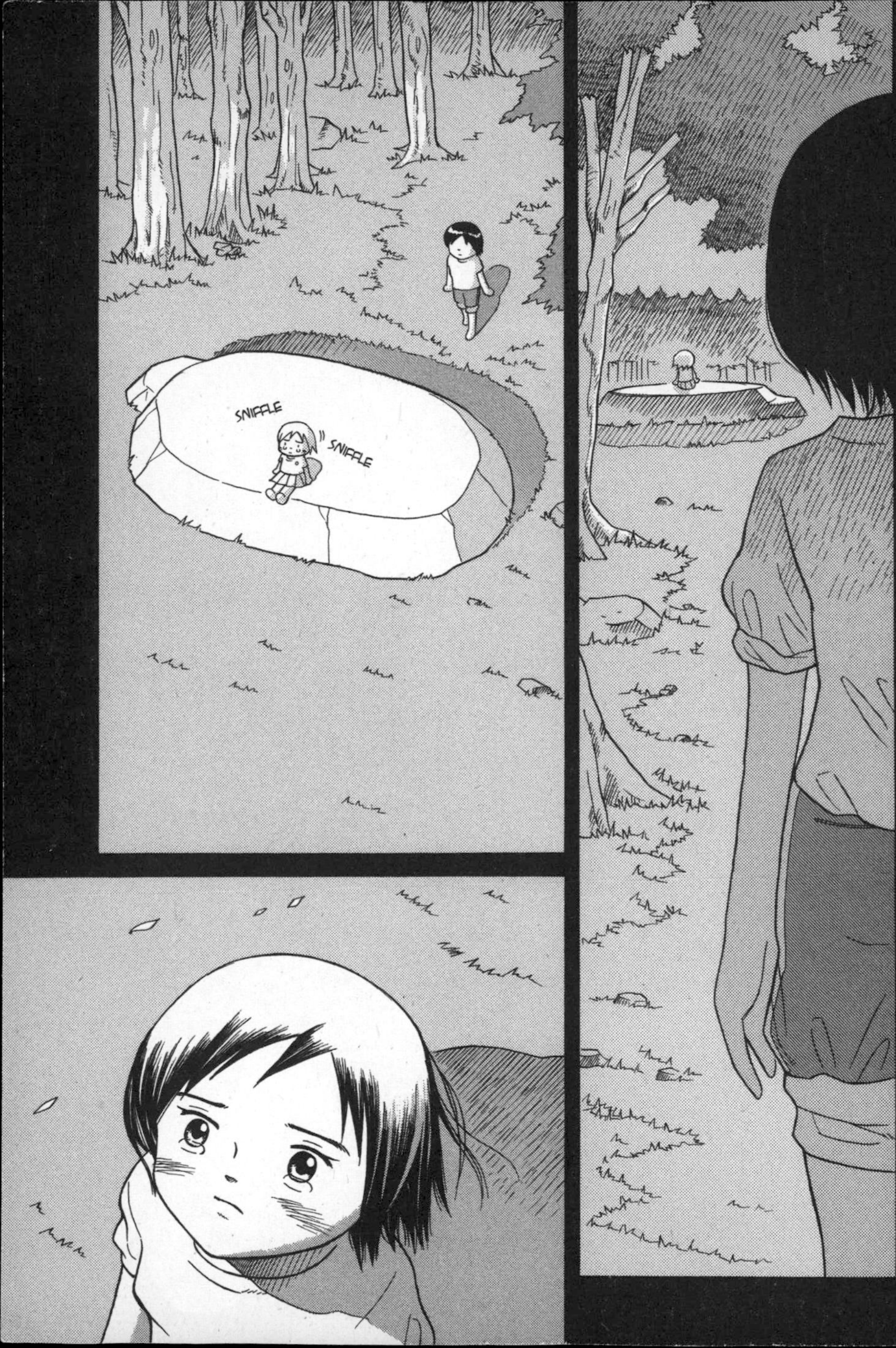
SNIFFLE
SNIFFLE

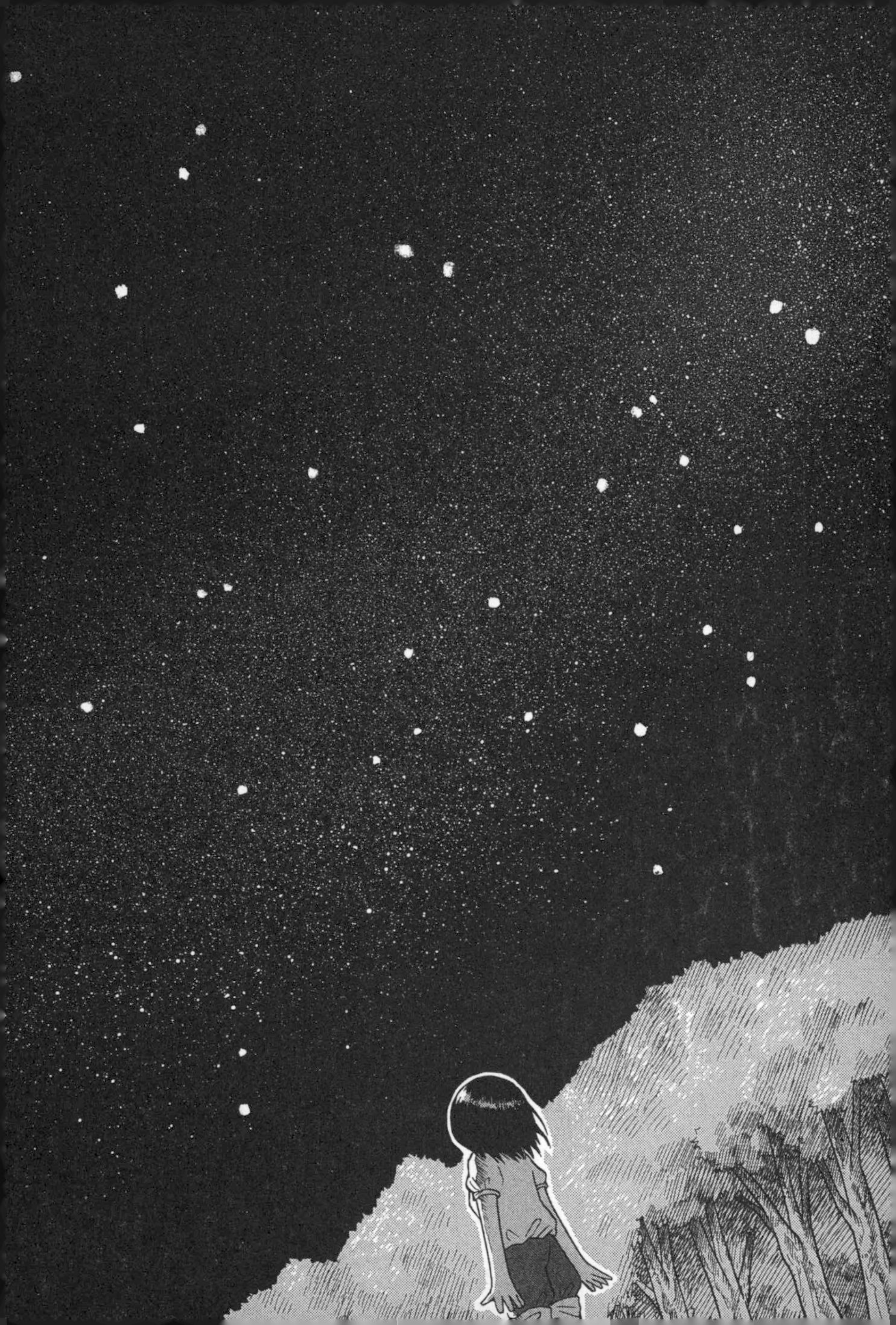

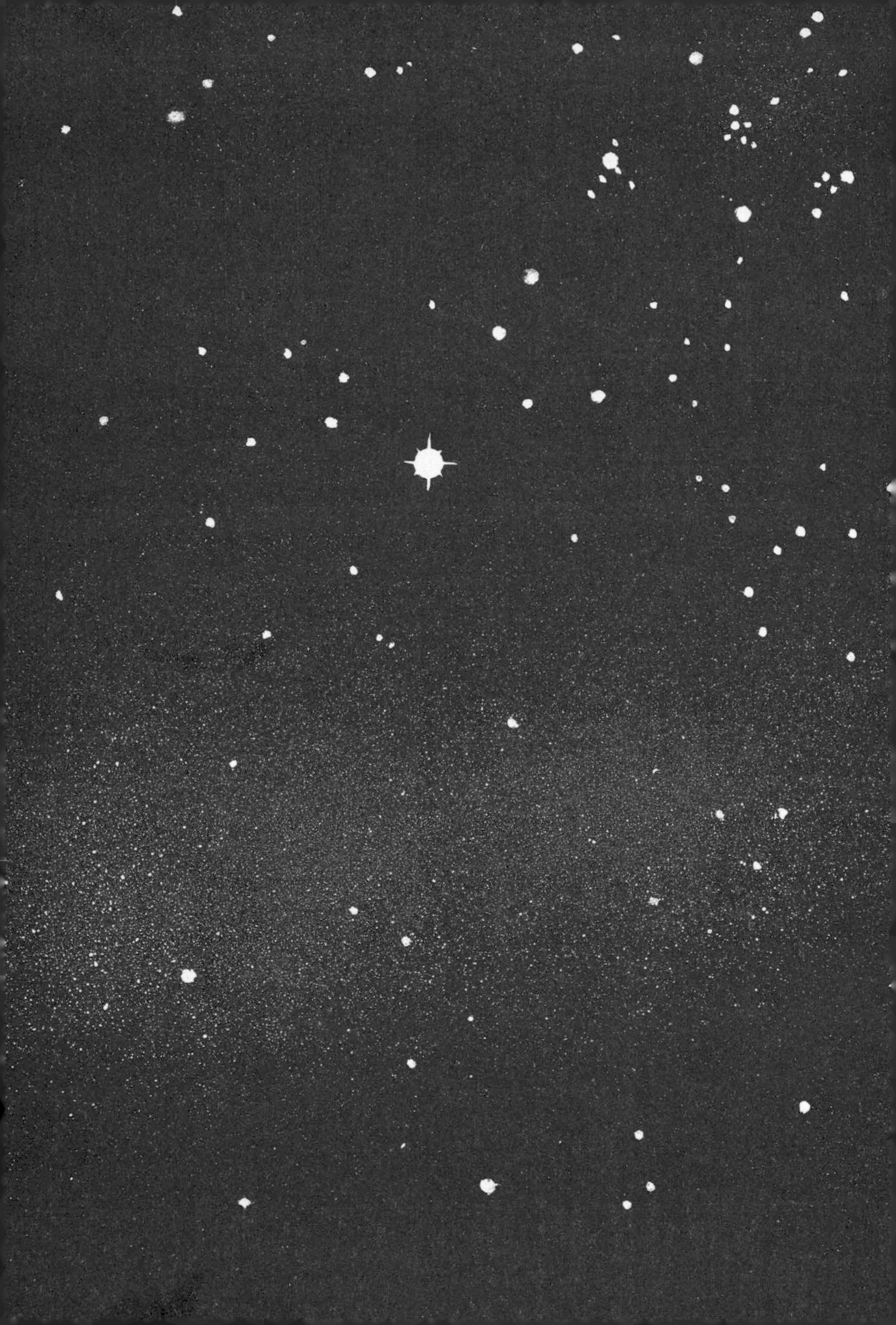

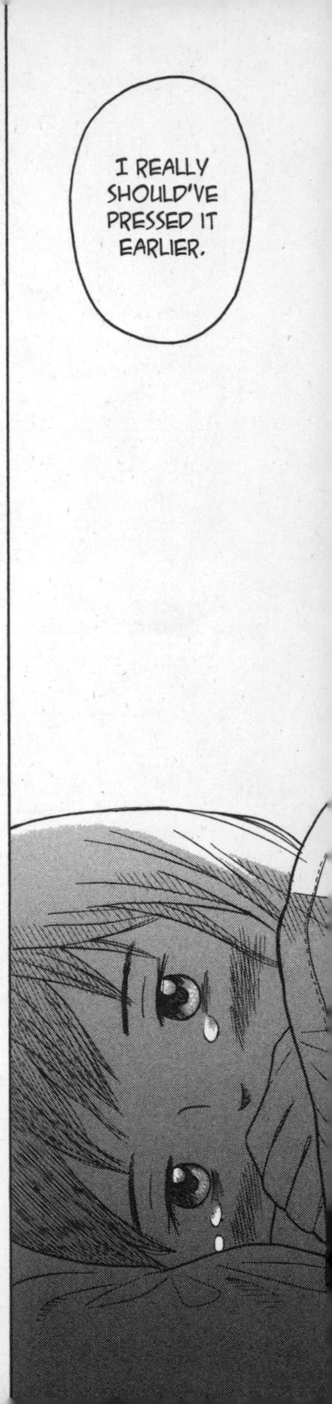
I REALLY SHOULD'VE PRESSED IT EARLIER.

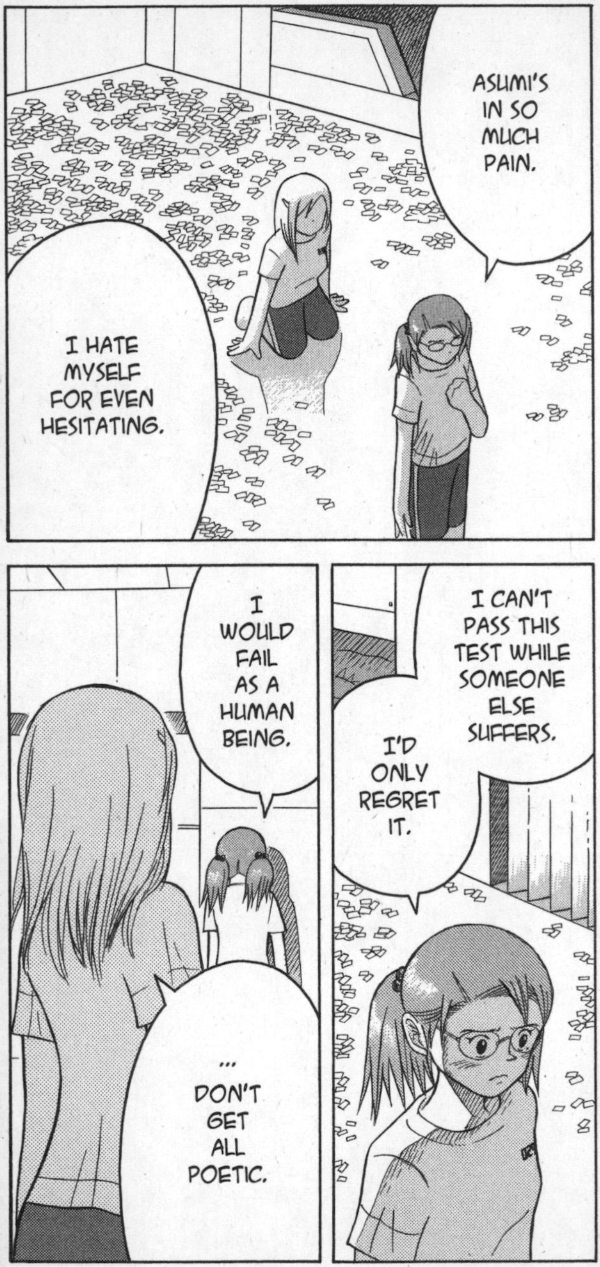
ASUMI'S IN SO MUCH PAIN.
I HATE MYSELF FOR EVEN HESITATING.
I CAN'T PASS THIS TEST WHILE SOMEONE ELSE SUFFERS.
I'D ONLY REGRET IT.
I WOULD FAIL AS A HUMAN BEING.
... DON'T GET ALL POETIC.

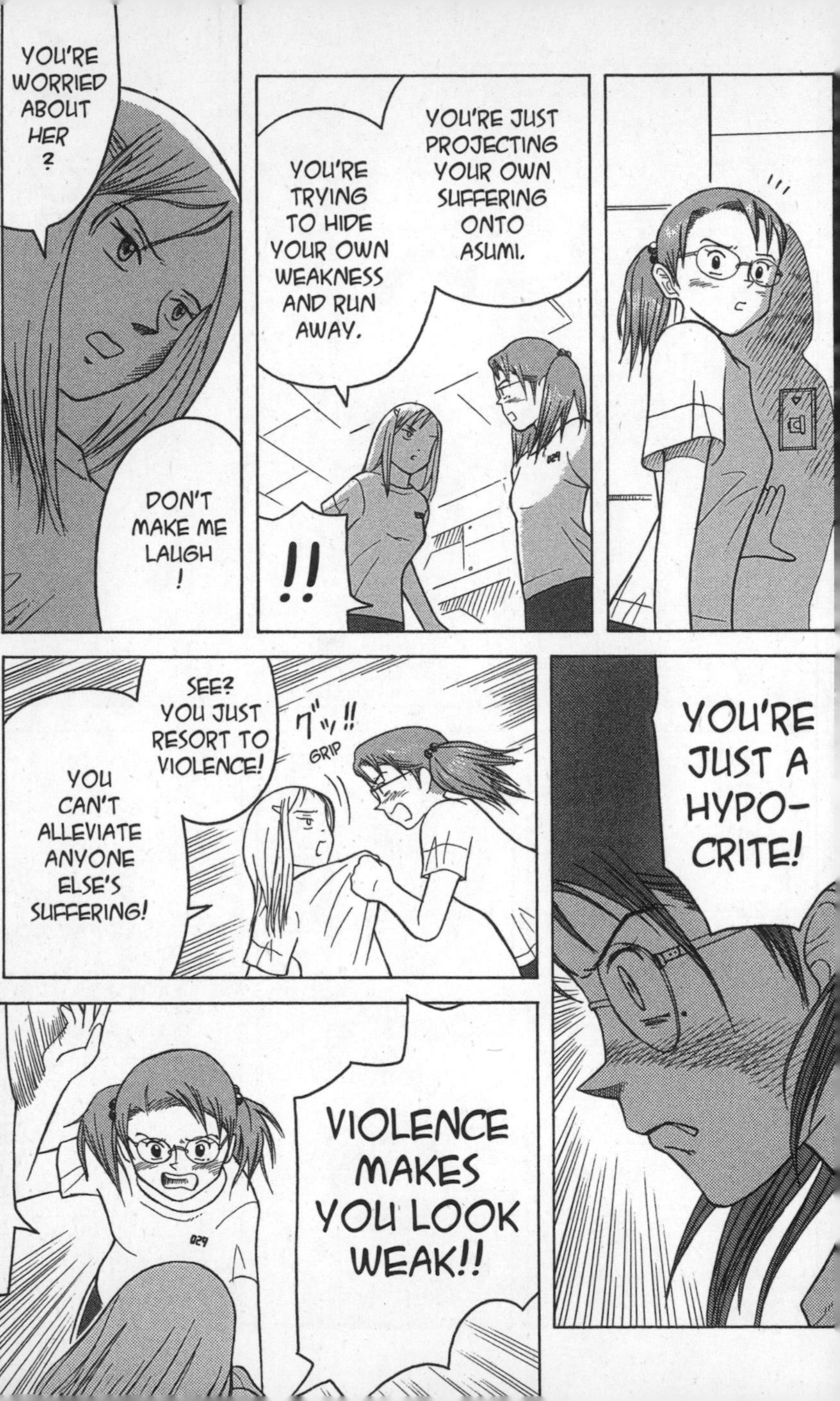
YOU'RE JUST PROJECTING YOUR OWN SUFFERING ONTO ASUMI.
YOU'RE TRYING TO HIDE YOUR OWN WEAKNESS AND RUN AWAY.
!!
YOU'RE WORRIED ABOUT HER?
DON'T MAKE ME LAUGH!
YOU'RE JUST A HYPOCRITE!
SEE? YOU JUST RESORT TO VIOLENCE!
グッ!!
GRIP
YOU CAN'T ALLEVIATE ANYONE ELSE'S SUFFERING!
VIOLENCE MAKES YOU LOOK WEAK!!
BITCH!

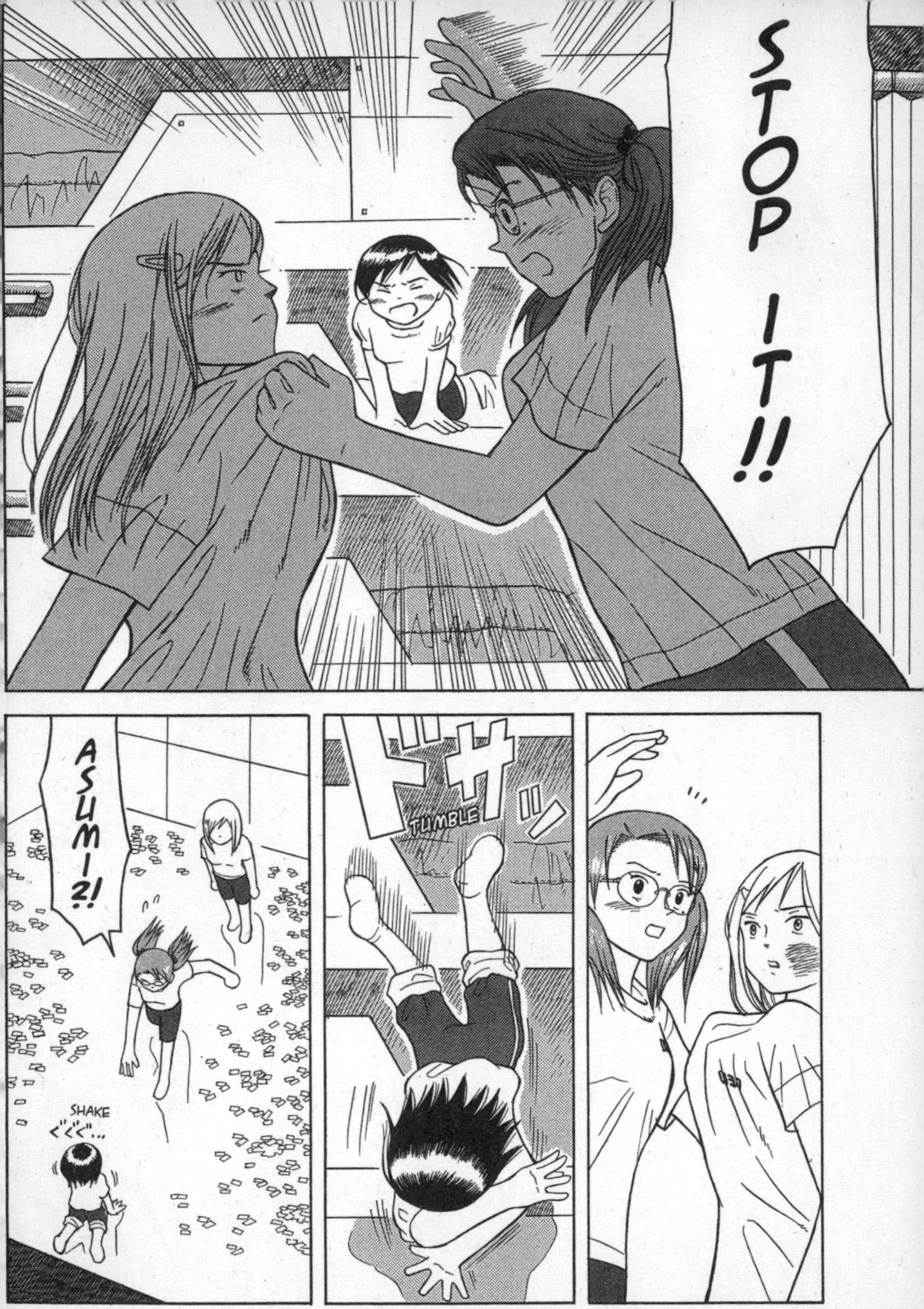
STOP IT!!
ドサッ
TUMBLE
ASUMI?!
SHAKE
ぐぐぐ...

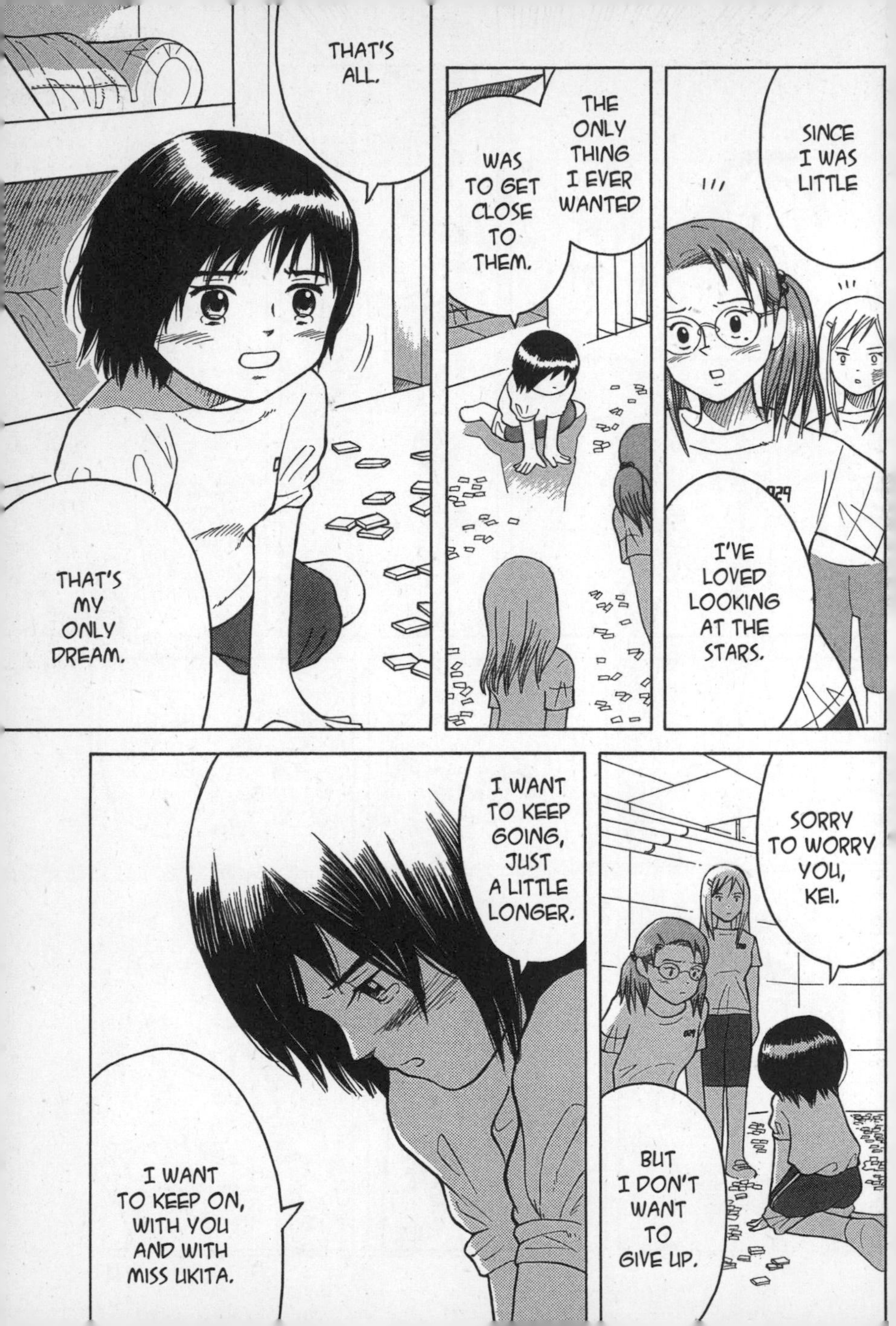
SINCE I WAS LITTLE
I'VE LOVED LOOKING AT THE STARS.
THE ONLY THING I EVER WANTED
WAS TO GET CLOSE TO THEM.
THAT'S ALL.
THAT'S MY ONLY DREAM.
SORRY TO WORRY YOU, KEI.
BUT I DON'T WANT TO GIVE UP.
I WANT TO KEEP GOING, JUST A LITTLE LONGER.
I WANT TO KEEP ON, WITH YOU AND WITH MISS UKITA.

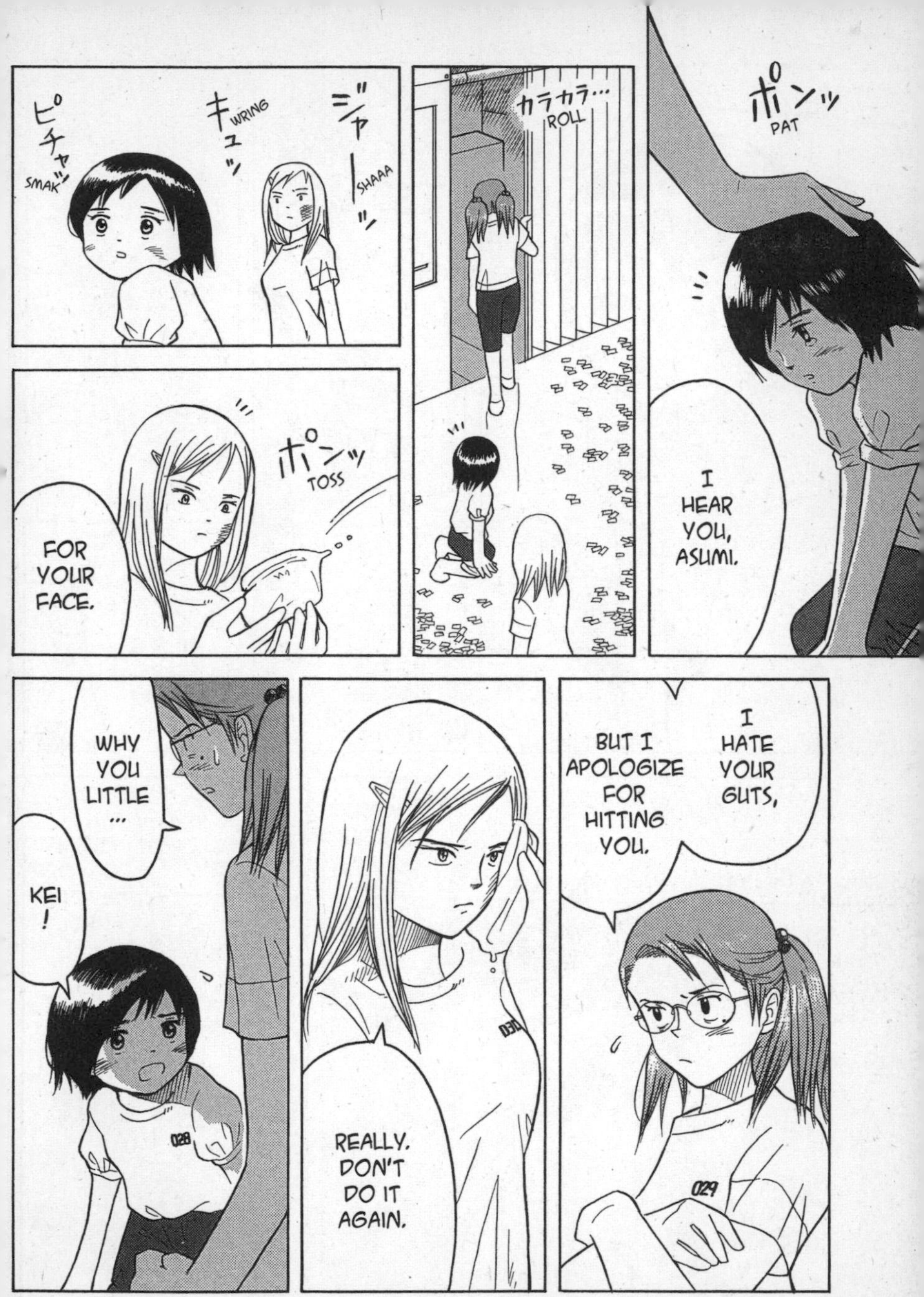
ポンッ
PAT
I HEAR YOU, ASUMI.
カラカラ…
ROLL
ジャーッ
SHAAA
キュッ
WRING
ピチャッ
SMAK
ポンッ
TOSS
FOR YOUR FACE.
I HATE YOUR GUTS,
BUT I APOLOGIZE FOR HITTING YOU.
REALLY. DON'T DO IT AGAIN.
WHY YOU LITTLE ...
KEI!

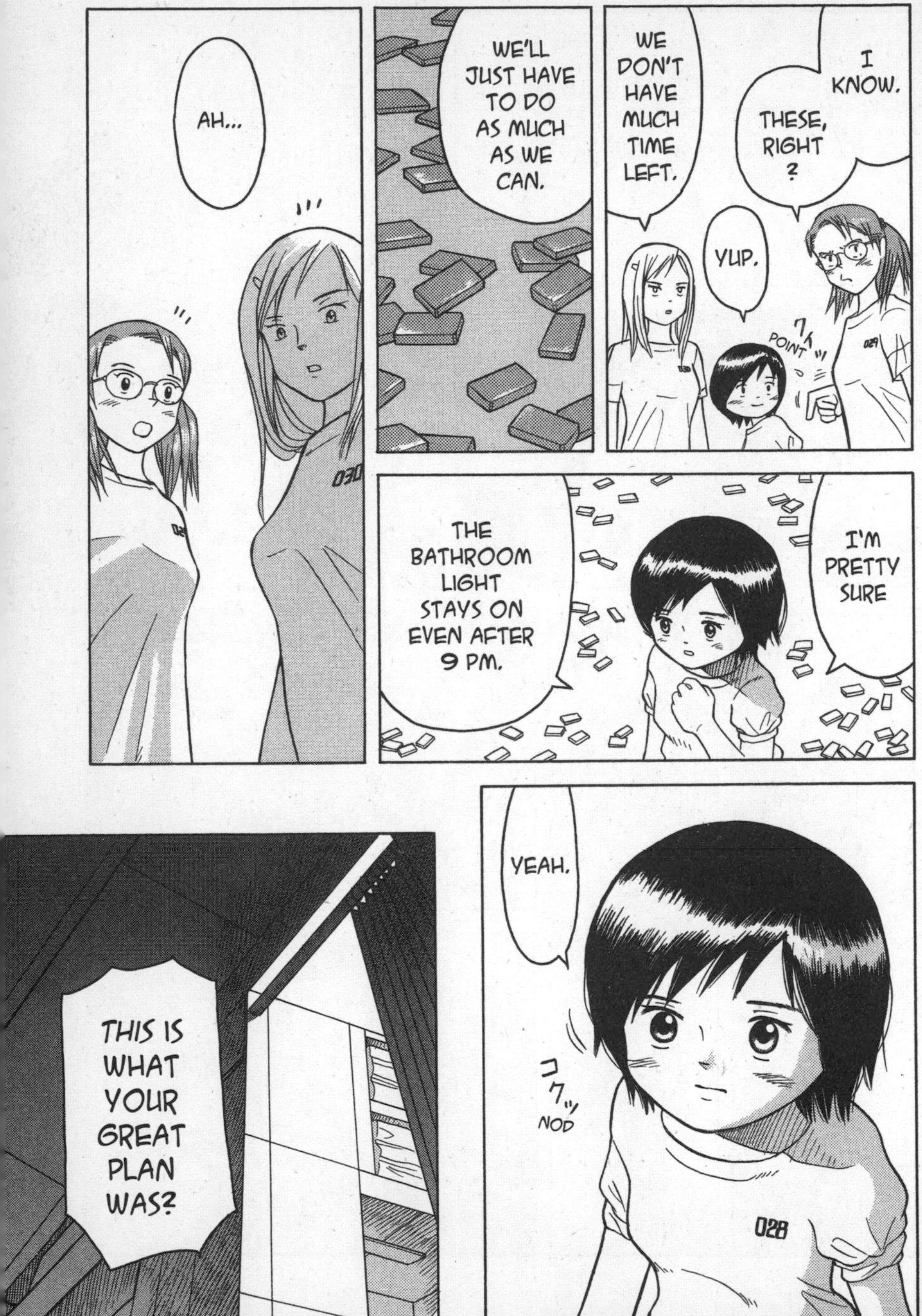
I KNOW.
THESE, RIGHT?
WE DON'T HAVE MUCH TIME LEFT.
YUP.
POINT
WE'LL JUST HAVE TO DO AS MUCH AS WE CAN.
I'M PRETTY SURE
THE BATHROOM LIGHT STAYS ON EVEN AFTER 9 PM.
AH...
YEAH.
NOD
THIS IS WHAT YOUR GREAT PLAN WAS?

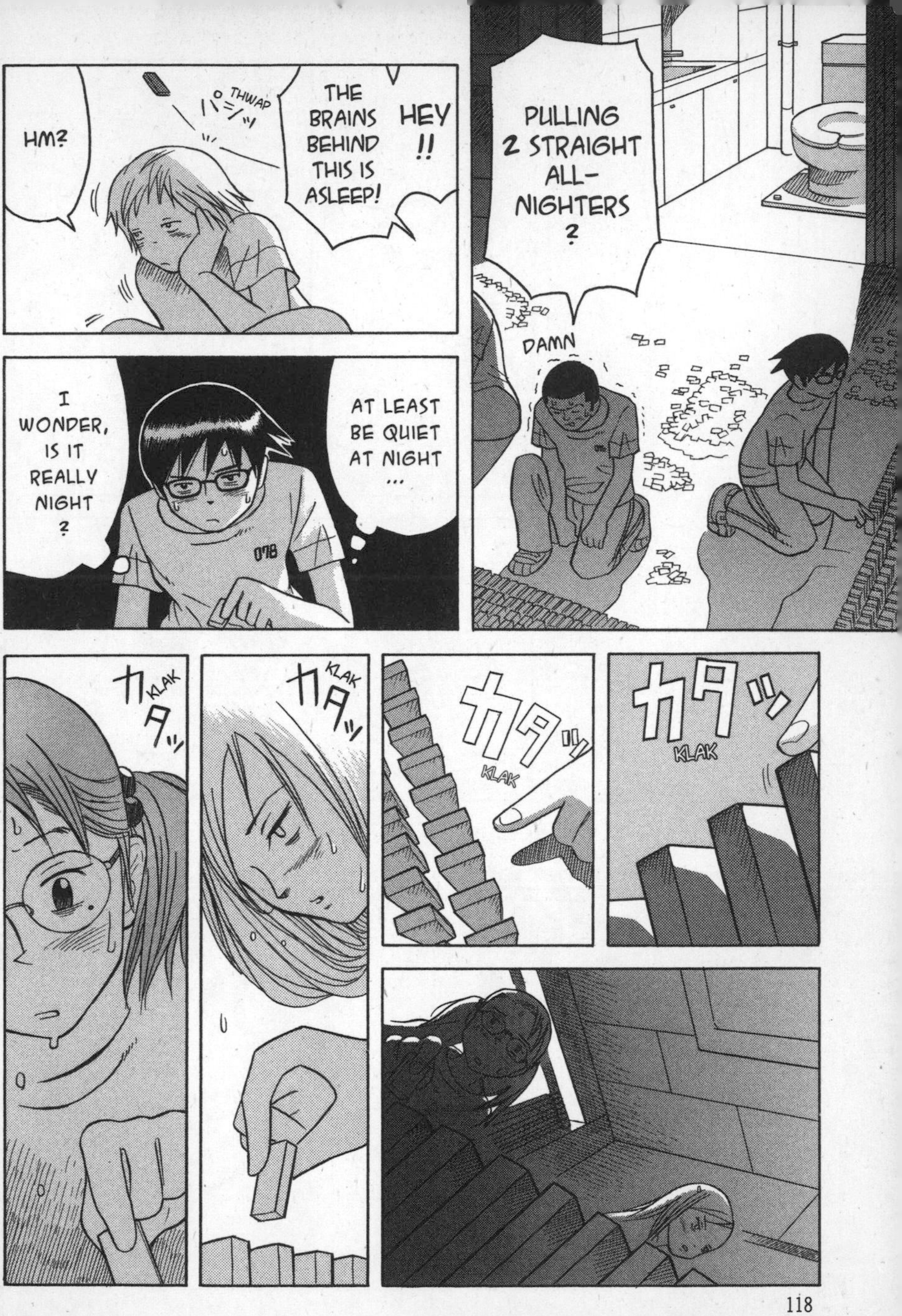
PULLING 2 STRAIGHT ALL-NIGHTERS ?
DAMN
HEY !!
THE BRAINS BEHIND THIS IS ASLEEP!
パシッ THWAP
HM?
AT LEAST BE QUIET AT NIGHT ...
I WONDER, IS IT REALLY NIGHT ?
カタッ KLAK
カタッ KLAK
カタッ KLAK
カタッ KLAK

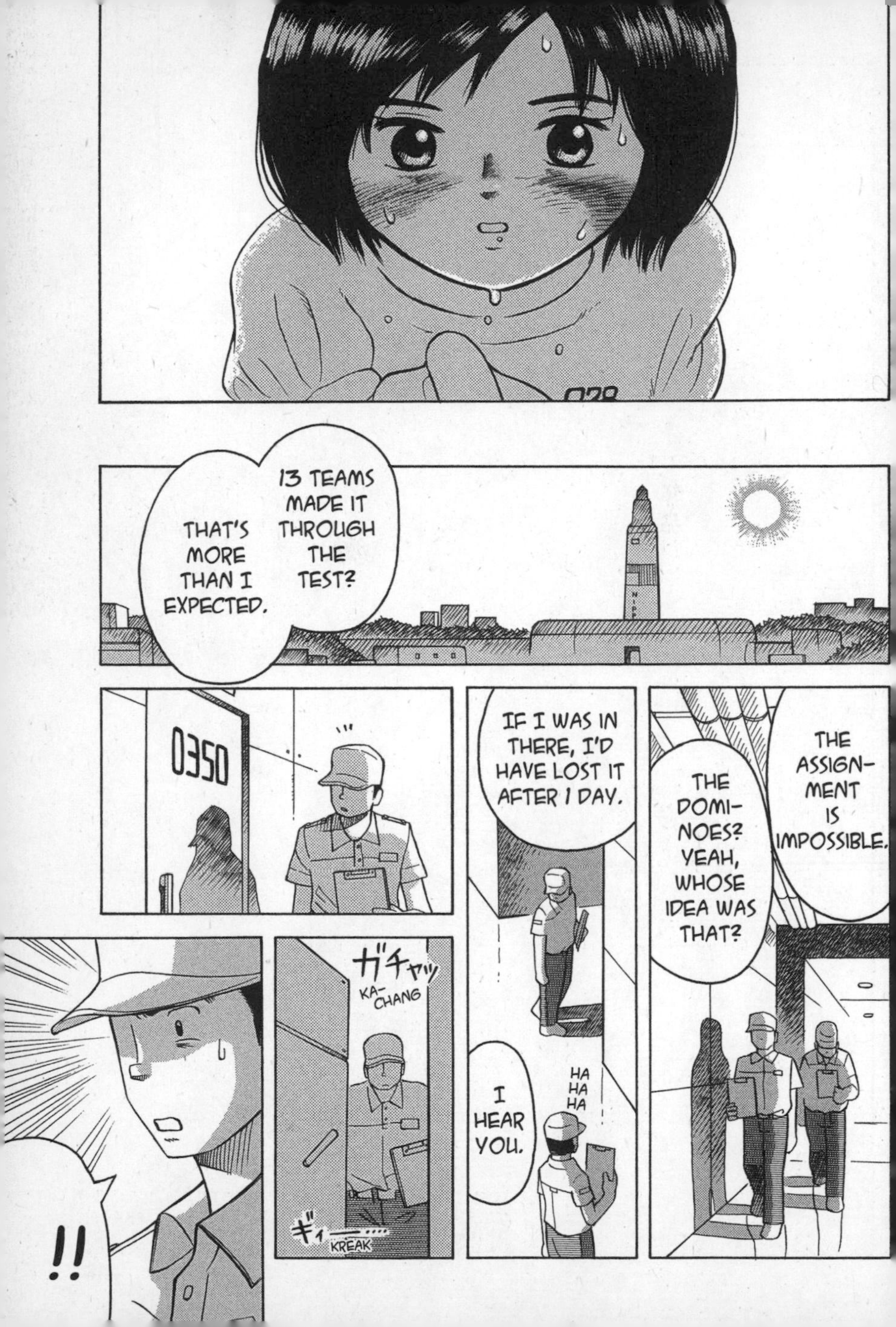
13 TEAMS MADE IT THROUGH THE TEST?
THAT'S MORE THAN I EXPECTED.
THE ASSIGNMENT IS IMPOSSIBLE.
THE DOMINOES? YEAH, WHOSE IDEA WAS THAT?
IF I WAS IN THERE, I'D HAVE LOST IT AFTER 1 DAY.
HA HA HA
I HEAR YOU.
0350
ガチャッ
KA-CHANG
ギィー……
KREAK
!!

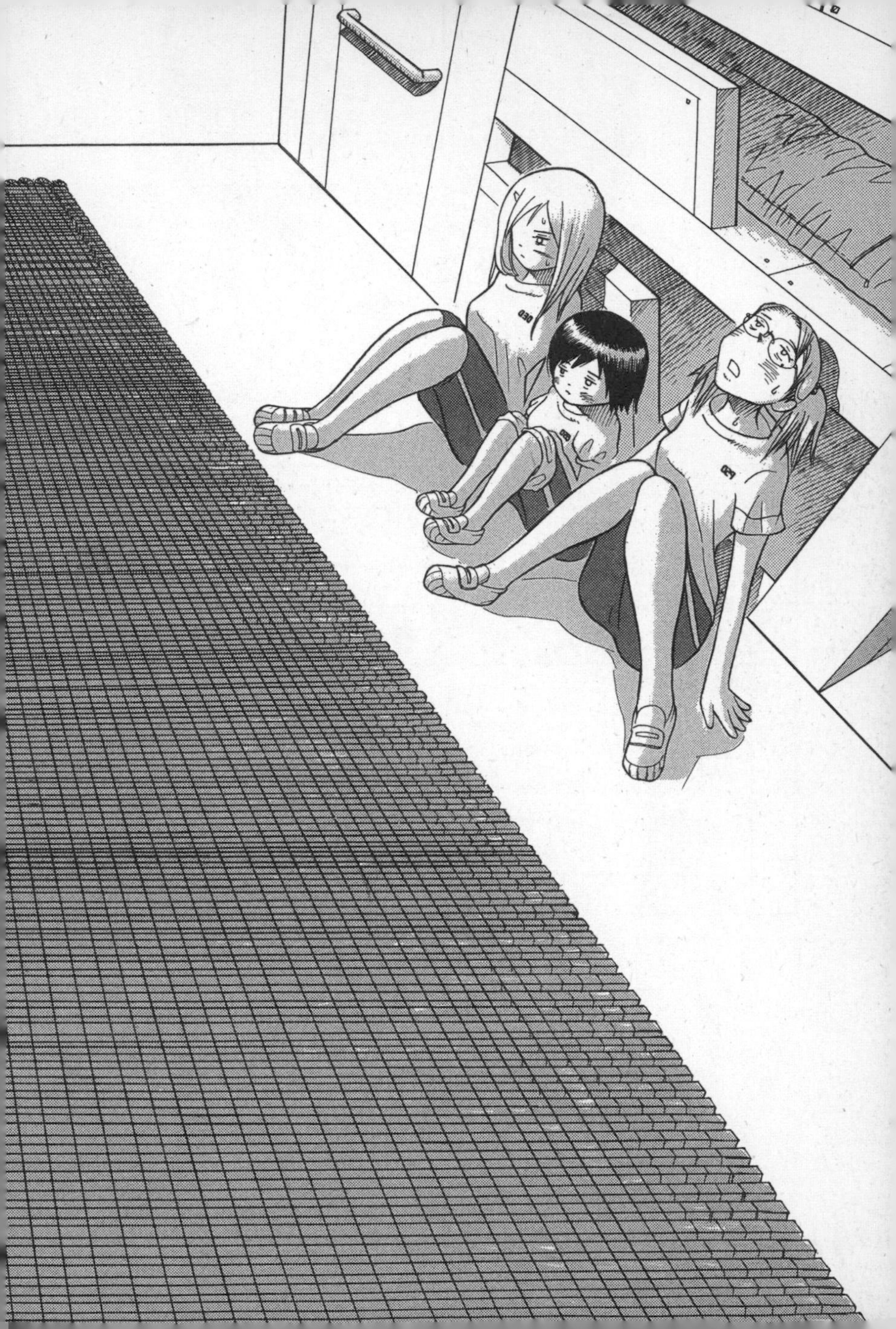

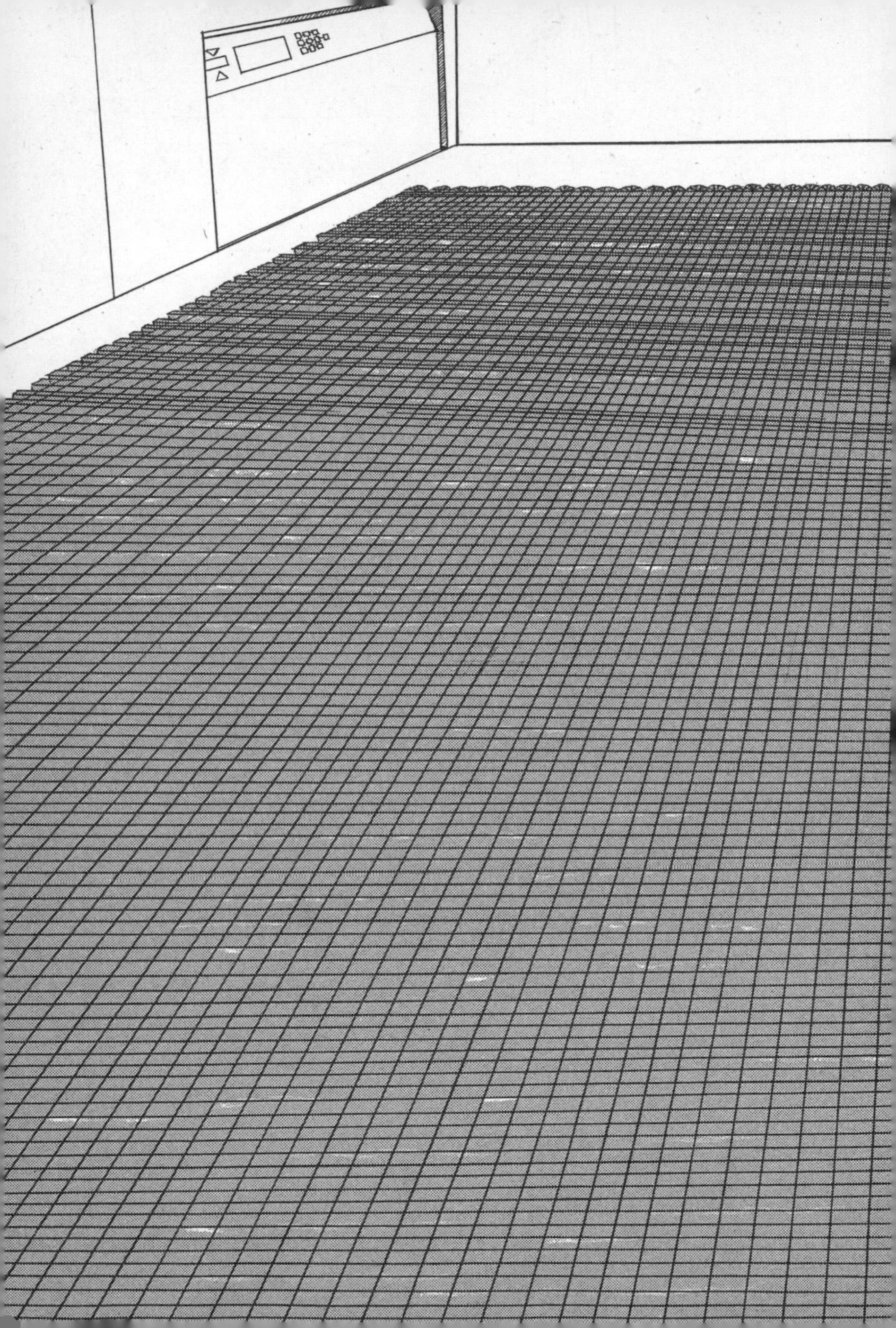

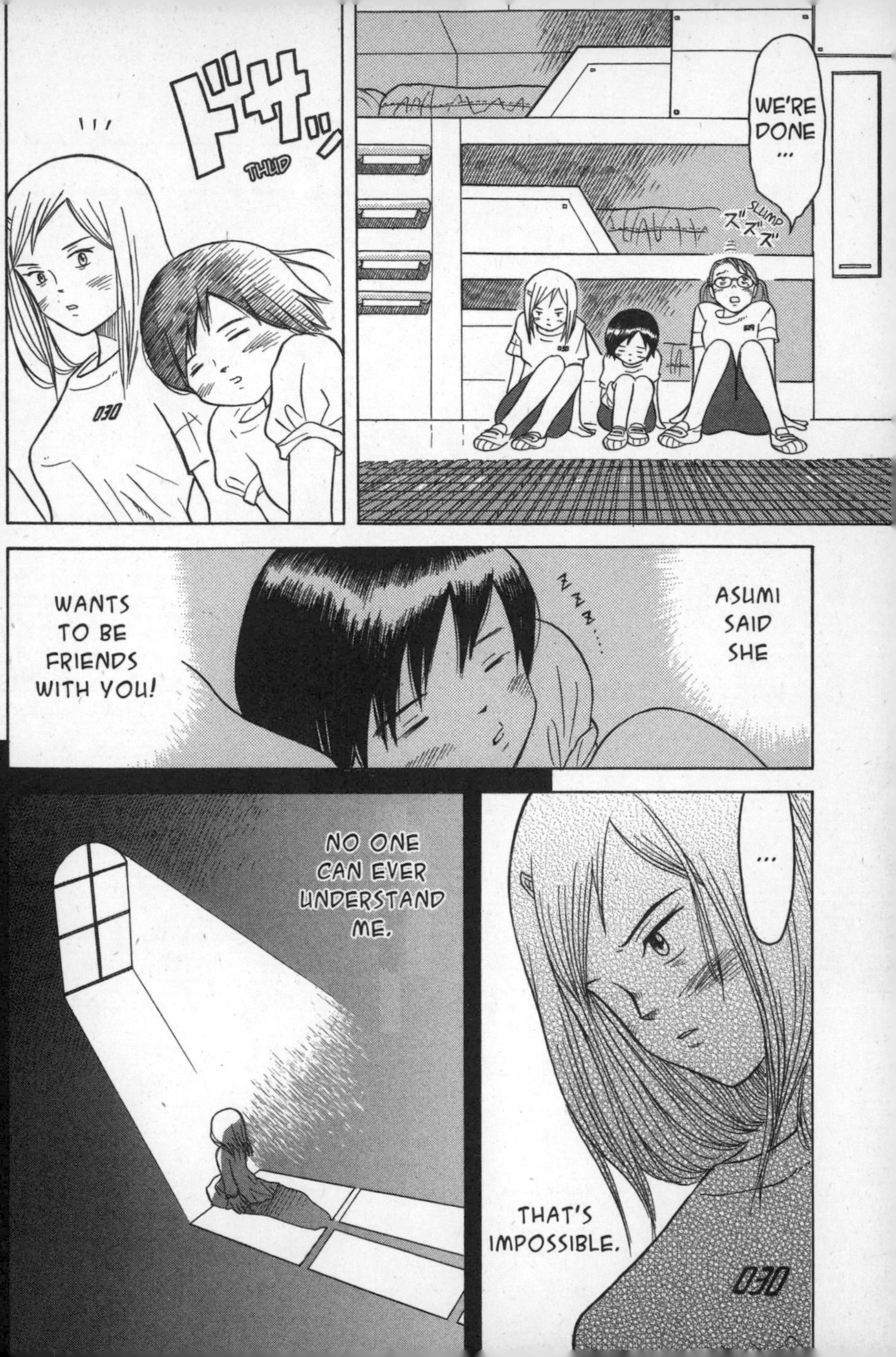
WE'RE DONE ...
SLUMP
ズズズ
ドサッ
THUD
ASUMI SAID SHE
WANTS TO BE FRIENDS WITH YOU!
ZZZ....
...
THAT'S IMPOSSIBLE.
NO ONE CAN EVER UNDERSTAND ME.

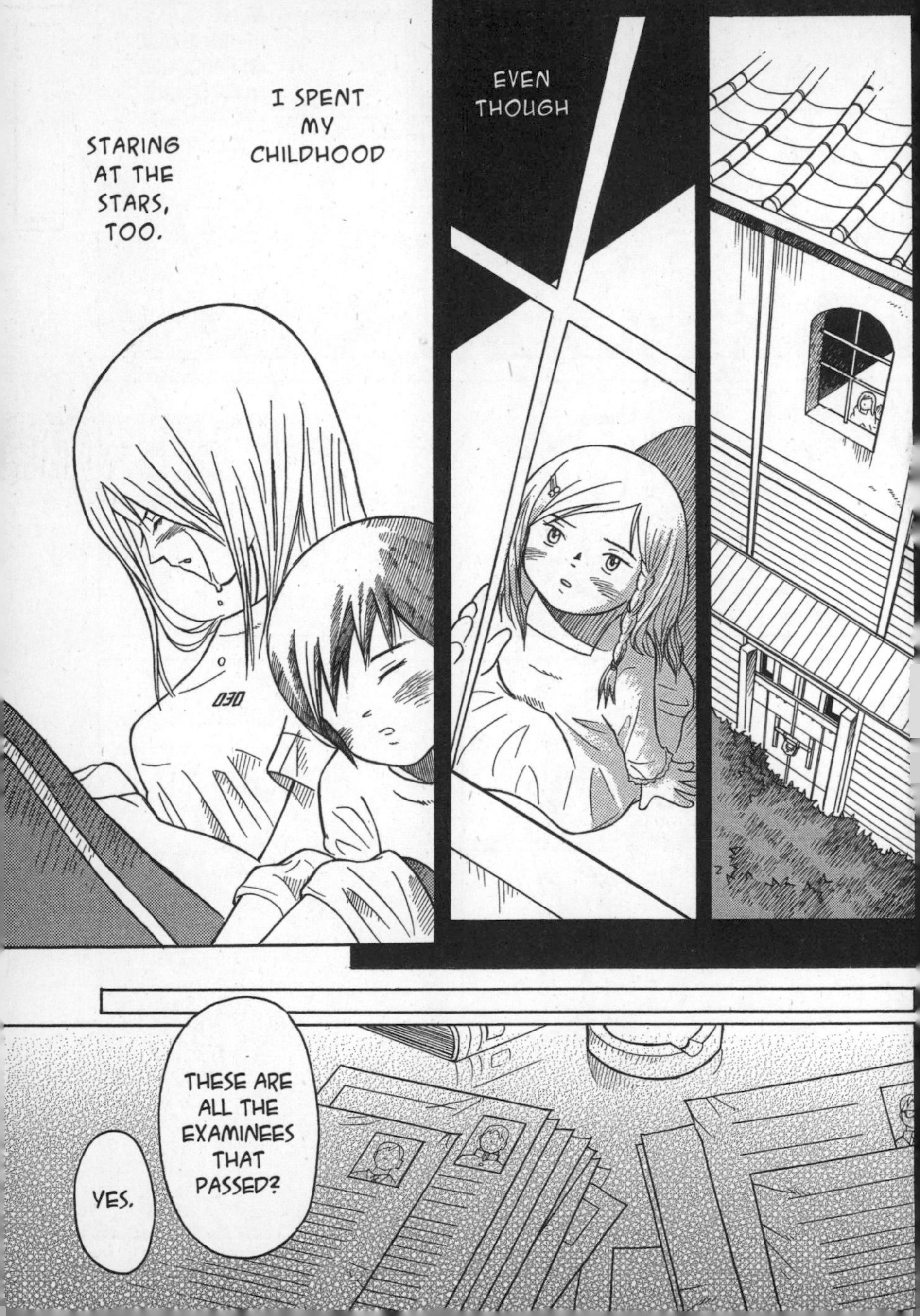
EVEN THOUGH
I SPENT MY CHILDHOOD
STARING AT THE STARS, TOO.
THESE ARE ALL THE EXAMINEES THAT PASSED?
YES.

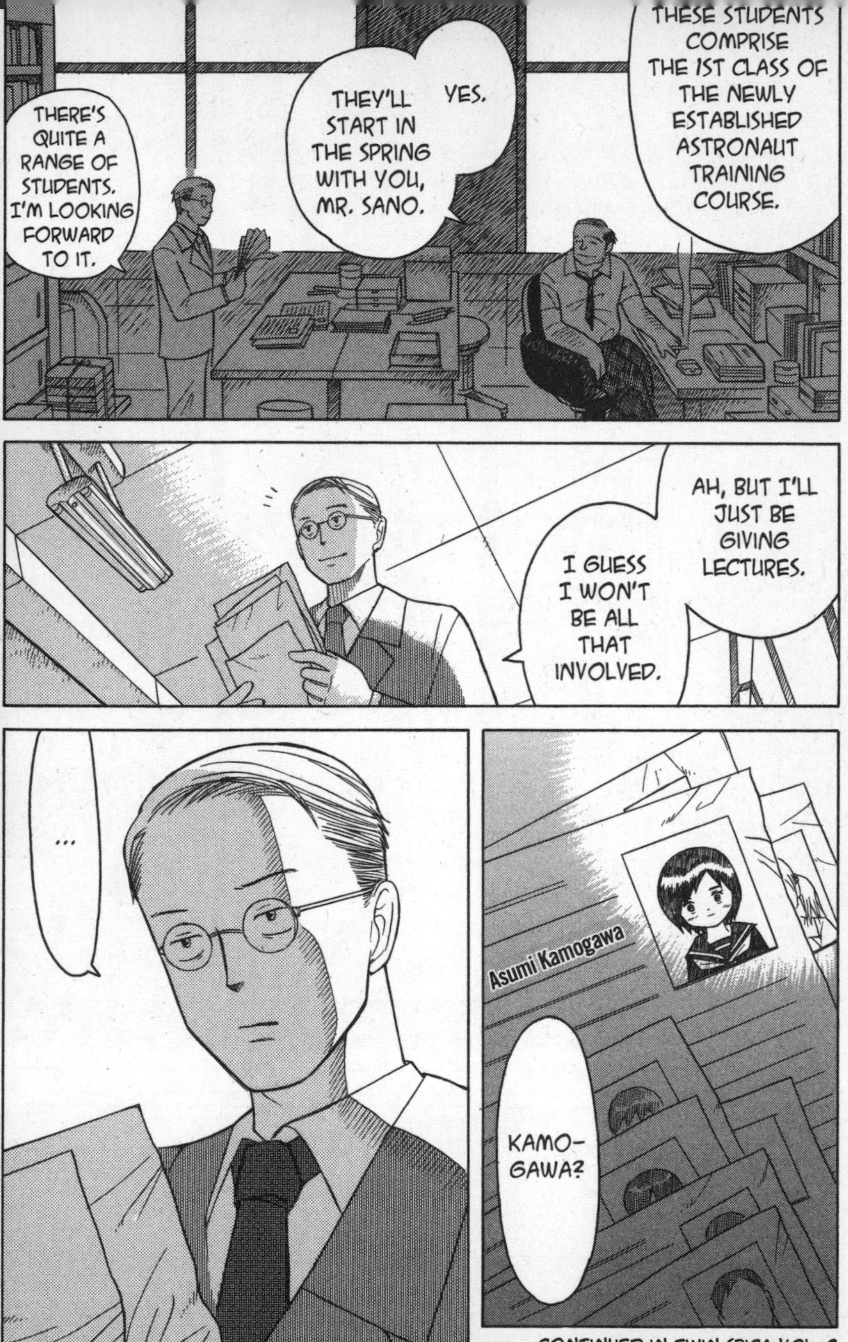
THESE STUDENTS COMPRISE THE 1ST CLASS OF THE NEWLY ESTABLISHED ASTRONAUT TRAINING COURSE.
YES.
THEY'LL START IN THE SPRING WITH YOU, MR. SANO.
THERE'S QUITE A RANGE OF STUDENTS. I'M LOOKING FORWARD TO IT.
AH, BUT I'LL JUST BE GIVING LECTURES.
I GUESS I WON'T BE ALL THAT INVOLVED.
Asumi Kamogawa
KAMO-GAWA?
...

CONTINUED IN TWIN SPICA VOL. 2

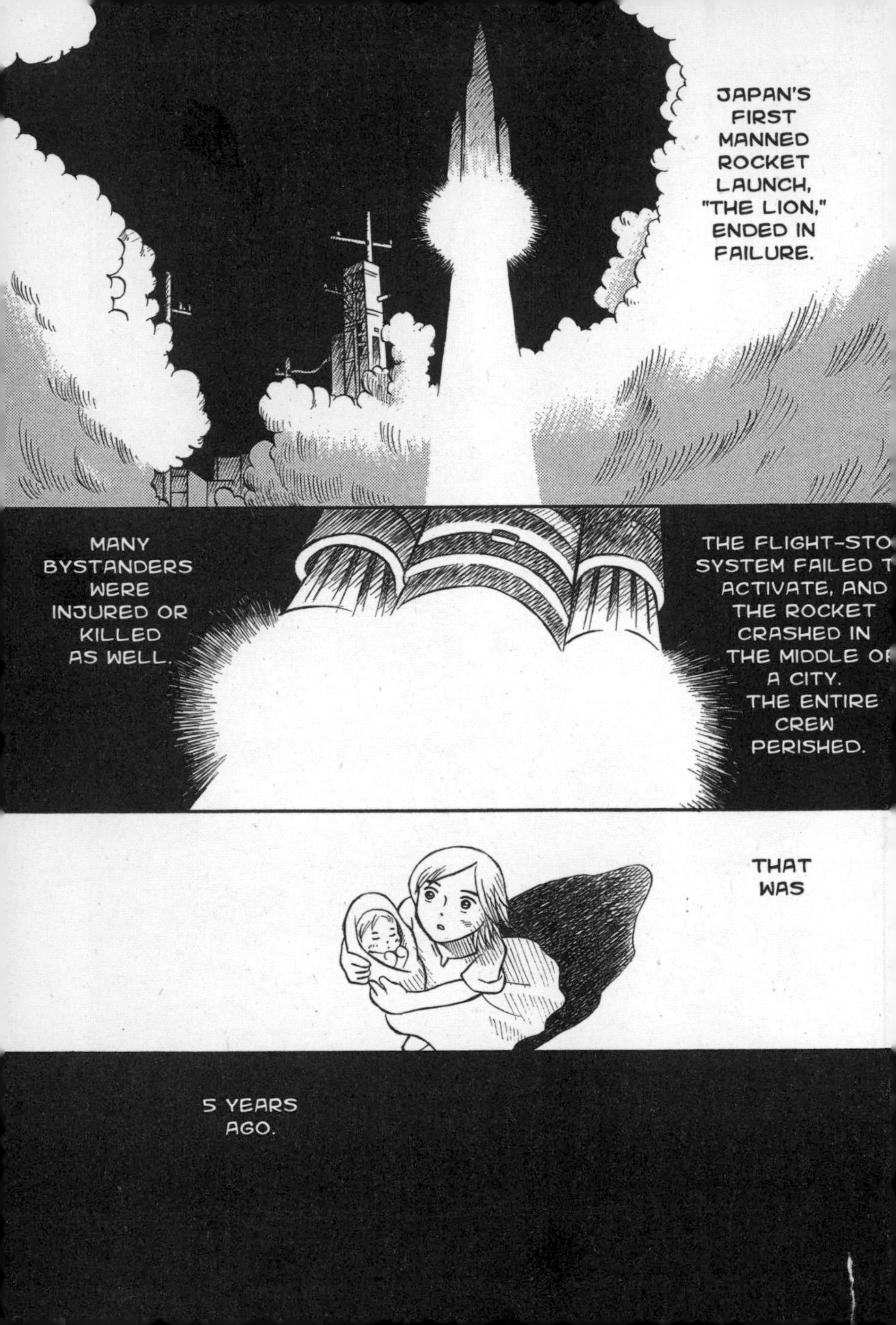
JAPAN'S FIRST MANNED ROCKET LAUNCH, "THE LION," ENDED IN FAILURE.
THE FLIGHT-STO SYSTEM FAILED T ACTIVATE, AND THE ROCKET CRASHED IN THE MIDDLE OF A CITY. THE ENTIRE CREW PERISHED.
MANY BYSTANDERS WERE INJURED OR KILLED AS WELL.
THAT WAS
5 YEARS AGO.

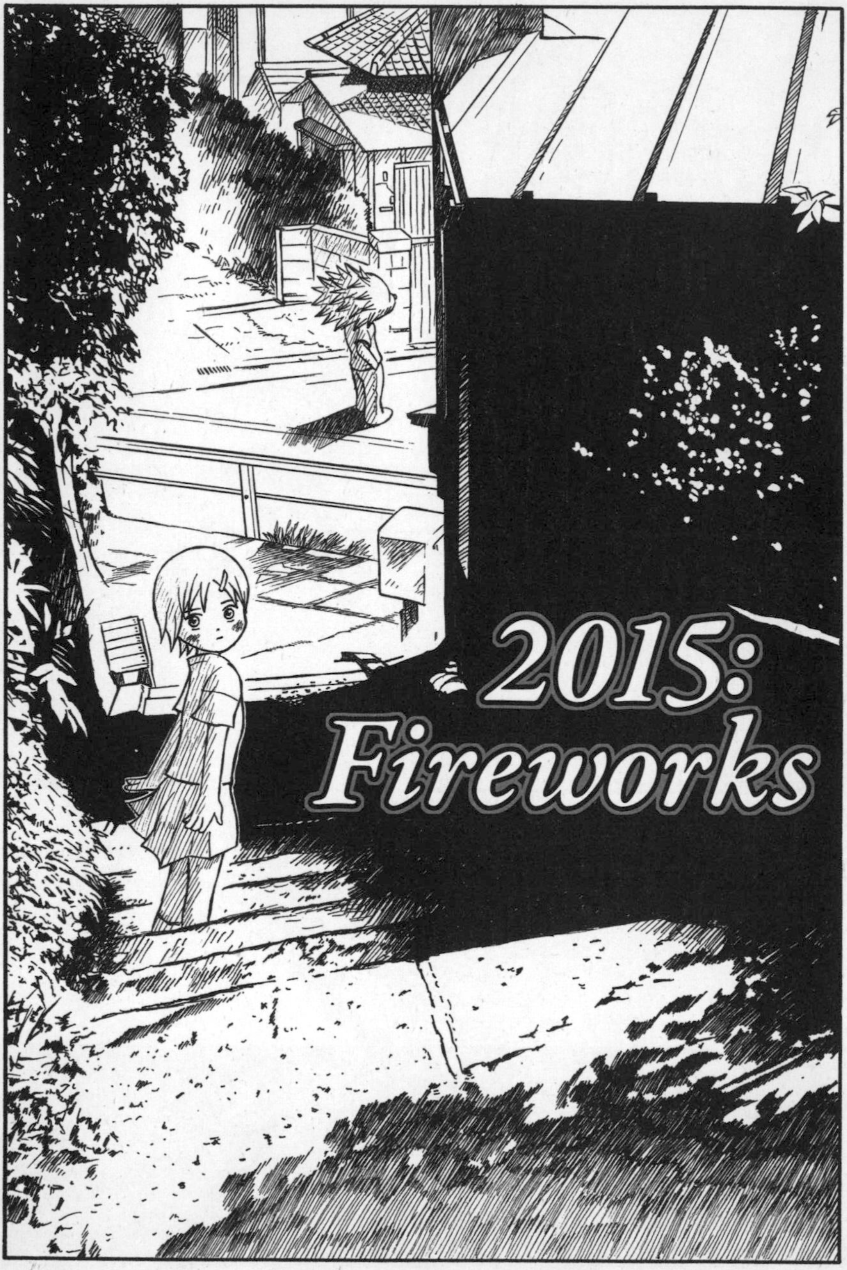
2015:
Fireworks

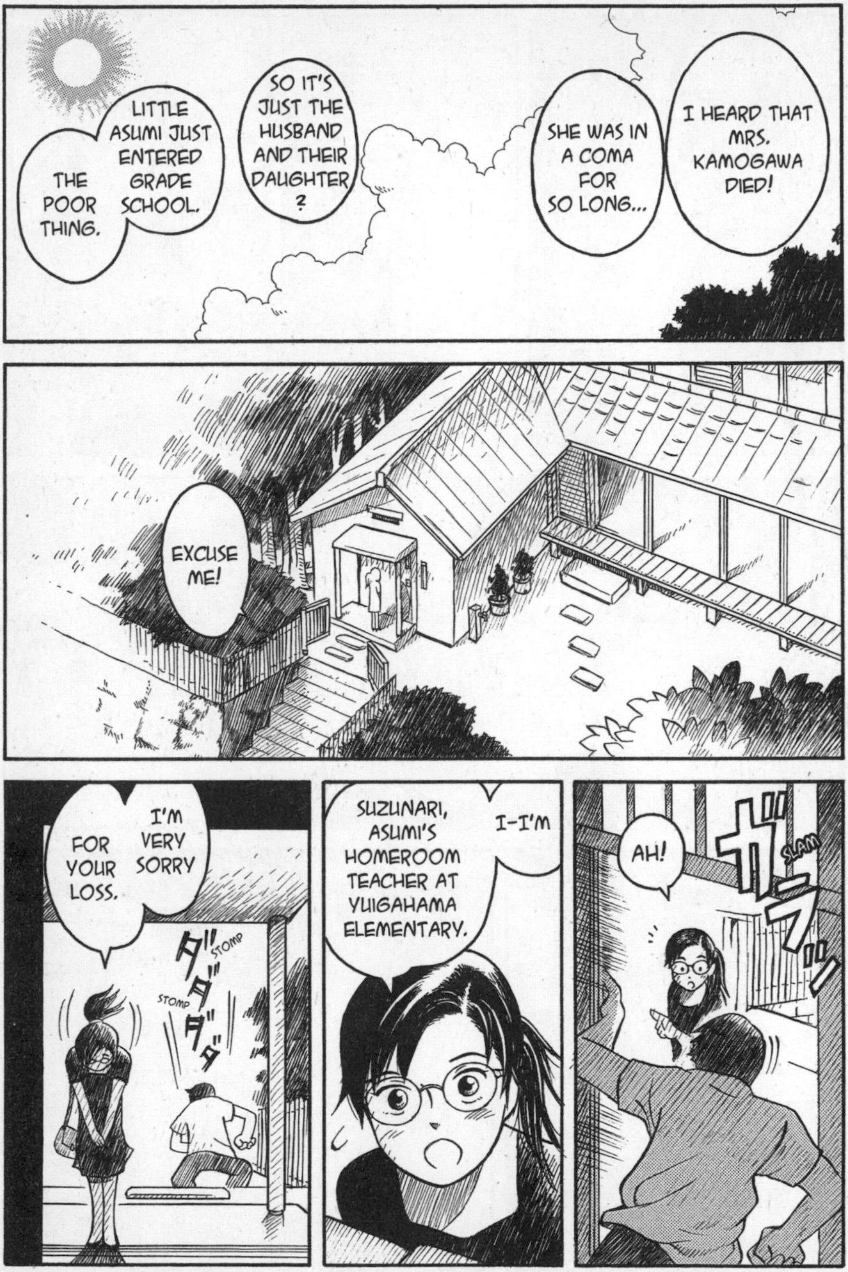
I HEARD THAT MRS. KAMOGAWA DIED!
SHE WAS IN A COMA FOR SO LONG...
SO IT'S JUST THE HUSBAND AND THEIR DAUGHTER ?
LITTLE ASUMI JUST ENTERED GRADE SCHOOL.
THE POOR THING.
EXCUSE ME!
SLAM
AH!
I-I'M
SUZUNARI, ASUMI'S HOMEROOM TEACHER AT YUIGAHAMA ELEMENTARY.
I'M VERY SORRY
FOR YOUR LOSS.
STOMP
STOMP

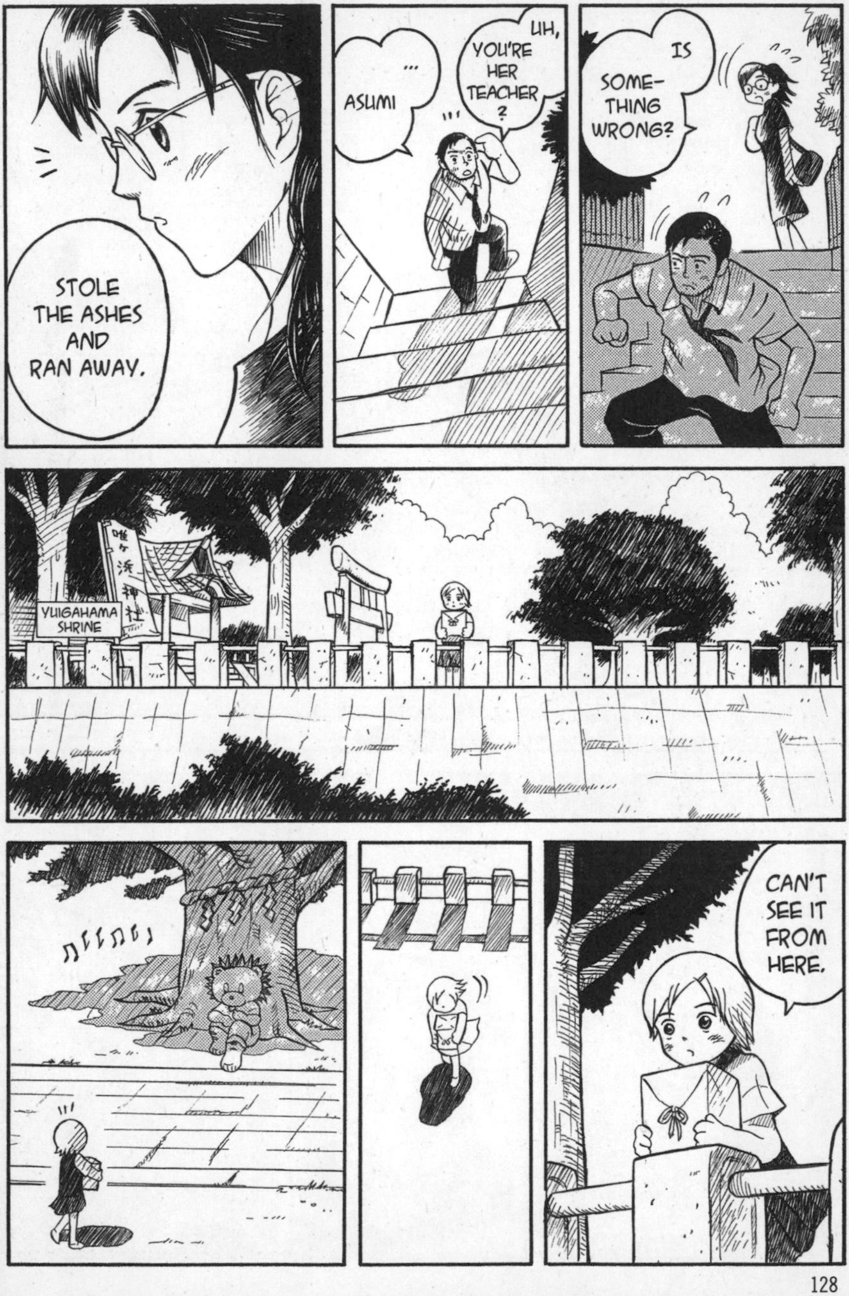
IS SOMETHING WRONG?
UH, YOU'RE HER TEACHER?
... ASUMI
STOLE THE ASHES AND RAN AWAY.
唯ヶ浜神社
YUIGAHAMA SHRINE
CAN'T SEE IT FROM HERE.

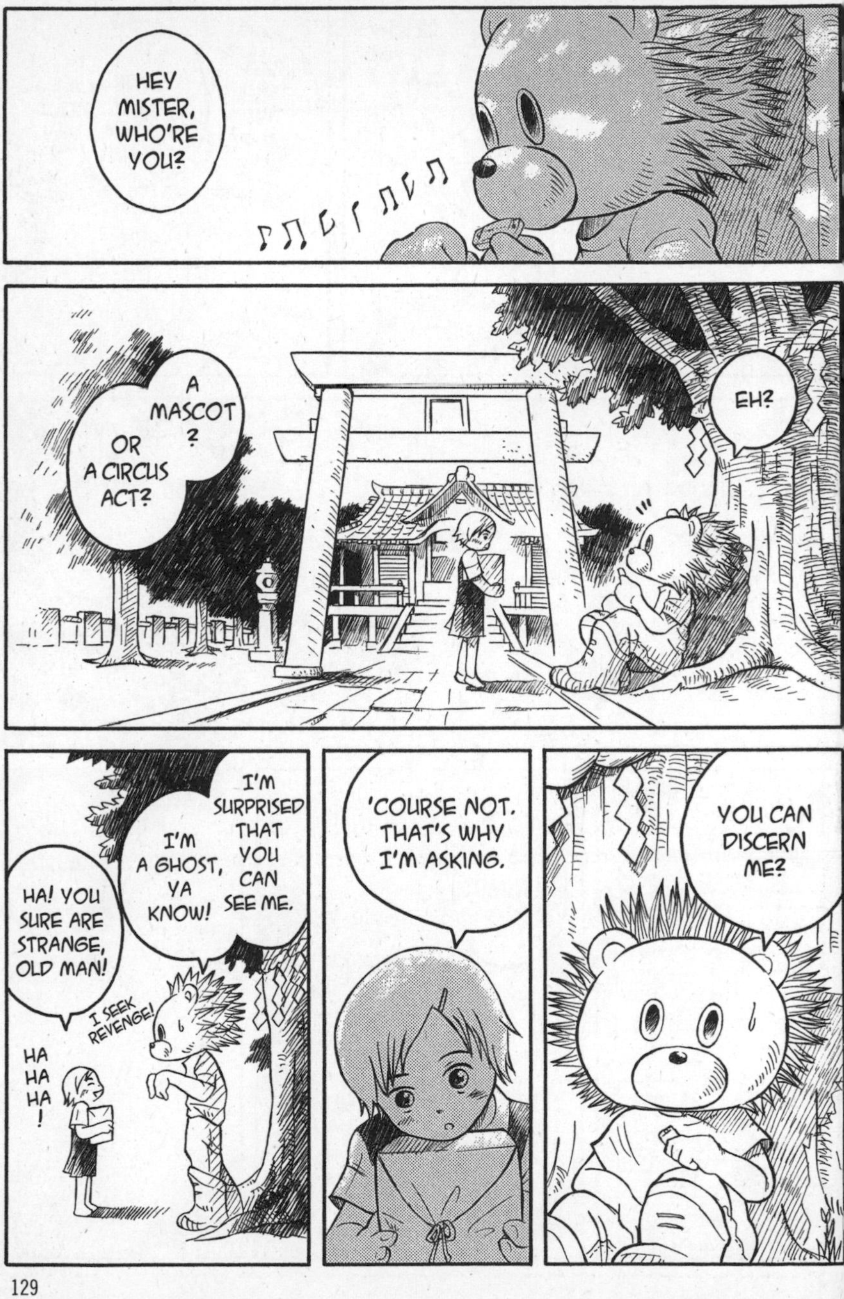
HEY MISTER, WHO'RE YOU?
EH?
A MASCOT?
OR A CIRCUS ACT?
YOU CAN DISCERN ME?
'COURSE NOT. THAT'S WHY I'M ASKING.
I'M SURPRISED THAT YOU CAN SEE ME.
I'M A GHOST, YA KNOW!
HA! YOU SURE ARE STRANGE, OLD MAN!
I SEEK REVENGE!
HA HA HA!

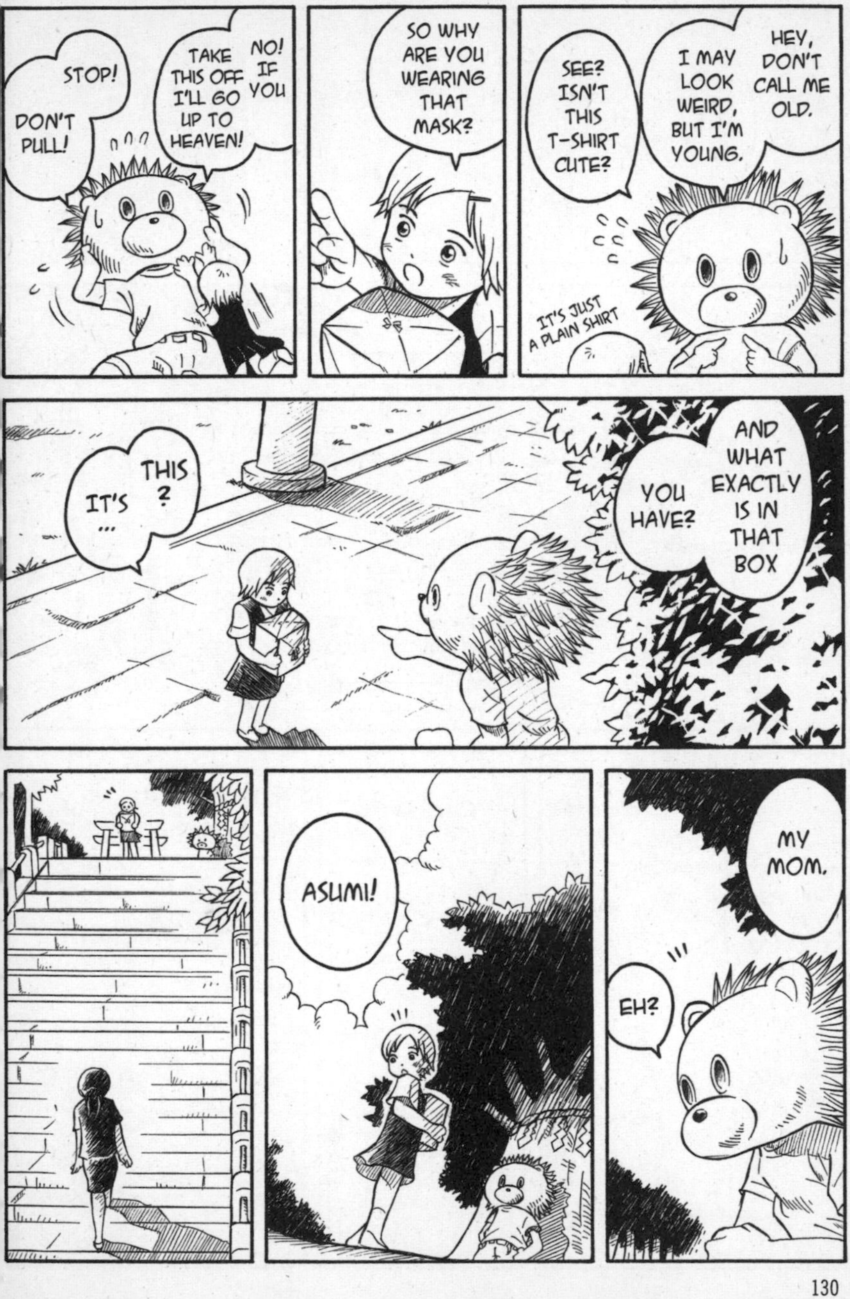
HEY, DON'T CALL ME OLD.
I MAY LOOK WEIRD, BUT I'M YOUNG.
SEE? ISN'T THIS T-SHIRT CUTE?
IT'S JUST A PLAIN SHIRT
SO WHY ARE YOU WEARING THAT MASK?
NO! IF YOU TAKE THIS OFF I'LL GO UP TO HEAVEN!
STOP!
DON'T PULL!
AND WHAT EXACTLY IS IN THAT BOX YOU HAVE?
THIS?
IT'S...
MY MOM.
EH?
ASUMI!

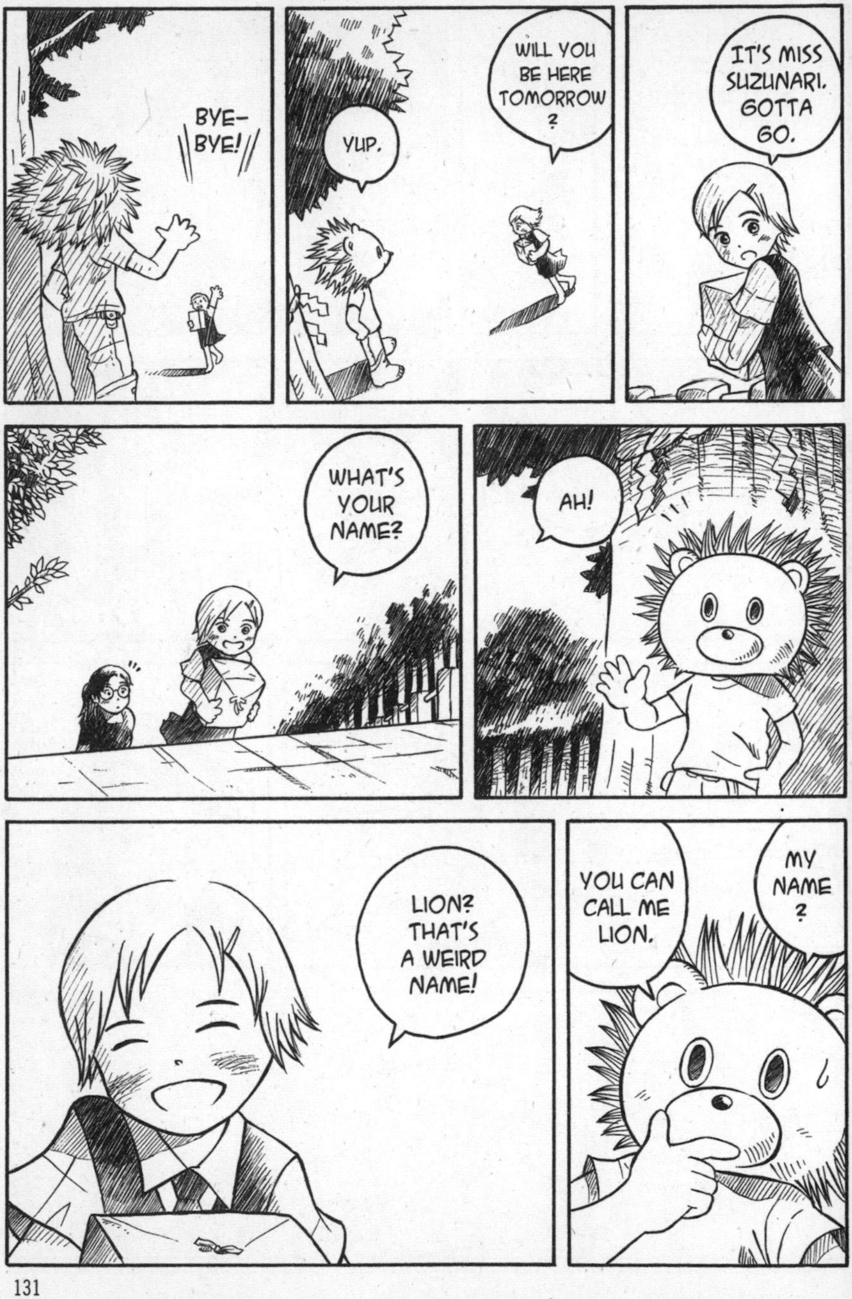
IT'S MISS SUZUNARI. GOTTA GO.
WILL YOU BE HERE TOMORROW?
YUP.
BYE-BYE!
AH!
WHAT'S YOUR NAME?
MY NAME?
YOU CAN CALL ME LION.
LION? THAT'S A WEIRD NAME!

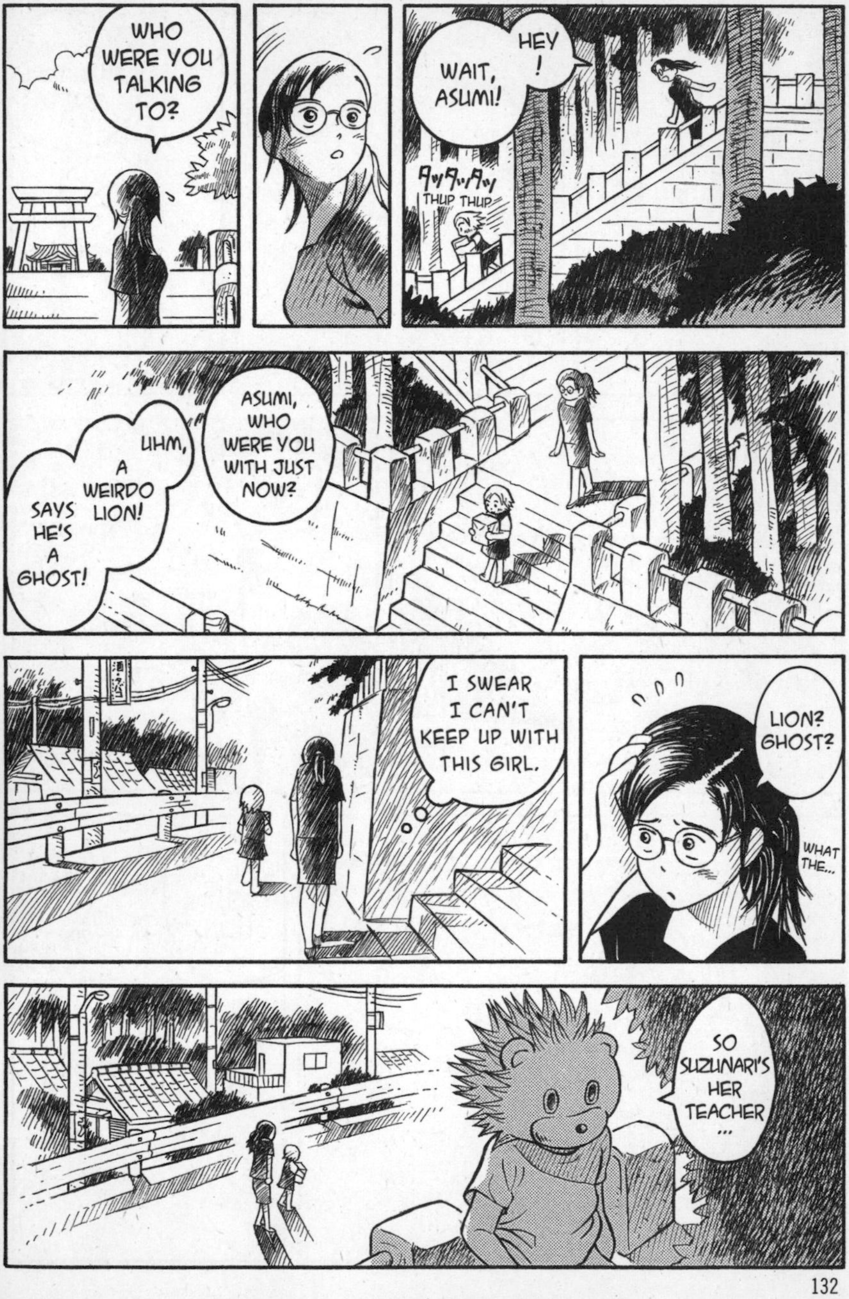
HEY! WAIT, ASUMI!
タッタッタッ
THUP THUP
WHO WERE YOU TALKING TO?
ASUMI, WHO WERE YOU WITH JUST NOW?
UHM, A WEIRDO LION! SAYS HE'S A GHOST!
LION? GHOST?
WHAT THE...
I SWEAR I CAN'T KEEP UP WITH THIS GIRL.
SO SUZUNARI'S HER TEACHER ...

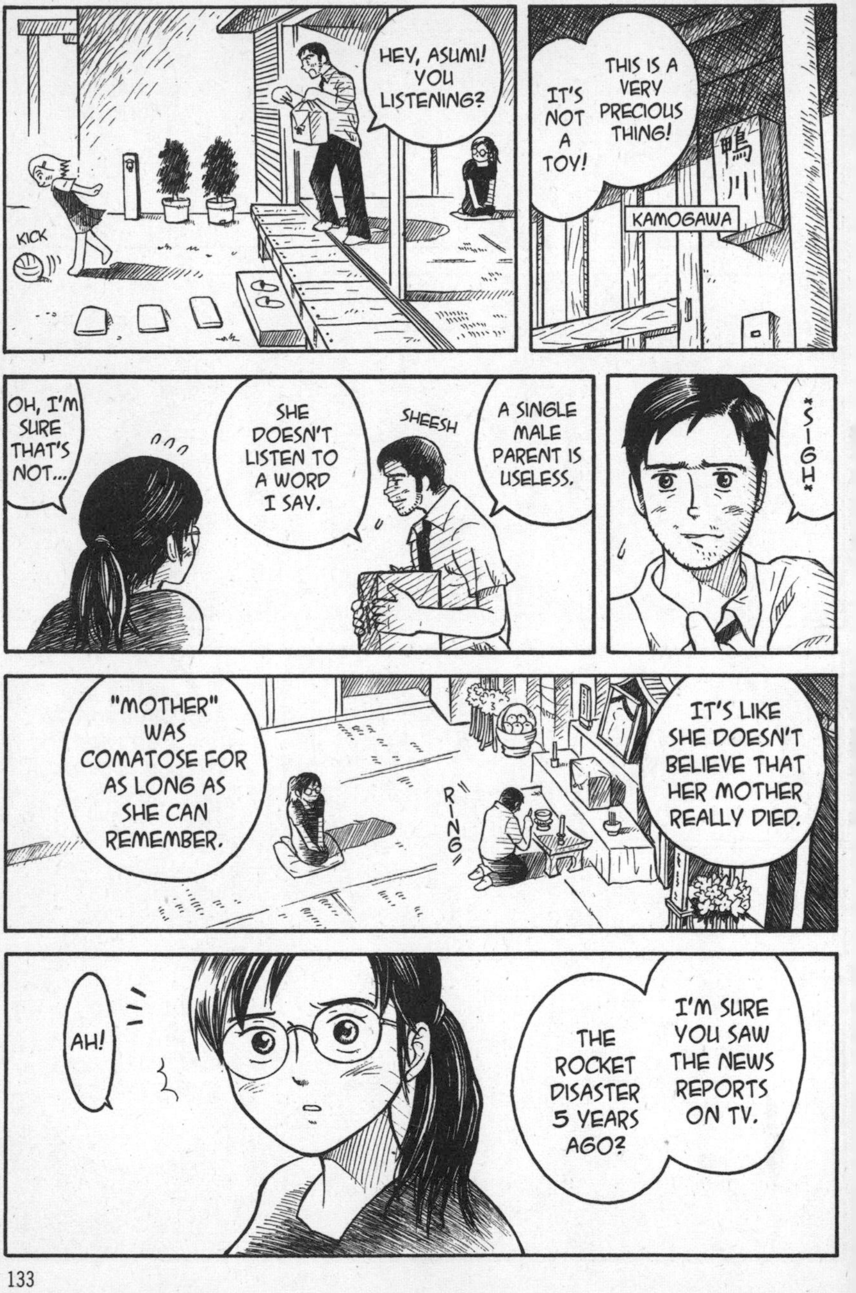
THIS IS A VERY PRECIOUS THING!
IT'S NOT A TOY!
鴨川
KAMOGAWA
HEY, ASUMI! YOU LISTENING?
KICK
SIGH
A SINGLE MALE PARENT IS USELESS.
SHEESH
SHE DOESN'T LISTEN TO A WORD I SAY.
OH, I'M SURE THAT'S NOT...
IT'S LIKE SHE DOESN'T BELIEVE THAT HER MOTHER REALLY DIED.
RING
"MOTHER" WAS COMATOSE FOR AS LONG AS SHE CAN REMEMBER.
I'M SURE YOU SAW THE NEWS REPORTS ON TV.
THE ROCKET DISASTER 5 YEARS AGO?
AH!

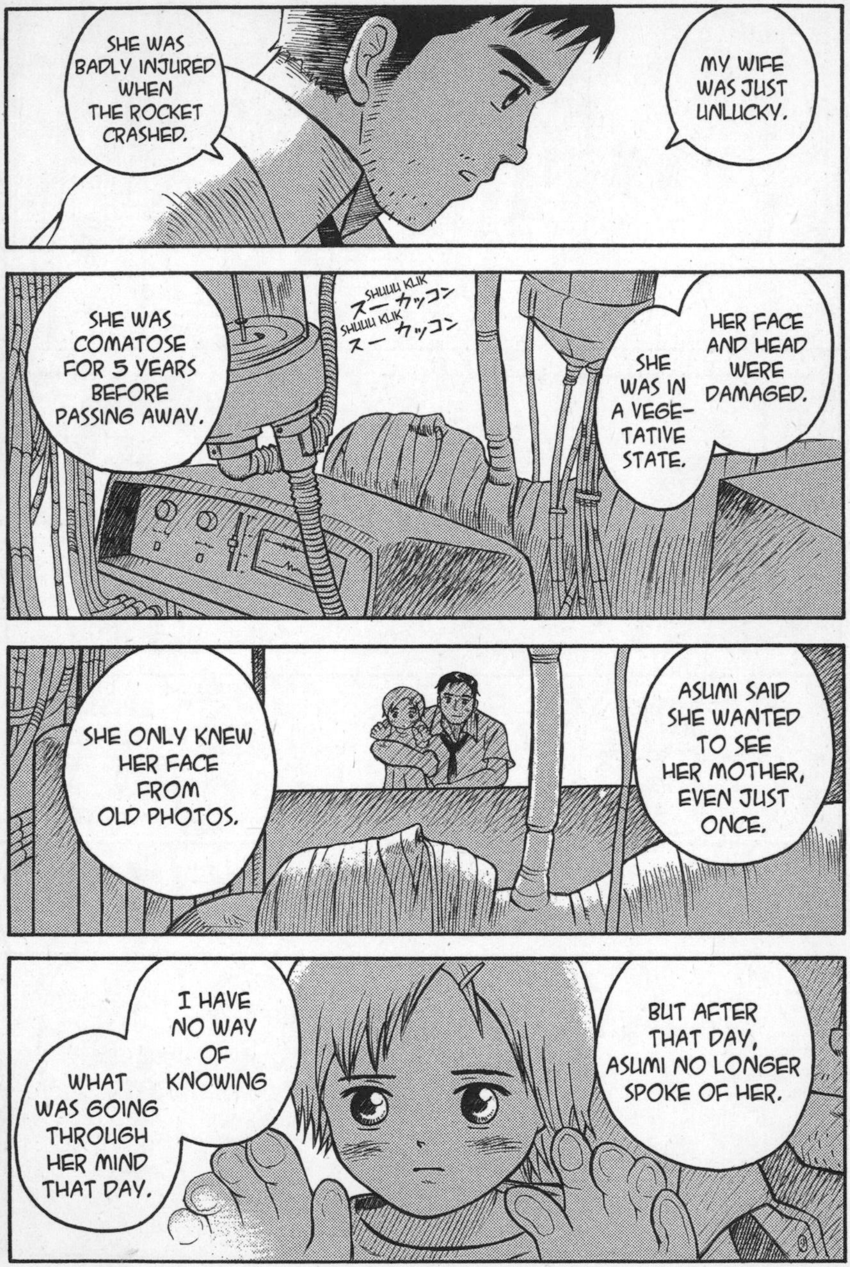
MY WIFE WAS JUST UNLUCKY.
SHE WAS BADLY INJURED WHEN THE ROCKET CRASHED.
HER FACE AND HEAD WERE DAMAGED.
SHE WAS IN A VEGE-TATIVE STATE.
SHUUU KLIK スーカッコン
SHUUU KLIK スーカッコン
SHE WAS COMATOSE FOR 5 YEARS BEFORE PASSING AWAY.
ASUMI SAID SHE WANTED TO SEE HER MOTHER, EVEN JUST ONCE.
SHE ONLY KNEW HER FACE FROM OLD PHOTOS.
BUT AFTER THAT DAY, ASUMI NO LONGER SPOKE OF HER.
I HAVE NO WAY OF KNOWING
WHAT WAS GOING THROUGH HER MIND THAT DAY.

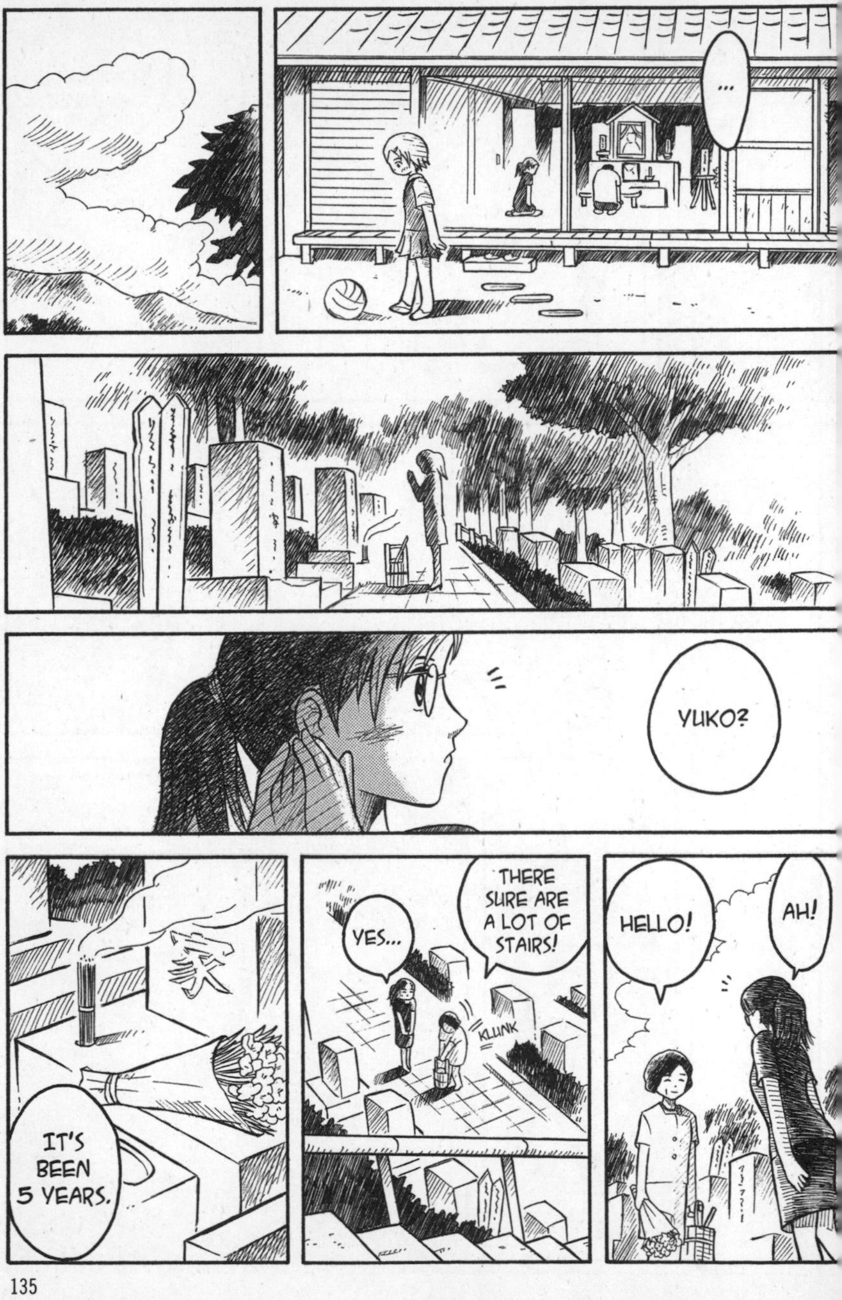
...
YUKO?
AH!
HELLO!
THERE SURE ARE A LOT OF STAIRS!
YES...
KLUNK
IT'S BEEN 5 YEARS.

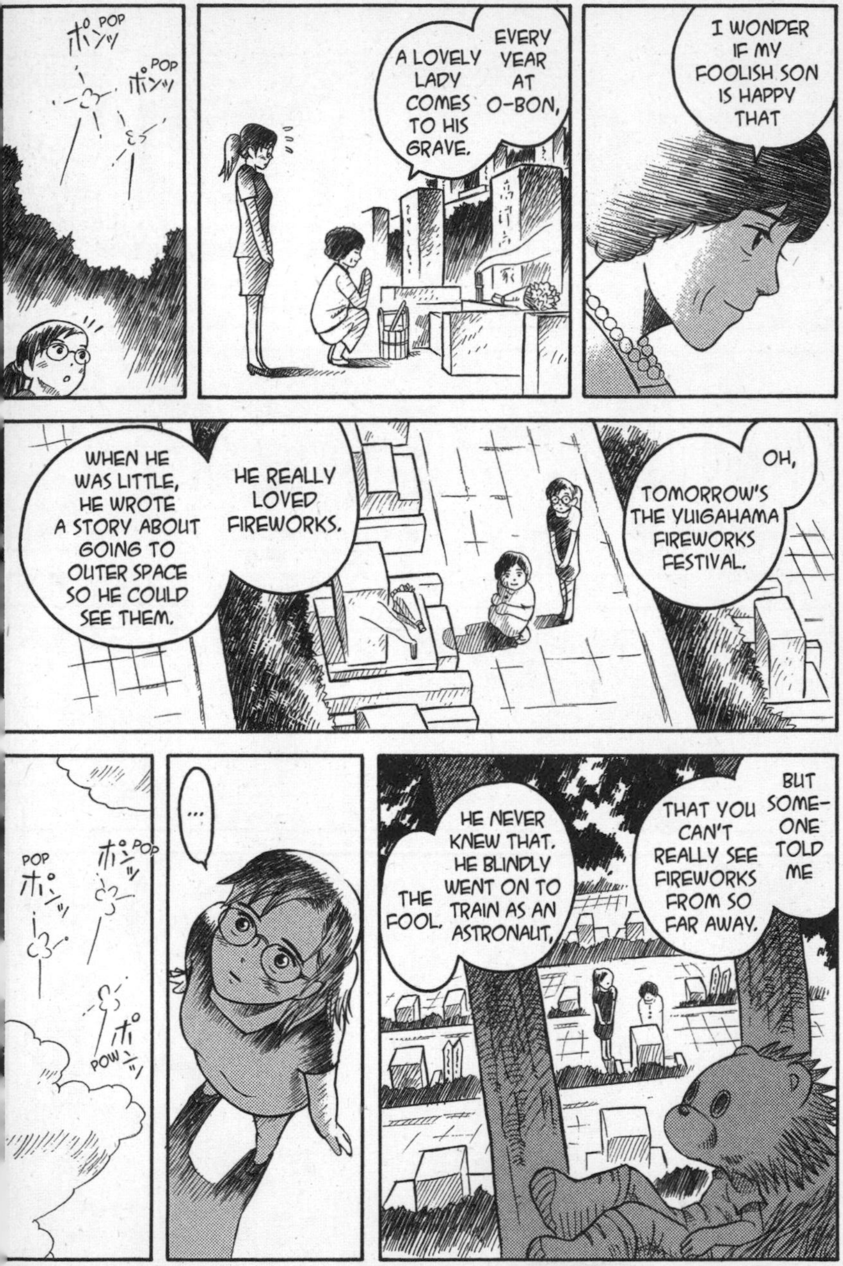

I WONDER IF MY FOOLISH SON IS HAPPY THAT
EVERY YEAR AT O-BON,
A LOVELY LADY COMES TO HIS GRAVE.
ポンッ POP
ポンッ POP
OH,
TOMORROW'S THE YUIGAHAMA FIREWORKS FESTIVAL.
HE REALLY LOVED FIREWORKS.
WHEN HE WAS LITTLE, HE WROTE A STORY ABOUT GOING TO OUTER SPACE SO HE COULD SEE THEM.
BUT SOMEONE TOLD ME
THAT YOU CAN'T REALLY SEE FIREWORKS FROM SO FAR AWAY.
HE NEVER KNEW THAT. HE BLINDLY WENT ON TO TRAIN AS AN ASTRONAUT,
THE FOOL.
...
ポンッ POP
ポンッ POP
ポンッ POW

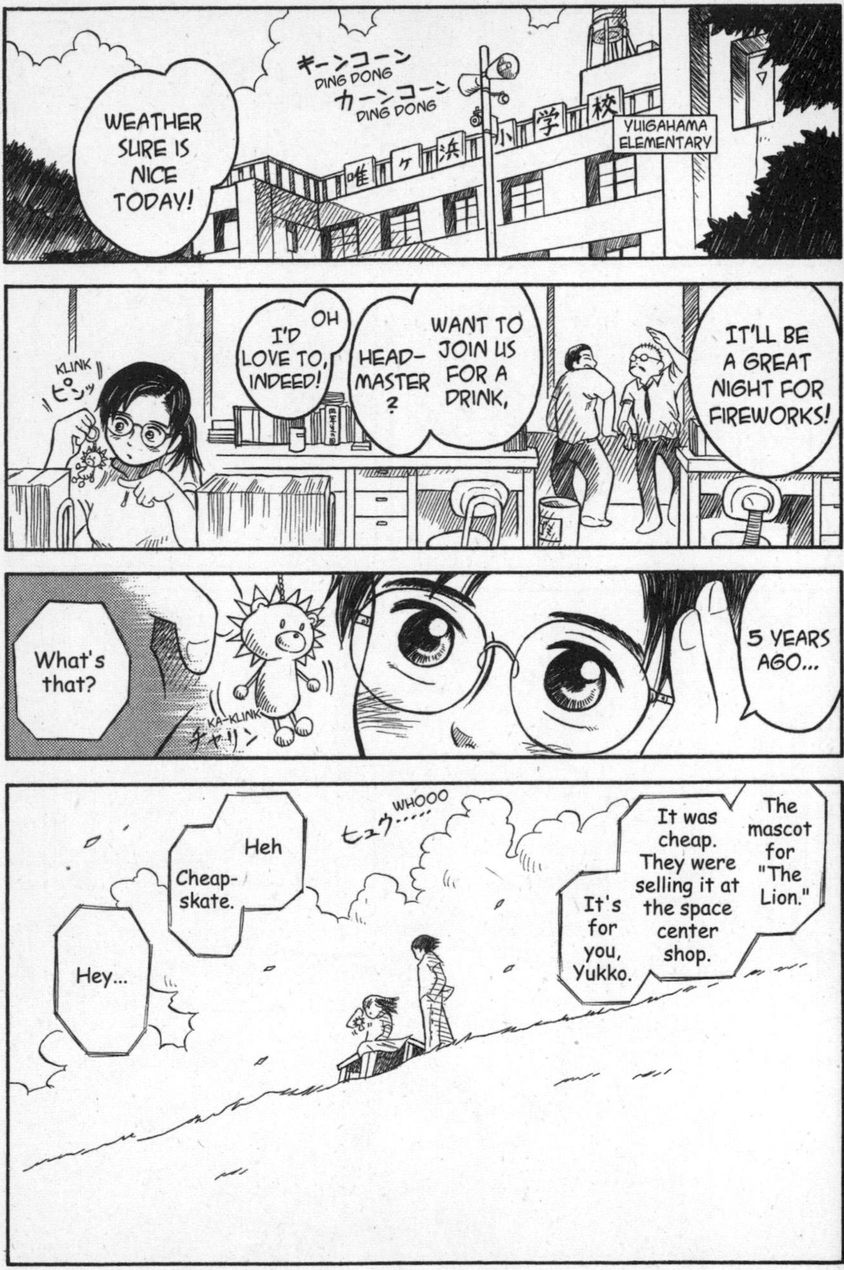
唯ケ浜小学校
YUIGAHAMA ELEMENTARY
キーンコーン
DING DONG
カーンコーン
DING DONG
WEATHER SURE IS NICE TODAY!
IT'LL BE A GREAT NIGHT FOR FIREWORKS!
WANT TO JOIN US FOR A DRINK, HEAD-MASTER?
OH I'D LOVE TO, INDEED!
KLINK
ピンッ
5 YEARS AGO...
KA-KLINK
チャリン
What's that?
The mascot for "The Lion."
It was cheap. They were selling it at the space center shop.
It's for you, Yukko.
WHOOO
ヒュウ……
Heh
Cheap-skate.
Hey...

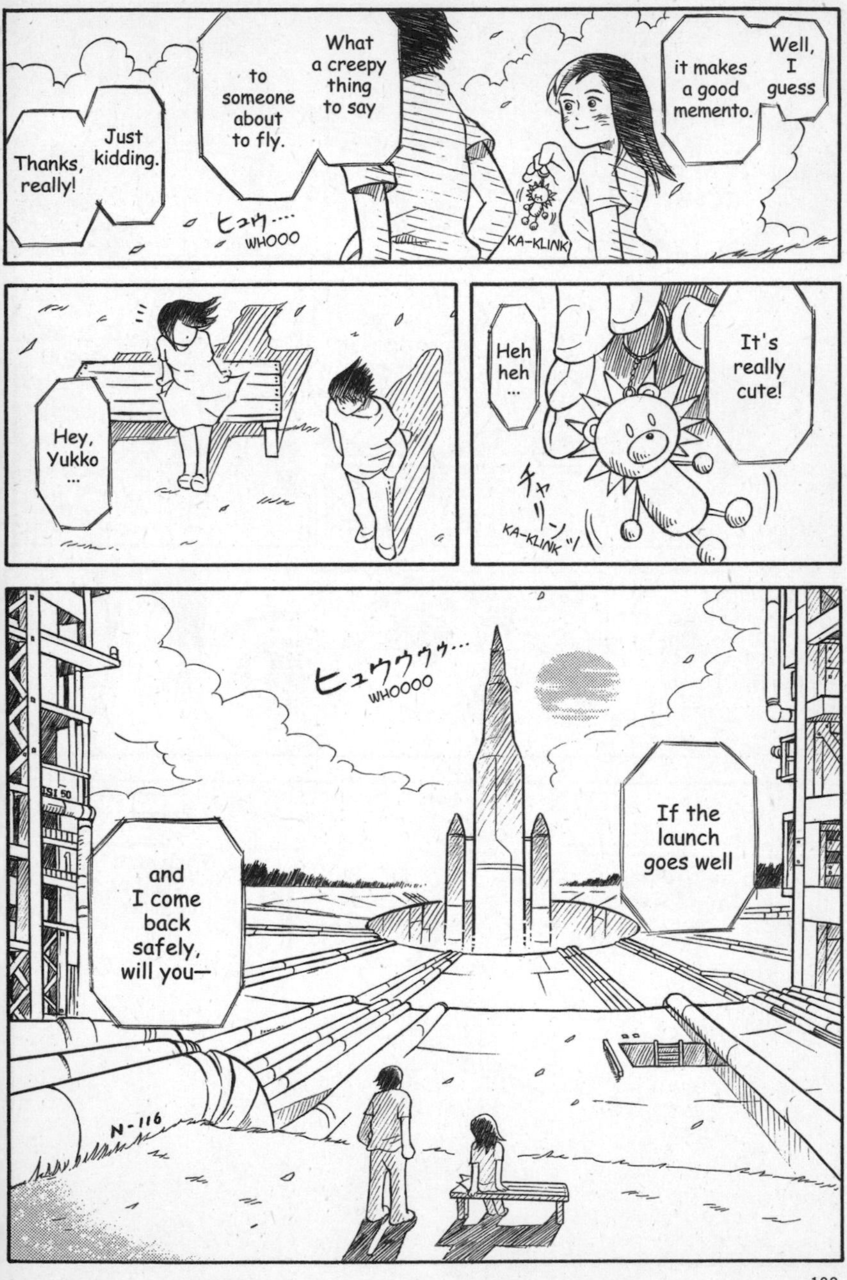
Well, I guess it makes a good memento.
What a creepy thing to say to someone about to fly.
Just kidding. Thanks, really!
KA-KLINK
ヒュウ….
WHOOO
It's really cute!
Heh heh …
チャリンッ
KA-KLINK
Hey, Yukko …
ヒュウウウウ…
WHOOOO
If the launch goes well
and I come back safely, will you—
N-116

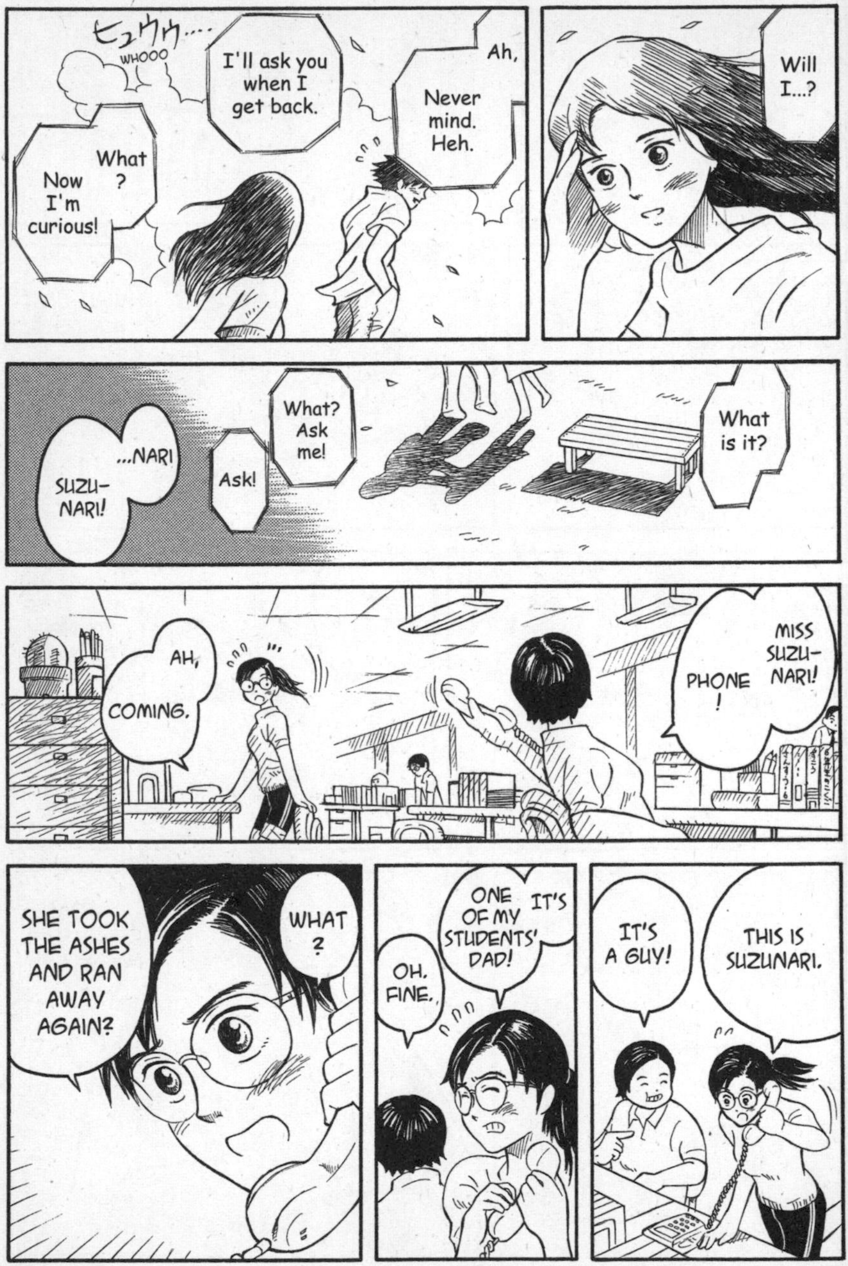
Will I...?
Ah, Never mind. Heh.
I'll ask you when I get back.
ヒュウゥ....
WHOOO
What? Now I'm curious!
What is it?
What? Ask me!
Ask!
...NARI SUZUNARI!
MISS SUZUNARI! PHONE!
AH, COMING.
THIS IS SUZUNARI.
IT'S A GUY!
IT'S ONE OF MY STUDENTS' DAD!
OH, FINE.
WHAT?
SHE TOOK THE ASHES AND RAN AWAY AGAIN?

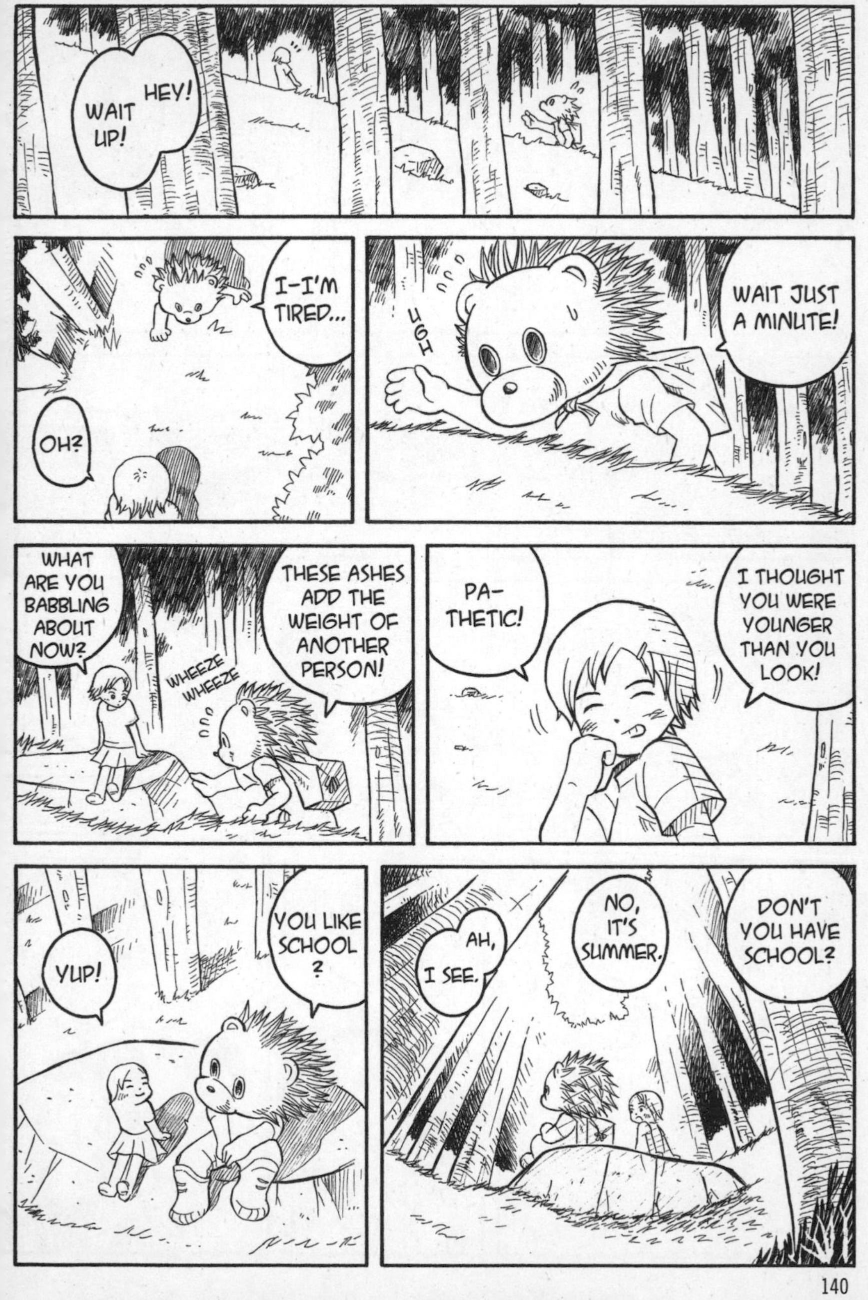
HEY! WAIT UP!
WAIT JUST A MINUTE!
UGH
I-I'M TIRED...
OH?
I THOUGHT YOU WERE YOUNGER THAN YOU LOOK!
PA-THETIC!
THESE ASHES ADD THE WEIGHT OF ANOTHER PERSON!
WHEEZE WHEEZE
WHAT ARE YOU BABBLING ABOUT NOW?
DON'T YOU HAVE SCHOOL?
NO, IT'S SUMMER.
AH, I SEE.
YOU LIKE SCHOOL?
YUP!

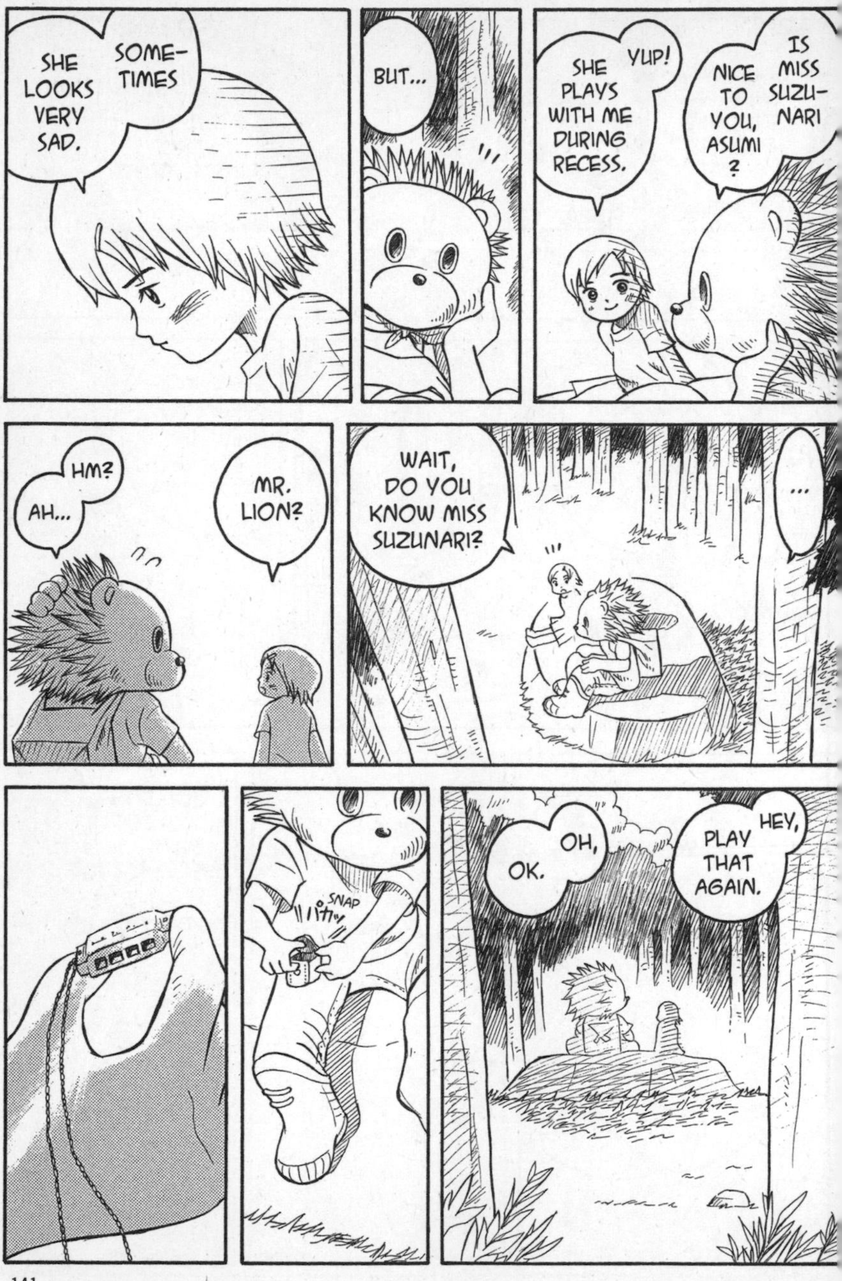
IS MISS SUZUNARI NICE TO YOU, ASUMI?
YUP! SHE PLAYS WITH ME DURING RECESS.
BUT...
SOMETIMES SHE LOOKS VERY SAD.
...
WAIT, DO YOU KNOW MISS SUZUNARI?
MR. LION?
HM? AH...
HEY, PLAY THAT AGAIN.
OH, OK.
SNAP
パチッ

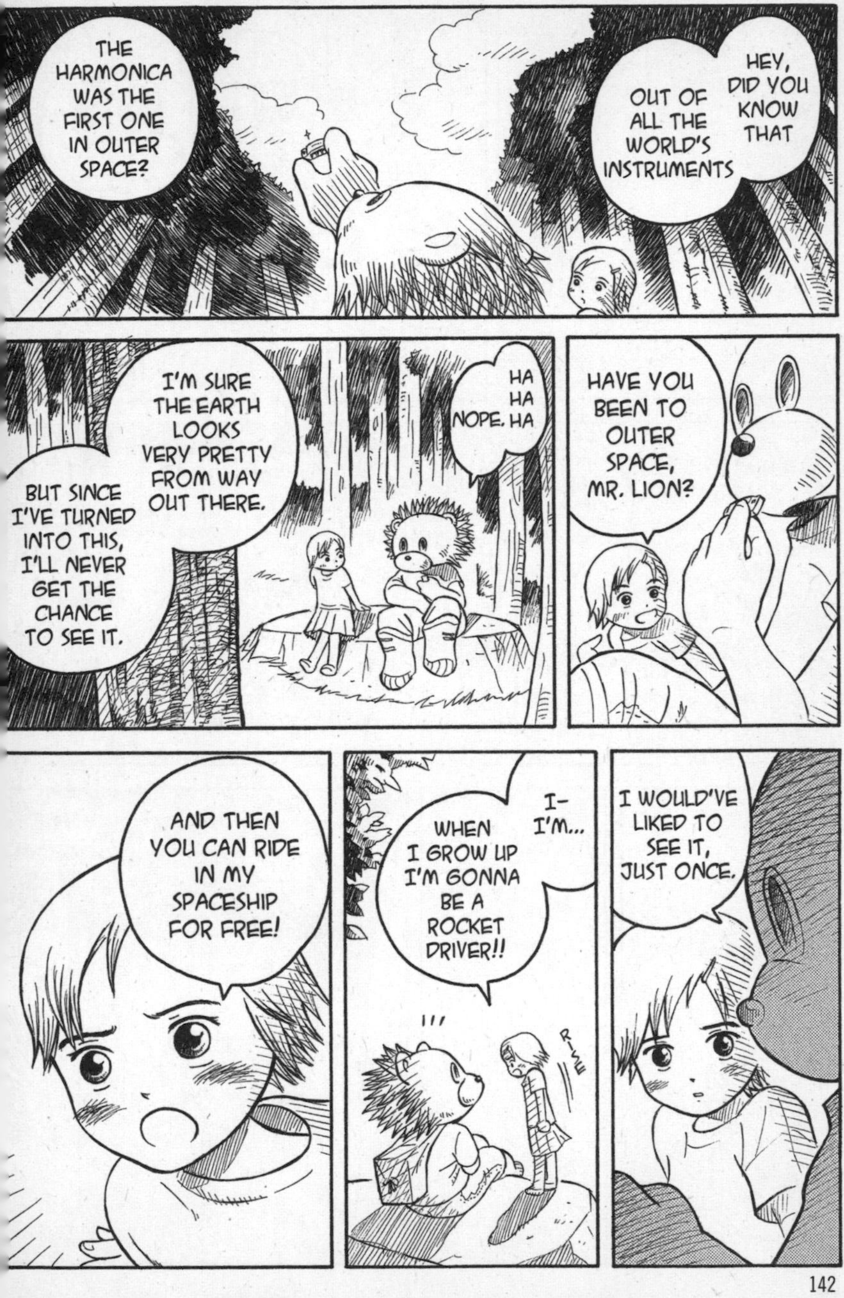
HEY, DID YOU KNOW THAT
OUT OF ALL THE WORLD'S INSTRUMENTS
THE HARMONICA WAS THE FIRST ONE IN OUTER SPACE?
HAVE YOU BEEN TO OUTER SPACE, MR. LION?
NOPE. HA HA HA
I'M SURE THE EARTH LOOKS VERY PRETTY FROM WAY OUT THERE.
BUT SINCE I'VE TURNED INTO THIS, I'LL NEVER GET THE CHANCE TO SEE IT.
I WOULD'VE LIKED TO SEE IT, JUST ONCE.
I- I'M...
WHEN I GROW UP I'M GONNA BE A ROCKET DRIVER!!
RISE
AND THEN YOU CAN RIDE IN MY SPACESHIP FOR FREE!

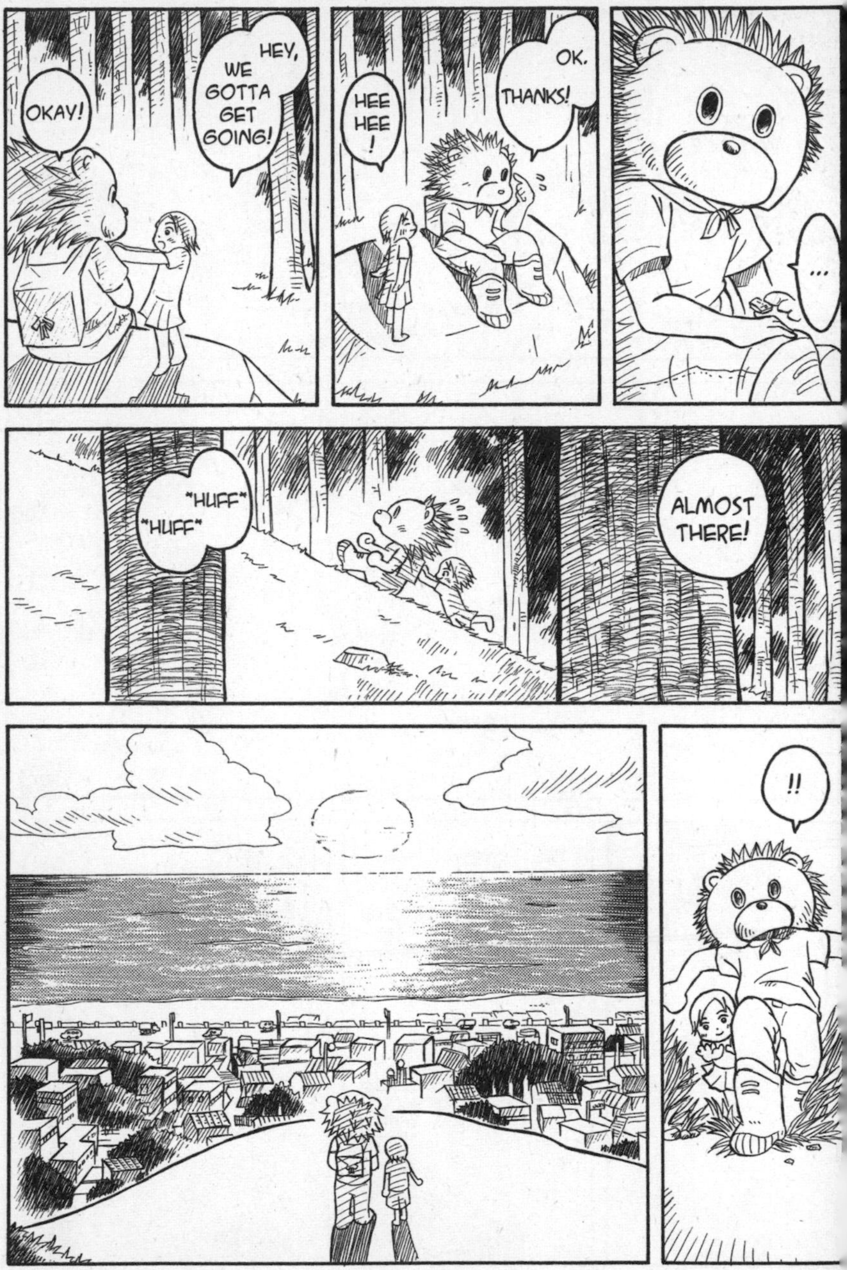
...
OK. THANKS!
HEE HEE!
HEY, WE GOTTA GET GOING!
OKAY!
ALMOST THERE!
HUFF *HUFF*
!!

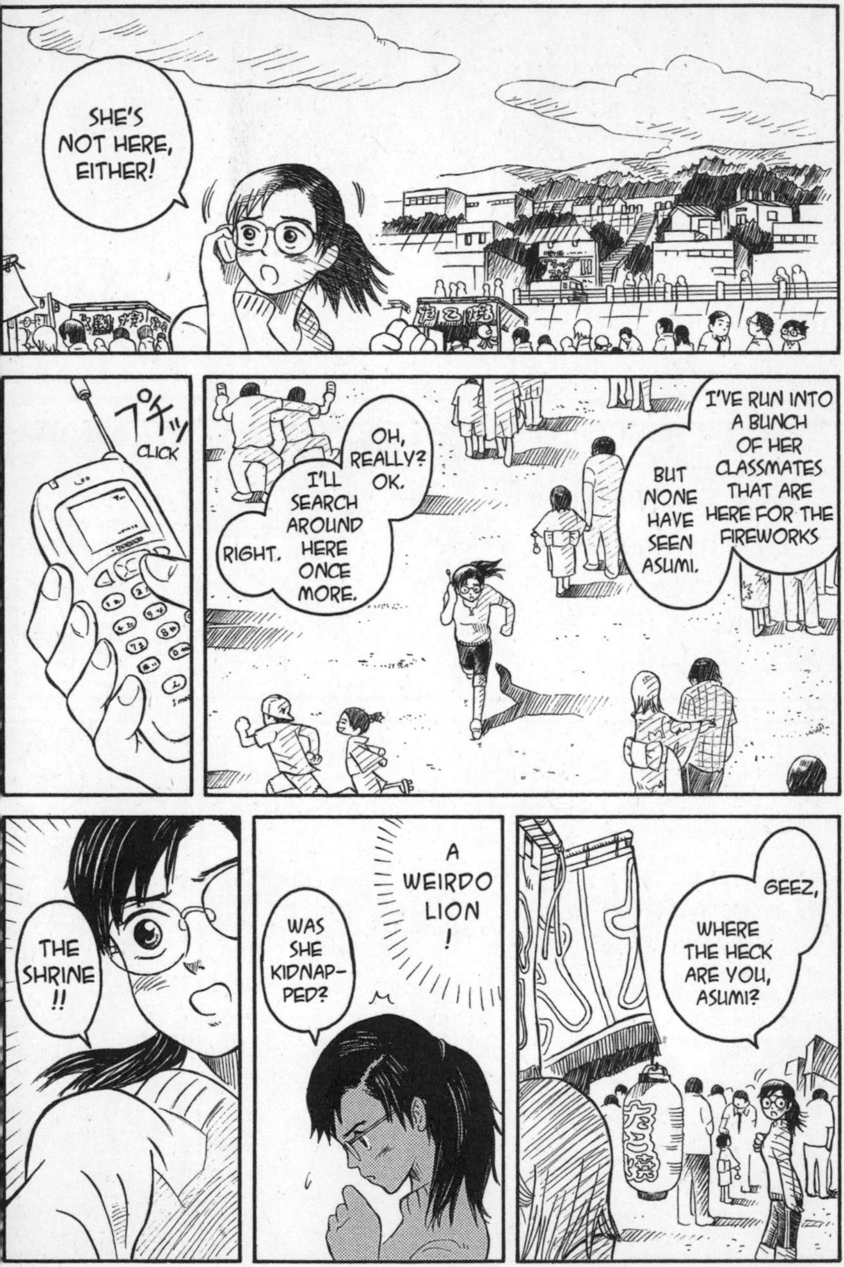
SHE'S NOT HERE, EITHER!
I'VE RUN INTO A BUNCH OF HER CLASSMATES THAT ARE HERE FOR THE FIREWORKS
BUT NONE HAVE SEEN ASUMI.
OH, REALLY? OK.
I'LL SEARCH AROUND HERE ONCE MORE.
RIGHT.
プチッ
CLICK
GEEZ,
WHERE THE HECK ARE YOU, ASUMI?
A WEIRDO LION!
WAS SHE KIDNAP-PED?
THE SHRINE!!

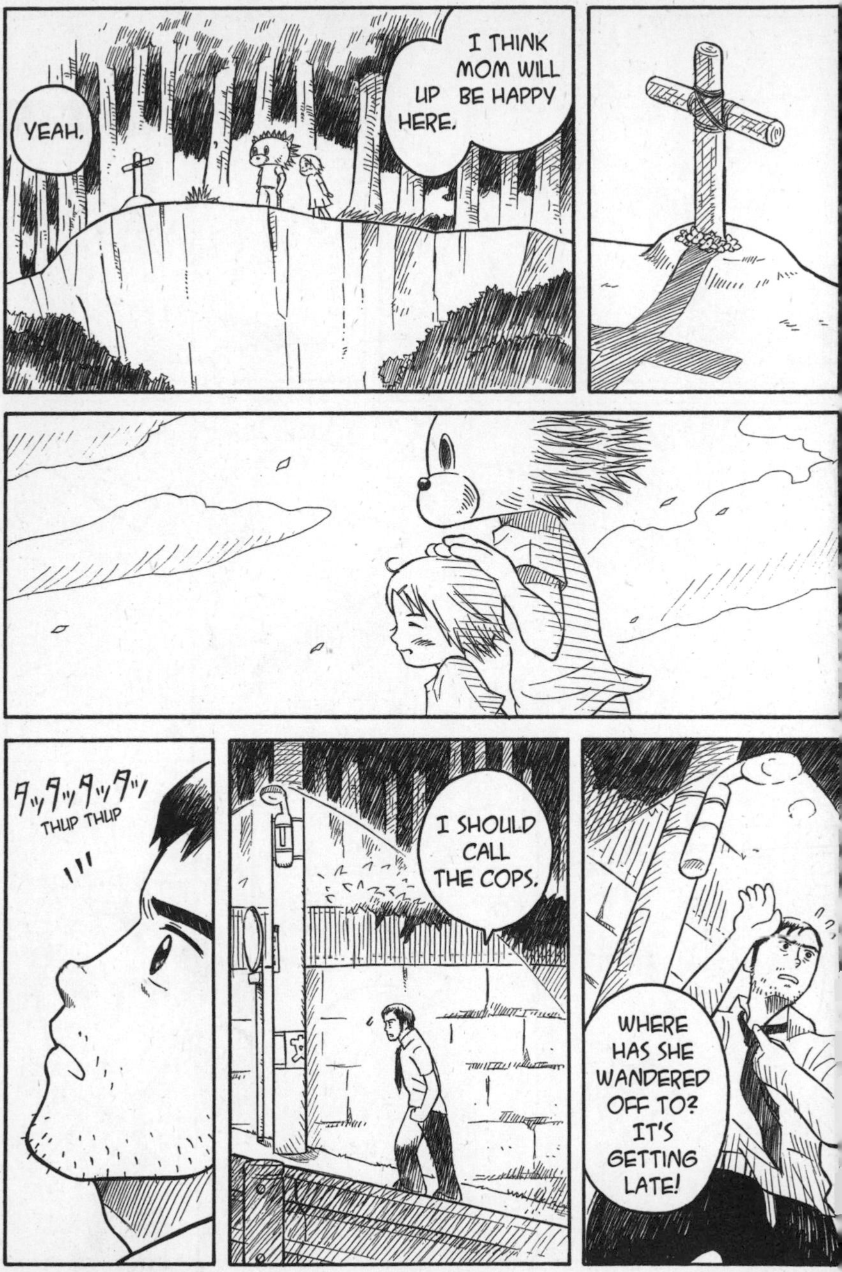
I THINK MOM WILL BE HAPPY UP HERE.
YEAH.
WHERE HAS SHE WANDERED OFF TO? IT'S GETTING LATE!
I SHOULD CALL THE COPS.
タッタッタッタッ
THUP THUP

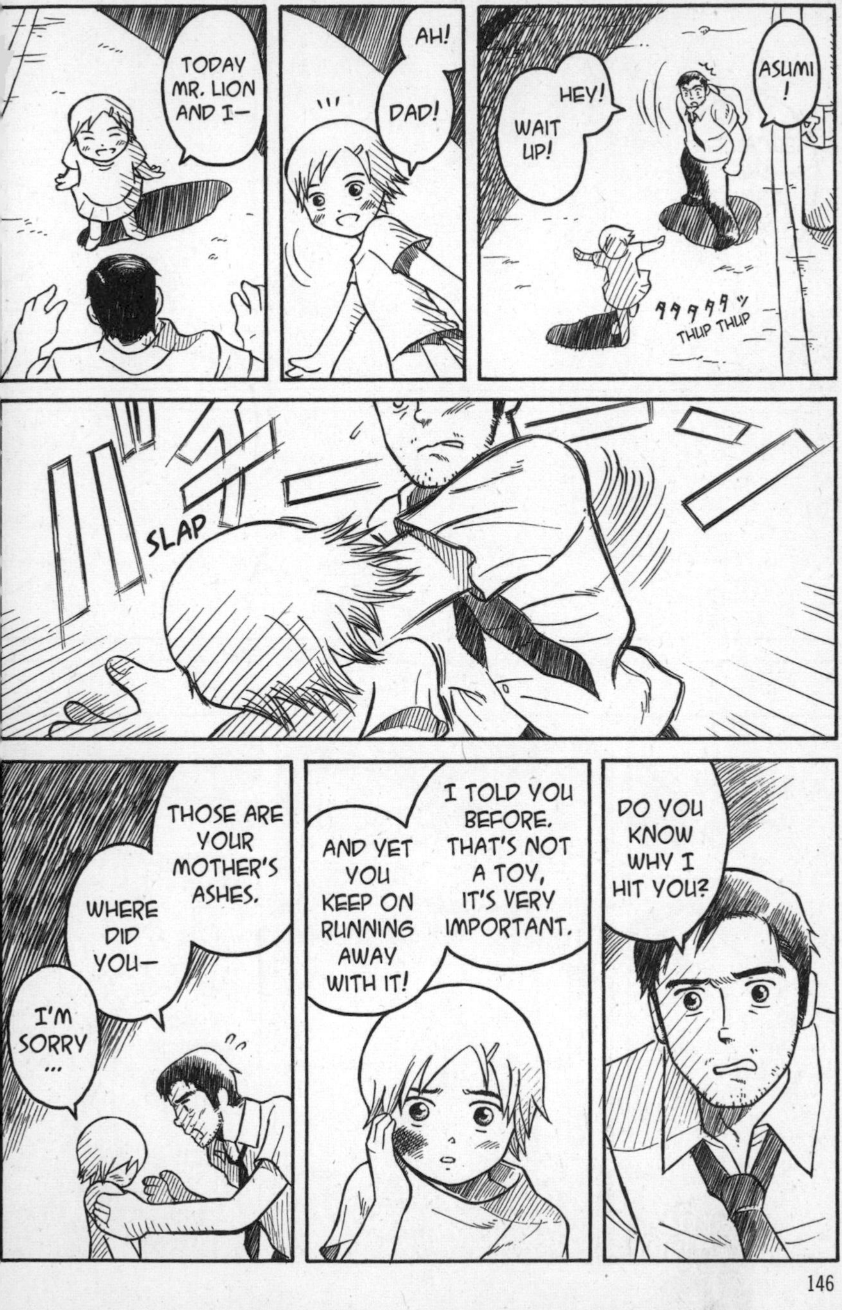
ASUMI!
HEY! WAIT UP!
タタタタッ THUP THUP
AH! DAD!
TODAY MR. LION AND I—
SLAP
DO YOU KNOW WHY I HIT YOU?
I TOLD YOU BEFORE. THAT'S NOT A TOY, IT'S VERY IMPORTANT.
AND YET YOU KEEP ON RUNNING AWAY WITH IT!
THOSE ARE YOUR MOTHER'S ASHES.
WHERE DID YOU—
I'M SORRY ...

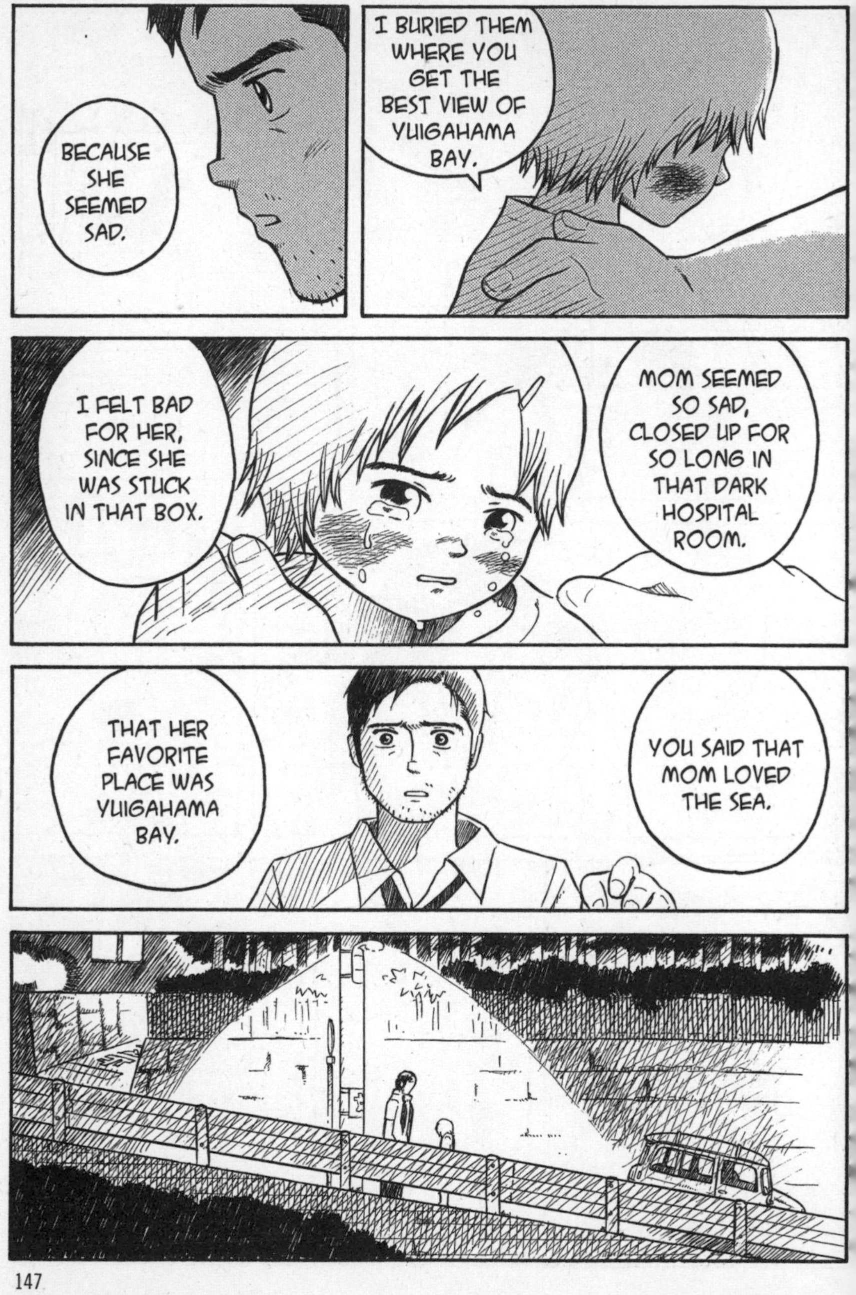
I BURIED THEM WHERE YOU GET THE BEST VIEW OF YUIGAHAMA BAY.
BECAUSE SHE SEEMED SAD.
MOM SEEMED SO SAD, CLOSED UP FOR SO LONG IN THAT DARK HOSPITAL ROOM.
I FELT BAD FOR HER, SINCE SHE WAS STUCK IN THAT BOX.
YOU SAID THAT MOM LOVED THE SEA.
THAT HER FAVORITE PLACE WAS YUIGAHAMA BAY.

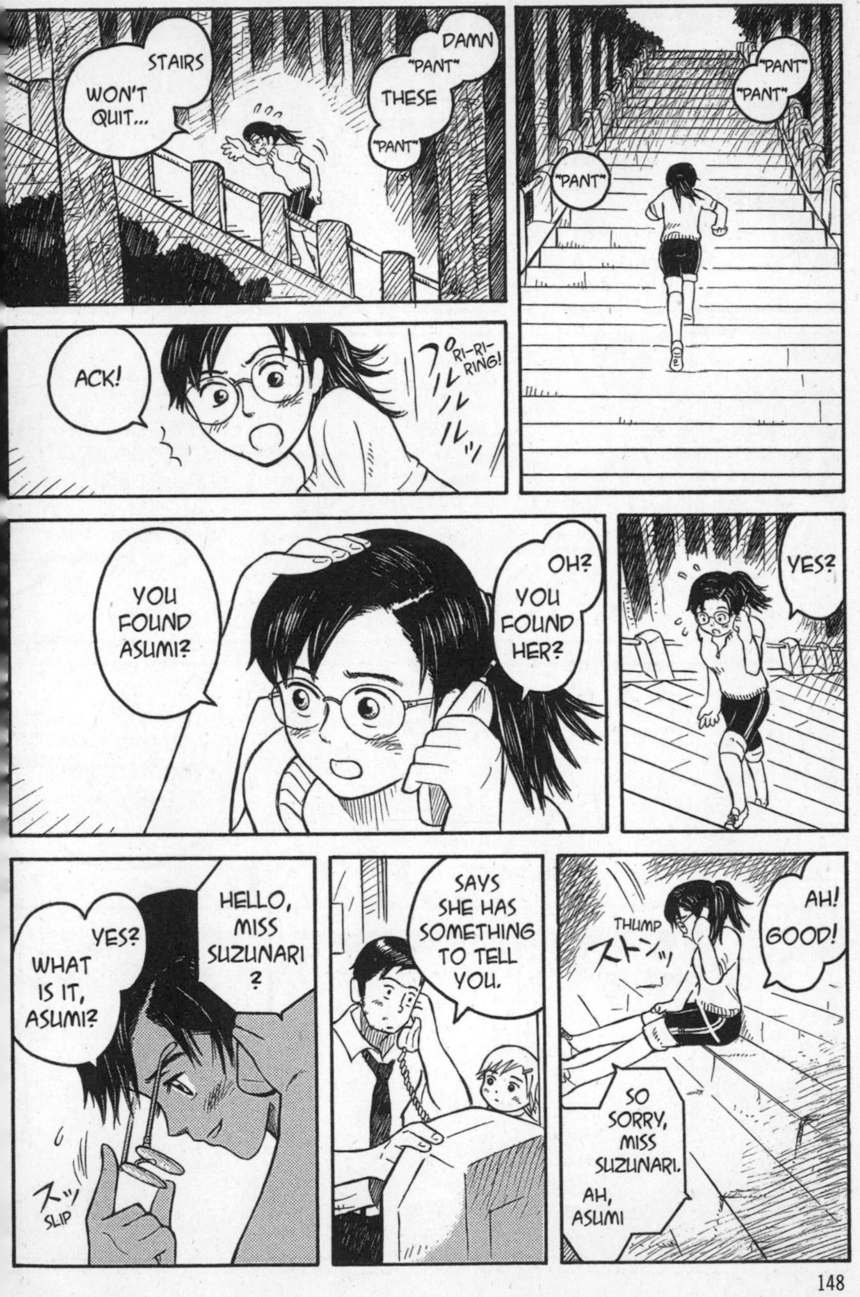
"PANT"
"PANT"
"PANT"
DAMN "PANT" THESE "PANT"
STAIRS WON'T QUIT...
RI-RI-RING!
ACK!
YES?
OH? YOU FOUND HER?
YOU FOUND ASUMI?
AH! GOOD!
THUMP
SO SORRY, MISS SUZUNARI.
AH, ASUMI
SAYS SHE HAS SOMETHING TO TELL YOU.
HELLO, MISS SUZUNARI?
YES? WHAT IS IT, ASUMI?
SLIP

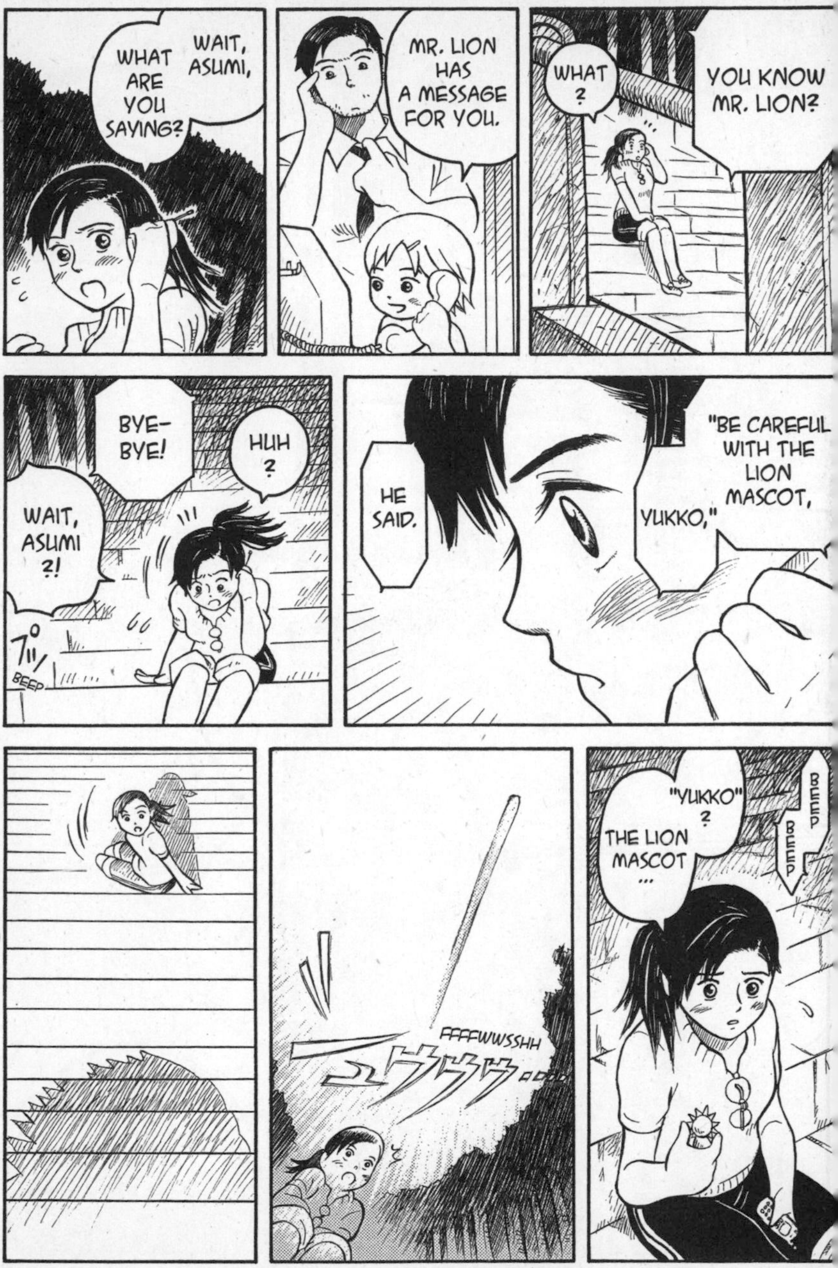
YOU KNOW MR. LION?
WHAT ?
MR. LION HAS A MESSAGE FOR YOU.
WAIT, ASUMI,
WHAT ARE YOU SAYING?
"BE CAREFUL WITH THE LION MASCOT, YUKKO,"
HE SAID.
HUH ?
BYE-BYE!
WAIT, ASUMI ?!
BEEP
BEEP BEEP BEEP
"YUKKO" ?
THE LION MASCOT ...
FFFFWWSSHH

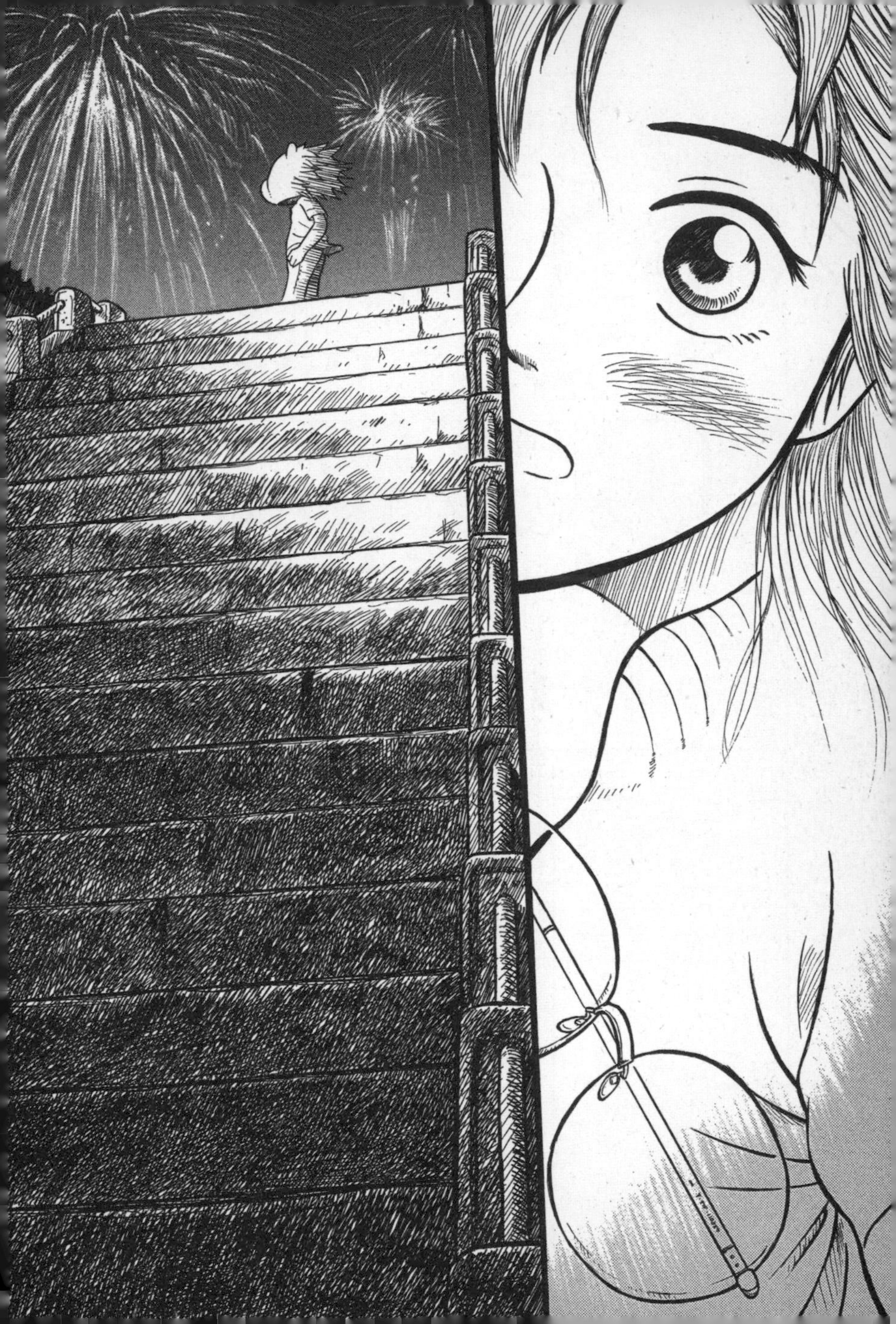

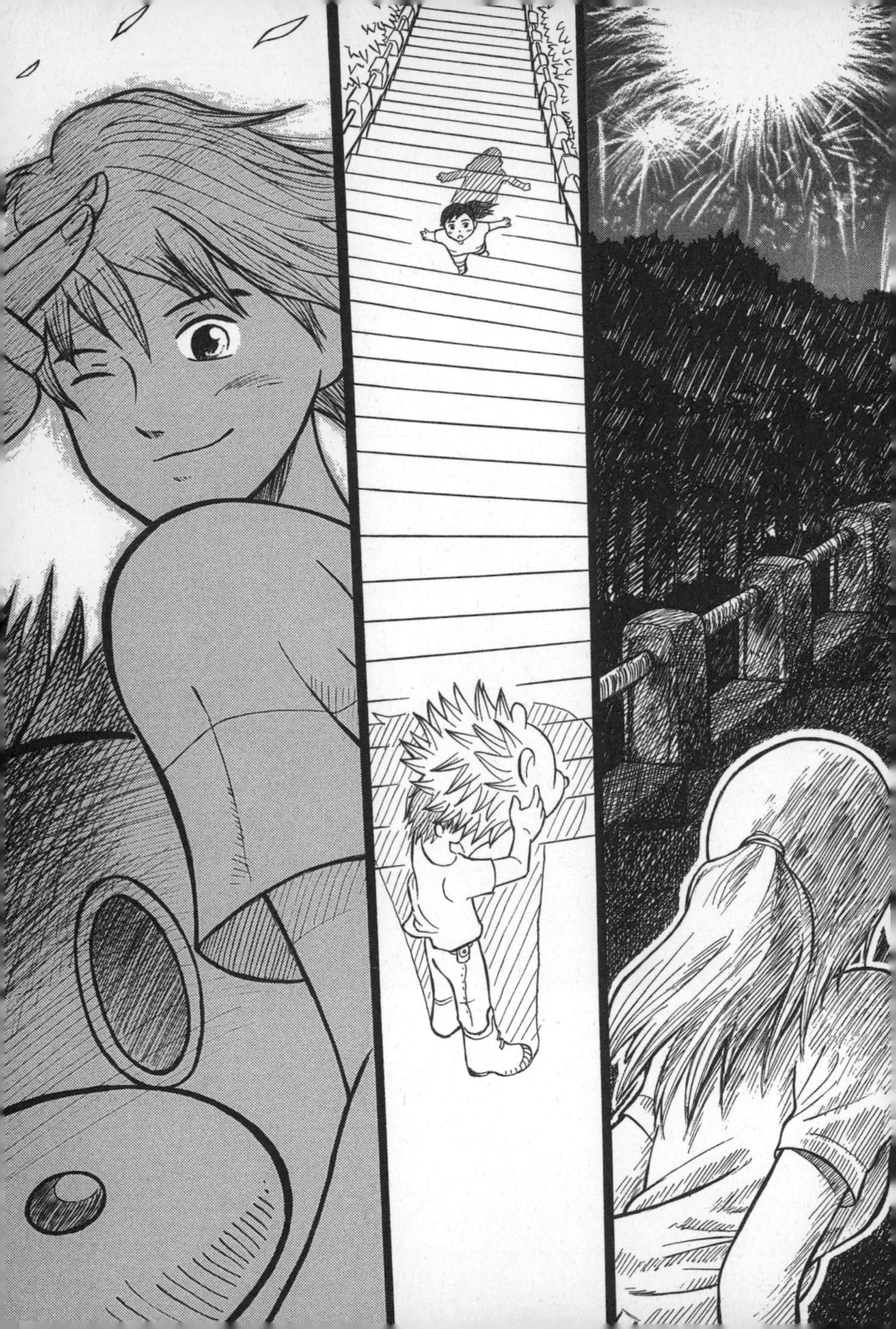

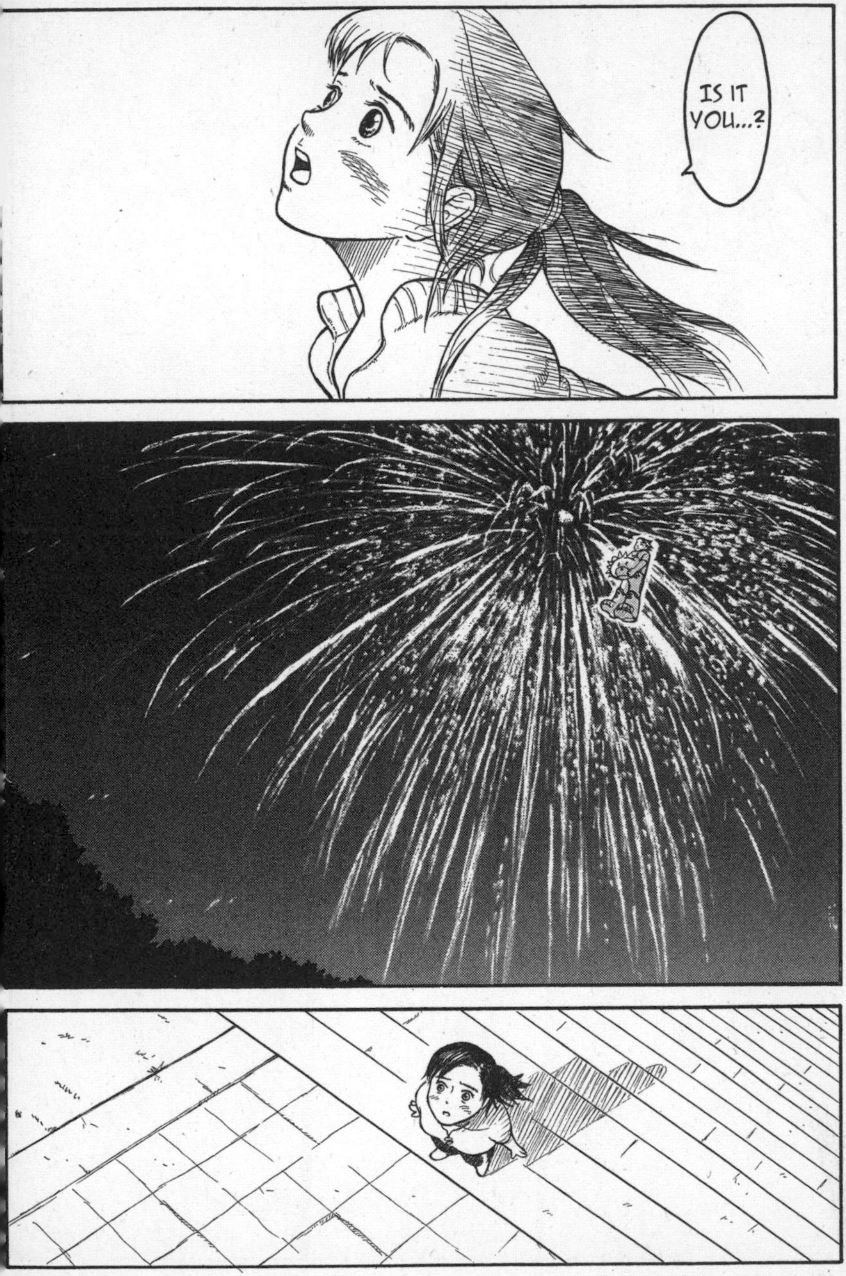
IS IT YOU...?

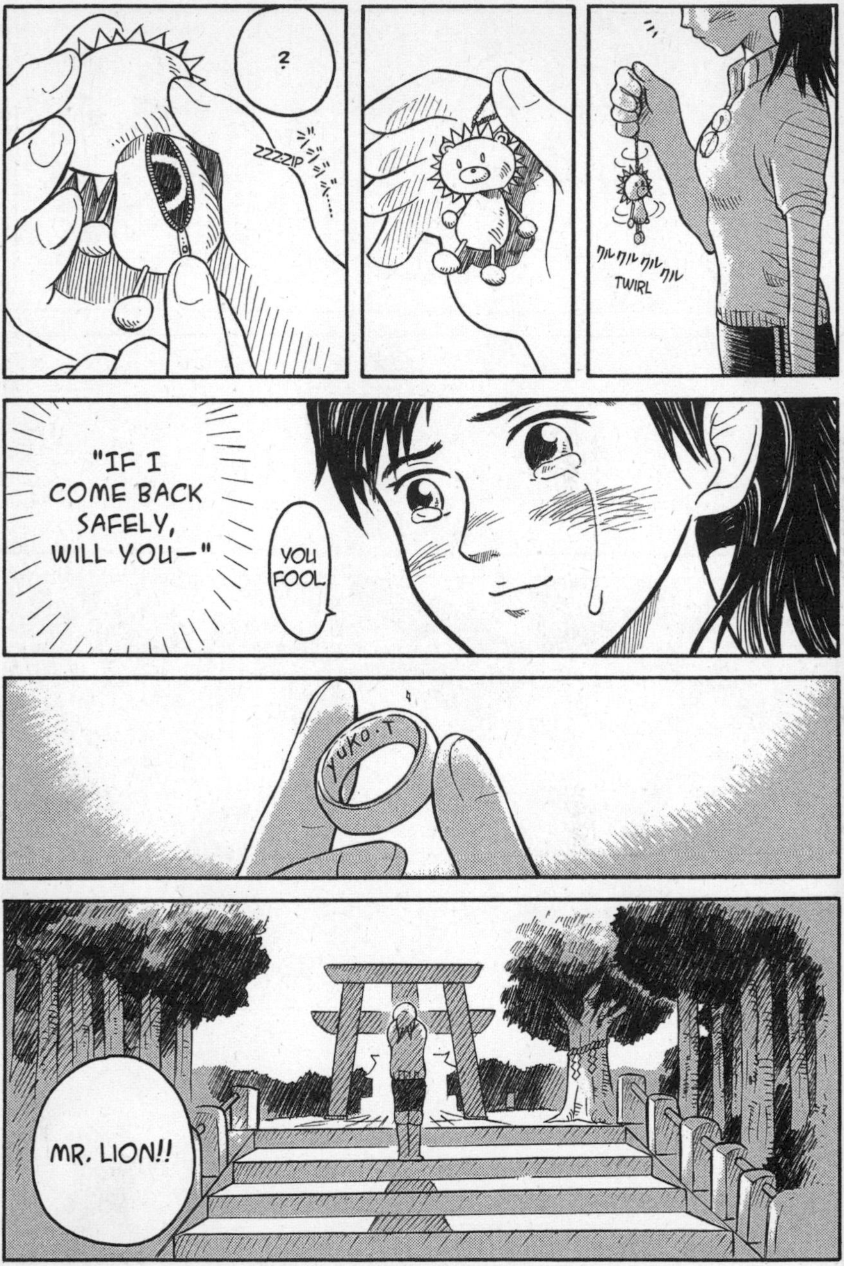

クルクルクルクル
TWIRL
?
ZZZZIP
YOU FOOL.
"IF I COME BACK SAFELY, WILL YOU—"
yuko.T
MR. LION!!

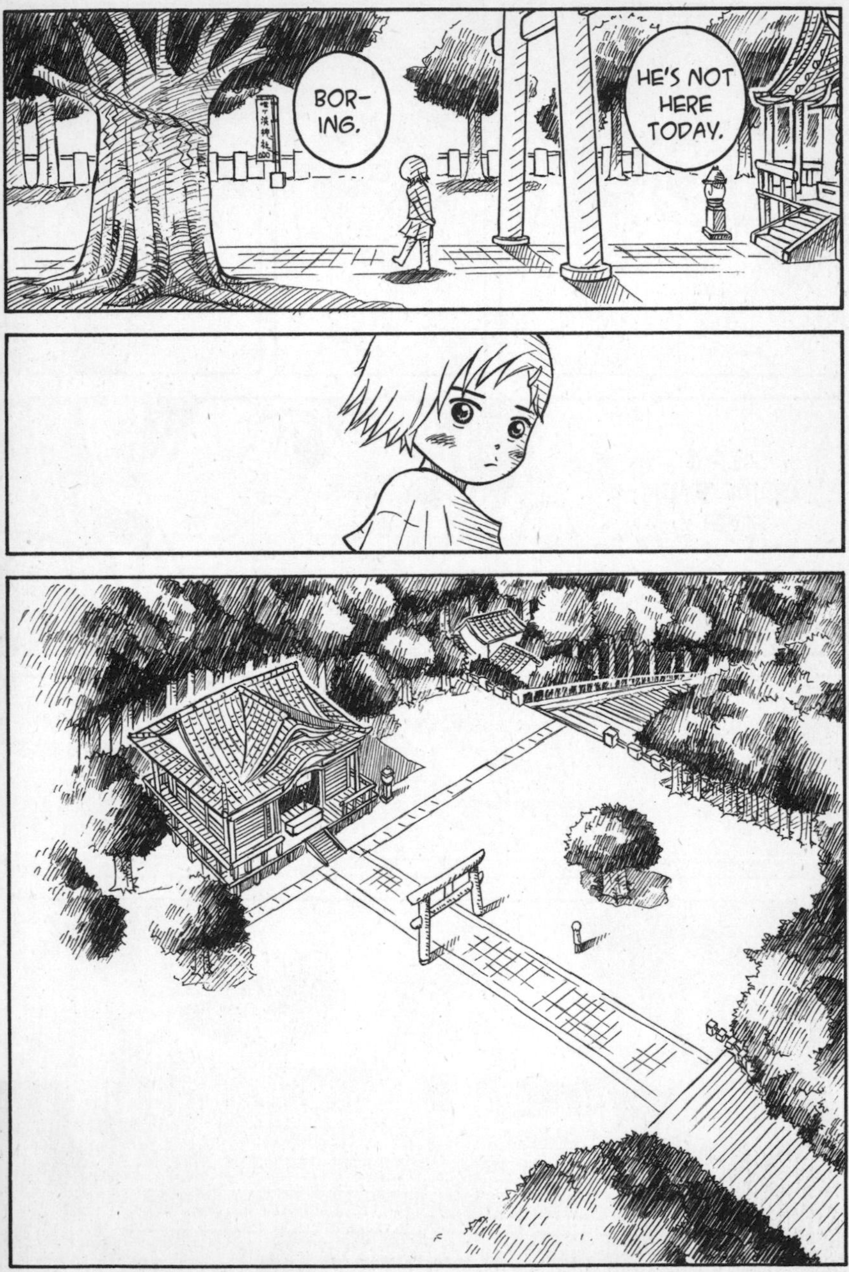
HE'S NOT HERE TODAY.
BOR-ING.

"2015: FIREWORKS" —THE END

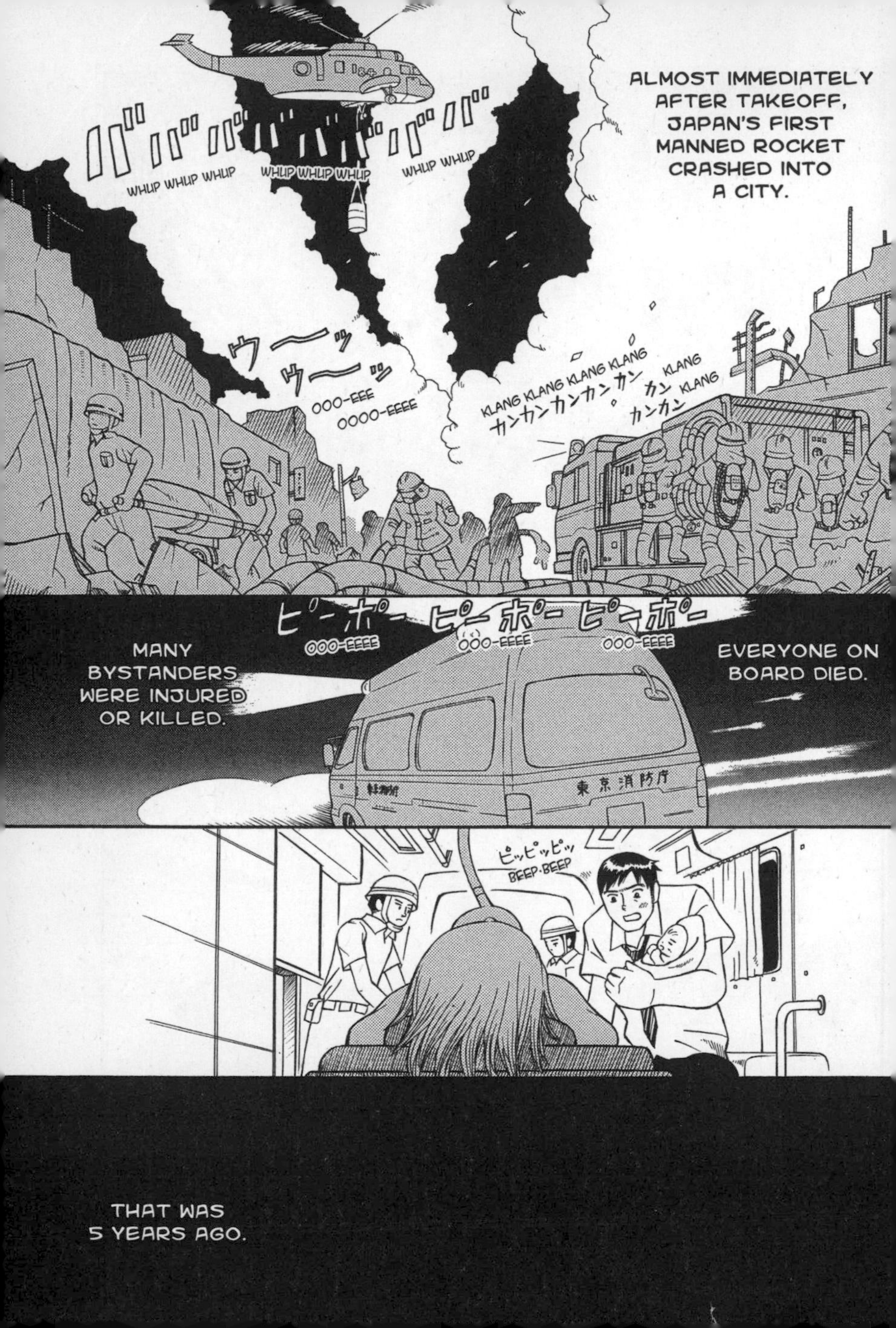
ALMOST IMMEDIATELY AFTER TAKEOFF, JAPAN'S FIRST MANNED ROCKET CRASHED INTO A CITY.
WHUP WHUP
WHUP WHUP WHUP
WHUP WHUP WHUP
カンカン KLANG
カン KLANG
カンカンカンカンカン KLANG KLANG KLANG KLANG
ウーッ ウーッ
OOO-EEE
OOOO-EEEE
EVERYONE ON BOARD DIED.
ピーポー ピーポー ピーポー
OOO-EEEE
OOO-EEEE
OOO-EEEE
MANY BYSTANDERS WERE INJURED OR KILLED.
東京消防庁
ピッピッピッ
BEEP·BEEP
THAT WAS 5 YEARS AGO.

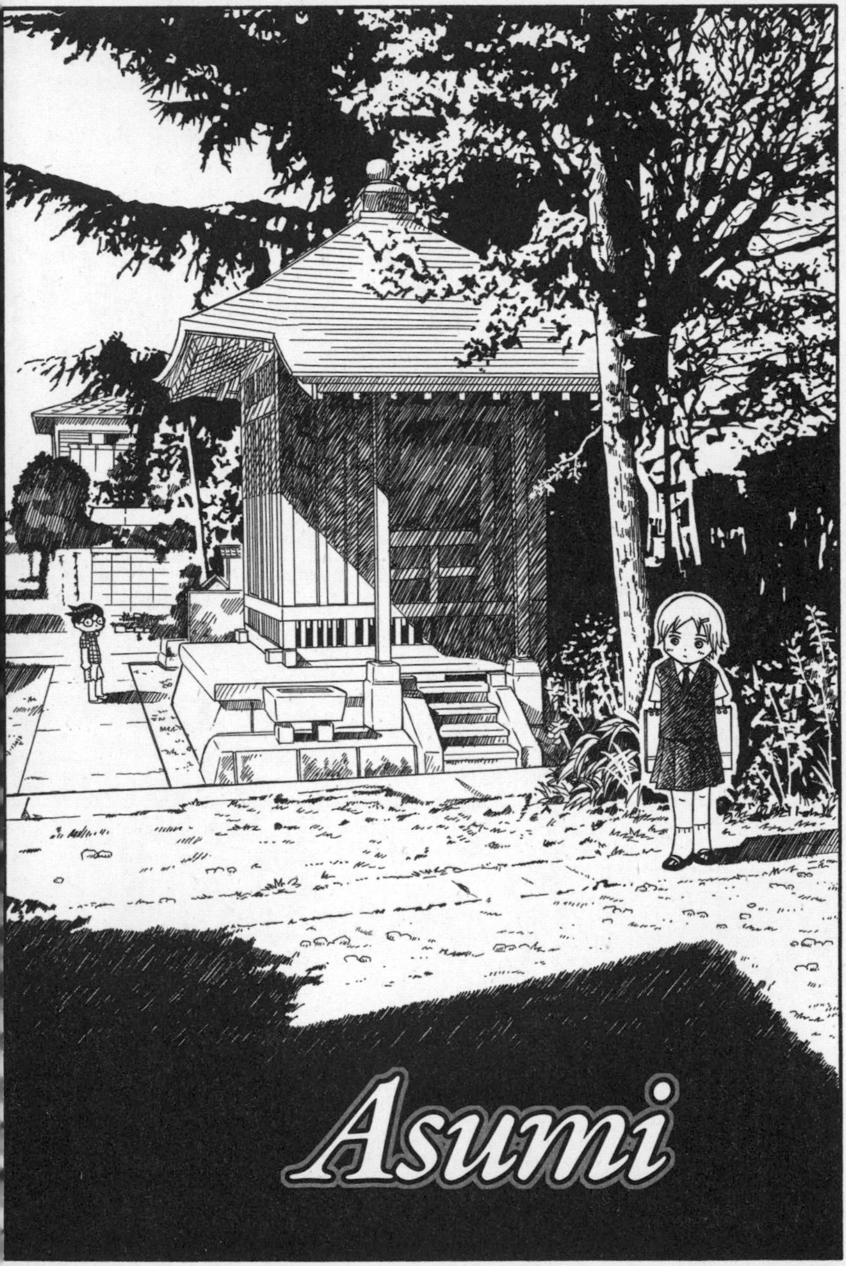
Asumi

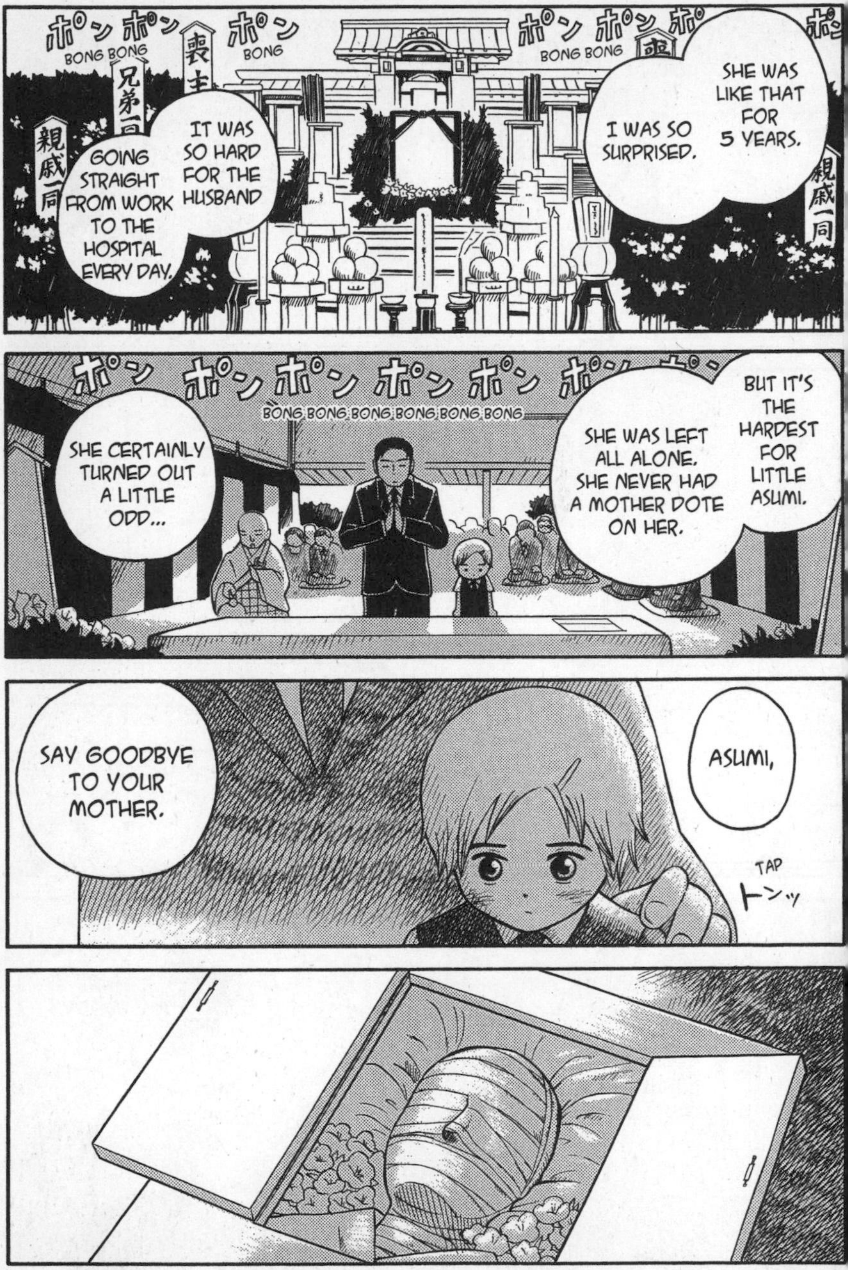
ポンポンポ
BONG BONG
SHE WAS LIKE THAT FOR 5 YEARS.
I WAS SO SURPRISED.
親戚一同
ポン
BONG
IT WAS SO HARD FOR THE HUSBAND
GOING STRAIGHT FROM WORK TO THE HOSPITAL EVERY DAY.
ポンポン
BONG BONG
親戚一同
ポンポンポンポンポンポン
BONG BONG BONG BONG BONG BONG
BUT IT'S THE HARDEST FOR LITTLE ASUMI.
SHE WAS LEFT ALL ALONE. SHE NEVER HAD A MOTHER DOTE ON HER.
SHE CERTAINLY TURNED OUT A LITTLE ODD...
ASUMI,
SAY GOODBYE TO YOUR MOTHER.
TAP
トンッ

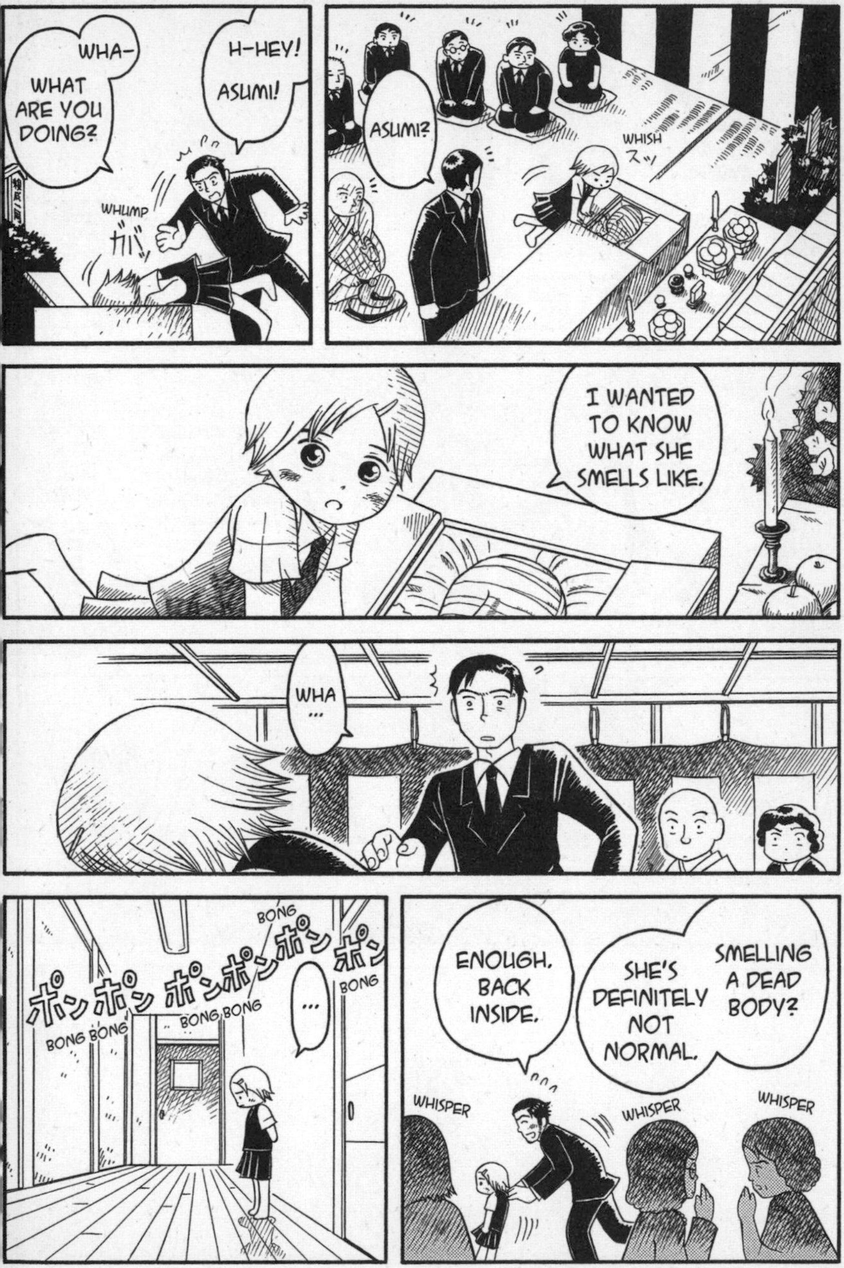
ASUMI?
WHISH
スッ
H-HEY!
ASUMI!
WHA-
WHAT ARE YOU DOING?
WHUMP
ガバッ
I WANTED TO KNOW WHAT SHE SMELLS LIKE.
WHA...
SMELLING A DEAD BODY?
SHE'S DEFINITELY NOT NORMAL.
ENOUGH. BACK INSIDE.
WHISPER
WHISPER
WHISPER
BONG
ポンポンポンポンポンポン
BONG
BONG BONG
BONG BONG
...

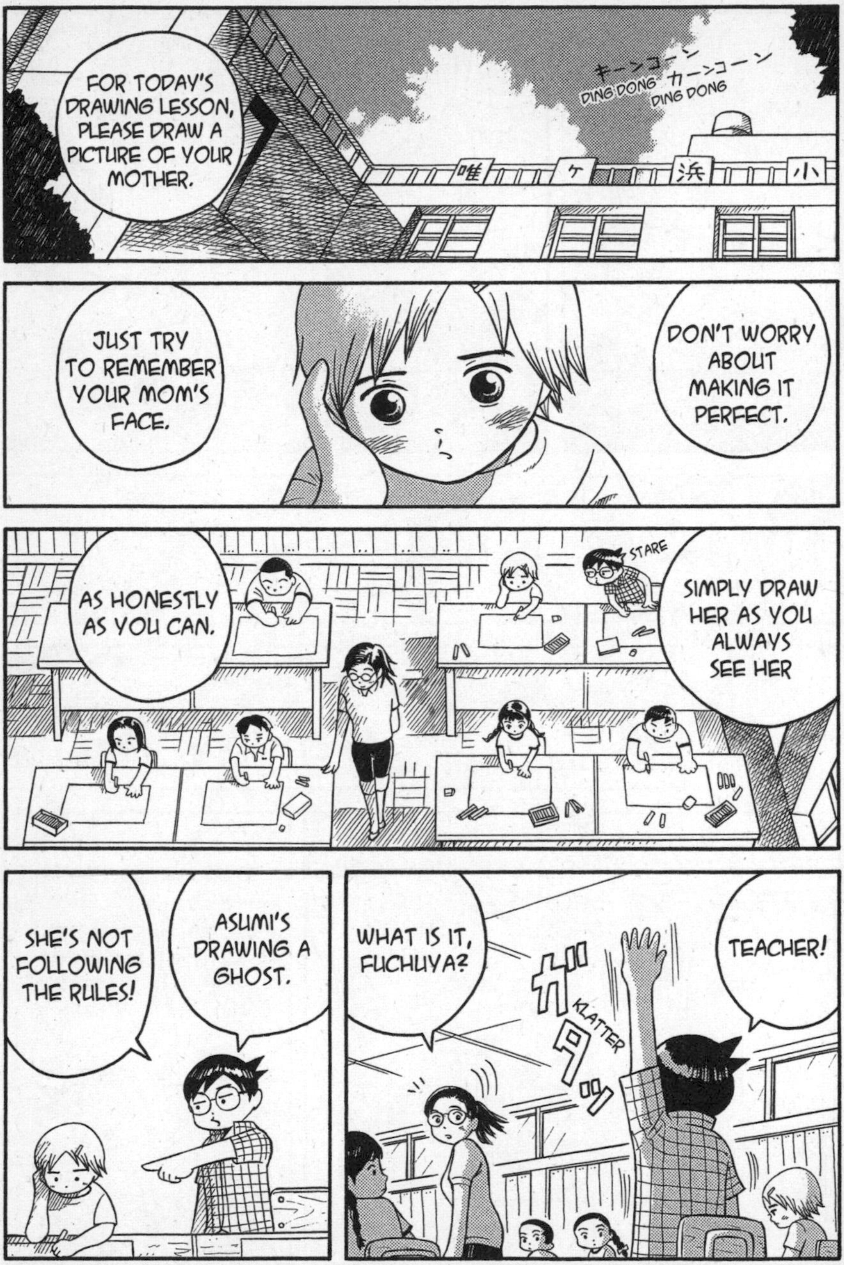
キーンコーン
DING DONG
カーンコーン
DING DONG
唯 ケ 浜 小
FOR TODAY'S DRAWING LESSON, PLEASE DRAW A PICTURE OF YOUR MOTHER.
DON'T WORRY ABOUT MAKING IT PERFECT.
JUST TRY TO REMEMBER YOUR MOM'S FACE.
SIMPLY DRAW HER AS YOU ALWAYS SEE HER
STARE
AS HONESTLY AS YOU CAN.
TEACHER!
ガタッ
KLATTER
WHAT IS IT, FUCHUYA?
ASUMI'S DRAWING A GHOST.
SHE'S NOT FOLLOWING THE RULES!

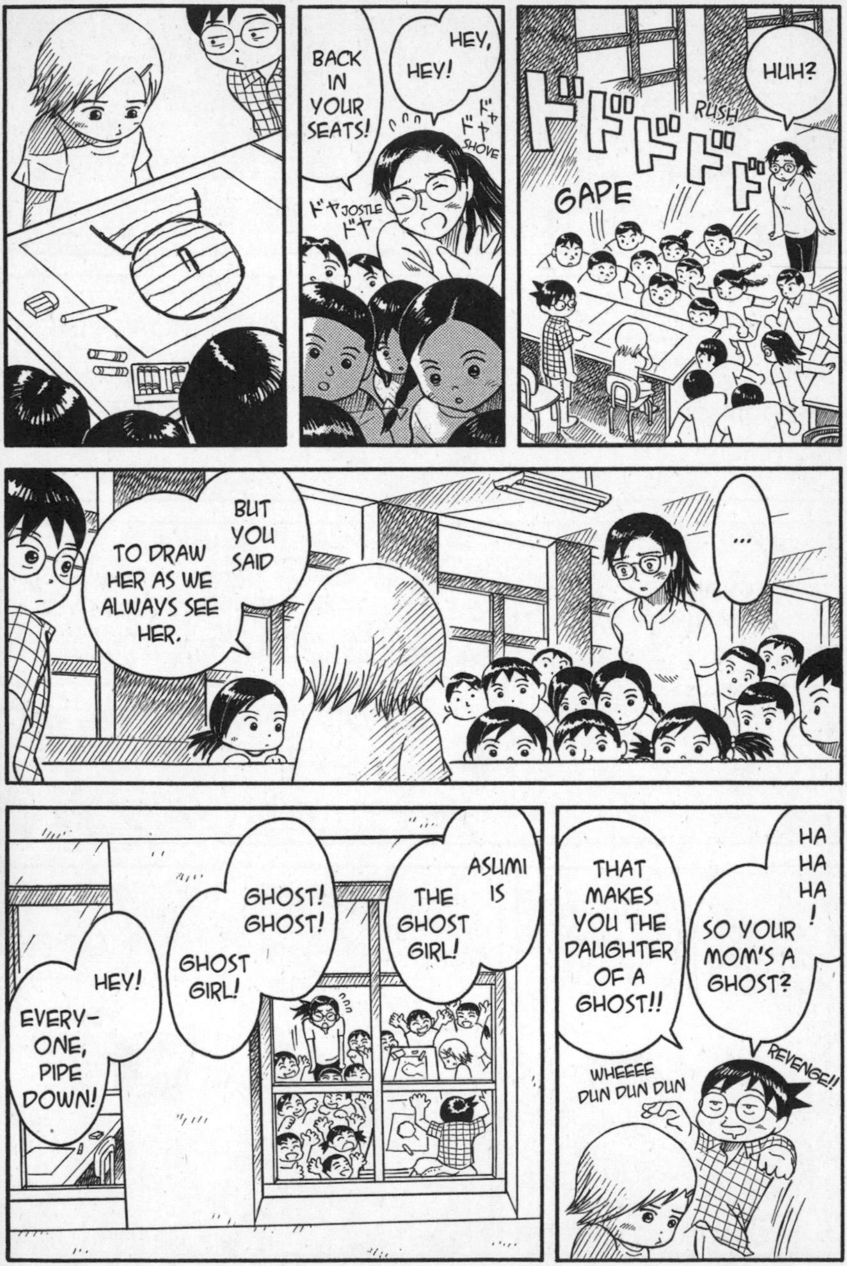
HUH?
RUSH
ドドドドドドド
GAPE
HEY, HEY!
BACK IN YOUR SEATS!
ドヤドヤ SHOVE
ドヤドヤ JOSTLE
...
BUT YOU SAID
TO DRAW HER AS WE ALWAYS SEE HER.
HA HA HA!
SO YOUR MOM'S A GHOST?
THAT MAKES YOU THE DAUGHTER OF A GHOST!!
REVENGE!!
WHEEEE DUN DUN DUN
ASUMI IS
THE GHOST GIRL!
GHOST! GHOST!
GHOST GIRL!
HEY!
EVERYONE, PIPE DOWN!

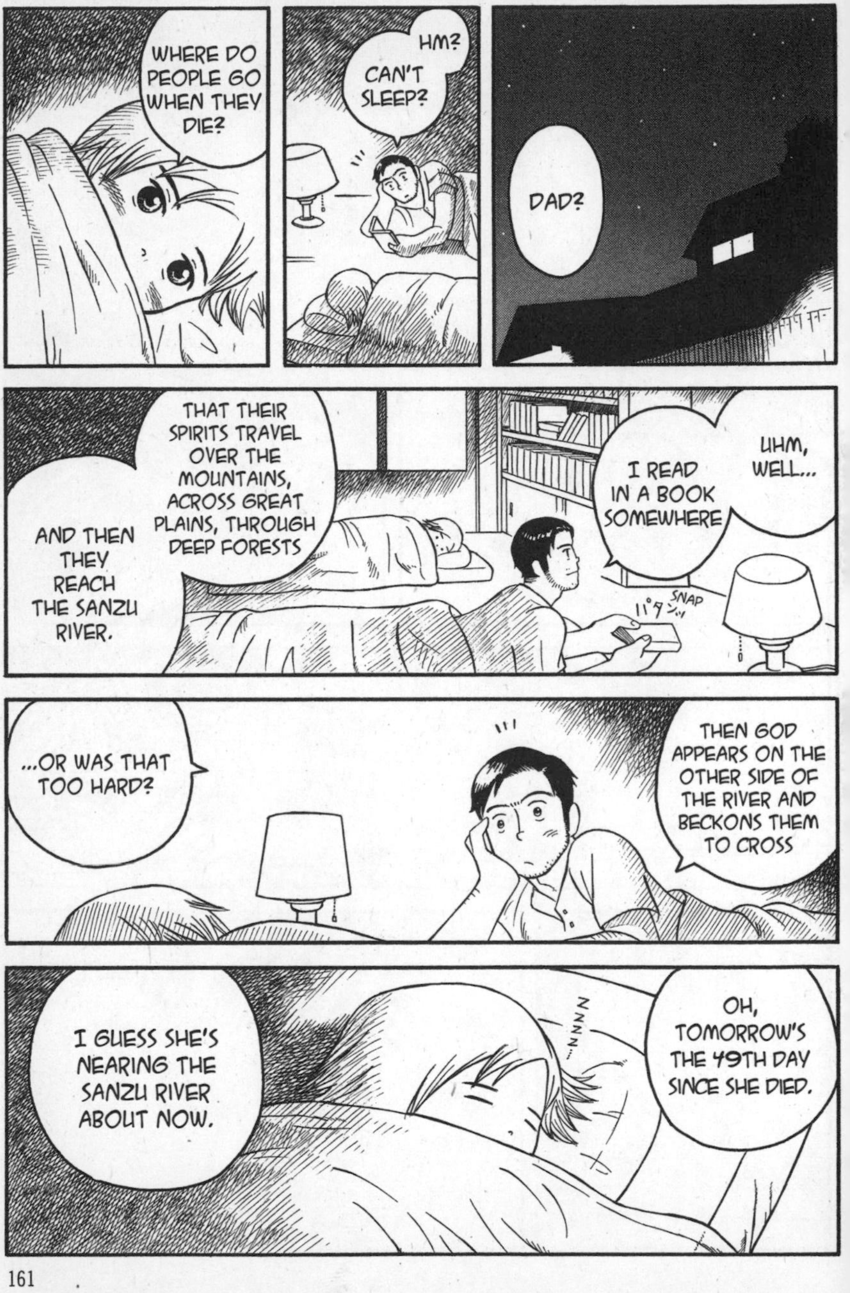
DAD?
HM?
CAN'T SLEEP?
WHERE DO PEOPLE GO WHEN THEY DIE?
UHM, WELL...
I READ IN A BOOK SOMEWHERE
SNAP
パタンッ
THAT THEIR SPIRITS TRAVEL OVER THE MOUNTAINS, ACROSS GREAT PLAINS, THROUGH DEEP FORESTS
AND THEN THEY REACH THE SANZU RIVER.
THEN GOD APPEARS ON THE OTHER SIDE OF THE RIVER AND BECKONS THEM TO CROSS
...OR WAS THAT TOO HARD?
OH, TOMORROW'S THE 49TH DAY SINCE SHE DIED.
ZZZZ...
I GUESS SHE'S NEARING THE SANZU RIVER ABOUT NOW.

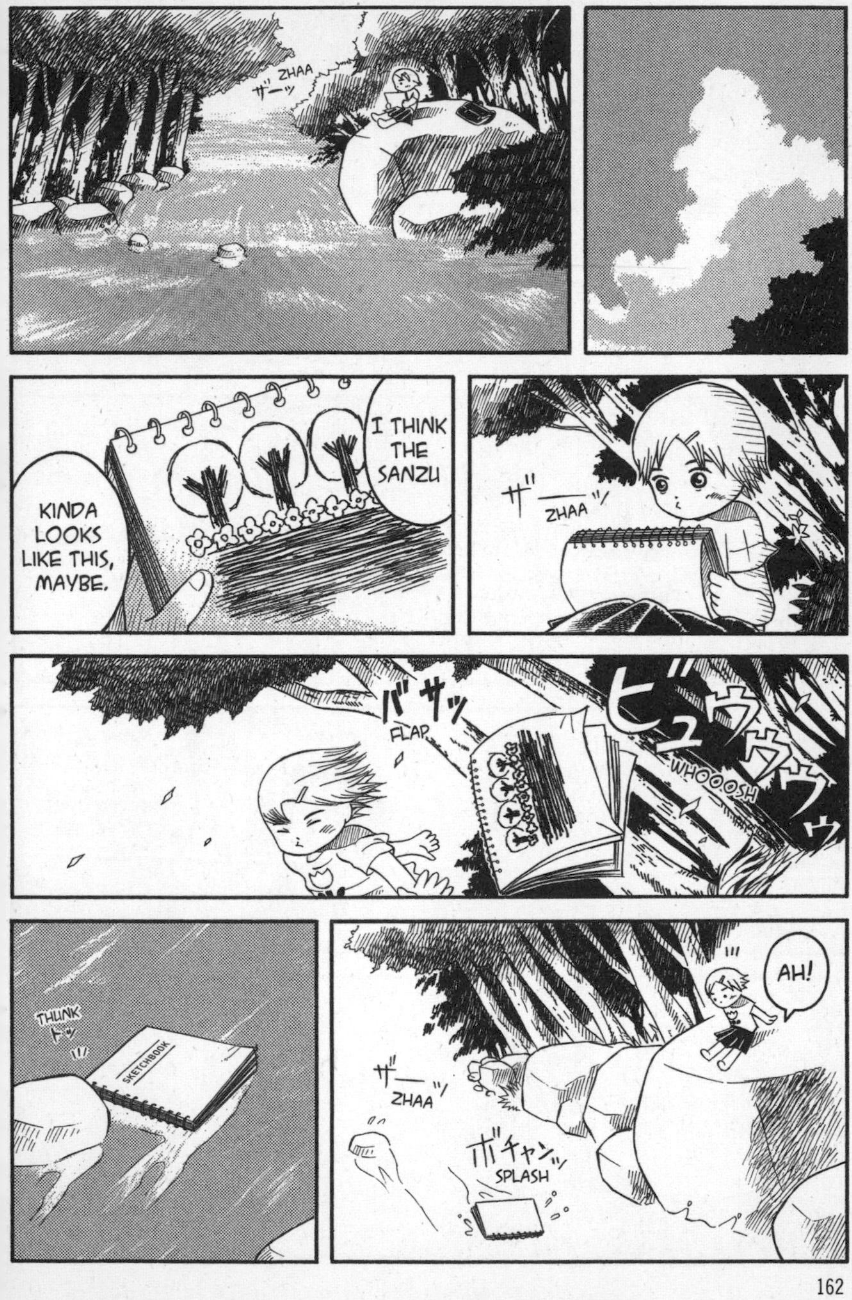
ザーッ
ZHAA
ザー
ZHAA
I THINK THE SANZU
KINDA LOOKS LIKE THIS, MAYBE.
ビュウウウウ
WHOOOSH
バサッ
FLAP
AH!
ザー
ZHAA
ボチャン
SPLASH
トッ
THUNK
SKETCHBOOK

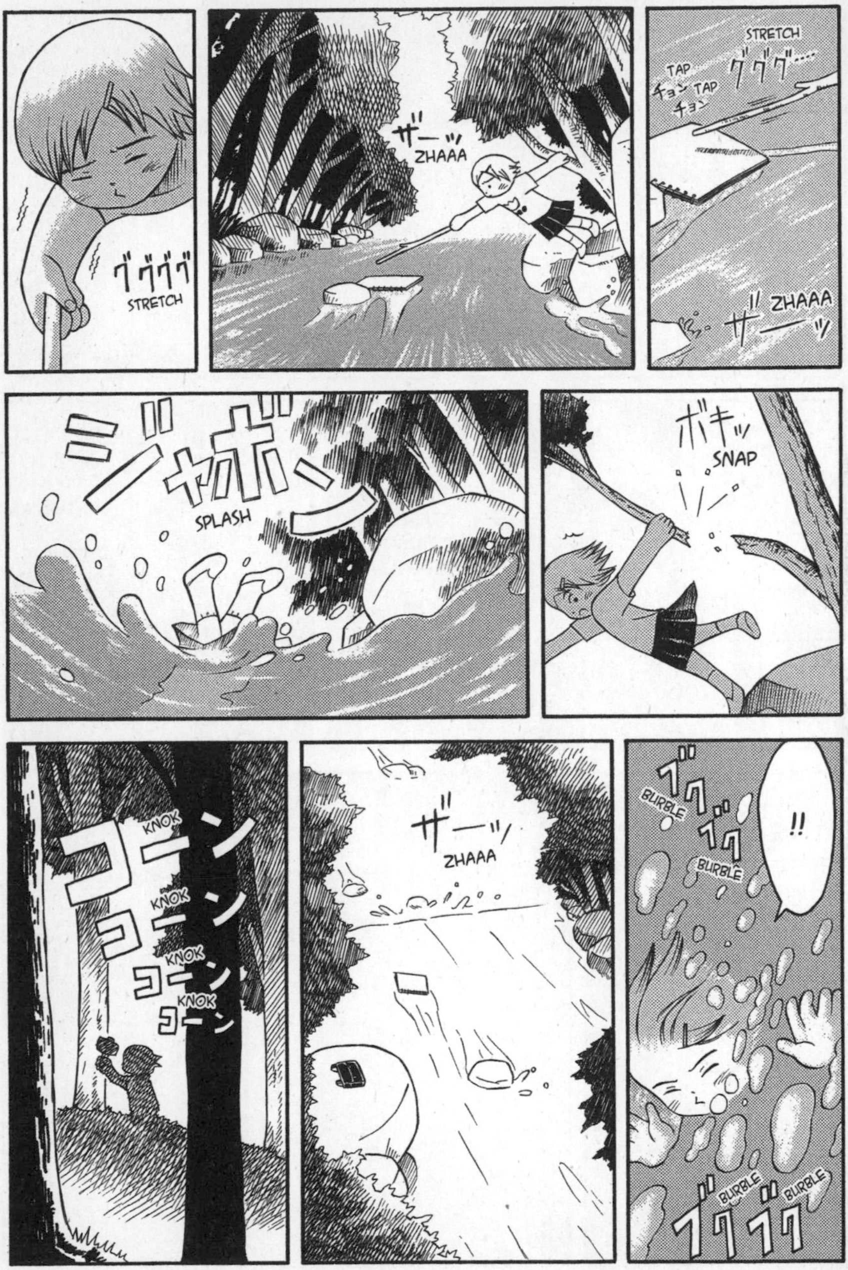
STRETCH
グググ…
TAP
チョン
TAP
チョン
ZHAAA
ザーッ
ザーッ
ZHAAA
ググググ
STRETCH
ボキッ
SNAP
ジャボーン
SPLASH
!!
ブク
BURBLE
ブク
BURBLE
BURBLE
BURBLE
ブクブク
ザーッ
ZHAAA
KNOK
コーン
KNOK
コーン
KNOK
コーン
KNOK
コーン

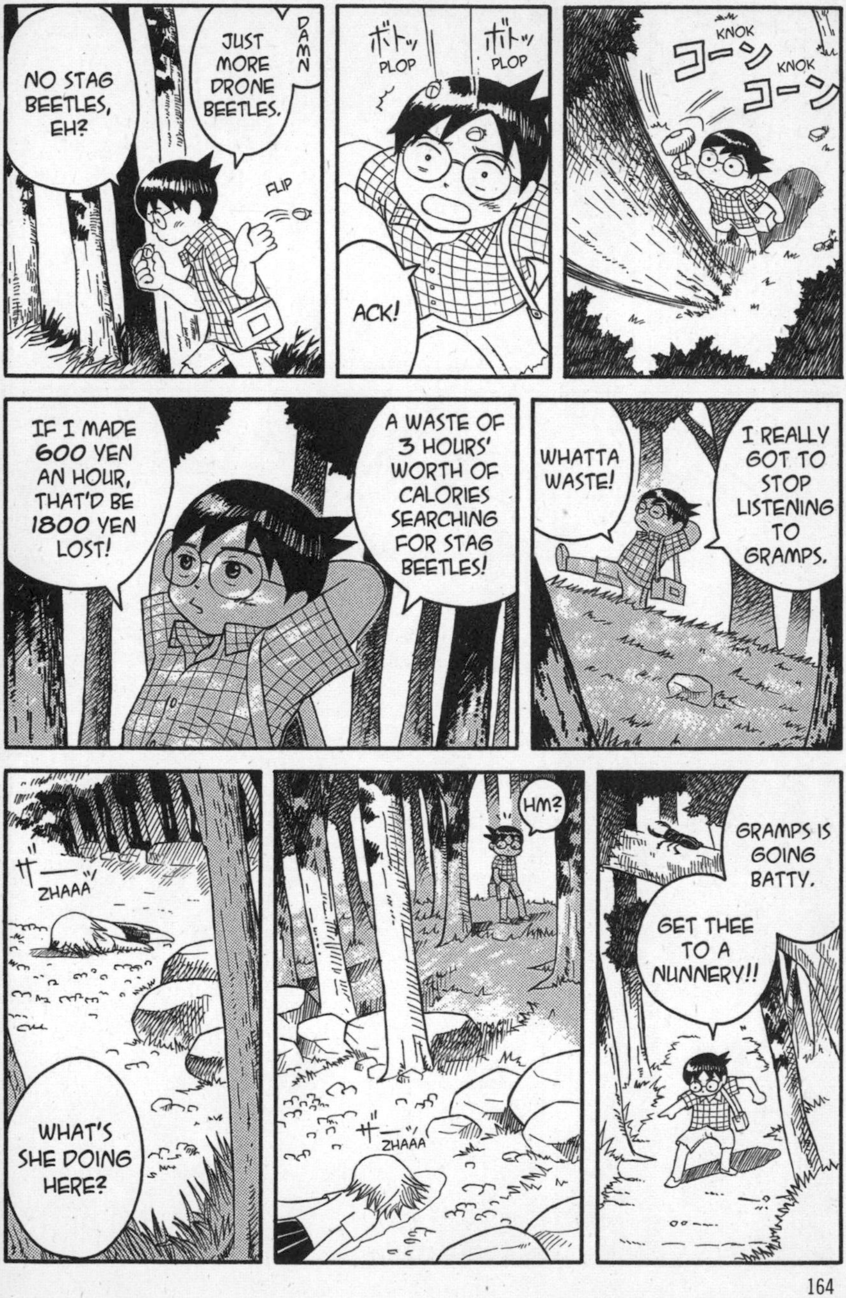

KNOK
コーン
KNOK
コーン
ボトッ
PLOP
ボトッ
PLOP
ACK!
DAMN
JUST MORE DRONE BEETLES.
NO STAG BEETLES, EH?
FLIP
I REALLY GOT TO STOP LISTENING TO GRAMPS.
WHATTA WASTE!
A WASTE OF 3 HOURS' WORTH OF CALORIES SEARCHING FOR STAG BEETLES!
IF I MADE 600 YEN AN HOUR, THAT'D BE 1800 YEN LOST!
GRAMPS IS GOING BATTY.
GET THEE TO A NUNNERY!!
HM?
ザー
ZHAAA
ザー
ZHAAA
WHAT'S SHE DOING HERE?

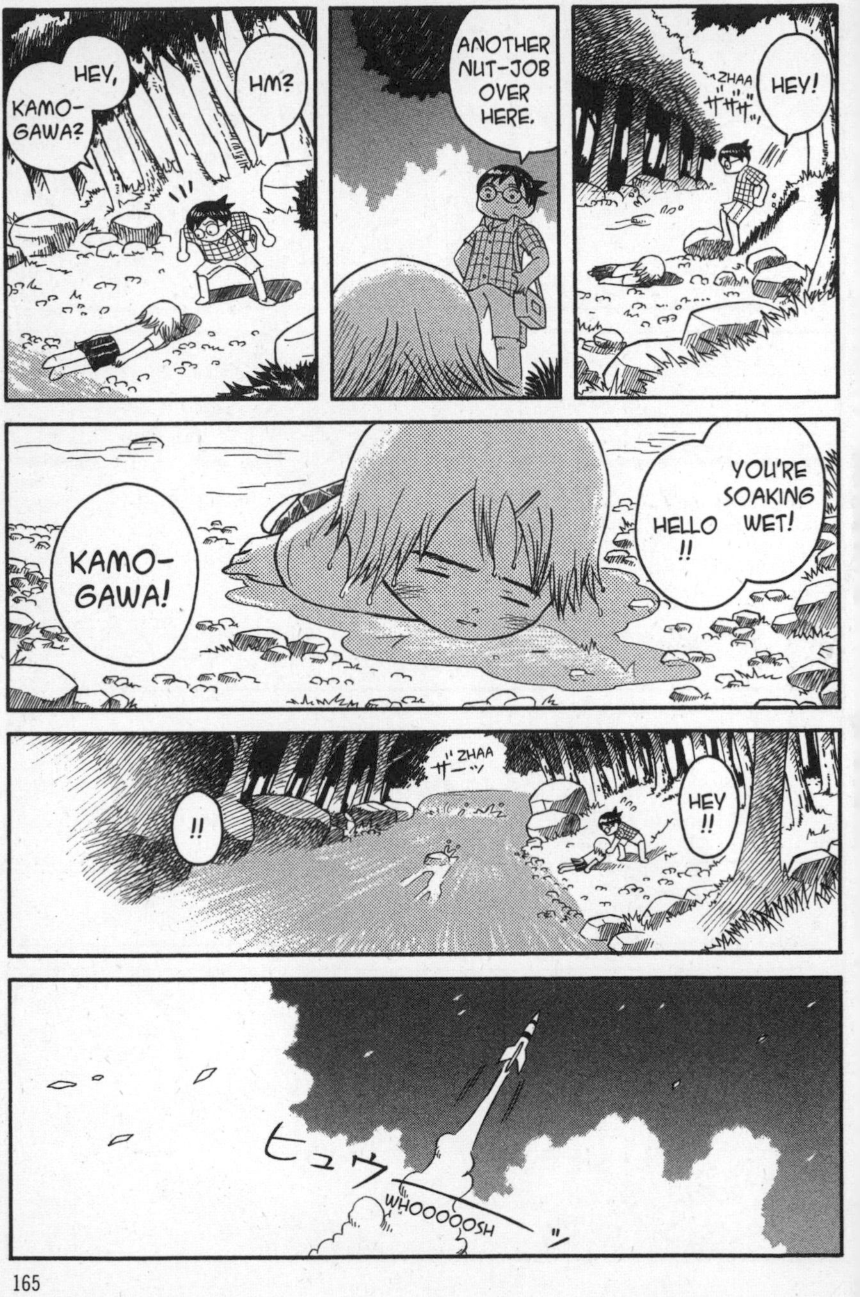
HEY!
ZHAA
ザザザ
ANOTHER NUT-JOB OVER HERE.
HEY, KAMO-GAWA?
HM?
YOU'RE SOAKING WET!
HELLO !!
KAMO-GAWA!
HEY !!
ZHAA
ザーッ
!!
ヒュウ
WHOOOOOOSH

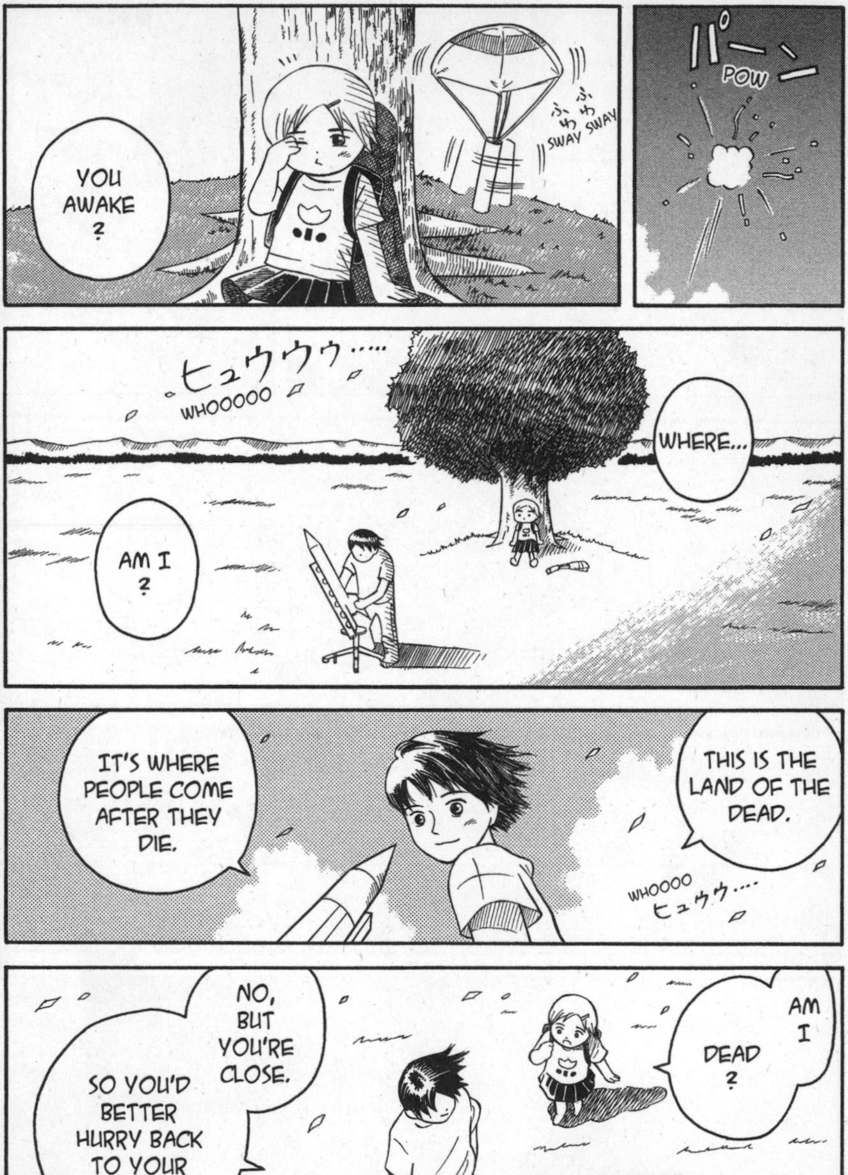
パーン
POW
ふわふわ
SWAY SWAY
YOU AWAKE ?
WHERE...
ヒュウウウ....
WHOOOOO
AM I ?
THIS IS THE LAND OF THE DEAD.
IT'S WHERE PEOPLE COME AFTER THEY DIE.
WHOOOO
ヒュウ....
AM I DEAD ?
NO, BUT YOU'RE CLOSE.
SO YOU'D BETTER HURRY BACK TO YOUR BODY.

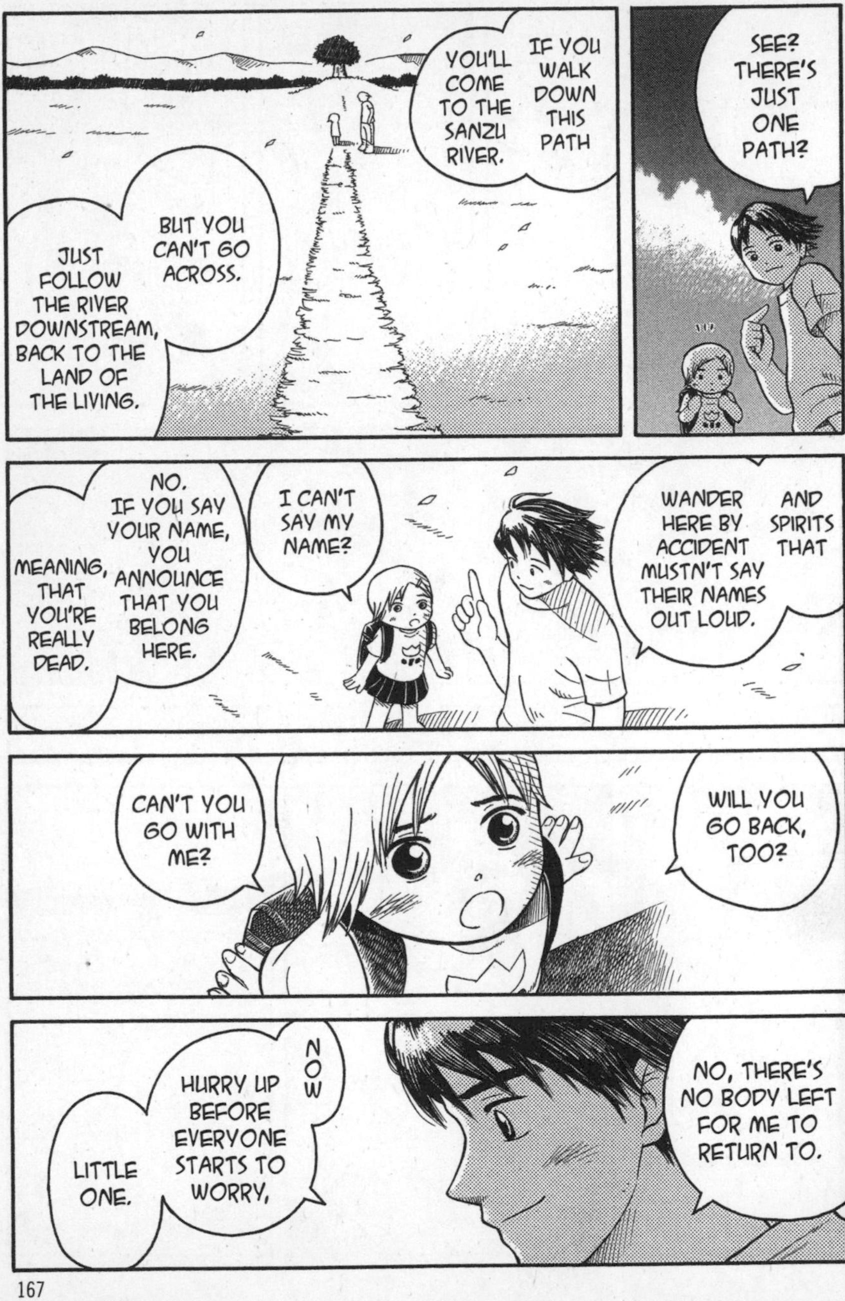
SEE? THERE'S JUST ONE PATH?
IF YOU WALK DOWN THIS PATH
YOU'LL COME TO THE SANZU RIVER.
BUT YOU CAN'T GO ACROSS.
JUST FOLLOW THE RIVER DOWNSTREAM, BACK TO THE LAND OF THE LIVING.
AND SPIRITS THAT
WANDER HERE BY ACCIDENT MUSTN'T SAY THEIR NAMES OUT LOUD.
I CAN'T SAY MY NAME?
NO. IF YOU SAY YOUR NAME, YOU ANNOUNCE THAT YOU BELONG HERE.
MEANING, THAT YOU'RE REALLY DEAD.
WILL YOU GO BACK, TOO?
CAN'T YOU GO WITH ME?
NO, THERE'S NO BODY LEFT FOR ME TO RETURN TO.
NOW
HURRY UP BEFORE EVERYONE STARTS TO WORRY,
LITTLE ONE.

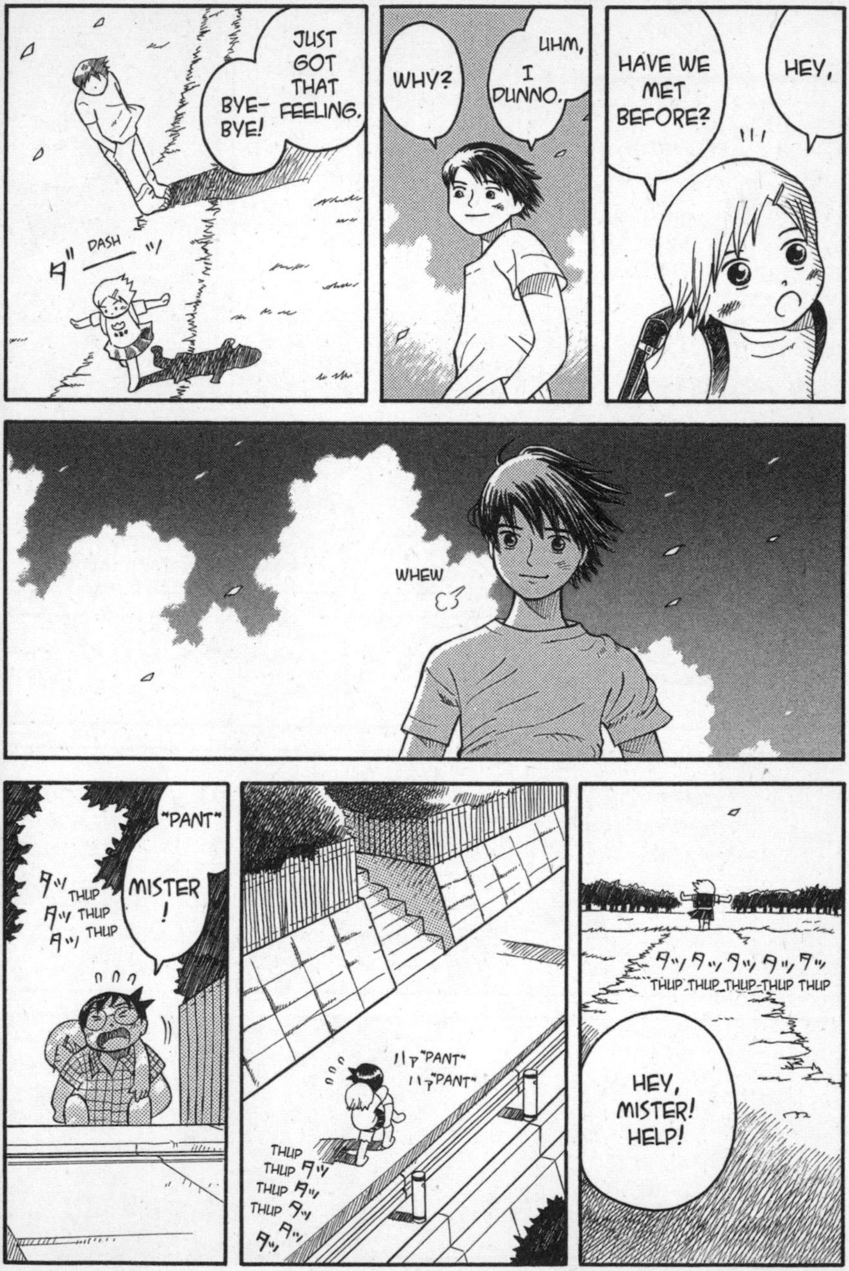
HEY,
HAVE WE MET BEFORE?
UHM, I DUNNO.
WHY?
JUST GOT THAT FEELING.
BYE-BYE!
ダッ DASH ッ
WHEW
タッタッタッタッタッ
THUP THUP THUP THUP THUP
HEY, MISTER! HELP!
ハァ *PANT*
ハァ *PANT*
THUP タッ
THUP タッ
THUP タッ
THUP タッ
タッ
PANT
MISTER!
タッ THUP
タッ THUP
タッ THUP

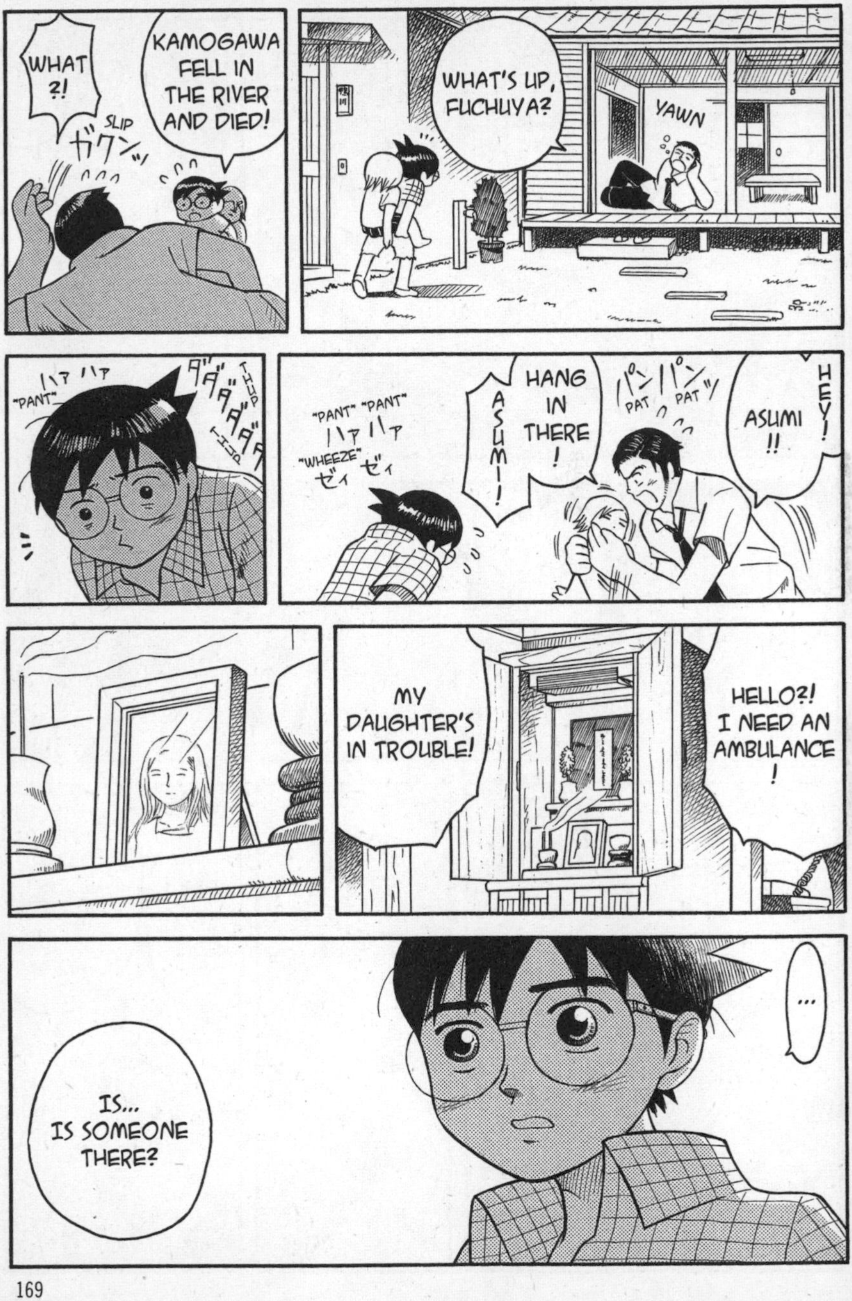
WHAT'S UP, FUCHUYA?
YAWN
KAMOGAWA FELL IN THE RIVER AND DIED!
WHAT?!
SLIP ガクンッ
HEY!
ASUMI!!
パンパンッ PAT PAT
HANG IN THERE!
ASUMI!
"PANT" "PANT" ハァハァ
"WHEEZE" ゼィゼィ
ダダダダ THUP
ハァハァ "PANT"
HELLO?! I NEED AN AMBULANCE!
MY DAUGHTER'S IN TROUBLE!
...
IS... IS SOMEONE THERE?

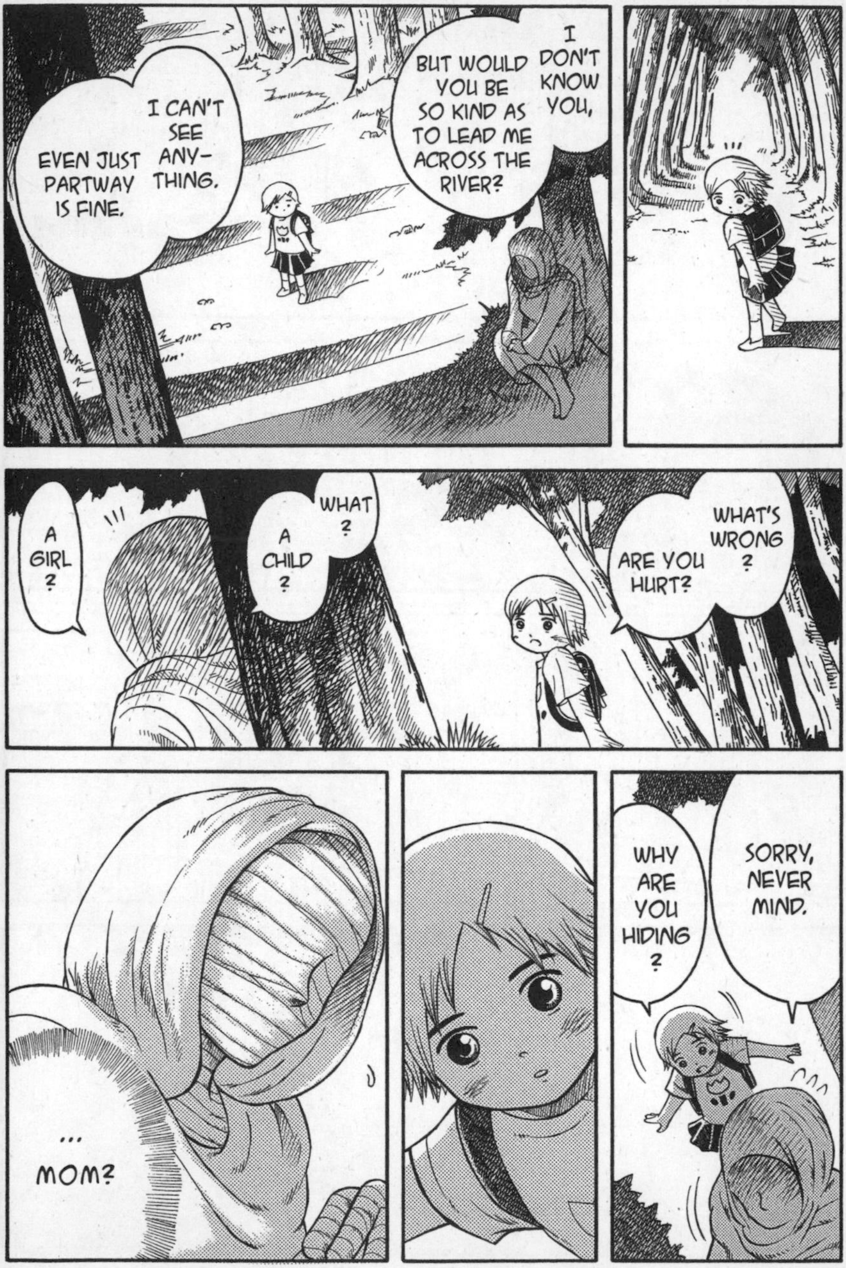
I DON'T KNOW YOU,
BUT WOULD YOU BE SO KIND AS TO LEAD ME ACROSS THE RIVER?
I CAN'T SEE ANYTHING.
EVEN JUST PARTWAY IS FINE.
WHAT'S WRONG?
ARE YOU HURT?
WHAT?
A CHILD?
A GIRL?
SORRY, NEVER MIND.
WHY ARE YOU HIDING?
... MOM?

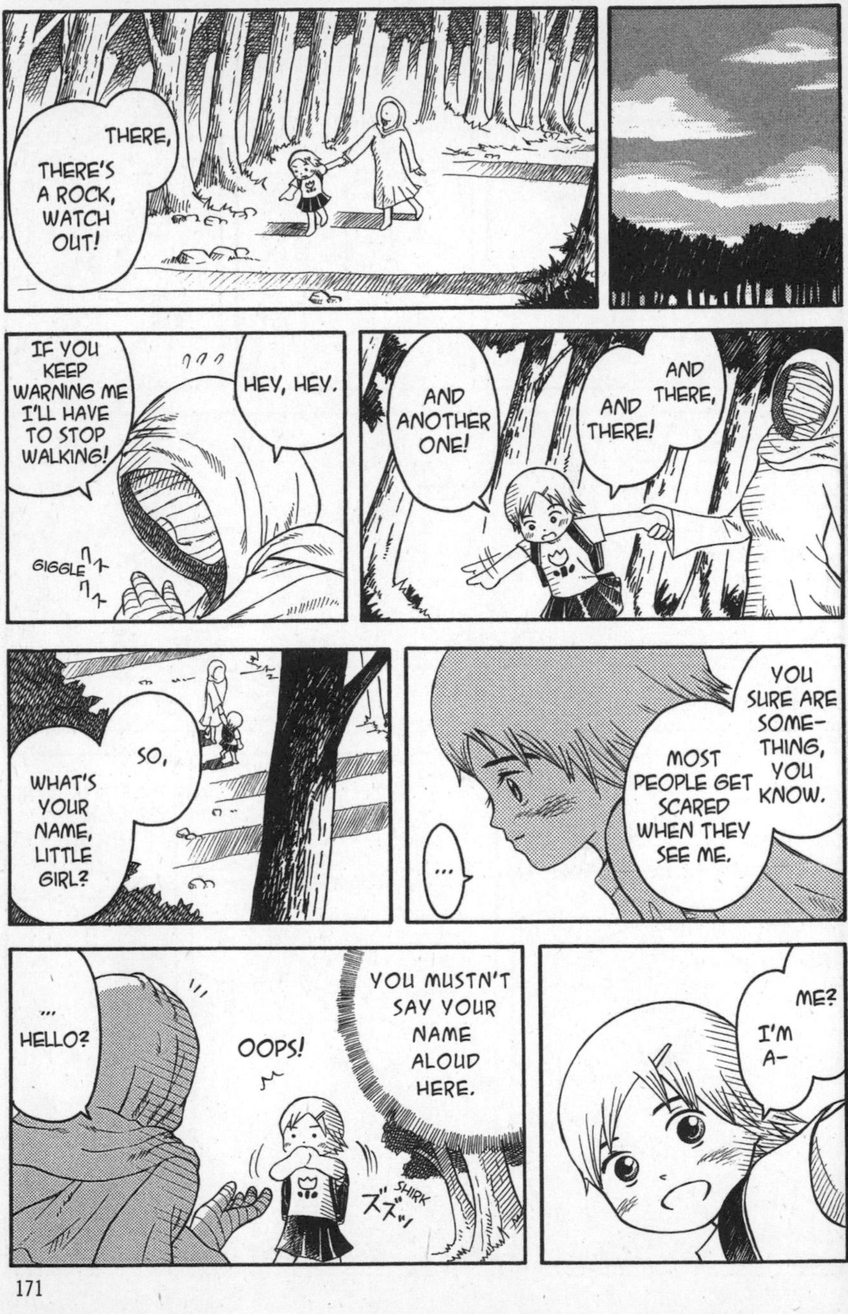
THERE,
THERE'S A ROCK, WATCH OUT!
AND THERE,
AND THERE!
AND ANOTHER ONE!
HEY, HEY.
IF YOU KEEP WARNING ME I'LL HAVE TO STOP WALKING!
GIGGLE
YOU SURE ARE SOME-THING, YOU KNOW.
MOST PEOPLE GET SCARED WHEN THEY SEE ME.
...
SO,
WHAT'S YOUR NAME, LITTLE GIRL?
ME?
I'M A-
YOU MUSTN'T SAY YOUR NAME ALOUD HERE.
OOPS!
SHIRK
... HELLO?

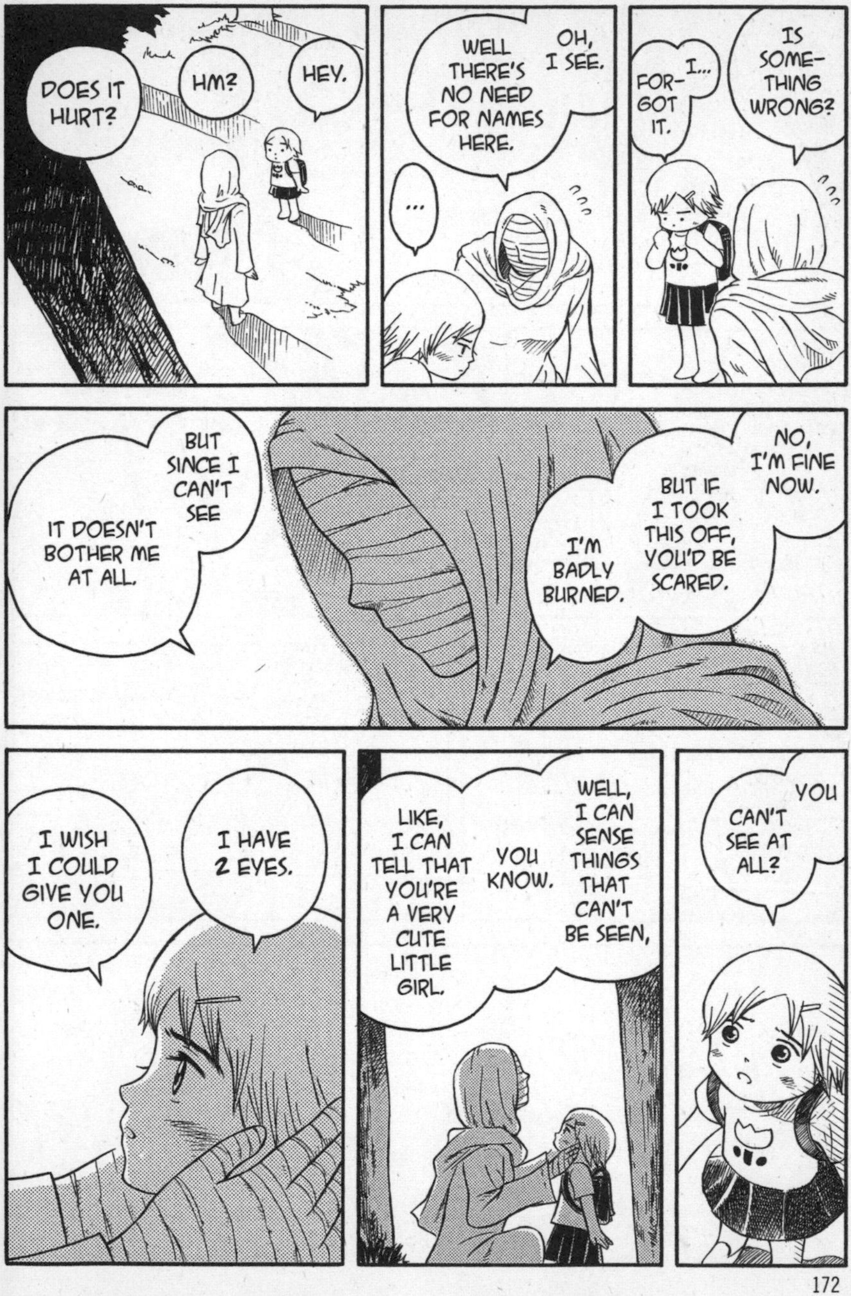
IS SOMETHING WRONG?
I... FORGOT IT.
OH, I SEE.
WELL THERE'S NO NEED FOR NAMES HERE.
...
HEY.
HM?
DOES IT HURT?
NO, I'M FINE NOW.
BUT IF I TOOK THIS OFF, YOU'D BE SCARED.
I'M BADLY BURNED.
BUT SINCE I CAN'T SEE
IT DOESN'T BOTHER ME AT ALL.
YOU CAN'T SEE AT ALL?
WELL, I CAN SENSE THINGS THAT CAN'T BE SEEN,
YOU KNOW.
LIKE, I CAN TELL THAT YOU'RE A VERY CUTE LITTLE GIRL.
I HAVE 2 EYES.
I WISH I COULD GIVE YOU ONE.

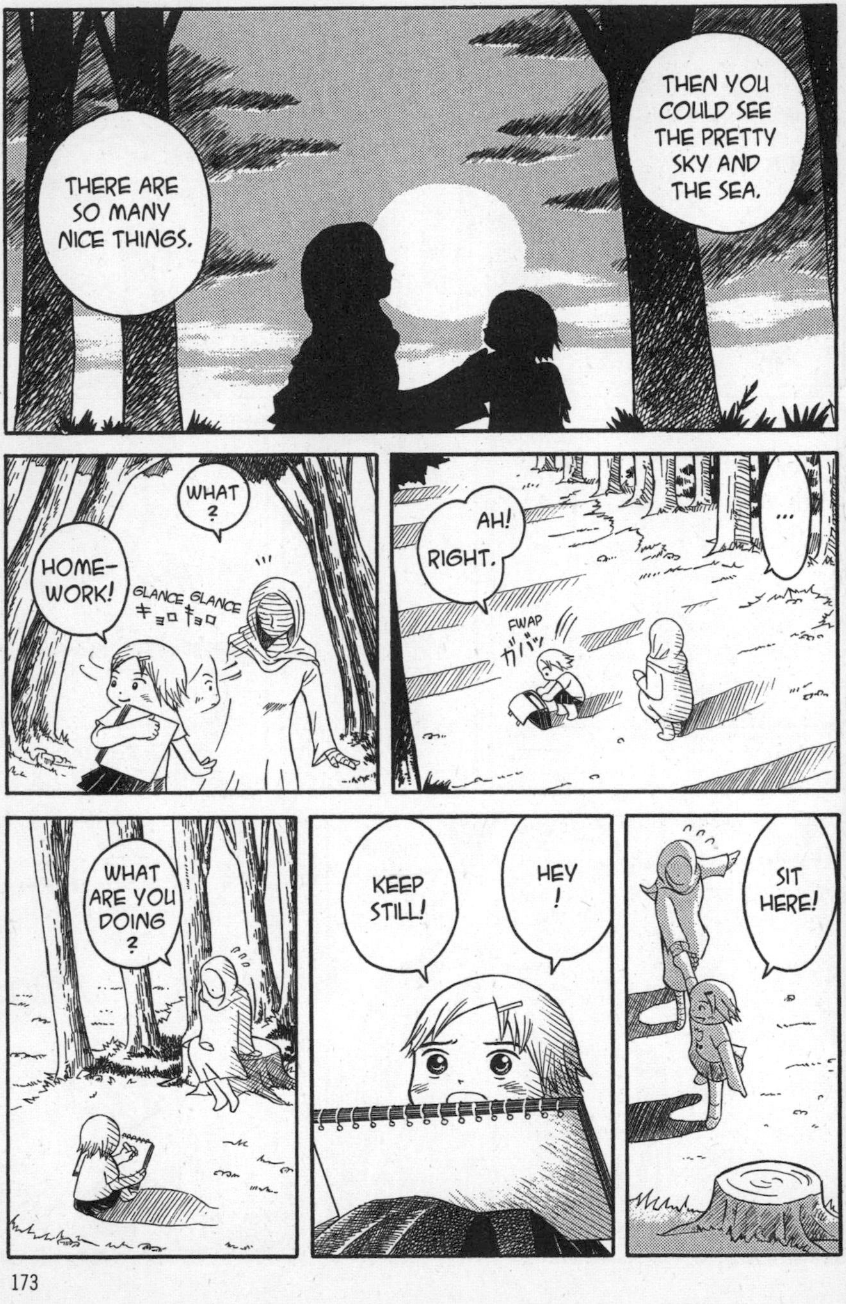
THEN YOU COULD SEE THE PRETTY SKY AND THE SEA.
THERE ARE SO MANY NICE THINGS.
...
AH! RIGHT.
FWAP ガバッ
WHAT?
HOME-WORK!
GLANCE GLANCE キョロキョロ
SIT HERE!
HEY!
KEEP STILL!
WHAT ARE YOU DOING?

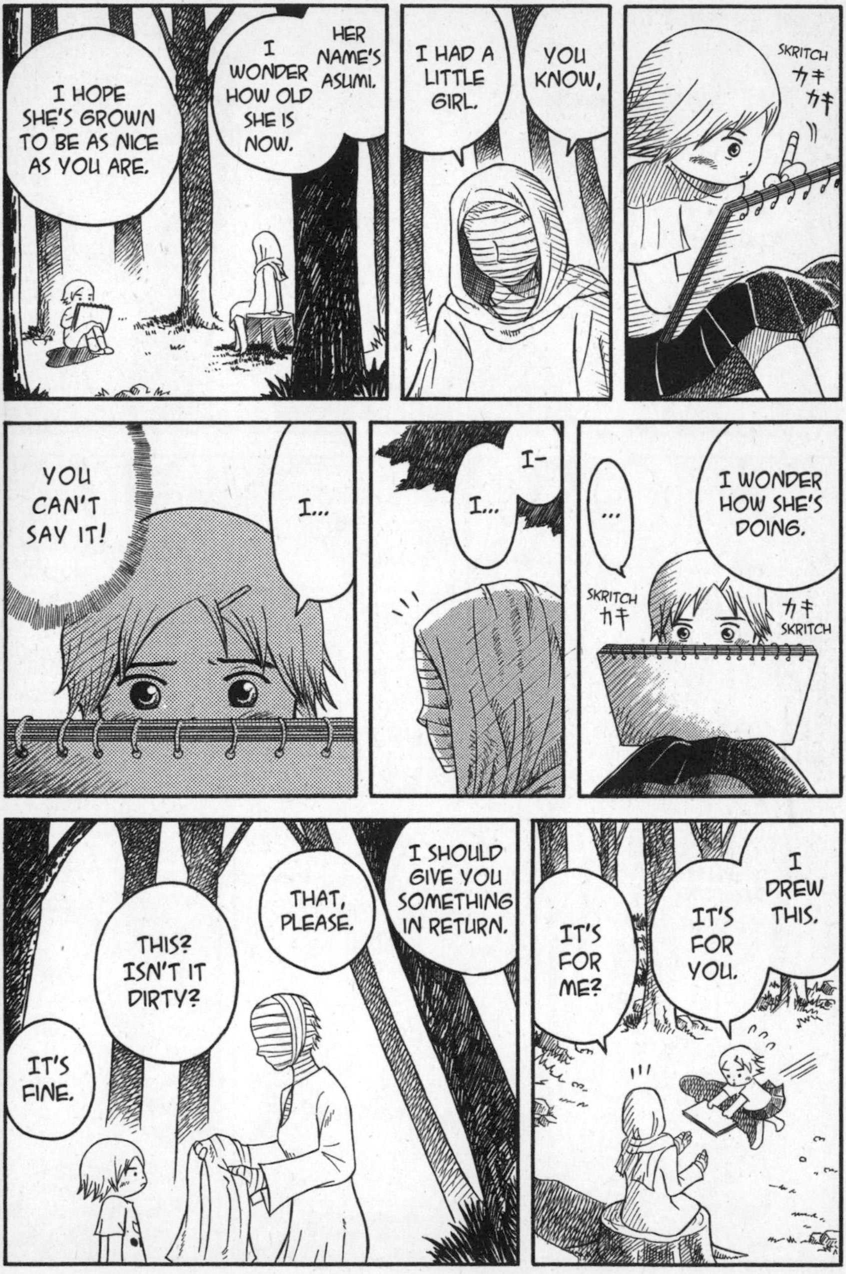
SKRITCH
カキ
カキ
YOU KNOW,
I HAD A LITTLE GIRL.
HER NAME'S ASUMI.
I WONDER HOW OLD SHE IS NOW.
I HOPE SHE'S GROWN TO BE AS NICE AS YOU ARE.
I WONDER HOW SHE'S DOING.
...
SKRITCH
カキ
カキ
SKRITCH
I-
I...
I...
YOU CAN'T SAY IT!
I DREW THIS.
IT'S FOR YOU.
IT'S FOR ME?
I SHOULD GIVE YOU SOMETHING IN RETURN.
THAT, PLEASE.
THIS? ISN'T IT DIRTY?
IT'S FINE.

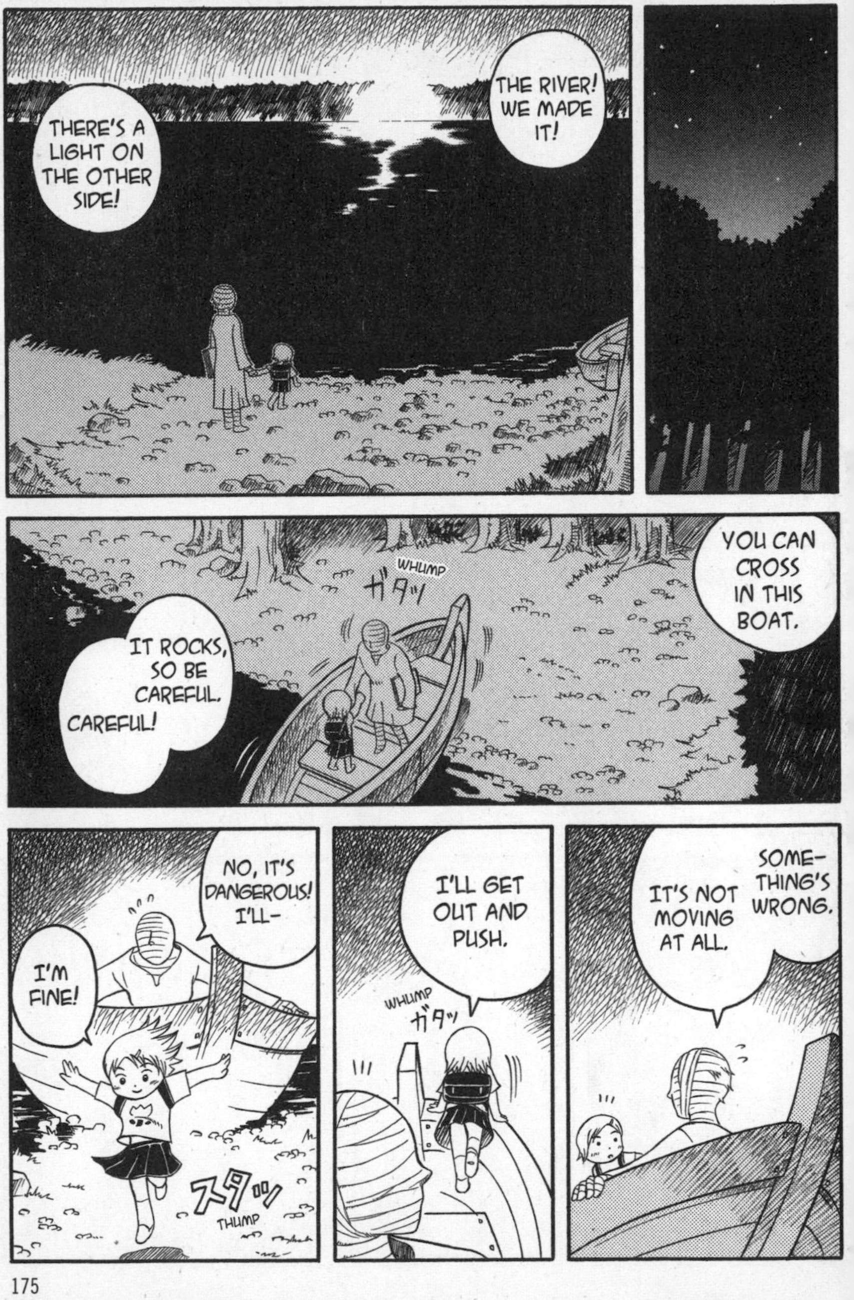
THE RIVER! WE MADE IT!
THERE'S A LIGHT ON THE OTHER SIDE!
YOU CAN CROSS IN THIS BOAT.
WHUMP
ガタッ
IT ROCKS, SO BE CAREFUL.
CAREFUL!
SOME-THING'S WRONG.
IT'S NOT MOVING AT ALL.
I'LL GET OUT AND PUSH.
WHUMP
ガタッ
NO, IT'S DANGEROUS! I'LL-
I'M FINE!
スタッ
THUMP

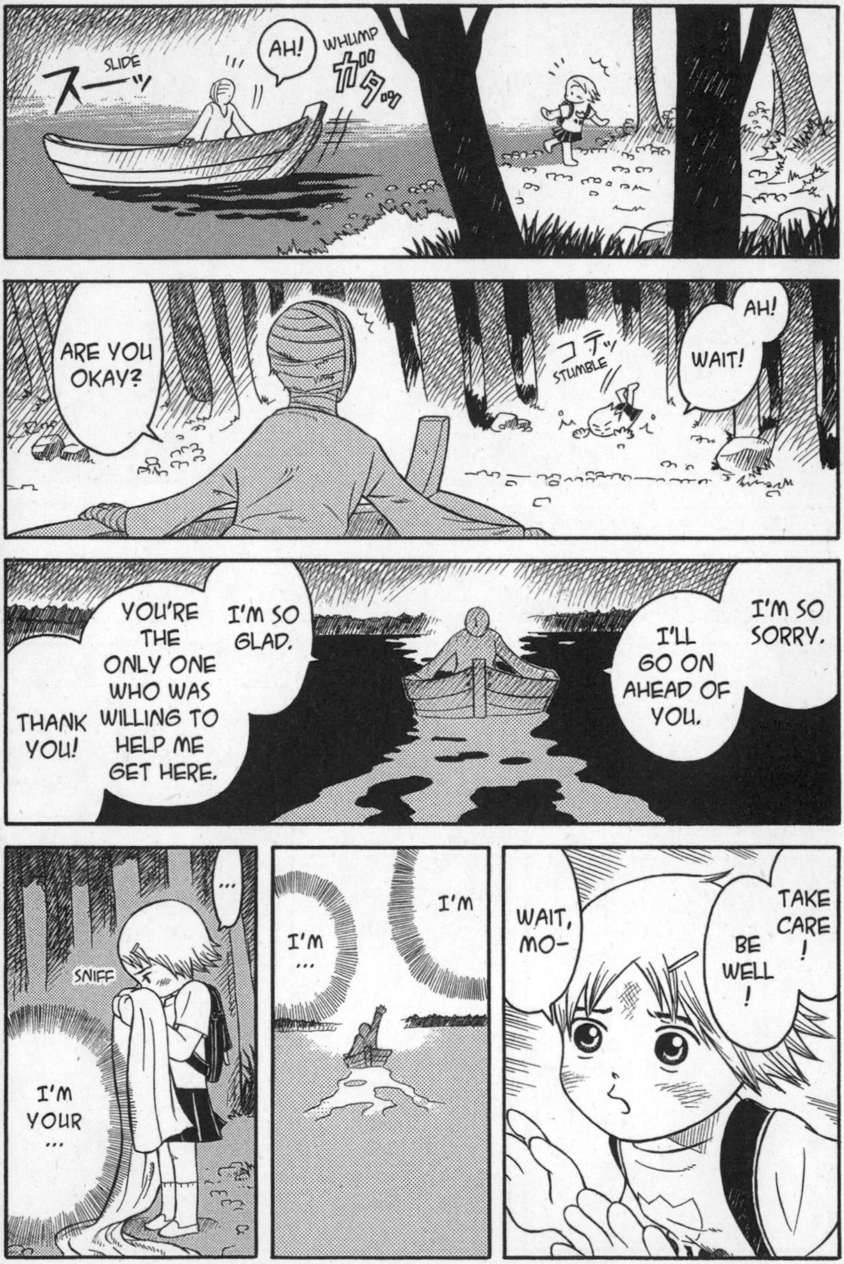
WHUMP
ガタッ
AH!
SLIDE
スーッ
AH!
WAIT!
コテッ
STUMBLE
ARE YOU OKAY?
I'M SO SORRY.
I'LL GO ON AHEAD OF YOU.
I'M SO GLAD.
YOU'RE THE ONLY ONE WHO WAS WILLING TO HELP ME GET HERE.
THANK YOU!
TAKE CARE!
BE WELL!
WAIT, MO-
I'M
I'M ...
...
SNIFF
I'M YOUR ...

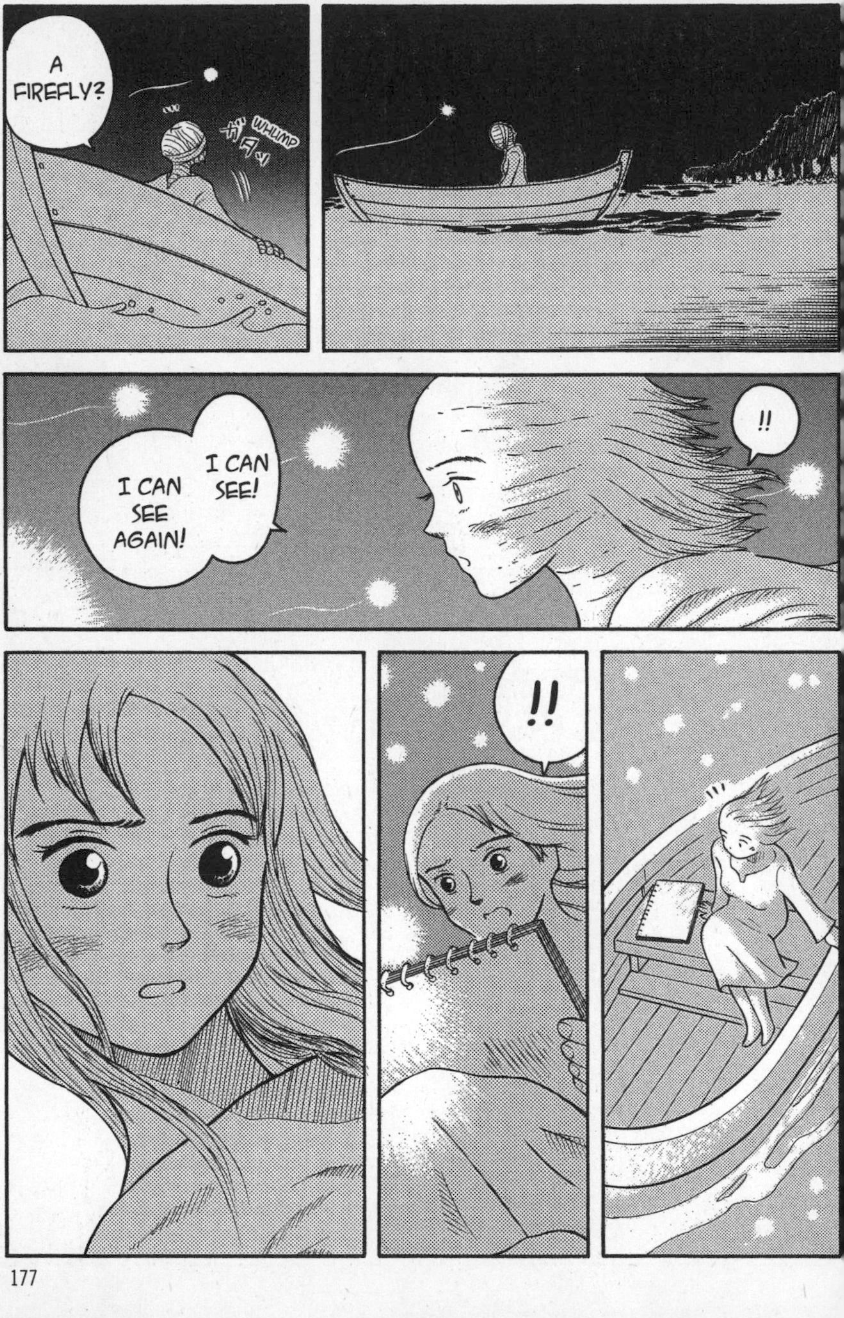
A FIREFLY?
ガタッ
WHUMP
!!
I CAN SEE!
I CAN SEE AGAIN!
!!

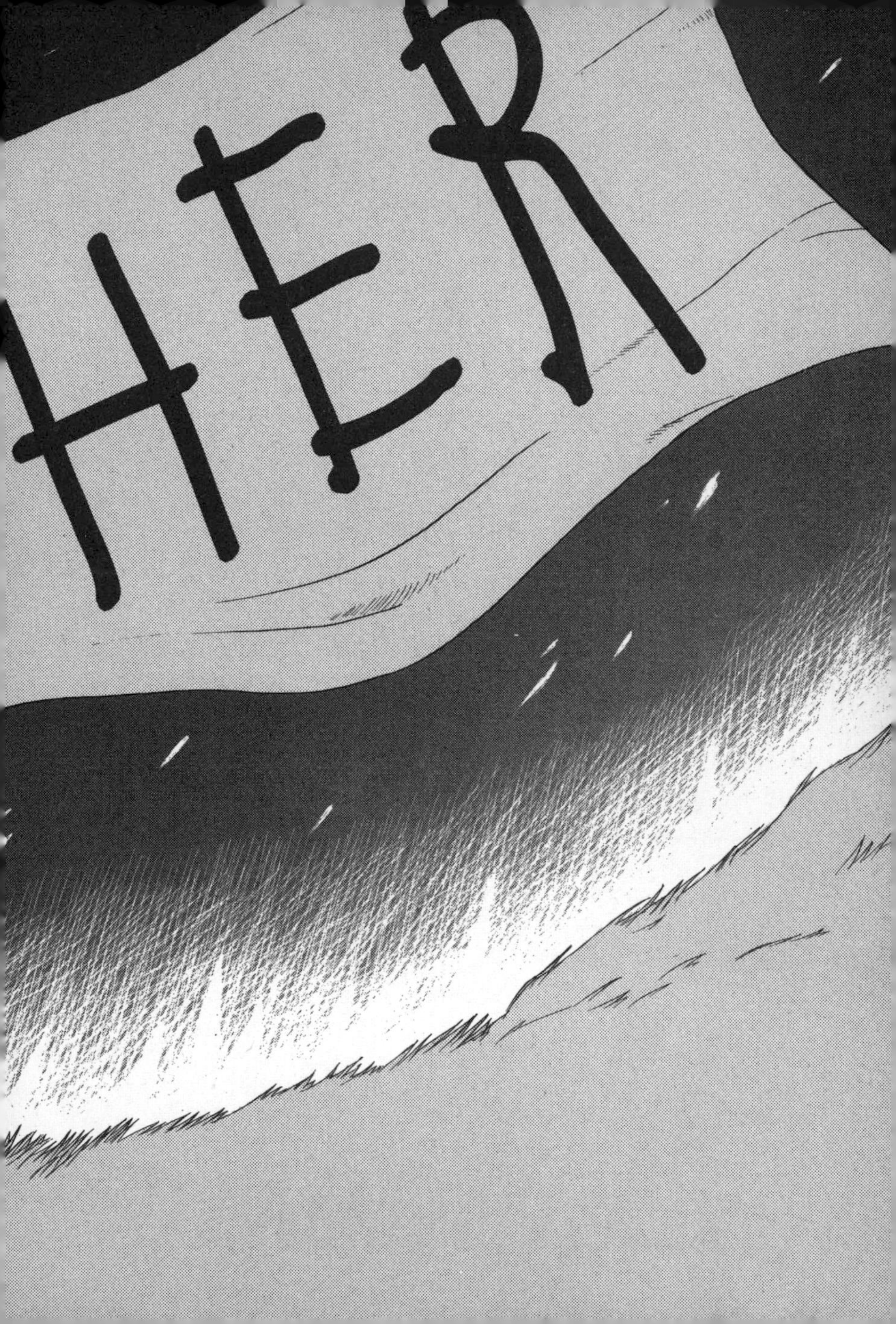
HER

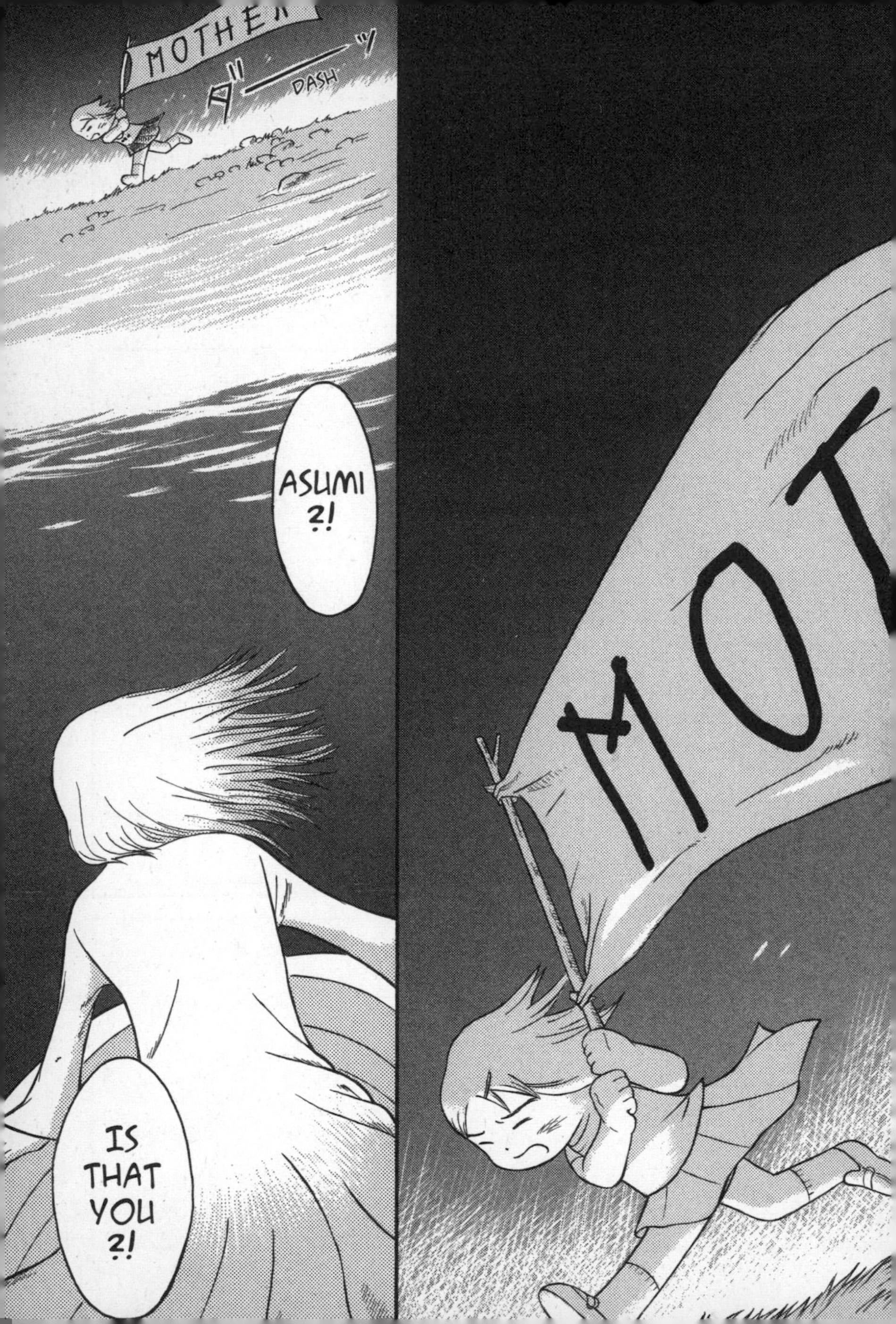
MOT
MOTHE
DASH
ASUMI ?!
IS THAT YOU ?!

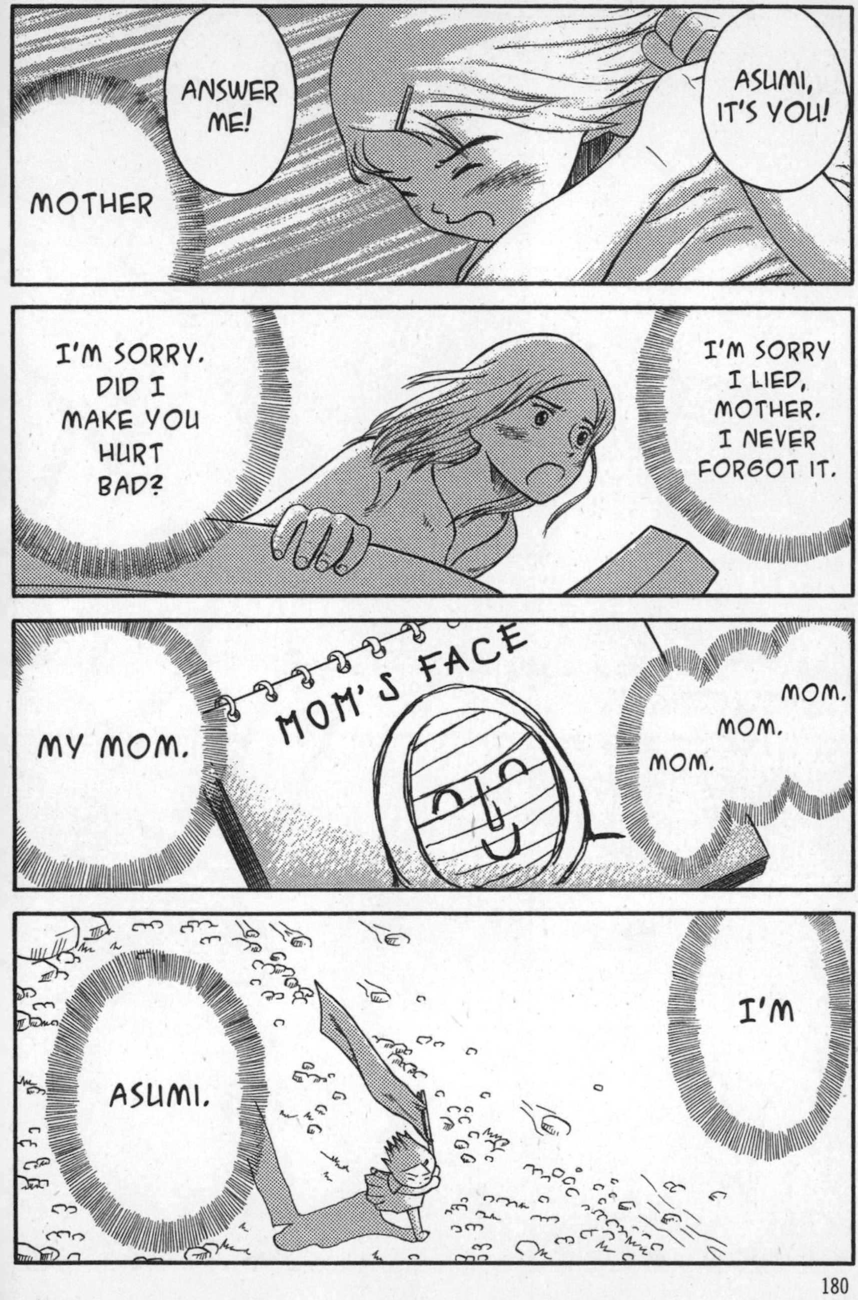
ASUMI, IT'S YOU!
ANSWER ME!
MOTHER
I'M SORRY I LIED, MOTHER. I NEVER FORGOT IT.
I'M SORRY. DID I MAKE YOU HURT BAD?
MOM.
MOM.
MOM.
MOM'S FACE
MY MOM.
I'M
ASUMI.

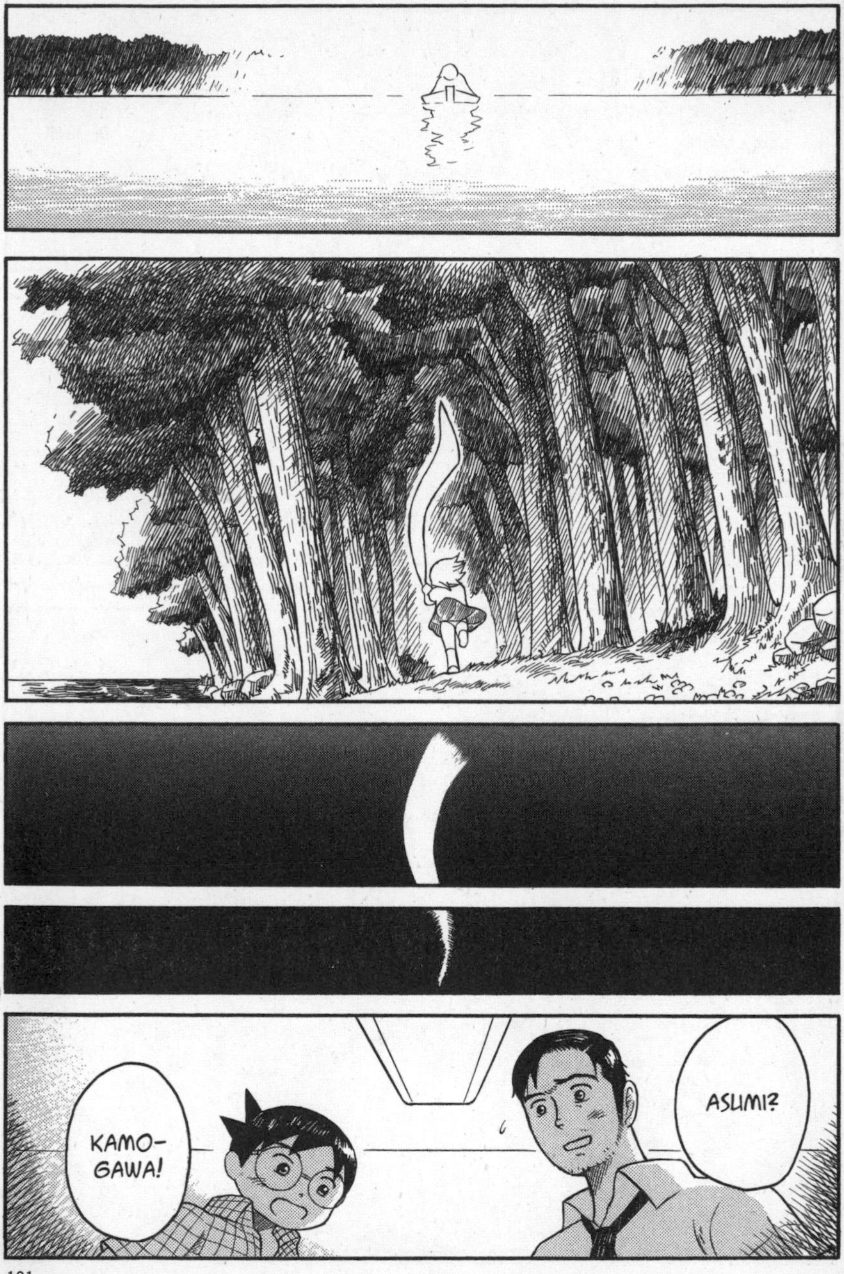
ASUMI?
KAMO-
GAWA!

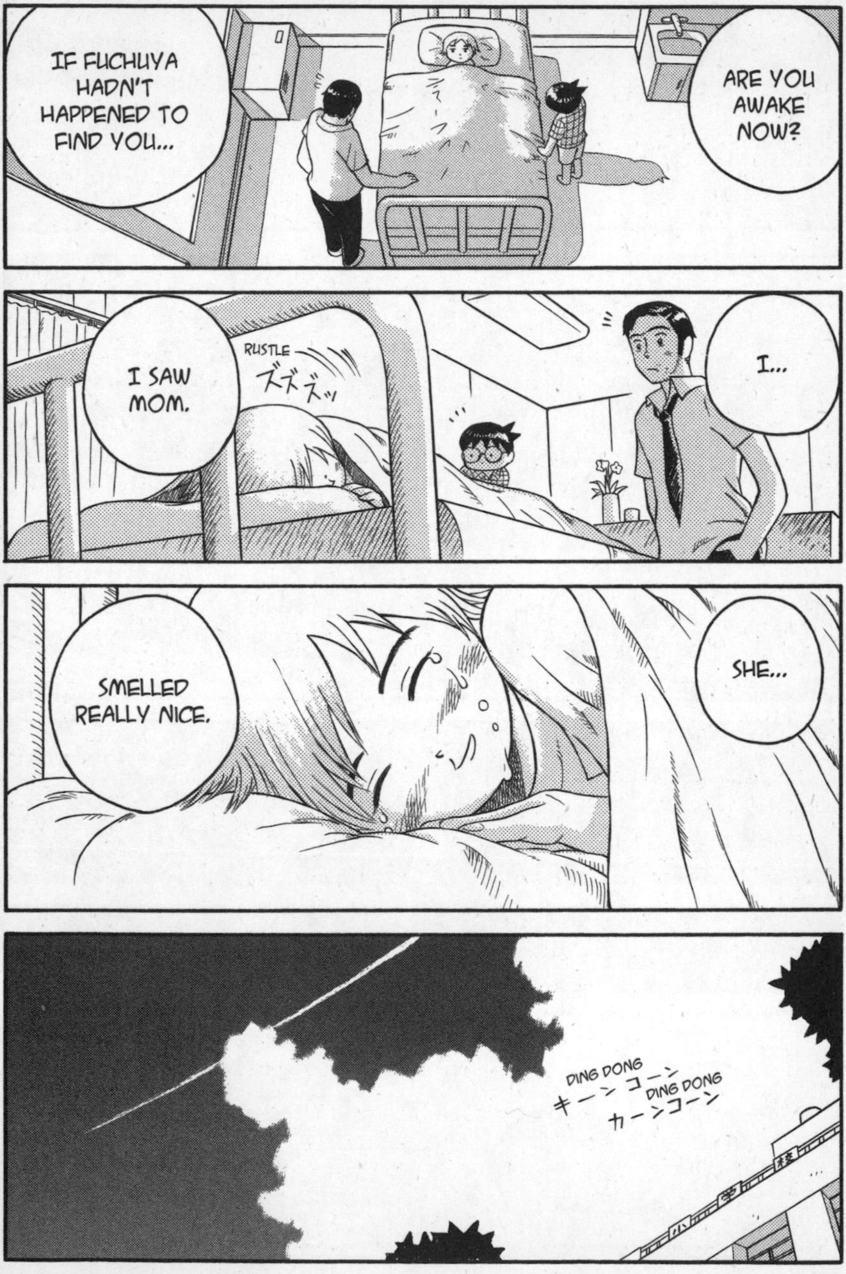
ARE YOU AWAKE NOW?
IF FUCHUYA HADN'T HAPPENED TO FIND YOU...
I...
RUSTLE
ズズズッ
I SAW MOM.
SHE...
SMELLED REALLY NICE.
DING DONG
キーンコーン
DING DONG
カーンコーン

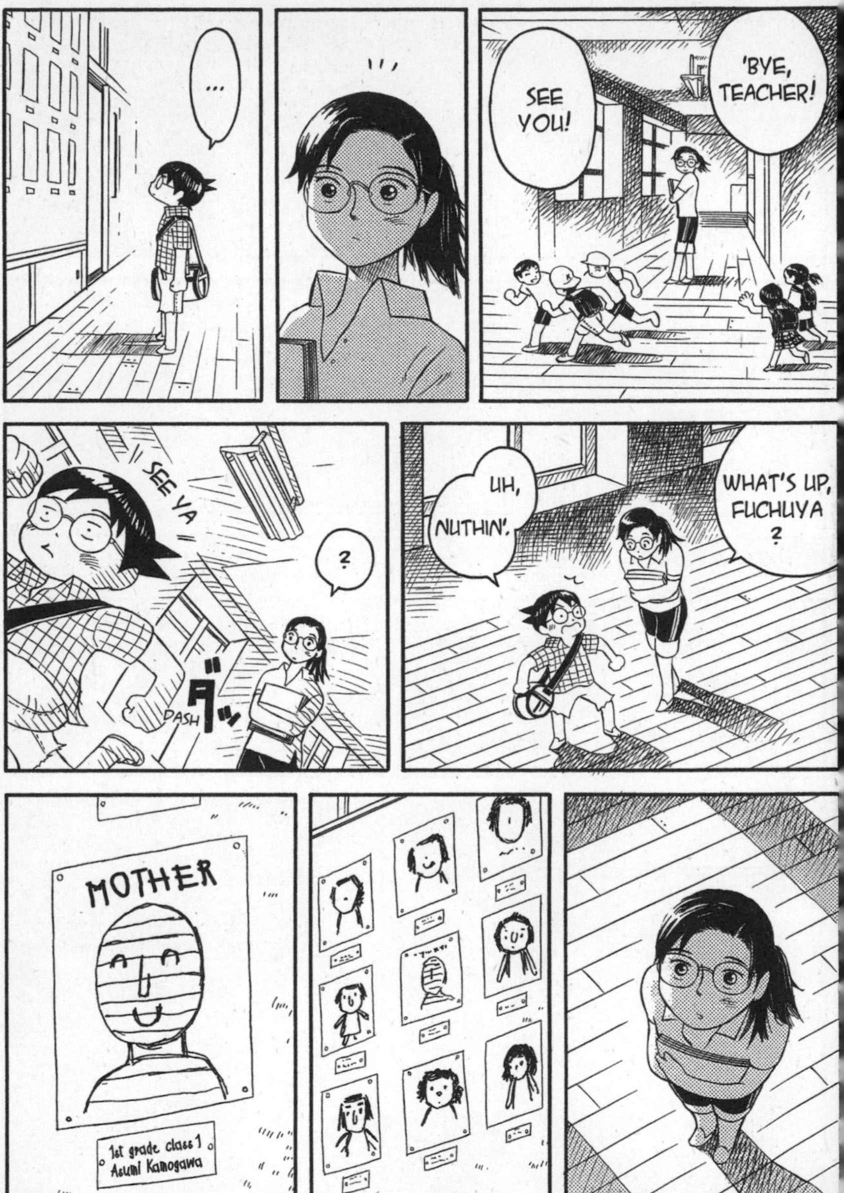

'BYE, TEACHER!
SEE YOU!
...
WHAT'S UP, FUCHUYA?
UH, NUTHIN'.
SEE YA
?
ダッ
DASH
MOTHER
1st grade class 1
Asumi Kamogawa

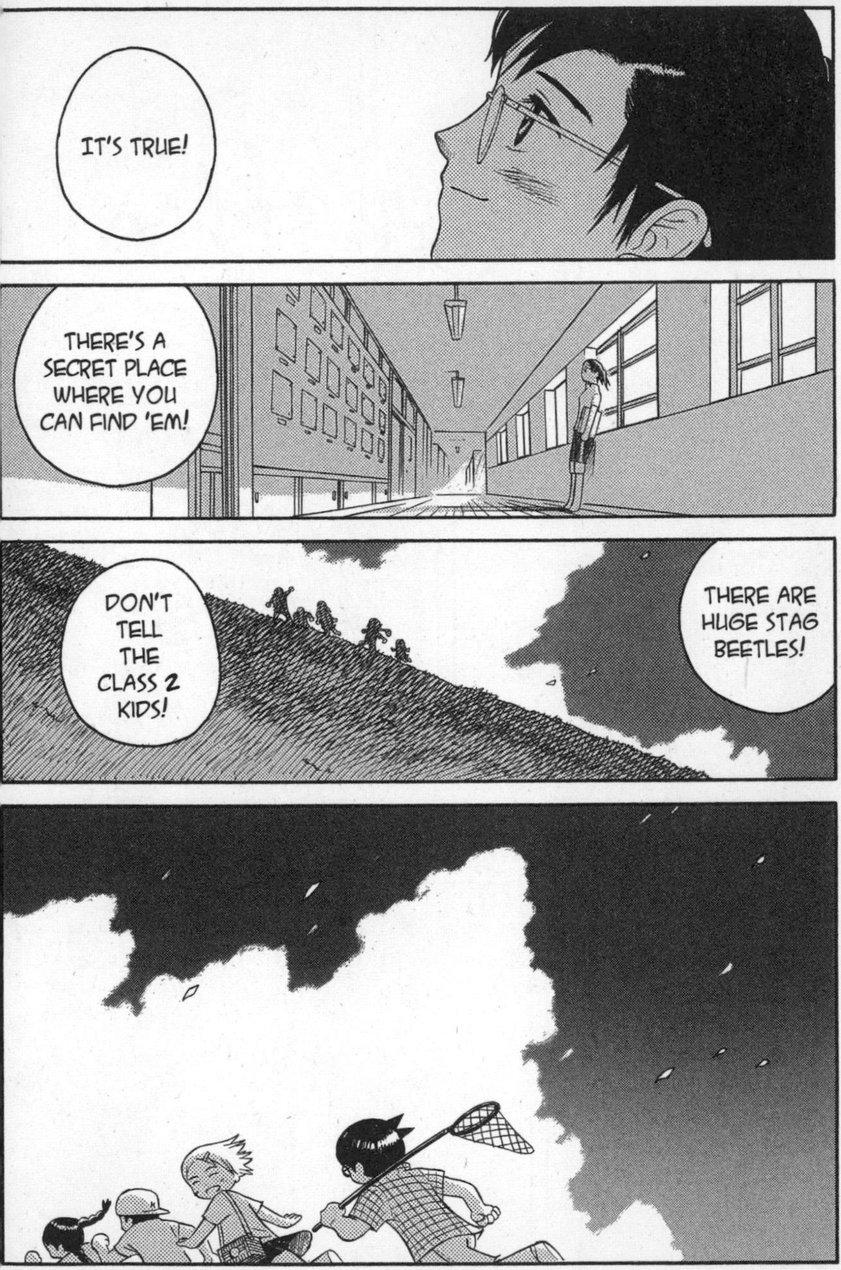
IT'S TRUE!
THERE'S A SECRET PLACE WHERE YOU CAN FIND 'EM!
THERE ARE HUGE STAG BEETLES!
DON'T TELL THE CLASS 2 KIDS!

"ASUMI" —THE END

ANOTHER SPICA

KOU YAGINUMA

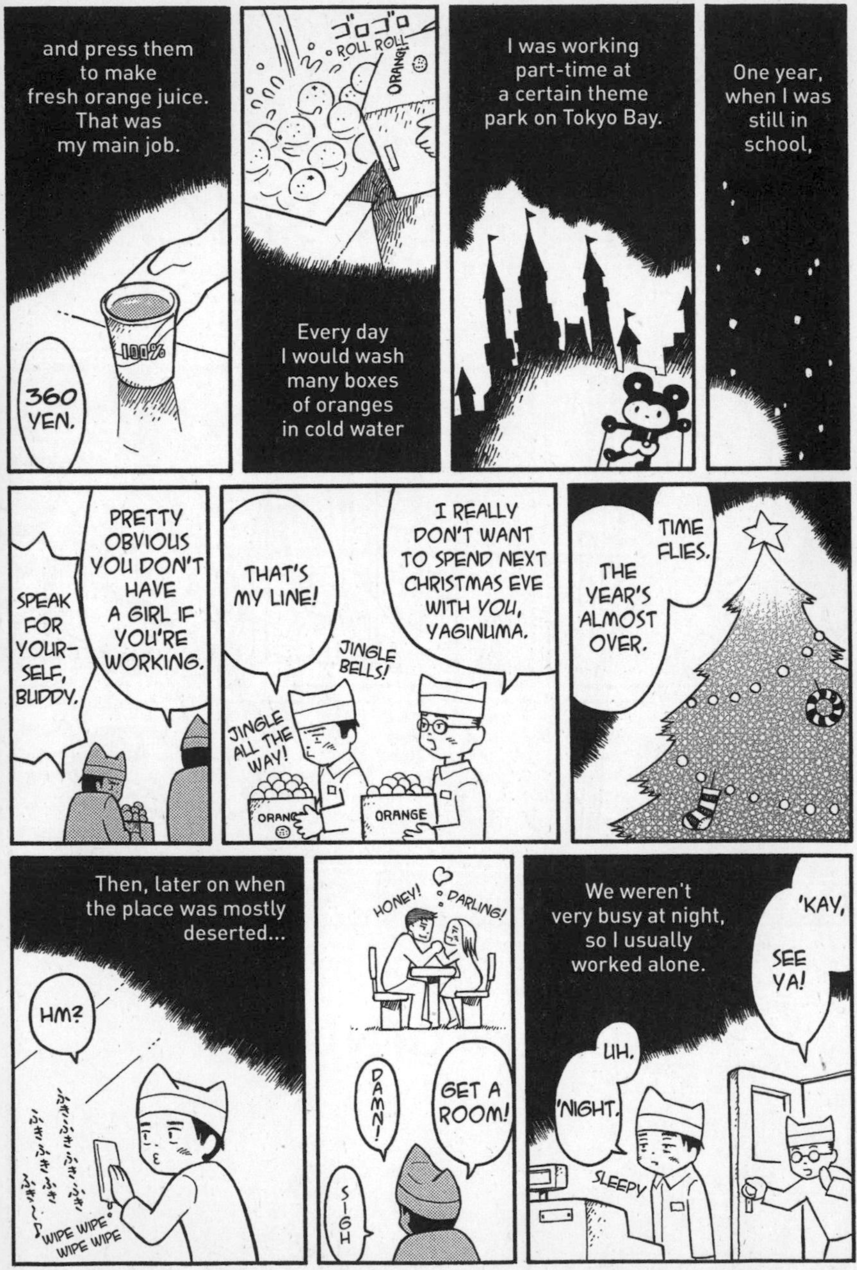
One year, when I was still in school,
I was working part-time at a certain theme park on Tokyo Bay.
ゴロゴロ
ROLL ROLL
ORANGE
Every day I would wash many boxes of oranges in cold water
and press them to make fresh orange juice. That was my main job.
100%
360 YEN.
TIME FLIES.
THE YEAR'S ALMOST OVER.
I REALLY DON'T WANT TO SPEND NEXT CHRISTMAS EVE WITH YOU, YAGINUMA.
THAT'S MY LINE!
JINGLE BELLS!
JINGLE ALL THE WAY!
ORANGE
ORANGE
PRETTY OBVIOUS YOU DON'T HAVE A GIRL IF YOU'RE WORKING.
SPEAK FOR YOURSELF, BUDDY.
We weren't very busy at night, so I usually worked alone.
'KAY,
SEE YA!
UH.
'NIGHT.
SLEEPY
HONEY!
DARLING!
GET A ROOM!
DAMN!
SIGH
Then, later on when the place was mostly deserted...
HM?
ふきふきふきふき
ふきふきふきふき
ふき～♪
WIPE WIPE
WIPE WIPE

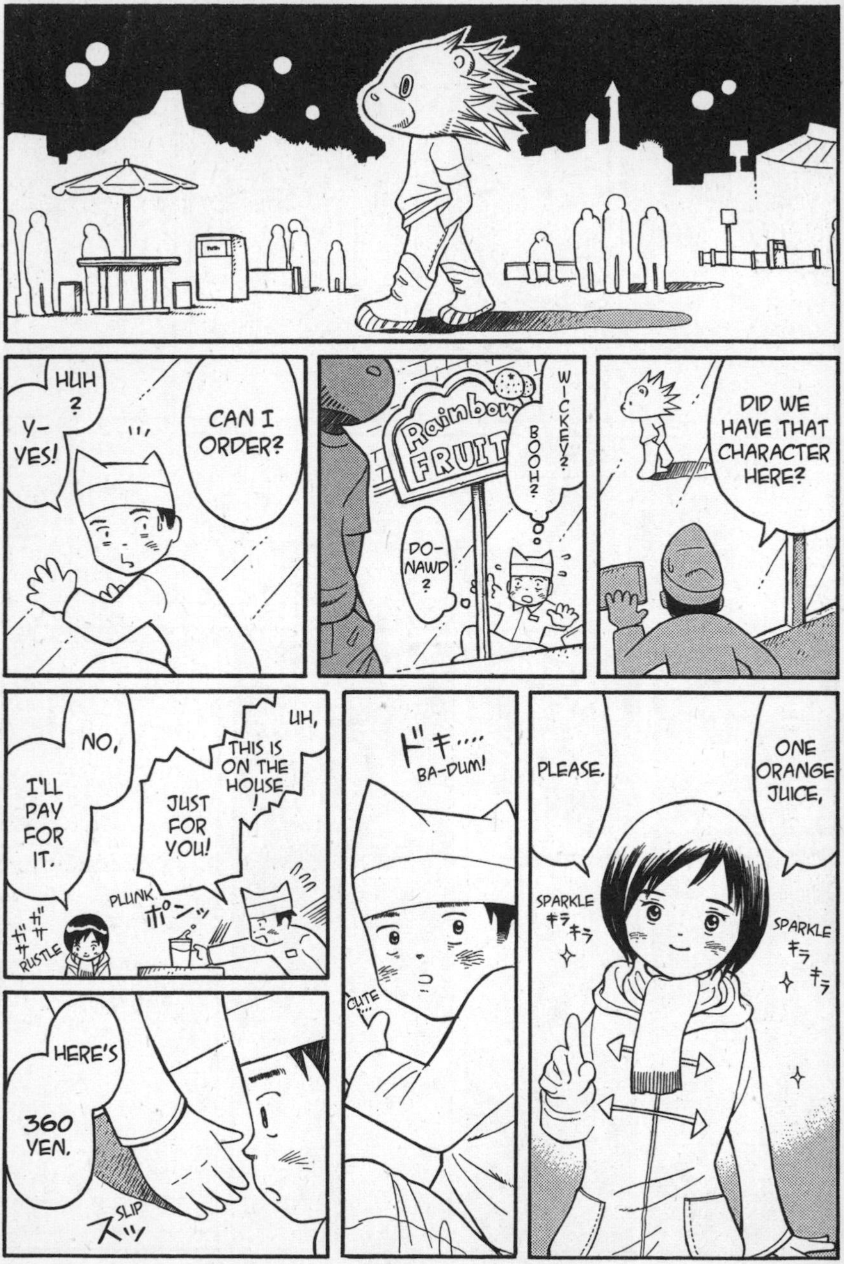
DID WE HAVE THAT CHARACTER HERE?
Rainbow FRUIT
WICKEY? BOOH?
DO-NAWD?
CAN I ORDER?
HUH?
Y-YES!
ONE ORANGE JUICE,
PLEASE.
SPARKLE キラキラ
SPARKLE キラキラ
ドキ....
BA-DUM!
CUTE...
UH, THIS IS ON THE HOUSE!
JUST FOR YOU!
NO, I'LL PAY FOR IT.
PLUNK ポンッ
ガサガサ RUSTLE
HERE'S 360 YEN.
SLIP スッ

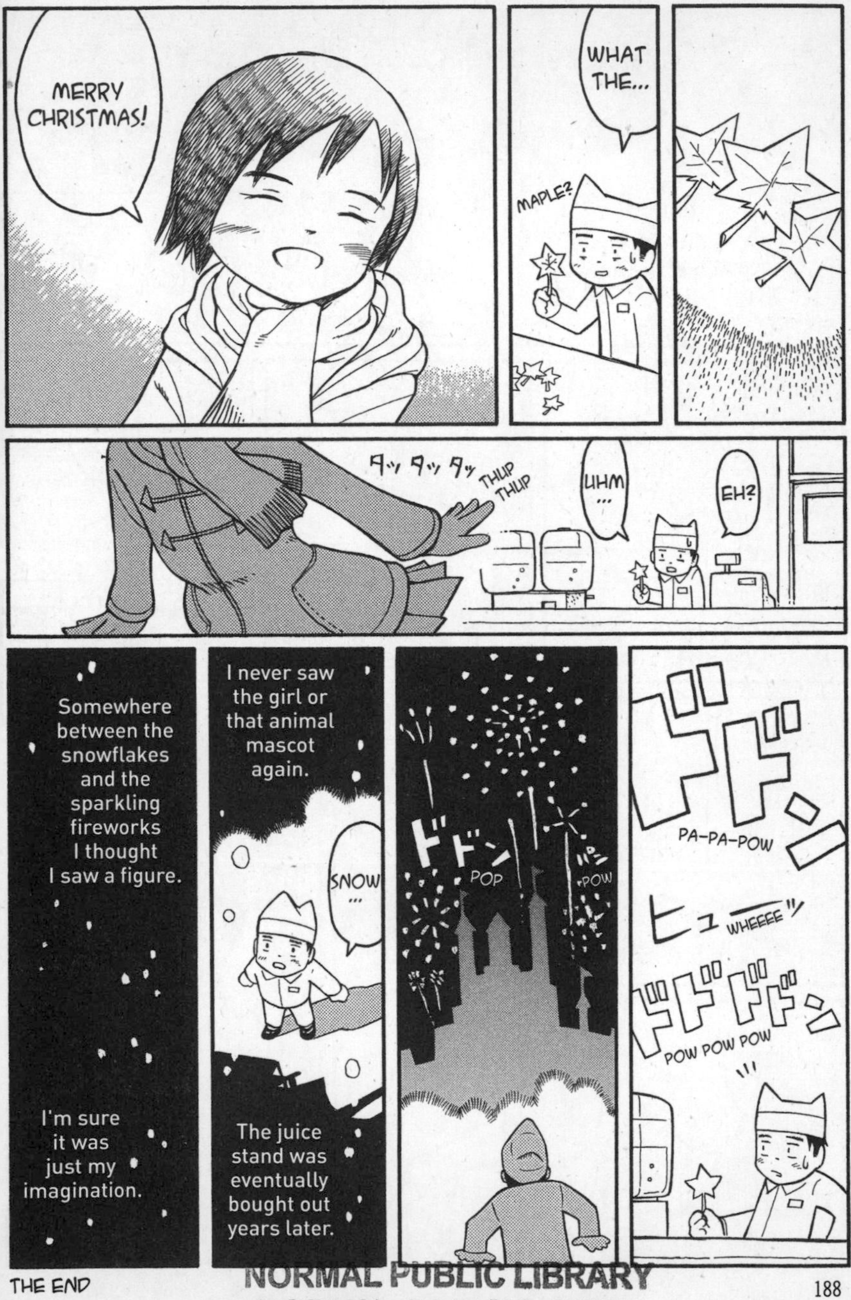
WHAT THE...
MAPLE?
MERRY CHRISTMAS!
EH?
UHM ...
タッ タッ タッ
THUP THUP
ドドン
PA-PA-POW
ヒュー
WHEEEE
ドドドドン
POW POW POW
ドドン
POP
POW
I never saw the girl or that animal mascot again.
SNOW ...
The juice stand was eventually bought out years later.
Somewhere between the snowflakes and the sparkling fireworks I thought I saw a figure.
I'm sure it was just my imagination.

THE END

Notes on the Translation

P. 64

When the author started this series, astronomy books gave the distance to Spica as 350 light-years. Current estimates, however, are in the 200 light-years. In the near future when this story takes place, who knows what the figure will be?

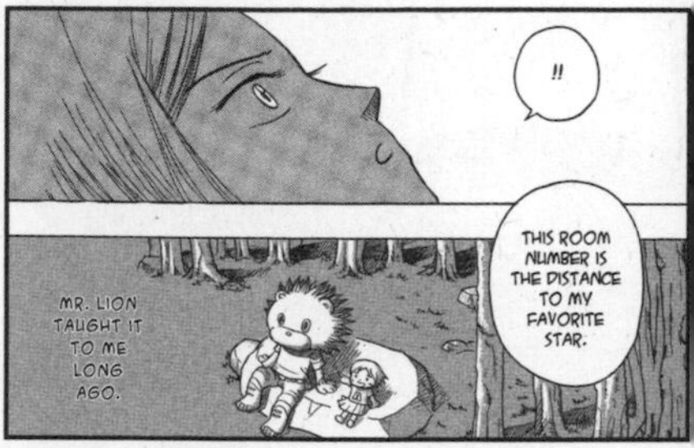
!!
THIS ROOM NUMBER IS THE DISTANCE TO MY FAVORITE STAR.
MR. LION TAUGHT IT TO ME LONG AGO.

P. 161

Sanzu River is the Japanese equivalent of the River Styx. The 49th day after a person's death is believed to be when the spirit crosses into the afterlife.

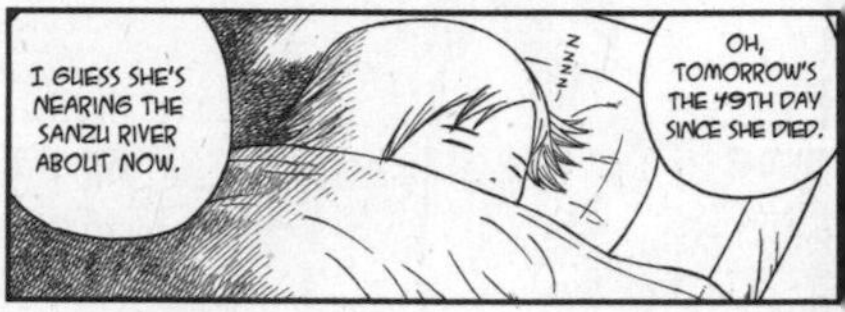
OH, TOMORROW'S THE 49TH DAY SINCE SHE DIED.
I GUESS SHE'S NEARING THE SANZU RIVER ABOUT NOW.

TWIN SPICA

Kou Yaginuma

Space has never seemed so close and yet so far!

Asumi has passed her exams and been accepted into the Tokyo Space School. Now even greater challenges await in the megalopolis. It's clear she is made of the right stuff, but can her little body put all those talents to use under the mental and physical rigors of astronaut training?

"*Twin Spica* is a pleasantly unexpected tear-jerker that hits the nostalgia key for those of us of a certain age who wanted desperately to go to space camp, even after the Challenger explosion."
—Erin Finnegan, Zero-Gravity Bride & *Anime News Network* writer

Volume 2
On Sale: July 2010
ISBN: 978-1-934287-86-6
$10.95 US / $12.99 CAN

© Kou Yaginuma

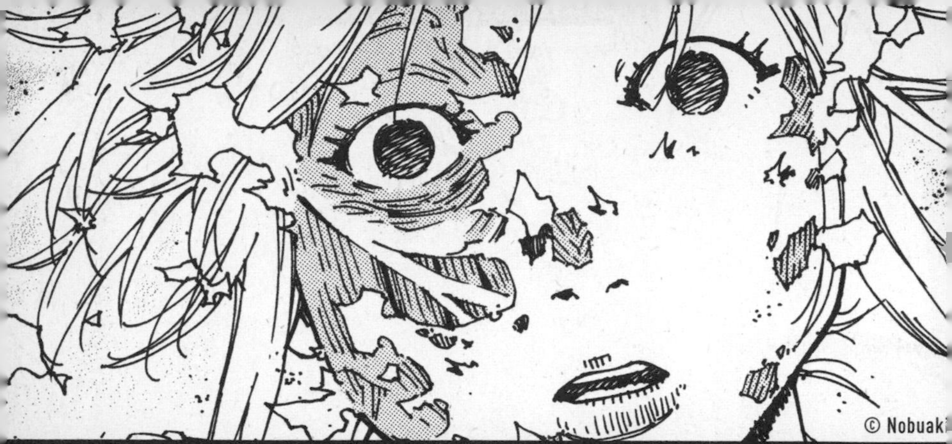
© Nobuaki

7 Billion Needles

BY NOBUAKI TADANO

A sci-fi comic this unique is like finding a needle in a haystack!

An interstellar manhunt comes to a conclusion on Earth when an aloof teenage girl unknowingly becomes mankind's last hope, in Nobuaki Tadano's *7 Billion Needles*. A homage to Hal Clement's golden age classic *Needle*, Tadano's debut series re-invents the sci-fi manga genre from the ground up. From its unique heroine to the intimate narrative constantly told from within her mind, *7 Billion Needles* challenges readers to step out of their comfort zones and take their destiny by the horns.

"A conflict between light and dark...That is the true meaning of a parasite. *7 Billion Needles* reimagines that struggle, and it must be experienced."
— Kia Asamiya, *Silent Mobius*

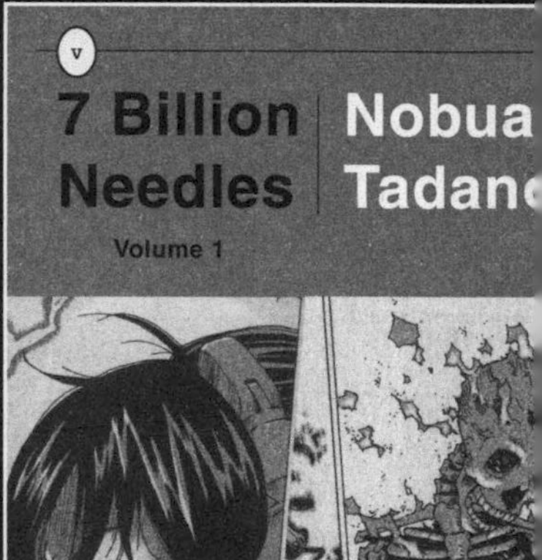
v
7 Billion Needles
Nobua
Tadan
Volume 1

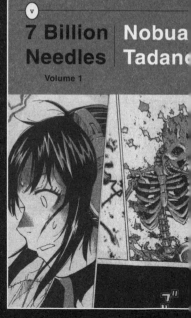

Volume 1: August 2010

ISBN: 978-1-934287-87-3, $10.95 US / $12

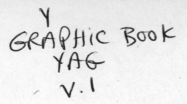

Y
GRAPHIC BOOK
YAG
V.1

Translation - Maya Rosewood
Production - Hiroko Mizuno
           Glen Isip
           Christine Lee

Originally published in Japanese as *Futatsu no Supika*
by MEDIA FACTORY, Inc., Tokyo 2002
Futatsu no Supika first serialized in Gekkan Comic Flapper,
MEDIA FACTORY, Inc., 2001-09
"2015-nen no Uchiage Hanabi" first published in Gekkan Comic Flapper,
MEDIA FACTORY, Inc, 2000
"Asumi" first published in Gekkan Comic Flapper,
MEDIA FACTORY, Inc., 2000

This is a work of fiction.

ISBN: 978-1-934287-84-2

Manufactured in Canada

First Edition

Vertical, Inc.
1185 Avenue of the Americas, 32nd Floor
New York, NY 10036
www.vertical-inc.com

A12005   470372